Well Body, Well Earth

Other Books by Mike Samuels and Hal Zina Bennett:
The Well Body Book
Spirit Guides
Be Well

By Mike and Nancy Samuels:
Seeing With the Mind's Eye
The Well Baby Book
The Well Child Book
The Well Child Coloring Book

By Hal Zina Bennett:
The Doctor Within
Cold Comfort
The Complete Bicycle Commuter
John Marino Bicycling Book (*with John Marino*)

Well Body, Well Earth

Mike Samuels, M.D. and Hal Zina Bennett

THE SIERRA CLUB ENVIRONMENTAL HEALTH SOURCEBOOK

Sierra Club Books   San Francisco

The Sierra Club, founded in 1892 by John Muir, has devoted itself to the study and protection of the earth's scenic and ecological resources—mountains, wetlands, woodlands, wild shores and rivers, deserts and plains. The publishing program of the Sierra Club offers books to the public as a nonprofit educational service in the hope that they may enlarge the public's understanding of the Club's basic concerns. The point of view expressed in each book, however, does not necessarily represent that of the Club. The Sierra Club has some fifty chapters coast to coast, in Canada, Hawaii, and Alaska. For information about how you may participate in its programs to preserve wilderness and the quality of life, please address inquiries to Sierra Club, 530 Bush Street, San Francisco, CA 94108.

Library of Congress
Cataloging in Publication Data

Samuels, Mike.
  Well Body, Well Earth

  Bibliography: p.
  Includes index.
  1. Environmental health. 2. Environmentally induced diseases. I. Bennett, Hal Zina, 1936–
  II. Sierra Club. III. Title.
  RA565.S33 1983   616.9'8   83-671

ISBN: 0-87156-801-2 cloth
ISBN: 0-87156-808-x paper

Cover design copyright © 1983
  by Lawrence Ratzkin
Book design by Jon Goodchild/Triad.
Illustrations by Jon Goodchild/Triad.

Printed in the United States of America
10 9 8 7 6 5 4 3 2 1

To Nancy and our sons
—Michael Samuels
To my sons,
and in memory of
my father Merle F. Bennett
—Hal Zina Bennett

To mother Earth. Zuni
Indians in ceremony at
sacred spring. 1921.
(Courtesy of Museum of the
American Indian, Heye
Foundation.)

The authors want to thank Daniel Moses and Jon Beckmann,
of Sierra Club Books, for encouraging us
to write a book about environmental health.
We want to thank Nancy Samuels for her love,
support, and generous editorial assistance.

Contents

Part 2
How the Earth's Health and Human Health Are One

Part 3
The Sourcebook

Part 4

A Prescription for Environmental Health

*H*e treats his mother, the earth, and his brother, the sky, as things to be bought, plundered, sold like sheep or bright beads. His appetite will devour the earth and leave behind only a desert.

You must teach your children that the ground beneath their feet is the ashes of our grandfathers. So that they will respect the land, tell your children that the earth is rich with the lives of our kin. Teach your children that the earth is our mother. Whatever befalls the earth, befalls the sons of the earth. If men spit upon the ground, they spit upon themselves.

This we know. The earth does not belong to man; man belongs to the earth. This we know. All things are connected like blood which unites one family. All things are connected.

Whatever befalls the earth befalls the sons of the earth. Man did not weave the web of life; he is merely a strand in it. Whatever he does to the web, he does to himself.

Chief Seattle, 1854

The Indians believed that Man did not weave the web of life; he is merely a strand in it. Whatever he does to the web, he does to himself. Web, 1971, by Michael Samuels.

Well Body, Well Earth

1

Evolution of a Balanced System

Throughout history there have been legends describing our Earth as a living being, "Mother Earth," an entity which nurtures and sustains us. For millions of years people believed that all animals and plants, even rocks, mountains, and the sky, evolved from a single source. Within this system of thinking, people viewed themselves as intimately connected to everything around them, from the tiniest insect or pebble to the greatest constellations in the heavens. Human life was not separate from other forms. Everything was related; everything was kin. Each member of the universal community supported each other member in perfect harmony.

The Earth is not a spaceship. Solid evidence establishes it as a living, breathing entity. (Apollo 10 CSM Viewed from LM Over Moon. Courtesy of NASA.)

By dance, music, or other offerings, people directed their energy toward aiding the Earth. (Rain Dance, 1921, by D.A. Cadzow. Zuni, New Mexico. Courtesy of the Museum of the American Indian, Heye Foundation.)

People not only saw the Earth as sustenance, but also saw themselves as nurturing and benefiting the Earth. It was not simply that humans were dependent on the Earth's bounty, but that the Earth was also dependent on human cooperation. Legends depict gods and goddesses, beings who appeared in human form, as creating the Earth or other elements of the universe. Similarly, we have records of ceremonies wherein people believed that, by means of dance, music, or other offerings, they brought the Earth much-needed rain, or encouraged the Sun to send energy for the crops to grow. We might now wonder how directly the dances and other offerings helped the planet, but the critical point here is that human beings did see their efforts as important to the Earth and religiously carried out whatever duties they felt were necessary to benefit it.

In *The Book of the Hopi,* Frank Waters recounts the Indians' view of the Earth, describing how they understood that the Earth was a living entity like themselves. They saw her as a mother; they came from her flesh, and they were nurtured by the grass and corn and the animals that she offered up for their nutriment.[1] Similarly, early in this century, the noted psychoanalyst C. G. Jung interviewed Ochiway Biano, then the chief of the Taos Indians, who told Jung, "we are a people who live on the roof of the world; we are the sons of Father Sun, and with our religion we daily help our father to go across the sky. We do this not only for ourselves, but for the whole world. If we were to cease practicing our religion, in ten years the sun would no longer rise. Then it would be night forever."[2]

How different are these views from the contemporary concept of the Earth as an inert mass whose movements were set in motion millions of years ago and whose destiny is fixed and unalterable! Indeed, this view of the Earth as a dead object, an insensate bit of rock, so dominates the thought of our day that even such original thinkers as Buckminster Fuller have compared the Earth to a spaceship, and have extrapolated from this metaphor that the solutions to the Earth's problems are comparable to repairing our automobiles or our television sets. From this we might suppose that keeping the Earth healthy and habitable would be like sweeping out the spaceship and polishing its hull regularly. Unfortunately, this vision of our world has not served us well in the past few decades. The failure lies in the metaphor: the Earth is not a spaceship, it is much more than that.

Throughout history, people have viewed themselves as intimately connected to everything around them. Human life was not separate from the Earth. (Shrine, Centre of the Earth, 1903, by George H. Pepper. Zuni, New Mexico. Courtesy of the Museum of the American Indian, Heye Foundation.)

Science now offers us a much richer view of our planet, with solid evidence establishing that it is not an inert mass or a machine, but a living, breathing entity. In the past few years scientific thought has come full circle, presenting us with a world vision much closer to that of the Indians than to that of Buckminster Fuller. Caring for our Earth is not at all like caring for our cars or our appliances, as it turns out. Since it is a living, breathing entity, the care we bestow upon our planet must be like the care we have for our mate, or parents, or our children, the people we love best and whose lives we often value more than our own.

If it is true that our Earth is a living entity, we must review the interactions between ourselves and our planet with far greater sensitivity than was ever thought necessary. We must accept, for example, the frightening but very real possibility that we are capable of creating substances that are incompatible with the Earth's needs. Whereas the use of fluorocarbons might pose no threat to a spaceship, they do pose a real danger to the Earth.

In a more positive vein, like all living things the Earth is homeostatic; that is, it can maintain itself in a healthy state by adjusting to changes in its environment or in itself. (We'll be discussing this further in Chapter Four.) This homeostatic capacity can play an extremely important role in our efforts to protect our planet's health—and thus our own health—now and in the future.

"We are a people who live on the roof of the world; we are the sons of Father Son, and with our religion we daily help our father to go across the sky": Ochwiaz Biano. (*Taos Pueblo at Sunrise,* 1982, by Michael Samuels.)

In this part of the book we'll be exploring what is essentially the life story of the living Earth and of humanity's intimate relationship with it. First, we'll describe the creation of the universe, the Earth, and the basic materials from which early life forms would evolve. Next, we'll trace how these early life forms evolved to become the millions of species we now enjoy. We'll explore the growth of human populations, from the smallest tribal groups, living intimately with their natural surroundings, to enormous urban populations, many of whose members have lost touch with their natural surroundings and no longer see the connections between their own welfare and the health of the planet.

The areas we'll be exploring in this part lay the groundwork for understanding why some of the changes imposed on the planet by our modern technology alter the natural environment so dramatically that the health of the Earth as well as of the millions of species it supports is deeply threatened.

CHAPTER ONE

The Birth of Our Planet

Everything in the universe is now built from the same elementary particles, those being *electrons, protons,* and *neutrons.* These three basic building blocks have combined and recombined in various patterns over the ages, to become everything in and on the Earth and in the universe beyond the Earth, from the tiniest grain of sand and the largest beasts in the forests, to the gaseous rings around Saturn and the most distant galaxies we can see. Since we can trace our own beginnings to these universal, elementary particles, it becomes obvious that *we are all kin.* Our kinship includes the air we breathe, the water we drink, the food we eat, every animal, plant, fish, fowl, pebble, and star in the heavens—in short, everything we could possibly encounter in our lifetimes.

Because of our kinship, we are affected by everything around us. We humans are not separate or impermeable. On the contrary, it is

Elementary particles have combined and recombined to become everything in the universe, from the tiniest grains of sand to the gaseous rings of Saturn. (a, *Sand Grains,* 1975, by Michael Samuels; b; Saturn, courtesy of Lick Observatory.)

our permeability and our kinship (through the elementary particles that we share with the universe) that makes our lives possible. Our very existence is a cooperation of these particles, an association that scientists tell us has evolved over billions of years. The stability (homeostasis) of our own bodies, as well as the

stability of the Earth and everything upon it, is made possible by this state of cooperation.

In the past fifty years human beings have learned to manipulate the same elementary particles from which we ourselves are made; this has allowed us to create vast numbers of new substances, from plastics to automobile fuels that by now flood our environment. Because we are in fact permeable and have a kinship with our world, we naturally interact with these newly introduced substances, just as we interact with substances that have evolved along with us, by natural means, during billions of years. Often our bodies have not yet developed ways to protect us from the toxins contained in our own inventions, nor do we have anything but the vaguest notions about how these substances might affect the generations to follow us.

Until very recently, the Earth had millions of years to adjust to new substances that appeared. For example, there was no oxygen on Earth, and all life forms were anerobic, until two billion years ago. Then plant life evolved and produced oxygen as a waste product. Biologists estimate that it then took approximately 1.5 million years for living cells to learn how to use oxygen; during that time oxygen, which we now consider essential to life itself, was *toxic,* and threatened all the life forms that then populated our planet.[1] (See Chapter Two.)

The rapid proliferation and vast variety of human-created substances introduced in the past fifty years guarantees that adjustment by genetic evolution is virtually impossible. Far too much is happening all at once for evolutionary processes to be able to work out the cooperative arrangements necessary for a healthy world. We can cope with our own capacity for creating new substances only by using our minds and directing our actions accordingly: we must learn to evaluate these changes in terms of how they affect our health and well-being.

A first step toward understanding the effects of the new substances in our environment is to learn the story of our kinship with the world. This understanding starts with an appreciation for the creation of the world itself.

The Myths That Shape the World

Every society has its own myths of creation, its cosmologies. These myths of creation are passed along from older generations to younger ones, and are extremely important in directing the thoughts and feelings of each individual toward goals that are beneficial to all. A cosmology gives people a reason for being, provides a framework from which they can make choices that will keep their way of life intact and healthy. In a very real way, a cosmology serves as a homeostatic mechanism, directing people's actions in ways that will benefit not only people but the living Earth itself.

As we look around and see all the environmental problems we have created for ourselves in recent times, we can hardly help wondering how our cosmology has gone wrong, how it has failed us. But has it failed? Our cosmology has not failed us at all; rather, we have lost touch with it. We no longer hear its message.

Although there are other voices, science is perhaps the most powerful one we have for expressing our myths of creation. There is a certain irony in this, since it is also through science that most of our environmental problems have been created. Nevertheless, the vision of the universe that science provides us is ultimately a healthy and positive one, a vision to which we can turn for guidance in evaluating a healthy course of action in the years ahead.

Our scientific cosmology begins with the material world, and its story focuses on the creation of matter and everything that followed. Although the work of astronomers, biologists, and nuclear physicists implies that there was a condition of nothingness—a condition that tasks the imagination—before the creation of matter, we must go to prescientific cultures for stories of the universe "before the beginning." There are dozens of cultures to which we could turn for this part of the cosmology, but the following ones are the most compatible with modern thinking.

From the Mayans:

All was in suspense, all calm, all in silence; all motionless and still; and the expanse of the sky was empty.[2]

From the Cheyenne of the Great Lakes region of the U.S.:

In the beginning there was nothing, and Maheo, the All Spirit, lived in the void. He looked around him, but there was nothing to see. He listened, but there was nothing to hear. There was only Maheo, alone in nothingness.[3]

From the Chinese, first century B.C.:

Before Heaven and Earth had taken form, all was vague and amorphous . . . That which was clear and light drifted up to Heaven, while that which was heavy and turbid solidified to become earth.[4]

The themes common to these myths are nothingness, and a spiritual force sitting in that nothingness and making the decision to create a world. Although these themes have no parallels in science, primitive and scientific cultures do share some common concepts in the next step explaining how the universe came to be. A great many prescientific peoples had "cosmic egg" myths that are roughly analogous to our most recent theories in science. According to Mircea Eliade, the cosmic-egg theory appeared in the cosmologies of people from every corner of the globe, and as far back as records exist.

Before Heaven and Earth had taken form, all was vague and amorphous. (*Untitled,* 1968, by John Griefen. Synthetic polymer on canvas, 44″ × 94″. Collection of the Whitney Museum of American Art, New York.)

From the Society Islands of the South Pacific:

Ta-aroa, ancestor of the gods, and creator of the universe, [was] sitting in his shell in darkness from eternity. The shell was like an egg revolving in endless space.[5]

From the Chinese, third century A.D.:

First there was the great cosmic egg. Inside the egg was chaos, and floating in chaos was P'an Ku, the Undeveloped, the divine Embryo.[6]

From Aristophanes, fifth century B.C.:

At first there was Chaos and Night, Darkness and broad Tartaros;
But there was neither Earth nor Air nor Sky.
Then blackwinged Night laid her egg,
Sired by the cyclone, in the unfathomed bosom of Darkness,
And from it, turned by the Seasons, sprang

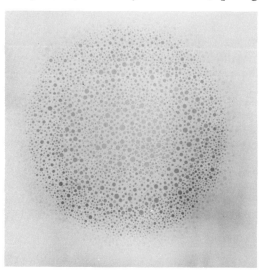

First there was the great cosmic egg. Inside was chaos. (*New Day,* 1967, by Paul Brach. Oil on canvas, 65″ × 65″. Collection of the Whitney Museum of American Art, New York. Gift of Margery and Harry Kahn.)

The big bang was unlike any explosion we can imagine. It occurred simultaneously everywhere, filling all space. (*Inner Red,* 1960, by Richard Anuszkiewicz. Oil on Canvas, 22″ × 18″. Collection of the Whitney Museum of American Art, New York. Gift of Honorable and Mrs. Nelson A. Rockefeller, in honor of John I.H. Bauer.)

Love the enchanter,
Brilliant, goldenwinged, a whirlwind of radiance![7]

Presenting us with the scientists' view of the cosmic egg, Carl Sagan tells us that "all the matter and energy now in the universe was concentrated at extremely high density—a kind of cosmic egg, reminiscent of the creation myths of many cultures.[8] George Gamow, who originated the important "big bang" theory of creation, called the material contained by the cosmic egg *ylem,* a Greek word, coined by Aristotle in the fourth century B.C., meaning "primordial substance," the basic material from which everything in the universe would be produced.

The Big Bang

Initially the cosmic egg was dense and hot, denser than any object now in the universe. Our Earth pressed into a ball of the same density would measure 200 feet in diameter. The temperature of the cosmic egg would have been measured in trillions of degrees.

The forces and temperatures within the cosmic egg continued to increase as it pressed in upon itself, until they became so immense that it exploded. Because the cosmic egg was, at that moment, literally all and everything, the explosion was unlike any explosion we know today. Steven Weinberg describes this moment of creation in his book *The First Three Minutes:*

Not an explosion like those familiar on Earth, starting from a definite center and spreading out to engulf more and more of the circumambient air, but an explosion that occurred simultaneously everywhere, filling all space from the beginning, with every particle of matter rushing apart from every other particle.[9]

At one second after the big bang, all the space in the universe was filled with nothing but intense light and electrons, with a relatively small number of protons and neutrons racing about.* This is what some scientists call the "cosmic soup," from which the universe as we know it today would eventually evolve. Everything in this soup moved at a great rate of speed, elementary particles bouncing off elementary particles, creating tremendous activity. Such a space, filled with pure energy racing everywhere at once, constantly expanding outward, glowing with a brightness greater than a million suns, is all but impossible to imagine.

The outward movement of the universe, that is, its expansion, meant that density was diminishing. As elementary particles traveled further and further away from each other, the temperature of the cosmic soup began to cool.

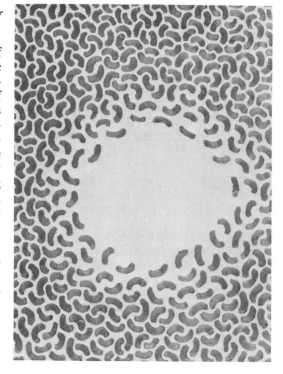

*There were also a great many neutrinos and antineutrinos, but we don't need to discuss them.

When the universe was about 100 seconds old, the temperature was low enough to allow a neutron and a proton to adhere to one other, forming a deuterium nucleus (earlier, they had simply bounced off in another direction whenever they collided). This was a very important moment, for suddenly the universe became engaged in a fairly singular activity: producing nuclei for building atoms.

To understand the importance of creating nuclei, let's compare the structure of the atom to that of a solar system, with a sun and its orbiting planets. The atom's sun—or nucleus—consists of at least one proton, but may consist of various combinations of protons and neutrons adhering to each other. Around the nucleus of the atom there will be one or more orbiting electrons, the planets of this microcosm.

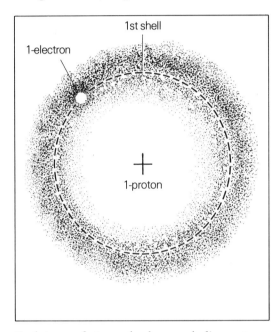

Each type of atom—hydrogen, helium, etc.—has a different number of protons that make up its nucleus.

The simplest of all atoms is the hydrogen atom, whose nucleus is a single proton. The hydrogen nucleus has existed in the universe since within a second after the big bang. At about 100 seconds after the big bang, pairs consisting of a proton and a neutron began to form; these were deuterium nuclei.* During the next 126 seconds, these nuclei each captured another proton and another neutron, making a new nuclear form consisting of two protons and two neutrons, which is the nucleus of the helium atom.

It had taken three minutes and 46 seconds since the explosion of the cosmic egg for the helium nucleus to form. The entire universe now consisted of light and a relatively small number of nuclei: about 73 percent hydrogen nuclei and 23 percent helium nuclei. There were also a few electrons floating freely. Although this does not seem like much, it was all the building material necessary for creating the stars and galaxies that would become the universe in which we live today.

After 10,000 years, the temperature had dropped far enough to allow electrons, attracted by protons, to establish stable orbits around the nuclei.* This step marked the birth of atoms. The universe then consisted of clouds of helium and hydrogen gases, filling all of space. Even today, some 20 billion years later, the universe still consists of 99 percent hydrogen and helium. It is from this vast pool of hydrogen and helium atoms that the Earth and everything on it was created, the same atoms being used again and again, over billions of years, for creating life. To get some perspective on what this means, consider that the hydrogen which makes up most of your body is 20 billion years old, and that the quanta that make up those atoms come directly from the cosmic egg. If we take a careful, scientific look at the most rudimentary building blocks from which we are made, we are all of the same age; we can trace our roots to the same cosmic conception.

The Birth Of the Galaxies

Scientists can envision the early universe as an endless cloud of hydrogen and helium. For reasons not yet understood, hydrogen and helium atoms began clumping together within the great cloud, forming some areas that were far denser than others. We know that all bodies attract each other: the larger the mass, the more material it attracts, that is, the greater the gravity of the mass becomes. Each dense area in the cloud therefore began to attract more and more atoms toward its centers, and this process continued until the density became so great that the area collapsed into itself, becoming a whirling body of gases. This swirling formation is called a *protogalaxy.*

Within each protogalaxy there were formed masses very much like the one that gave rise to the protogalaxy itself. But as these new masses collapsed into themselves, they became dense pockets of helium and hydrogen known as *protostars*. Since we can observe gas clouds collapsing into protostars in our own Galaxy today, we can discuss protostar and star formation as they are happening right now.

Because the protostar is dense, it has a strong gravity; so it continues to pull atoms toward its center. Its density increases, and it becomes smaller, as it packs ever more tightly. Atoms drawn into the protostar fall continuously toward its center, and gathering speed they get hotter and hotter. As speed and heat increase, helium and hydrogen atoms begin colliding with each other; the force of the collisions separates orbiting electrons from their nuclei.

When a hydrogen atom has its electron

The hydrogen atom is the simplest of all atoms. it has a nucleus consisting of a single proton with one electron circling the nucleus.

*Chemically, deuterium is "heavy hydrogen," and combined with oxygen as D_2O, it makes "heavy water."

*Each electron has one negative unit of electric charge, and each proton has one positive unit of charge. These charges are exactly equal in magnitude, but opposite in sign; so, like the opposite poles of magnets, they attract one another. Every atom, if undisturbed, always contains the same number of protons and electrons; so overall it is electrically neutral. The neutron has no electric charge: it is neutral; and its name was derived from this fact. The proton and the neutron each weigh about 1,800 times as much as the electron; so almost all your body weight is nuclear.

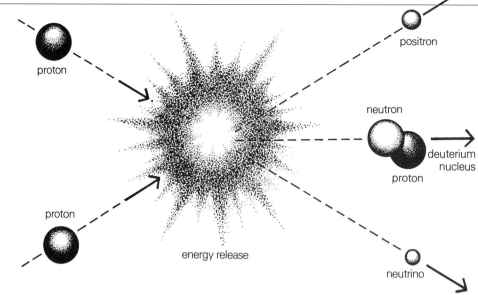

When protons collide they fuse. First a heavy hydrogen (deuterium) nucleus is formed. Next deuterium collides with another proton forming light helium (two protons and one neutron), and then two light helium nuclei collide and form a helium nucleus (two protons and two neutrons). In the process, great energy is released. This is how the sun produces light.

removed, it becomes a single, free proton. (Remember, each hydrogen nucleus is a single proton.) Then, the tremendous heat and speeds now present cause protons to be brought together and fused into new nuclei; this is what we commonly know as *nuclear fusion.* The processes that lead to fusion release tremendous amounts of energy, as is demonstrated by the detonation of a hydrogen bomb, which makes use of this principle.

As the process of nuclear fusion goes on in the protostar, hydrogen nuclei (protons) continue to fuse. When four protons have fused (by a process that transforms two of them into neutrons), they become a helium nucleus. Tremendous heat and light are produced as the helium nuclei form, and it is this phenomenon that makes the Sun and other stars shine, and provides the solar energy upon which all life on Earth is dependent.

When a protostar *turns on,* that is, when

nuclear fusion begins illuminating it, that protostar has become a *star.* It took 700,000 years after the big bang for the first star to form, and for synthesis of nuclei more complex than helium to become possible.

In a star, the atoms on the outer layer are held up by the radiation and particles flowing out from the fusion reaction at its center, just as air inside a balloon supports its outer membrane. This prevents the star from collapsing. The star remains stable until all the hydrogen it contains has been burned. Our Sun, for example, has burned approximately half its hydrogen; it has enough remaining to burn for another five billion years.

When a star has finally consumed all its hydrogen, its life is dramatically transformed. Because the fusion reactions at its center cease, the outer layers of the star are no longer supported. The star begins to collapse in on itself. As gravity draws the outer layers toward the

This picture shows the center of the Orion Nebula, a gaseous cloud of hydrogen and helium atoms, where new stars are coming into being in our own lifetimes. (Courtesy of Lick Observatory.)

center, temperatures rise, and continue to rise, until all the hydrogen once contained in these outer layers is consumed.

The universe was now racing toward an event which would create the atom most important for life: the carbon atom. As we will see, carbon atoms can link to one another, forming long, complex chains of atoms, which are necessary for life as we know it. All the building blocks of our bodies (our cells) are made from chains of carbon atoms linked with oxygen, hydrogen, nitrogen, and other atoms. But how, exactly, did the carbon atom come into existence?

After all the hydrogen is burned from a dying star, helium atoms begin to burn and fuse. The helium atom, with its nucleus of two neutrons and two protons, joins two other

temperature and pressure are great enough to enable nuclear burning of oxygen and carbon. As the oxygen and carbon burn, these atoms fuse together in a variety of new combinations, producing ever more complex elements: two carbon atoms join to become magnesium; two oxygen atoms join to make sulfur; one carbon atom joins with one oxygen atom to make silicon; one carbon atom joins with hydrogen to make nitrogen; etc. (There would eventually be 106 known elements in the universe, 90 of these being commonly found on our planet.)

The complexity, or heaviness, of an element is determined by the structure of its nucleus. The nucleus of an atom always consists of neutrons and protons; each type of nucleus has a particular number of protons within it. For example, the nucleus of a helium atom—

Table 1.1 The cosmic abundance of the elements

Elements[a]	10^-	0	10	10^2	10^3	10^4	10^5	10^6	10^7	10^8	10^9	10^{10}	10^{11}
Gold		●											
Hydrogen													●
Helium												●	
Oxygen										●			
Carbon									●				
Nitrogen									●				
Silicon								●					
Sulfur								●					
Iron								●					
Sodium							●						
Calcium							●						
Potassium						●							
Phosphorous						●							
Lithium				●									
Bromine				●									
Berilium			●										
Lead			●										
Silver		●											
Uranium	●												

[a]Each of the elements is compared to gold; its relative abundance, in atoms, in the universe is noted in multiples of 10. Thus, there are 100 lithium atoms for every atom of gold; 100,000 atoms of potassium for every atom of gold; etc.

helium atoms; their nuclei fuse, forming the carbon atom. (Carbon atoms therefore have six neutrons and six protons in their nuclei.) This fusing of nuclear material releases tremendous quantities of energy, and its end product is an atom that is extremely stable, lasting forever.

Almost immediately after they come into being, the carbon atoms are fused with helium atoms to form yet another new atom, one that is also essential to life as we know it: the oxygen atom.

Even as these new atomic structures are being born, the helium in the parent star is burning out. The star continues to burn until there is no helium left; all that remains is a hard core of oxygen and carbon.

What happens next depends on the size of the star. Small stars simply die out, producing no more new elements. But in the larger stars,

the simplest atomic structure after the hydrogen atom—always contains two protons, and usually contains two neutrons (an *isotope* of helium can have one or three neutrons in its nucleus). A "normal" oxygen atom always has 8 neutrons and 8 protons. Iron atoms, still more complex, have 26 protons and 30 neutrons.

Out of the cauldron of the burning star, heavy elements up to iron are forged. Iron has some unique features that are crucial to our understanding of the creation of our world. The nuclear synthesis of all the elements up to iron releases energy, vast amounts of energy, into the universe. But with the coming of iron, something quite different occurred. Instead of releasing energy, iron actually consumes it. The iron uses the energy provided by the synthesis of other atoms, and in the process it extinguishes the star.

A supernova is as bright as an entire galaxy. When a supernova explodes, it scatters heavy elements all through space. (The Crab Nebula, a remnant of the supernova explosion of A.D. 1054. Courtesy of Lick Observatory.)

The large star has now become an iron ball, hurtling through space, surrounded by all the elements it has created. Like the cosmic egg from which everything in the universe has come, the iron ball collapses into itself, becoming increasingly dense and hot until it explodes as a *supernova*, a heavenly body as bright as an entire galaxy.

When a supernova blows up, the temperature is so great that many neutrons and protons, released from the iron core, join surrounding elements to make new, even heavier elements, such as silver, gold, and uranium. (Since these elements are created *only* when a supernova explodes, they are extremely rare.)

Whenever a supernova explodes, all its elements are scattered out into space, like seeds cast into the wind. As the first generation of

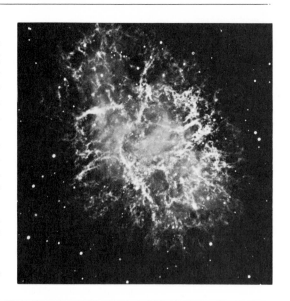

Dust grains coated with ice, surrounding our forming sun (called the protosun), collided with each other, forming larger and larger masses, finally becoming the terrestrial planets of our solar system.

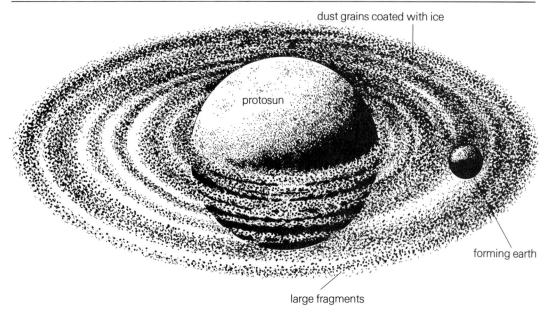

dust grains coated with ice

protosun

forming earth

large fragments

stars came to the end of its evolution, there were billions of supernovas, spewing out a cloud of material which diffused into space. This cloud, like the cloud of gases formed after the explosion of the cosmic egg, swirled about, forming some areas that were denser than others. The densest areas became slow, spiraling clouds collapsing in on themselves, forming even denser clouds. However, the type of cloud now forming was different from anything that had previously existed in the universe; unlike the cloud that formed after the big bang, this new one was filled with all the heavy elements created thus far. This process would occur time and time again throughout the universe, each time seeding space with large quantities of heavy elements.

Over time, space itself became denser and denser with heavy elements. Then something quite dramatic happened; the heavy elements

combined with each other, forming what we now call compounds, that is, combinations of different kinds of elements. Heavy elements, such as silicon, iron, and aluminum, joined with oxygen to form the materials for rocks and ores. Hydrogen combined with oxygen to make water (H_2O), with nitrogen to form ammonia, with carbon to form methane, and so on.

Even while the compounds were forming, the vast expanses of outer space were peppered with hydrogen and helium. In fact, 99 percent of the matter in space was—and still is—hydrogen and helium, with the remaining 1 percent being the heavy elements. The heavy elements The heavy elements appeared in the form of tiny dust grains, quartz grains coated with ice.

The stage was set for the creation of our own solar system: our Sun, the Earth, and all the Earth's sister planets.

Our Solar System Is Born

Approximately five billion years ago, our solar system was nothing more than a cloud of hydrogen and helium atoms, with the dust grains containing the heavy elements swirling in space. Its transformation probably began when a supernova exploded nearby; the force of the shock from this explosion caused the dust cloud to collapse in on itself. The collapsing cloud developed a dense, rotating core, destined to become our Sun. The material spinning around in the outer layers, outside the core, was eventually to form the planets, including our own Earth.

The core of the cloud collapsed into itself, and the heat rose, fueled by the hydrogen that became our Sun. The dust grains, ice-coated, revolving around our youthful Sun, grew denser. Whenever these grains collided with each other, they stuck, and like rolling snowballs they grew larger as they collected more and more dust grains around them. At first these balls were distributed more or less randomly around the Sun, but as the Sun spun on its axis, and the balls grew, they fell into a ring, pulled around by the tremendously powerful gravity of the Sun. Eventually they formed a thin band around the Sun, much like the rings around Saturn.

As the balls continued to orbit around the Sun, larger ones attracted smaller ones. Whenever they collided, they formed larger and larger balls. Eventually the largest masses swept the rings clean of smaller balls, and began to establish relatively stable orbits for themselves. These large surviving masses became the planets.

Our planet Earth, the third planet out from the Sun, is one of only four *terrestrial* planets in our solar system. Only the rocklike materials which make up these terrestrial planets could have survived the heat of the Sun. Those planets past Mars, which is the furthest from the Sun of the four terrestrial planets, are nonterrestrial. They are made of light gases, such as hydrogen and helium, with ices that can survive the extremely low temperatures at these greater distances from the Sun. These planets resemble clouds, but have not grown large enough to collapse into themselves to become stars; they are called *jovian* planets.*

When the planet Earth was still relatively young by universal standards (less than a billion years old), it had reached its full size. It was made of silicates, iron, nickel, and ice grains, and had established about the same

*From Jove, an alternative name of Jupiter.

At first the ice-coated balls were distributed randomly around the sun. As the sun spun on its axis, they formed a band. (The First Step, 1910, by Frantisek Kupka. Oil on canvas, 32″ × 51″. Museum of Modern Art, New York. Hillman Periodicals Fund.)

Mars (left) is a terrestrial planet, made of rocklike materials, but Jupiter (right) is nonterrestrial, made of hydrogen and helium gases. (Courtesy of Lick Observatory.)

The earth has four layers—the solid core, the liquid core, the mantle, and the outer crust.

gravity as today. It was following an elliptical orbit around the Sun. As the Earth traveled through space, it occasionally collided with smaller masses, dust particles and rocks, of the same material from which it was formed. This constant bombardment generated great heat, and created immense craters on the Earth's surface. The heat was, in fact, so great that it began to melt the outer crust of the Earth, causing vast rivers of lava to flow. This process was to continue until the Earth had swept its path through space clear of rocks and other materials.

At the center of the Earth were rare heavy metals produced by the last stages of the supernova explosion which had triggered the birth of our solar system from a cloud. These rare metals included uranium and thorium. The nuclei of the atoms that make up these metals are extremely unstable; so these nuclei disintegrate quickly. The nuclei began to fly apart with tremendous energy and speed. This process is very similar to what happens in a nuclear reactor: it is nuclear fission rather than nuclear fusion, a disintegration rather than an integration of nuclear materials.

The nuclear fission at the center of the Earth continued until the heat at the core reached approximately 9,000° Fahrenheit, a temperature nearly equal to that at the surface of the Sun, or three times hotter than a steel furnace. Most of the Earth, heated to these temperatures, was transformed into a molten mass. The iron, present throughout the material that made up the Earth, flowed to the center, establishing a core of iron, mostly molten, which exists to this day.

As time went on, the nuclear materials originally from the rare metals at the Earth's center began to be used up, and as a result the

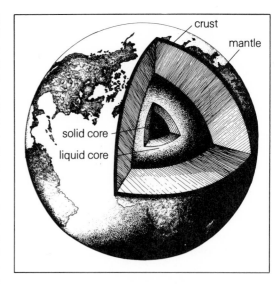

Earth cooled slightly. The metals which had the highest melting points began to solidify, and as this happened they were drawn back toward the center of the Earth.

The cooling of the Earth continued. Because the original molten mass was made up of many materials, each with a different melting point, layers began to be formed: the heaviest materials were closest to the core, with lighter and lighter materials appearing closer to the outermost crust of the Earth.

The Earth has three major layers: the core, the mantle, and the outer crust. The core is a ball about 3,600 miles in diameter. The mantle is 2,200 miles thick, and the crust upon which we live—soil, oceans, and rivers—is a mere ten miles thick.

Below the Earth's crust, in the outer regions of the mantle, is a layer which geologists call "slush." The slush consists of solid rock mixed with molten rock. This thick,

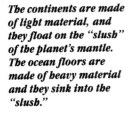

The continents are made of light material, and they float on the "slush" of the planet's mantle. The ocean floors are made of heavy material and they sink into the "slush."

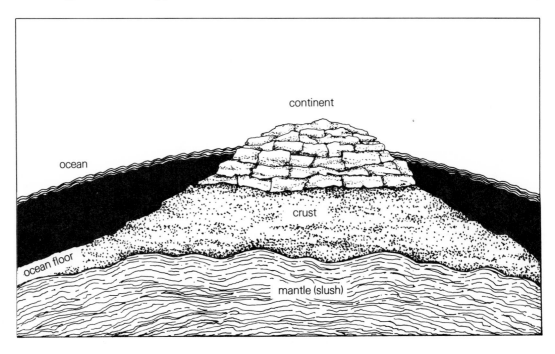

semiliquid slush acts like a cushion, on which rest solid slabs which geologists call "plates." (There are six major plates, and several minor ones, which make up the whole surface of the Earth.) The formation of oceans and continents is determined by the weight of the materials from which each is made: the ocean floors are made of the heaviest materials, and as a result they sink deep into the plates; the continents are made of the lightest materials, and so they float highest above the plates. The plates supporting our oceans and continents have been constantly in motion since their formation about 2.5 billion years ago. The edges of these plates are what is commonly known as "earthquake faults."

To give an illustration of how much the plates move, about 250 million years ago all the land on the Earth was joined into a single mass, a giant continent that the geologists called Pangaea. Pangaea was surrounded by a single ocean of water. Then the plates began shifting, rearranging the single land mass into many continents and oceans, as we have today. This process took millions of years, and it continues even to this day, as is evidenced by earthquakes the world over. As the plates shift, their edges bump together, cracking and buckling under the great forces exerted on them. It is this activity that shapes the mountains and valleys which create the highly individualized geography of each continent. The plates have been moving since the first continent was formed, and they will continue to move as long as the Earth lives.

The Oceans and Atmosphere Are Formed

The Earth formed from balls of dust grains coated with ice. There were probably three kinds of ices coating the dust grains: water ice (H_2O), ammonia ice (NH_3), and methane ice (CH_4). When the Earth's temperature began to rise, melting even the rocks that shaped it, the ices naturally melted too. As they melted, the ices turned into gases, escaping from the Earth like steam rising from baked apples, in a process called "outgassing." As the water rose, leaving the Earth, it struck the cool air of space and condensed. It fell back to Earth in the form of rain, and filled the indentation on the plates, becoming our oceans. The outgassing continued as the Earth's plates collided and volcanoes erupted. The saltiness of our oceans evolved as the waters continued to evaporate, condense into clouds, and rain down over the land,

The plates supporting our continents and oceans have been constantly in motion since their formation two and a half billion years ago. View of Earth. Courtesy of NASA.)

About 250 million years ago all the land on earth formed a single giant continent, called Pangaea.

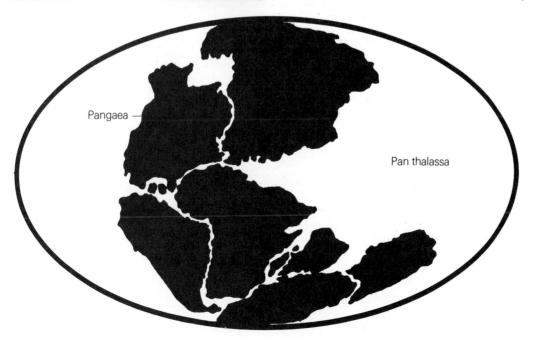

leaching minerals and carrying them back to the seas.

What happened to the other two ices—methane and ammonia—as they outgassed? Instead of becoming clouds that would turn to rain, these gases continued to move heavenward; eventually they were held in a wide band around the Earth by its gravitational pull, and thus became the planet's first atmosphere. Interestingly enough, our first atmosphere was not at all like the one we have today. Very few of the life forms now living on our planet could have survived more than a few seconds in that environment. The toxic gases that enveloped our Earth far exceeded any air pollution we would possibly imagine; they were a combination of chemicals that would be comparable to swamp gas and ammonia.

Oxygen released from H_2O during rains was responsible for transforming the toxic methane and ammonia into an atmosphere that could support some of the life forms we know today. Oxygen reacted with methane to form carbon dioxide, and with ammonia to release nitrogen. As this transformation took place, during millions of years, the atmosphere of the Earth became less and less poisonous, but it still didn't have oxygen. It had about the same nitrogen content as it has today (about 78 percent), but carbon dioxide, rather than oxygen, was the dominant gas in the remaining 22 percent.

Taking an inventory of the Earth's bounty at this stage of its life, we'd have found that it possessed all the minerals and elements it has today. There were several continents and oceans. There were great rains and lightning storms. There was sunlight, cosmic rays, ultraviolet light; gaseous atoms were provided by outgassing and evaporation. All sorts of elements bombarded the Earth's surface from outer space. And the seas had become a veritable soup of new alliances between atoms and compounds, with water vapor rising into the atmosphere, raining down into the oceans or down upon the land, collecting more minerals, and rushing back to the seas to establish still newer alliances. Steaming volcanoes, shifting continents, and dramatic ocean tides stirred the rich soup, readying our youthful planet for the coming of life as we know it today.

From the Hopis of northeastern Arizona:

Taiowa (the Creator) was pleased. "You have done a great work according to my plan, nephew. You have created the universes and made them manifest in solids, waters, and winds, and put them in their proper places. But your work is not yet finished. Now you must create life and its movement to complete the four parts of my universal plan . . . Here is this Earth we have created. It has shape and substance, direction and time, beginning and end. But there is no life upon it. We hear no joyful sound. What is life without sound and movement? So you have been given the power to help give us this life."[10]

The living Earth was ready for the emergence of life. (*Hopi Indian Snake Dancer Entering Kiva,* 1920. Library of Congress.)

CHAPTER TWO

The Beginnings of Human Life

All life on Earth began with the same four elements: carbon, hydrogen, oxygen, and nitrogen. These four building blocks have combined and recombined to form proteins, carbohydrates, and fats, which not only create living cells, but continue to nurture those cells throughout their lives. These basic substances have joined to form all the species that have existed since the beginning of time, from the bacteria and blue-green algae, which were the first life forms on Earth, to the hundreds of thousands of plant and animal species that abound today. Since we can trace our own beginnings to these four elements, it becomes obvious that *we are all kin.* Our kinship includes all plants and animals on the Earth.

Every life form can be scientifically envisioned as an *organization of molecules* which is not by any means haphazard. On the one hand, their formation depends on the availability of certain materials. Then, in order for that organization to succeed, there must be nutrients available. Beyond this, the stability of any organism's life depends on such factors as a particular temperature range, the absence of toxins against which it can't protect itself, the levels of radiation from the Sun, and the absence of predators that might annihilate it.

We each fit into an "ecological niche." This niche is not an arbitrary geographical territory. Rather, an organism's niche is determined by its particular behavior: how it transforms energy, how it responds to and changes its physical and biological surroundings, and how it interrelates with other species.

A species is shaped, in large part, by its interactions with its environment; its success depends on its ability to change as its environment changes. But the changing of a species requires thousands of years, not mere decades. If an environmental change is too abrupt, the organism may not be able to adapt and it will die. In our age of technology, we must take a long and careful look at this fact. *Homo*

sapiens, which like all other species grew out of a particular set of environmental conditions, and evolved in response to changes in the world that occurred over millions of years, has become responsible for some of the most dramatic environmental alterations the Earth has ever known. Within the last fifty years, and with increasing incidence and force, we have been changing our own ecological niche, a niche that we share with thousands of other species, many of which must remain healthy if we ourselves are to survive. That niche is becoming so different from the one in which we evolved that our bodies are no longer comfortable, no longer free of dis-ease. Even all the biological capabilities we have evolved to remain stable as a species in our niche may not be enough for us to successfully adapt to the environment we ourselves are creating. Time is a factor now; we have taken millions of years to develop our bodies to fit the environment, but in a short period of fifty years we have dramatically changed that environment.

A first step in understanding what may be the consequences of altering our ecological niche as we are doing is to understand the nature of our kinship with the other living things with whom we share that niche. This understanding begins with our appreciation for our own creation.

The Myths That Shaped Human Life

Just as myths of the Earth give us a perspective about our relationship with the universe, so myths of creation give us a perspective about relationships with our environment and other species around us. Interestingly enough, the myths of prescientific cultures roughly parallel the scientific views of creation.

From the Cheyennes of the Great Lake area of the U.S.:

With his power, Maheo (the All Spirit) cre-

ated a great water, like a lake, but salty. Out of this salty water, Maheo knew, he could bring all life that ever was to be. The lake itself was life if Maheo so commanded it. In the darkness of nothingness, Maheo could feel the coolness of the water and taste on his lips the tang of the salt.

"There should be water beings," Maheo told his Power. And so it was. First the fish, swimming in the deep water and then the mussels and snails and crawfish lying on the sand and mud Maheo had formed so his lake should have a bottom. . . .

"Our grandmother Earth is like a woman; she should be fruitful. Let her begin to bear life. Help me, my Power."

When Maheo said that, trees and grass sprang up to become the grandmother's hair.

The flowers became her bright ornaments, and the fruits and seeds were the gifts that Earth offered back to Maheo.[1]

From the Hopi of northeastern Arizona:

Sotuknang [the first Power, according to Hopi legend] was happy seeing how beautiful it all was—the land, the plants, the birds and animals, and the power working through them all. Joyfully he said, "Taiowa [the Creator], come see what our world looks like now!"

"It is very good," said Taiowa. "It is ready now for human life, the final touch to complete my plan."

So Spider Woman gathered earth, this time of four colors, yellow, red, white and black; mixed them with tüchvala, *the liquid of*

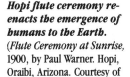

Hopi flute ceremony reenacts the emergence of humans to the Earth.
(*Flute Ceremony at Sunrise,* 1900, by Paul Warner. Hopi, Oraibi, Arizona. Courtesy of the Museum of the American Indian, Heye Foundation.

her mouth; molded them and covered them with her white-substance cape, which was the creative wisdom itself. As before, she sang over them the creation song, and when she uncovered them those forms were human beings in the image of Sotuknang. Then she created four other beings after her own form. They were Wuty, female partners, for the first four male beings.[2]

The scientific view of human origins is not dissimilar. In Carl Sagan's words:

And one day a molecule arose that quite by accident was able to make crude copies of itself out of the other molecules in the broth. As time passed, more elaborate and more accurate self-replicating molecules arose. Those combinations best suited to further replication were favored by the sieve of natural selection. Those that copied better produced more copies. And the primitive oceanic broth gradually grew thin as it was consumed by and transformed into complex condensations of self-replicating organic molecules. Gradually and perceptively, life had begun.

Single-celled plants evolved, and life began to generate its own food. Photosynthesis transformed the atmosphere. Sex was invented. Once free-wheeling forms bonded together to make a complex cell with specialized functions . . . One-celled organisms evolved into multicelled colonies, elaborating their various parts into specialized organ systems. . . . Plants and animals discovered that the land could support life. . . And then, only a moment ago, some small arboreal animals scampered down from the trees.[3]

The Chemical Synthesis of Life

Somewhere around four billion years ago, less than a billion years after the formation of the Earth, the sea and the Earth's atmosphere cooperated to give birth to chemical compounds that would eventually lead to life. The four basic elements—hydrogen, oxygen, nitrogen, and carbon—were among the most common substances in the universe. Because of their structures, they were ideal for building longer, more complex combinations of atoms. These combinations are known as *chemical compounds.*

Compounds made of the four basic elements are extremely stable, and for this reason they held great potential for creating life. The primordial soup which was our ocean four billion years ago contained methane and ammonia from the atmosphere. Within the hot, salty soup, these compounds dissolved into their component ions—ions of carbon, oxygen, hydrogen, and nitrogen—and these ions began to combine and recombine in a variety of new ways.

Box 2.1. Building blocks of life found in interstellar space

Acetaldehyde (CH_3CHO)
Acetonitrile (CH_3CN)
Cyanimide (NH_2HCO)*
Cyanoacetylene (HC_3N)
Formaldehyde ($HCHO$)*
Formamide (NH_2HCO)
Formic acid ($CHOOH$)*
Hydrogen cyanide (HCN)*
Isocyanic acid ($HNCO$)
Methanol (CH_3OH)*
Methyl acetylene (CH_3C_2H)
Methylamine (CH_3NH_2)*

*These compounds combine with other simple molecules to form amino acids, which are DNA precursors.   Adapted from Cloud, 1978.

Within the primordial soup are all the elements necessary for life. (Primordial Soup, 1972, by Michael Samuels.)

The energy to stir this primordial soup, meanwhile, was being provided by vast electric storms above the seas, and by ultraviolet rays from the Sun, rays that were especially strong at this time because the Earth had not yet developed an ozone layer to filter them out. Within the primordial soup the four basic elements began to form larger, more complex molecules, including formaldehyde ($HCHO$), hydrogen cyanide (HCN), formic acid ($CHOOH$), and methanol (CH_3OH).

Formaldehyde, hydrogen cyanide, formic acid, and methanol are called *intermediate molecules;* that is, they react with other molecules to make amino acids. For example, when formaldehyde reacts with hydrogen cyanide, then with water and methane, it produces the amino acid *alanine.* Amino acids are the substances from which proteins are made.

In 1951, Stanley Miller and Harold Urey, at the University of Chicago, passed an electric charge through a mixture of methane, ammo-

The four basic elements —hydrogen, carbon, nitrogen, and oxygen—combined to form complex molecules, called amino acids, that are the building blocks necessary for creating life. The amino acids formed huge molecules called proteins, which eventually combined to form the basic cellular structures of our bodies.

Large proteinoid microspheres can be made in the laboratory. They resemble fossils seen in early rocks.

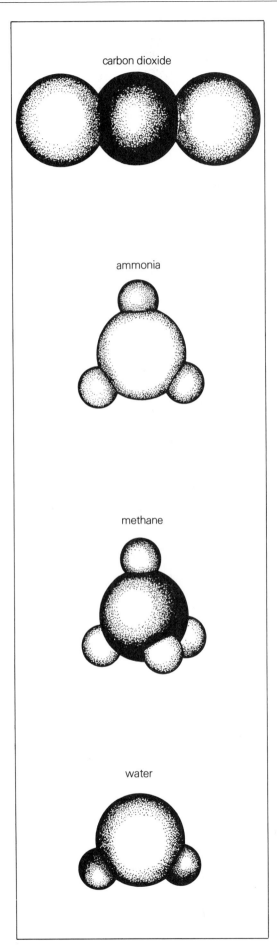

carbon dioxide

ammonia

methane

water

nia, and steam, without oxygen, reproducing conditions that had probably occurred four billion years ago. The Miller–Urey experiments produced amino acids, proving that the Earth might have done the same. (It is fascinating to note that all the elements necessary for producing amino acids are present throughout the universe.)

Sidney Fox provided the next piece in the puzzle of how life was created on Earth. At the University of Miami, Fox warmed mixtures of amino acids and water, and the amino acids miraculously joined together into long, protein-like chains. These chains folded into themselves and became microscopic balls; the balls then connected each other into structures that resemble some bacteria that exist today. At this point, a sudden leap occurred, from simply

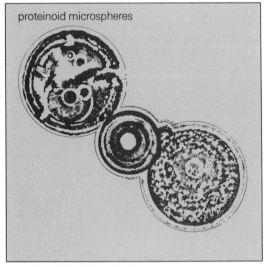

proteinoid microspheres

producing new combinations of chemicals to producing life-like structures. One of the exciting things about the Fox experiments was that these strings of balls closely resembled fossils that scientists had dated at 3.5 to 4 billion years old.

From a Random to an Ordered System

Up to this point, new forms were being created more or less randomly, that is, by molecules bumping into each other and joining. But in order for more complex forms to develop, there had to be a system for passing along specific information. The random system worked all right as long as the forms being created were simple, but in order for a complex bacteria or a plant or an animal to develop, there had to be a "blueprint," a stock of information telling molecules exactly what to do, a set of rules, a way of storing and passing along information for organizing molecules and reproducing whole, intricate life forms. The piece of the puzzle that would accomplish all this is what we now call DNA, which is, in essence, pure information in a material form.

DNA, which stands for *deoxyribonucleic acid*, is made up of very simple compounds. Chemically, it is sugar, phosphate, and nucleic acid. All these compounds are constructed of the simple molecules that were abundant in the primordial soup. (For example, five formaldehyde molecules join together to make one molecule of the kind of sugar that appears in DNA.) Although chemically simple, the task this special combination of sugar, phosphate, and nucleic acid accomplishes is profound.

Just as an ethical code stores and communicates information that enables groups of people to organize into harmonious and productive societies, so DNA stores and communicates information that enables groups of molecules to organize into harmonious and productive life forms.

The structure of DNA resembles two intertwined corkscrews. Along each corkscrew are many balls of nucleic acid, and each ball can combine with only one very specific kind of molecule. When the DNA is dipped into the primordial soup, it picks up those molecules it needs, organizing them in a definite order along the corkscrew.

The first life on Earth was a tiny sphere filled with a liquid mixture of amino acids and proteins, with DNA-like material floating loosely inside it. All this was contained in a cellular membrane made of fatty substances. This most primitive of all life forms closely resembles bacteria that exist today.

These first bacteria-like creatures had some serious limitations, the main one being that

The most primitive of all ancient life forms closely resembled bacteria that exist today. (Cells of E-coli, magnified 22,500 times. Courtesy of S. Abraham and E.H. Beachey. V.A. Medical Center, Memphis, Tenn.)

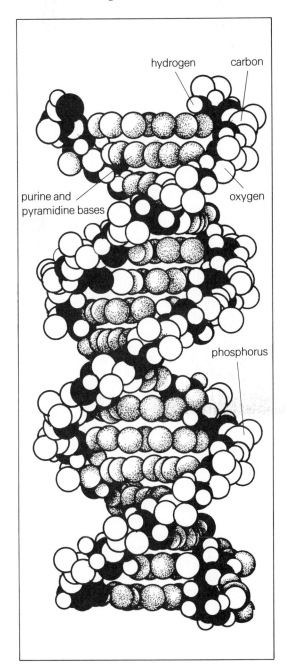

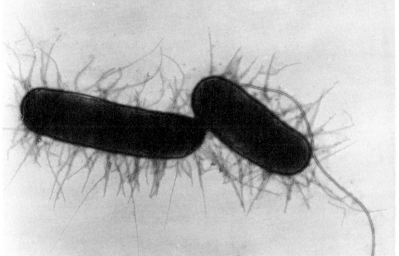

they fed on the same materials in the primordial soup out of which they had been formed. Obviously, if this went on for too long they would have eaten each other. Then, after thousands of years, the creature developed proteins, which allowed it to use some important new resources. With protein contained inside its membrane, the creature was able to take carbon dioxide, abundant in the water, join it with water molecules, and use the energy of the Sun to produce valuable carbohydrates to nurture itself. This was the first appearance on Earth of *photosynthesis*, the process by which plants create their own nutrients from the Sun's energy and minerals in the water. The first creatures capable of this amazing process were the blue-green algae.

Wherever photosynthesis occurs, it produces not only carbohydrates for the plant but oxygen as well. For the first time in the history of the Earth, due to the proliferation of blue-green algae, there was an expanding bounty of free oxygen. Ironically, this same oxygen was a real threat to the blue-green algae, because the oxygen was actually toxic to the creature who

Just as ethical codes store and communicate information by which groups of people organize into harmonious and productive societies, so DNA stores and communicates information by which groups of molecules organize into harmonious and productive life forms. When the DNA was dipped into the primordial soup of simple chemical compounds, it picked up those molecules it needed and arranged them in a definite order.

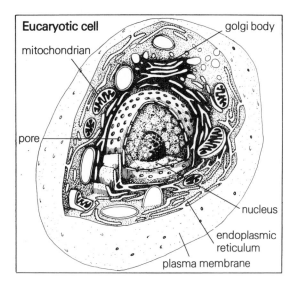

Eucaryotic cell

golgi body

mitochondrian

pore

nucleus

endoplasmic
reticulum

plasma membrane

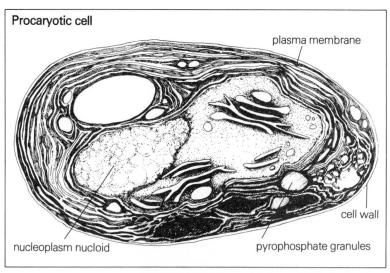

Procaryotic cell

plasma membrane

cell wall

nucleoplasm nucloid

pyrophosphate granules

*The first cells on Earth
were procaryotic cells.
They were simple struc-
tures that had no
nucleus; their DNA was a
single coil floating freely
in the cell. Modern blue-
green algae resemble
these early cell
structures.*

*The eucaryotic cell
represented an important
evolutionary jump be-
cause it had a nucleus
that formed a packet of
DNA. These were the first
cells that had the ability
to detoxify oxygen.*

*After blue-green algae
learned to photosynthe-
size, producing oxygen,
our aerobic environment
evolved. All the Earth's
creatures have a common
ancestor, two billion
years back, in the blue-
green algae. (Algae, 1972,
by Michael Samuels.)*

*Ozone is O_3; it arises in the
atmosphere when an ultraviolet
ray splits an ordinary, diatomic
oxygen molecule, O_2, into two
monatomic molecules, which may
recombine, or may combine with
an O_2 molecule to form O_3. It is
the splitting of oxygen molecules
which uses up the potentially
harmful energy of the ultraviolet
rays; the ozone is the result of the
filtering process.

had produced it. In one respect, we might view this as the first case of mass pollution produced by one of the Earth's inhabitants.

Up to now the creatures that inhabited the Earth reproduced themselves by simply splitting in half, thus producing two organisms where there had previously only been one. Each new generation was exactly like its parent—or nearly so. Because of this close duplication, there was little opportunity for broad change or adaptation to varying environmental conditions. The only opportunity for change was through *mutation*, which occurred when the DNA was accidentally altered, either by exposure to the ultraviolet rays of the Sun or by other mechanisms offered by the environment. Because there was no ozone layer to filter out the Sun's rays, the DNA had no particular need to develop more sophisticated mechanisms for change. However, this cooperation between the Sun and what was then the Earth's most advanced creature on the evolutionary scale was not to last.

As the amount of oxygen in the atmosphere increased, it created an ozone layer, which filtered out the ultraviolet rays.* Thus the blue-green algae lost their primary mechanism for change. Had the blue-green algae failed to evolve new life forms at this point, all further development of life on Earth might have ceased.

To solve the problem posed by the absence of ultraviolet rays, the blue-green algae developed an entirely new system for change. It developed a membranous sack within itself that held the DNA in a neat little bundle. Once the DNA was enveloped in this membrane, its structure was altered. Instead of being a double corkscrew-like shape, floating loosely around inside the organism, it became many small strands of nucleic acid. This arrangement made possible a whole new system of reproduction, that is, sexual reproduction, by which two individuals, often with different charac-

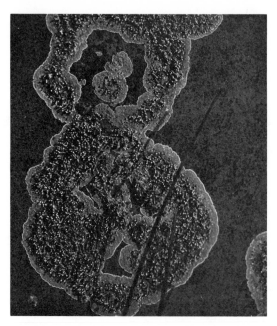

teristics, could contribute DNA to produce new generations of organisms similar to, but not copies of, themselves. Great varieties of nucleic acid could be brought together in this way. And at this point in the development of the primordial soup, a great many mutations were already in existence, left over from the days before ultraviolet rays had been filtered out by the ozone layer. These were now able to come together, providing a vast number of variables.

One of the more dramatic changes to come out of this new system of reproduction was an organism that could detoxify oxygen and could actually benefit from the presence of this gas. This new breed of blue-green algae grew and became abundant, producing increasing quantities of oxygen until our Earth was totally enveloped by an oxygen-rich atmosphere, with a permanent ozone layer to filter out the ultraviolet rays.

Once our oxygen-rich atmosphere was in

place, the circumstances that had allowed life to develop from chemical compounds were completed. A lid was placed on further evolution of this kind. The step-by-step process of combining elements until an actual living organism emerged had to occur in an anerobic (oxygen-less) environment. After blue-green algae learned to photosynthesize, producing oxygen, and our aerobic environment was set, life would have to evolve from whatever living organisms were in existence at that time.

If we trace our roots back to this stage in the Earth's history, as indeed we can do, we see our kinship not only with the blue-green algae, but with all the other species who also evolved —along different, though parallel, lines with our own—from this common ancestor. By comparing protein molecules and reconstruct-

bers increased, and the generations that followed continued to change, making better and better use of their environment, even developing capabilities for moving to new environments when that of their parents altered radically or became overcrowded.

The environment is as important as the DNA itself in fostering change. When, for example, the oxygen level increased on the Earth—nearly doubling in a half-billion years— those organisms that could detoxify and use oxygen thrived, but those that were poisoned by it died out. This change in the environment resulted in the natural selection of organisms that could thrive in the new environment and produce offspring that could thrive as well.

The more rapid and dramatic a change in the environment is, the more rapid is the pro-

---

Box 2.2. Evolution time scale

20 billion years ago:	the big bang
6.6 billion years ago:	supernovation, the formation of the seeds of our solar system
4.6 billion years ago:	formation of our solar system
3.8 billion years ago:	first cells, bacteria
1 to 2 billion years ago:	blue-green algae
1 billion years ago:	green algae, increased abundance of oxygen
600 million years ago:	first multicelled sea animals, such as starfish, jellyfish, flatworms, also mosses, liverworts, and vascular plant life
490 million years ago:	first animals with backbones
300 to 400 million years ago:	first fish
200 to 300 million years ago:	reptiles, insects, ferns, some dinosaurs
190 million years ago:	first mammals
100 million years ago:	the age of dinosaurs
60 million years ago:	earliest primates
20 million years ago:	monkeys
2 to 3 million years ago:	early human ancestors, hominoids, Australopithecus
500 thousand years ago:	*Homo erectus*
50 thousand years ago:	*Homo sapiens*
5 to 10 thousand years ago:	beginnings of agriculture
2 to 5 thousand years ago:	first cities
2 hundred years ago:	industrial revolution
50 years ago:	nuclear and computer age

Sexual reproduction offered the opportunity for unique combinations of genetic material derived from two different parent chromosomes.

chromosome

crossbands

ing our evolutionary paths, geneticists have been able to demonstrate that all the Earth's creatures—bacteria, plants, fishes, insects, birds, and other animals—have a common ancestor, two billion years back, in the blue-green algae.

How Did So Many Species Come from One?

The potential for change presented by sexual reproduction meant that a wide variety of creatures could evolve to fit diverse environments. Out of the unique combinations of DNA that two parent organisms enjoyed, there would evolve an immense variety of species, each with special characteristics that allowed it to thrive in the environment into which it was born. As each species endured, its num-

cess of evolution. When, for example, mountains are formed by the collision of the Earth's plates, opportunities arise for new species to develop to fit into those untried environments. The most dramatic environmental change of this type took place when the ozone layers formed, shielding the Earth from ultraviolet rays and making it possible for organisms to live on the land. Until then the ocean was the only environment which could support life, but suddenly there were millions of new environmental possibilities.

This brings us to an important concept in evolutionary theory: whenever large new environments open up, there are suddenly a broad variety of environmental *niches* to be filled. When the filtering of ultraviolet rays opened up the land to life, there were suddenly deserts and mountains, rivers and valleys, hot areas and cold ones, each of which, because of its unique characteristics, offered different environmental opportunities. Theoretically a species could form to fill each and every niche offered by the land.

When an organism makes an evolutionary breakthrough, as happened when life forms began leaving the sea to live on the land, the offspring evolve broadly to fill a huge variety of niches. Great variations of species develop within the lineages, each with its own specialized physical characteristics that allow it to use a special place in the environment. As an organism specializes, becoming a master of its particular niche, organisms without the same mastery tend not to do as well. Thus, competition for each niche tends to be limited by this process of adaptation.

When a single species finds a broad new environment and begins fanning out to take advantage of all the possibilities, the process is called *adaptive radiation*. This can be seen in the first fish that adapted lizardlike features and moved to the land. With this vast unused territory open to it, virtually every individual offspring of that lizardlike creature was able to find an environmental niche and succeed in it. If an individual was born lacking the characteristics needed to thrive in the environment of its parents, it could find a new niche, where it could survive and start a whole new lineage of its own. Sometimes these new lineages, given a million years of evolution, would change so much that they seemed not to resemble their ancestors at all.

Sometimes the events that lead to the development of new species seem abrupt and accidental, rather than part of a smooth, natural progression. For example, new species arise sometimes when members of one group are separated from another. Floods, the formation of mountains, the drifting apart of continents, have all caused such separation. When isolation occurs, one group may develop entirely different characteristics from another, and finally the two become distinct species.

In the processes of sexual reproduction, natural selection, adaptive radiation, and isolation of one group from another, we have all the evolutionary mechanisms through which single-cell organisms would evolve into the human race.

Major Steps in Human Evolution

The story of human evolution, from blue-green algae to the present, is a story of endless challenge and the triumph of the life force itself. The abilities to diversify and to evolve increasingly complex forms encouraged the development of organisms that could thrive in virtually every environmental niche the Earth had to offer. As new organisms developed, each one made changes in the environment by its very presence, and in a real sense each became an integral part of the environment. For example, when blue-green algae became capable of producing oxygen, they transformed the Earth's atmosphere; these creatures became a force in the evolution of the Earth.

The next big evolutionary step after blue-green algae was the organization of single cells into multicelled structures. It was almost as if single cells made a cooperative decision to join together and work as a larger unit, in order to take advantage of more diverse environmental opportunities. This banding together of cells first resulted in digestive systems that could nourish the organism on a diet of blue-green algae and other single-celled organisms. It also resulted in the development of muscles for locomotion, shells for protection, and sense organs for gathering information. The species that grew from this step included sponges, corals, jellyfish, worms, clams, and starfish, as well as multicelled plants. (Remember, blue-green algae were the only forms of vegetation up to this moment in the Earth's history.) The new, more complex forms of vegetation included a variety of seaweed that had a circulatory system, roots, and leaves, which enabled them to move to environments outside the sea.

Plants preceded animals in their move from the sea to the land. Indeed, the plants would need to change the face of the earth, creating a vast new set of environmental conditions, before animals could find the land habitable. The first land plants were mosses, rushes, and ferns. All the changes, brought about when single-celled organisms cooperated to create multicelled organisms, began 680 million years ago.

When multicelled organisms moved from the sea to the land, they had to change the way they reproduced. In the sea, the water served as a medium for exchanging genetic material and for nourishing the soft, permeable egg during gestation. This process obviously wouldn't have worked on the land; besides the problem that the Sun's rays would dry out a soft-shelled egg, the soil and the air didn't supply the materials the egg needed to mature. Before animals could fully adapt to life outside the sea, they had to evolve hard-shelled eggs which contained all the nutrients needed to support the infant organism inside.

In a similar way, supplying each cell with a steady supply of oxygen poses special problems for multicelled organisms. Whereas each single-celled organism living in the sea is bathed in a medium containing oxygen, many cells in a multicelled organism may have no direct contact with the external environment. In order to carry oxygen and other nutrients to every cell in its body, the multicelled organism, whether plant or animal, had to develop a circulatory system.

Plants moved to the land approximately 500 million years before the animals did. In that period of time the plants transformed the barren surface of the land into a jungle of green. Not until the plants had established themselves on the land did animal life venture out from the seas. And the first animal life to make that bold move was an insect. The insects were so successful that they thrive even to this day, boasting a greater population than any other type of animal.

The insects got along very well with the plants. In fact, the insects came to serve an important function for the plants; the tiny winged creatures carried pollen from plant to plant, something plants couldn't do for themselves. Plants did their best to make the most of this, developing scents and bright-colored

moving ever outward into all the environmental niches available, some fish adapted to environments that were muddy rather than simply watery. These fish developed especially muscular fins for moving around in the sticky goo of their world, and from them evolved the first *amphibians*, creatures who divided their time between the land and the sea. As the amphibians ventured further and further from the sea, they developed an appetite for plants and insects that were part of the land environments. These marsh creatures also developed a hard-shelled egg, freeing them from having to return to the sea to reproduce.

The first amphibians depended on a damp environment to provide moisture for their bodies. But in time they developed a protective skin, to shield them from the heat of the

As dinosaurs disappeared from our planet, new environmental opportunities opened up for mammals. (Ichthyosaurus Vertebra, 1982, by Michael Samuels.)

flowers to attract the insects, and locating their reproductive organs within the flowers so that pollination would be accomplished when the insect came to visit.

At this point most animals were still very limited in mobility. The largest creatures in the seas were snails and clams, which have limited mobility. The development of a backbone—the next big evolutionary step—meant that organisms could develop a rigid structure that was not a type of hard, outer shell. They could go on to evolve complex nervous systems, skeletons, and muscular organs well-suited for moving across great expanses of sea or land and for manipulating objects in the physical environment. Scientists believe that starfish and sea urchins provided the first models for this next evolutionary step, since these creatures, in the larval stage, possess a kind of rudimentary backbone.

The backbone was an extremely successful innovation, producing thousands of different kinds of fish. As the populations of fish grew,

Sun, and a system for retaining water within their own bodies. These innovations allowed the amphibians to move out of the swamps into drier and drier territories, and it marked the coming of the age of reptiles. The age of reptiles began about 300 million years ago, and reptiles dominated the Earth until about 60 million years ago.

Around 250 million years ago the Earth's weather patterns began to change. The tropical climates that had supported reptilian life so comfortably began to cool. Most of the larger cold-blooded creatures (the dinosaurs) died out. As always, the altered physical environment pushed the evolutionary processes of the animals toward change. A few creatures began to appear who could regulate their own body temperatures, freeing them of their dependence on the Earth's weather.

Fossils have been found of an animal that resembled a rat as much as a reptile; it lived on Earth some 190 million years ago. This creature, the prototype for mammals, had fur on its body, could maintain its own body heat, and produced milk to feed its young. Descendents of this modest little mammal, about the size of a shrew, would eventually dominate the Earth's land populations.

By 60 million years ago large animals who could not regulate their own body temperatures were dying out in great number. They simply couldn't survive in the cooler temperatures now characteristic of the Earth's weather. As these reptiles disappeared forever from the face of our planet, new environmental opportunities were opened up for the mammals. The mammals proliferated, evolving special adaptations to fit every imaginable niche. One mammal even took up residence in the trees.

Our early tree-living mammals looked very much like modern-day shrews and, in the beginning, their diet was limited to insects. In the long process of adapting to their new environment, they changed in several important ways. First, their diet expanded to include nuts and fruits, which were, of course, abundant. This led them to develop a shorter jaw, with teeth suited for masticating fruits and nuts. They developed grasping fingers, both for picking nuts and fruits, and for helping them get around in the trees. In time their eyes moved from the sides of their heads to the front, thus providing them with stereoscopic vision and the ability to judge depth, an important skill for animals living in the trees. The completion of these adaptations marked the coming of the age of primates.

The first primates probably looked like modern-day lemurs. They had eyes facing forward, a long, muscular tail, and well-articulated grasping fingers.

Out of the lemur-like species grew the first anthropoids, a class of animals that includes

monkeys, apes, and humans. About 30 million years ago, the anthropoids' evolution separated into two distinct branches: the monkeys on one hand, the apes and humans on the other. The family to which humans and apes belong is known as the *hominids*. They have no tail, and they have both larger brains and larger bodies than monkeys. For the first time we begin to see behavior among animals that closely resembles human behavior.

Life Among the Hominids

The earliest hominids were three to four feet tall, and looked very much like modern-day apes. They had no tail, canine teeth, and mobile faces, with rather sophisticated muscles of expression. They lived in bands that included between ten and thirty individuals, each band dominated by a single male. Most of the band members were females with their offspring.

These hominids were territorial; their territories were usually limited to the trees where they nested and to the ground area immediately beneath them. They spent most of their time in the trees, eating, sleeping, breeding, and raising their offspring. They came down to the ground only rarely, but when they did they walked more or less upright.

There is good evidence that the hominids used sticks and stones for tools, and, thanks to their ability to walk upright, were able to carry things in their arms. Their diet consisted largely of fruits and nuts, with occasional supplements of insects or small game that they either captured or scavenged.

These early hominids nursed their young, holding them to their breasts much as humans do today. The young were reared by the band for several years, reaching maturity at 9 to 10 years of age. The average lifetime was around 30 years of age. Females bred the year around, with menstrual cycles not unlike those of humans.

The social structure of the band was based on age and sex, with the oldest and strongest male dominating. Social activities were focused on reproduction and raising offspring. Young hominids played with others in their peer group, all under the watchful eyes of the parents.

The adults of the band probably spent much time teaching the young the traditions of the group and acceptable behavior. We can suppose the young were also taught the vocal signals the band used to communicate with each other; there would have been signals for danger, food, friendship, sexual activity, and maternal care, and calls to tell others of their location.

Although territorial, the hominids did not seek out conflicts with neighboring bands, but

As early hominids left the trees, they developed large brains along with upright stature. (Plesianthropus Broom. Courtesy of the American Museum of Natural History.)

neither did they seek out their friendship or cooperation. They were neutral at best, defensive and hostile at worst.

Climatic Changes

Around the time of the early hominids, the Earth began undergoing some tremendous geological changes. The plates began shifting rapidly and dramatically, and changes in the wobble of the Earth's axis caused the coming of a series of ice ages. What is now the Indian subcontinent was pressed north, bumping into Asia and producing what was to become the majestic Himalayan mountain range. This new formation blocked the northward flow of warm air from Africa toward Asia and Europe. Warm ocean currents shifted, because of the change in the continents, and glaciers from the north polar regions moved as far south as the middle of Europe and America.

As glaciers from the north crept south, rains in South Africa increased, turning once arid deserts into rain forests. Meanwhile, the climates of North America and Europe were transformed from semitropical to frigid, like that of regions now close to the North Pole.

Scientists speculate that the glaciers extended southward and then receded on a 26,000-year cycle. (In evolutionary time this is not a long period, since it probably takes a million years for a new species to form.) The 26,000-year span is based on the wobble of the Earth's axis, which completes its cycle in that time. During the part of each cycle when the glaciers were receding, Africa once more became arid, but Europe, parts of Asia, and the northern regions of the American continent became warmer, with rich, dense forests. What is important to note here is that there

have been not just one ice age, but 15, since the appearance of the first hominids.

We said earlier that changes in the environment stimulate changes in species; the individuals that are most able to adjust to the changed environments are the ones who survive, and who therefore reproduce. Their offspring will also have the characteristics needed to live in the new environments. Imagine, then, the evolutionary challenge to those species that lived on the Earth during these vast changes in the Earth's weather patterns!

The changes that occurred within each of the 26,000-year cycles were complex and multifaceted, but for our purposes we can focus on the most important of these changes: the disappearance of dense tree growth after each period of glaciation. With the disappearance of the trees, our hominid ancestors were robbed of their former habitat. Those who could only live in the trees eventually evolved into modern-day gibbons and siamangs. Those individuals who learned how to live on the ground started a whole new evolutionary line, a line that led directly toward human beings.

Those Who Left the Trees

In order to survive, the hominids who moved from the trees to the ground needed to develop a whole new set of habits. The most obvious of these was an upright posture. By walking erect, they were able to see over the tall grasses that grew in their new environment, allowing them to get a better view of the landscape, not only to search for food, but also to see predators. In addition, the upright stance, once fully mastered, left their hands free for carrying things: tools, weapons, food, and offspring.

Obviously the diet of these animals had to change. They became increasingly dependent on meat, since the fruits and nuts that had been their mainstays were in shorter and shorter supply. As they became meateaters, they also had to find sources for water. As residents of the trees, and vegetarians, their diet had not required a separate water source. The new need for water introduced a whole new set of problems for the hominids, problems centered on behavior patterns at the water hole. In the wild, all meateaters congregate at the water holes; and so the traffic between predators and their prey is extensive. In order to use the water holes, the hominids had to learn to defend themselves against larger animals; at the same time, they would want to take smaller game for nourishment. In order to succeed as hunters and to survive, they had to develop social systems of cooperation.

Early hominids were relatively small and weak to succeed as hunters; to survive their frequent visits to the water hole, they had to be

Early humans chose sharp rocks for cutting or scraping and often chipped away pieces to form more efficient shapes. (Flint implement, pointed form. Courtesy of the American Museum of Natural History.)

As evolution continued, large brains developed, providing increased intellectual ability to adapt to a rapidly changing environment. Innovation had become an adaptive mechanism. (Skull of *Pithecanthropus Robustus.* Courtesy of the American Museum of Natural History.)

innovative. Innovation and intelligence led to tool building, as well as to planning and cooperation between members of their groups. Planning and cooperation required the development of a language, something more than a crude set of signals to call others, warn them of danger, or express pleasure or pain.

It is interesting to note that dietary patterns brought about a new set of social standards among the hominids. As vegetarians living in the trees, our earliest forerunners picked and ate their food immediately and continuously throughout the day. But when they became meateaters, patterns changed. Game was hunted, captured, and brought back to the group's camp to be shared. Rituals of planning the hunt, catching the animals, preparing the food, and then eating it required a degree of social interchange that the vegetarians had never required.

Changes in Brain, Bone, and Muscle

Physical changes took place in hominids and early humans over millions of years. Archaeologists have been able to put together, from thousands of pieces of evidence, a picture of the major changes that led up to our present stage of evolution. These changes may seem large and dramatic to us, but millions of generations passed between us and the beginning of life on Earth; changes from one generation to another would have been so subtle that parents would rarely have perceived any changes in their offspring.

Bones discovered in recent archaeological digs show that as animals began walking on two feet, their spine, pelvis, feet, and skull underwent some specific alterations. The spinal column, arched horizontally in animal that walk on all fours, had to develop an S-curve to support the upright posture. In addition, the shape of the spines on each vertebra had to change, since muscles that attach to these spines needed new angles of support in the bipedal animal. The hole and joint at the base of the skull had to move from the rear to the bottom of the head, while the jaw shortened and the face became flatter so that the skull would balance atop the spine. For the legs to be aligned parallel to the erect spine, the pelvis had to completely alter in shape. The hip sockets changed to accommodate the new position of the legs, and the pelvis grew larger to support the greater weight it would be carrying. Large muscles—the buttocks—formed to support the weight of the upright body; these muscles essentially had to balance in midair the upper part of the body. In an animal that walks on all fours, the chest is carried by the front feet. Feet developed arches, and the big toes grew larger and more muscular. These changes in the physical struc-

ture took between 5 and 10 million years to complete, and they attained completion only 2 or 3 million years ago.

An upright stature was fully developed before the large brain evolved. Archaeological evidence about our own ancestors during the period of brain development is scant, but the species *Australopithecus* offers us some clues to fill in the gaps in our history. Australopithecus, like monkeys, developed along a line that was separate from, but parallel to, our own development. This creature lived in Africa until approximately a million and a half years ago; Australopithecus first appeared nearly six million years ago, and there is no doubt that early *Homo sapiens* lived in some regions with this earlier species.

From bones and artifacts discovered by archaeologists, we have been able to put together a fairly complete picture of life among the australopithecines. These creatures went beyond merely using sticks and stones as weapons or tools, as some of the earlier hominids had done. Although not adept toolmakers, they were observant enough, and presumably intelligent enough, to choose sharp-edged rocks for cutting or scraping. And there is ample evidence that they knew how to shape a sharp edge on a stone by chipping away pieces until they had attained a crude wedge or point. Their heads were about the same size as those of apes. They lived on the ground, and often found protection in caves; they could probably craft crude shelters of rocks with their hands. They lived in small groups, probably no more than forty individuals in all. They were migratory, traveling many miles over the land in search of food. Evidence of murder, and even cannibalism, has been found; such behavior is found in the study of most primates, but is extremely rare in all other species.

As evolution proceeded for early humans, those individuals with the largest brains began

For humans to walk upright, the spinal column had to evolve into an s-shaped curve.

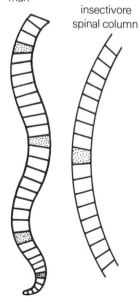

spinal column
man

insectivore
spinal column

to be favored. Larger brains meant an increasing ability to think and discover innovative solutions to problems, thus early humans were able to make adjustments that otherwise would have been impossible. For example, during the various ice ages, with radical shifts in weather patterns, large-brained species were able to figure out ways to keep themselves warm when the weather turned cold: building fires, building shelters, and seeking out enclosed structures. They could also increase their own warmth with animal hides to make fast adjustments to shifting climates when they could not evolve hair patterns quickly enough to have survived.

As early humans developed larger and larger brains, language patterns became increasingly complex. More deliberate activities centered on toolmaking, and more efficient approaches to hunting and gathering food, began to appear. Basketmaking, food preparation, and even religious activities were becoming a part of these peoples' lives.

Brain size continued to increase, from the estimated 400-cc capacity of Australopithecus, to the 1,500-cc capacity of Neanderthal man, a period of time spanning some 5.5 million years. Modern human beings, that is, *Homo sapiens sapiens,* appeared between 25,000 and 50,000 years ago, and have about the same average brain capacity as Neanderthal man. The variety of artifacts left behind by our ancestors indicates that as brain capacity increased, so did the capacity for craftsmanship, imagination, and invention.

As humans developed a larger brain and increasingly sophisticated skills in language, social organization, and toolmaking, there emerged two areas of concern that were entirely new to our planet. These concerns are religion and medicine.

In recent years archaeologists have made a discovery that radically changed our popular view of Neanderthal man as a brutish, insensitive creature. In the Shanidar Cave in the Zagros Mountains of Iraq, there was discovered the evidence of a human burial that had taken place some 60,000 years ago. The pollens of many species of flowers were found, indicating that bunches of flowers had been deliberately arranged around the body, leaving evidence that a ceremony, in which many people had participated, had taken place.

The archaeologist Richard E. Leakey found the Shanidar Cave discovery interesting for several reasons. He points out that deliberate burial of the dead shows a "keen self-awareness and a concern for the human spirit." Such concepts are the rudiments of religion. Leakey goes on to tell us that several of the species of flowers found at the Shanidar burial ceremony were used in local herbal medicines, even in modern times. He reflects, "That the

Shanidar people were aware of at least some of the medicinal properties of these flowers is not unlikely."[4]

Although we are not the direct descendents of Neanderthal man, it is quite likely that we both descend from the same stock. And the picture of these people we are given by the Shanidar discovery quite likely also gives us an accurate picture of our own ancestors' sensitivities.

Shaping Mankind from the Atoms

The story of our evolution provided by scientists seems, in the final analysis, no less miraculous or mysterious than the stories of creation provided by religious texts. From science's vantage point, there are far more questions than there are answers. Though the cosmic egg and the big bang give us events and images on which to hang the story of our beginnings, we are still left with one important, unanswered question: "From where did the cosmic egg come?" In the face of this single question, all of humanity's most sophisticated works are humbled.

Still, there is great value in reconstructing our story, in tracing our development from the random wanderings of elementary particles in space, through the collisions that shaped our planet, and finally to the emergence of life itself, triumphing in its long, eventful journey from the first pressings of the cosmic egg.

And we cannot help but be uplifted when we consider the tenacity of the life force itself, a force that has not only endured but progressed in the face of vast challenges, ranging from the blue-green algae's production of toxins (oxygen), through millions of years of dramatic and violent geological shifts (including ice-age cycles), through droughts and storms and famines we cannot even begin to recount. We are left in awe of this great force, the life

As early humans developed, they evolved keen self-awareness and concern for the spriritual/cultural side of life, expressed in the development of language, healing, art, and sophisticated tools. (Top, cave paintings; bottom, Neanderthal Man. Courtesy of the American Museum of Natural History.)

force, that has lived on even as millions of species have been extinguished.

Compared with the age of the universe, the emergence of an animal with intelligence and consciousness is a late event. And it is even more recently that we have solved the mysteries that allow us to manipulate the elementary particles from which we ourselves have sprung. The clues that might tell us how to use this knowledge are found, we feel, in an understanding of our social institutions, which we will discuss in Chapter Three.

From the Cheyenne of the Great Lakes area, United States:

Maheo reached into his right side, and pulled out a rib bone. He breathed on that bone, and laid it softly on the bosom of the Earth Woman. The bone moved and stirred, and stood upright and walked. The first man had come to be.

"He is alone with Grandmother Earth as I once was with the void," said Maheo. "It is not good for anyone to be alone." So Maheo fashioned a human woman from his left rib, and set her with the man. Then there were two persons on the Grandmother Earth, her children and Maheo's. They were happy together, and Maheo was happy as he watched them.

After a year, in the Springtime, the first child was born. As the years passed, there were other children. They went their ways, and formed many tribes.[5]

From the Hopi, southwestern United States:

The First People of the First World did not answer her; *they could not speak. Spider Woman said, "As you commanded me, I have created these first people. They are fully and firmly formed; they are properly colored; they have life; they have movement. But they cannot talk. That is the proper thing they lack. So I want you to give them speech, also the wisdom and power to reproduce, that they may enjoy their life and give thanks to their creator."*

So Sotuknang gave them speech, a differ-

ent language to each color, with respect for each other's differences. He gave them wisdom and the power to reproduce and multiply.

Then he said to them, "With all these I have given you, this world to live on and be happy, there is only one thing I ask of you. To respect the Creator at all times. Wisdom, harmony, and respect for the love of the Creator who made you. May it grow and never be forgotten among you as long as you live."

So the First People went their directions, were happy, and began to multiply.

Sophisticated tools were an important step in the development of early man.
(*Late Paleolithic Artifacts.* Courtesy of the American Museum of Natural History.)

One of ancient man's first discoveries in the realm of the human spirit involved healing. There is evidence that 60,000 years ago Neanderthal man used healing medicines in ceremonies.
(*Jo Bad, Medicine Man,* 1900. Edward Curtis, Library of Congress.)

**Her* refers to Spider Woman, who in Indian legend is the helper of Taiowa, the Creator, who lives on Earth.

CHAPTER THREE

The Shaping of Human Culture

With the evolution of the large brain, the human race gained the power to reason and invent. And with these powers we gained greater flexibility and a broader range of adaptive choices than are possessed by any other species on our planet.

In a sense, culture is the sum total of our efforts to use our mental capacities to adapt to our environment. In this respect, culture may be the chief adaptive tool that distinguishes us from other animals. With our powers we have gone a step beyond any other species to create our own environment, one which, ironically, now poses at least as many hazards as benefits.

In his book, *Culture: Man's Adaptive Dimension,* Ashley Montagu tells us:

The most important setting of human evolution is the human cultural environment. That setting will not only continue to be the principal mise-en-scène *of man's future development, but . . . increasingly be his chief and most important means of adapting himself to the complexities of the world he has created. Hence, it is important to understand not only what human culture is, how it acts, but also how it came about. And not only for its own sake, or simply because it is so extraordinarily interesting, but principally because the understanding such knowledge of man's nature confers will enable us more intelligently to control and direct our future development.*[1]

The first significant evidence of human culture is to be found in the hunter-gatherer societies. Next came the agriculturalists, and finally the scientific-industrial culture that dominates the present. Examples of all these cultural forms, from the smallest hunter-gatherer tribes to the largest industrialized nations, can be found living on the Earth today, sometimes within only miles of one another.

Each culture is a people's way of adapting to a particular environmental niche. The Eski-

mos of the northernmost regions of our globe have evolved a culture that allows them to live in their frigid, snow-covered home. In the cities, culture helps us adapt not only to the advantages and pressures of a natural environment, but also to advantages and pressures of our own making, the products of a scientific-industrial society.

Every evolutionary change can be measured not in terms of complexity or sophistication, but in terms of the success or failure of a species to adapt to its particular niche. However sophisticated we who live in the industrialized nations may consider ourselves to be, this principle of successful adaptation continues to be as valid for us as it was for blue-green algae billions of years ago. Successful adaptation is a final measure for us all.

The Ancient Roots of Modern Culture

We can trace our roots to the hunter-gatherer societies, and in the process see the similarities between ourselves and the Kalahari Bushmen of South Africa, the Bakhtiari nomads of Persia, and the peasant farmers of India and China. Our kinship with these peoples runs deep.

One cannot help but be humbled to realize how short a period of time our technological societies have existed: less than 200 years. Agricultural societies date back five to ten thousand years. Beyond that, the hunter-gatherer cultures, including predecessors of *homo sapiens sapiens,* can be said to date back three million years. Technological society has not existed long enough to have changed human nature at all.

Thousands of subtle evolutionary changes took place during the millions of years that the hunter-gatherers dominated the Earth. And like all evolutionary changes up to that time, shaped by the rigorous demands of the environment, these allowed humans to live in har-

It is important to understand not only what human culture is, but also how it came about. The understanding such knowledge confers will better enable us to control our future development. (Village near Gomodino Pan, Courtesy of American Museum of Natural History.)

mony with the natural world. Many anthropologists, looking back over the centuries upon centuries of hunter-gatherer cultures, have concluded that the hunter-gatherer era marks the only period in history when humans existed in balance with the environment; that is, humans took no more than the Earth could easily provide, and what they took allowed the species to thrive.

During the past ten thousand years, beginning with the first agrarian societies, which initiated the practices of cultivating crops and domesticating animals, human cultural values went through some radical changes. Instead of gathering and hunting local, harvestable foods, whole cultures developed that were based on fencing in cattle, cultivating fields, and storing food. The cultural changes since that time have

sary for our survival, that is, evolutionary changes in our bodies, cannot come about quickly enough to make the adjustment. Our brains, the same organs that helped our ancestors to devise ways of keeping themselves warm and of organizing into increasingly more efficient social groups, offer our only hope. In addition, our brains have not changed since we were all hunter-gatherers; it is with this same organ of adaptation, one that has not changed significantly in ten thousand years, that we must meet the challenge. As Richard Leakey comments,

It is a mere ten thousand years since agriculture first became established, and from that momentous change have flowed the industrial and technological societies in

It is possible to trace our roots to the hunter-gatherer societies. Our kinship with these peoples runs deep. (Two Families Go Out to Hunt and Gather. Irven DeVore. Courtesy of Anthro-Photo.)

taken us further and further out of balance with nature. At this point in our history, our relationship with the Earth is precarious indeed: populations rising beyond what the land can support; the poisoning of our water, air, and soil; the annihilation of thousands of species of plants and animals; and, the ultimate threat of a nuclear holocaust that can destroy all life on our planet.

Most responsible scientists writing on the subject today predict that if world population patterns continue along present trends, the Earth will cease to be able to support us in another 50 years. If these population trends do continue, the changes that we will be facing will be the most far-reaching since the last ice age. The standard of living will plummet to desperate levels, and millions of people will not survive the challenge.

As we race toward that moment when the Earth can no longer support us, we must accept the fact that the physical changes neces-

which we now live. Because that period is so short in biological terms, we can be sure that the brains of the hunter-gatherers ten thousand years ago were exactly the same as ours today: their experience was different, but the mental equipment with which they analyzed their world was identical to that inside 20th-century human skulls.[2]

If it is true that brain structure has not changed significantly in all this time, the first task, if we wish to solve our present problems, will be to stand back and study this organ of adaptation itself. What is this tool on which so much depends? What are its limits, and what are its greatest powers? Is there something about it that others before us have enjoyed, but which we have lost? Are there reflexes of this organ that pose a threat if acted upon? And, if that is true, can our knowledge of these reflexes help us guard against foolish acts of destruction and find truly healthy alternatives?

History provides us with a few of the answers to these questions.

The stories told by hunter-gatherer and ancient agrarian peoples, myths that instruct new generations in the ways of the culture, provide us with insights into the brain we ourselves possess. Part of the insight comes in our recognition of how clearly even the most primitive peoples were able to see themselves and their changing relationship with the Earth. In reading the myths of prescientific cultures, we are struck by the poignancy of their insights, which surprisingly parallel the best speculations offered by science. Often the intuitive skills of early people are at least equal to the scientific processes in which we place so much trust today, and one cannot help but wonder what power there may be in combining these two capacities.

According to Indian legend a twin found reeds growing at his end of the stream and with them he shaped a storage basket. Winnowing Corn. 1908. Hopi Arizona. (Courtesy of the Museum of American Indian, Heye Foundation.)

From the Navajo, southwestern U.S.:

On the surface of the Earth, people found a world unlike any they had seen before. There were mountains and plains, streams and trees, stones and growing plants. At first the people did not know how to live in this new world, but the Twins* soon found out. One of them took some clay from the stream bed and held it in his hand, and it shaped itself into a food bowl. Then the clay he held formed a water jar, and again a dipper and finally a pipe.

At the same time, the other Twin found reeds growing at his end of the stream, and with them he shaped a water basket, and a storage basket, and other kinds of mats and baskets. The Twins showed one another what they had made. "These shall be the women's work," they said to one another.

"What shall the man's work be?" the Twins asked each other. They looked and saw stones lying on the ground. As the Twins picked up the stones, the pieces became axes and hammers, knives and spear points in their hands, and the men had weapons.

Last of all, the Twins shaped digging sticks from branches of mountain mahogony, and hoes from deer shoulder blades. Then the men had tools. They found the Kisani, a stranger people, living in the mountains and growing gardens in the valleys, and the people traded their tools and baskets and bowls and weapons for seeds to plant in their own places along the rivers. They learned how to build dams and spread the water on dry ground where it was needed. The people were very happy, learning all their new skills."[3]

From the Kalahari tribes of South Africa:

We who were made first, have come to be last. And those who were created last have come to be first . . .

One day long ago Kara/tuma was out

hunting. And in the bush he discovered a cow. When he saw the cow, he said, "Is this a cow? Is this a buffalo?"

And the cow was not afraid of him; it did not run away. It just stood there. But Kara/tuma did not take it home with him to the village. Instead, he shot it. . . .

Later Kara/tuma told the black people [Bantus] about the cow. (The black men were his younger brothers. For Kara/tuma's parents first bore him, then bore a black man, and last of all gave birth to a European. All of you Europeans here are small children compared to us.) He told a black man about the cows, and the black man said, "Let's go have a look at these things."

So they went to see the cows. As soon as the black man saw that the cows didn't run away

like the other animals, he said, "Ay! A thing like this that doesn't fear you, you certainly don't want to kill. Let's make a Kraal [corral] and drive them into it, and see what will happen."

So they chopped down thorn trees and made a Kraal and drove the cows into it. One of the cows gave birth in the Kraal. So the black man took a thong and ties her hind legs, and she still just stood there, and he milked her and brought the milk to Kara/tuma.[4]

The Navajos and Kalahari describe the sensibilities of the hunter-gatherer and their transitions to an agricultural way of life. Carl Sagan speculates on the cultural challenges that lie ahead for us:

Human history can be viewed as a slowly dawning awareness that we are members of a larger group. Initially our loyalties were to ourselves and our immediate family, next, to bands of wandering hunter-gatherers, then to tribes, small settlements, city-states, nations. We have broadened the circle of those we love. . . . If we are to survive, our loyalties must be broadened further, to include the whole human community, the entire planet Earth.[5]

Balance with Nature in Hunter-Gatherer Cultures

In their book *Man the Hunter,* the noted anthropologists Richard Lee and Irvin Devore reflect that, "To date, the hunting way of life has been the most successful and persistant adaptation man has ever achieved."[6] This way of life, by which human life sustained itself for millions of years, is still at the core of all our thinking. William Laughlin, an anthropologist at the University of Wisconsin, states that,

ple as now live in the entire state of California.

Although it is difficult to generalize about hunter-gatherer societies, anthropologists often turn to the Kalahari tribesmen to paint a picture of the earliest known cultural form. There are several reasons for studying these people: first, they live on the savannahs of South Africa, which may have been humanity's birthplace; second, they are the last of a culture that once dominated the entire continent; and third, they are incredibly successful in their way of life. Still in existence today, these people provide us with insights into a way of life that once extended into virtually every environmental niche the Earth offered.

The Bush people live in small groups of between 16 and 90 people, with most such groups averaging around 34 people. They are

Standing on the outskirts of a !Kung camp, one thinks of birds' nests clinging with frail strength to the branches of bushes. (*San Camp,* by Mel Konner. Courtesy of Anthro-Photo.)

"Hunting is the master behavior pattern of the human species. Hunting has placed a premium on inventiveness [and] problem solving, and has imposed a real penalty for the failure to solve the problem."[7] Laughlin points out that hunting involves a highly complex set of skills, including teaching children the ways of the group, observing animal behavior, learning and devising ways to capture and kill the game, and finally organizing activities around bringing the game back to the home base, where it can be prepared for eating and portioned out to other members of the family, tribe, or village.

To gain some perspective on the balance that existed between humans and nature at the time when hunter-gatherers were the only forms of culture yet evolved, it is helpful to look at land/person ratios. For example, prior to 10,000 B.C. the total population of the Earth was around 10 million, fewer people than now live in Greater London, or about half as many peo-

seminomadic, and have open and friendly associations with neighboring encampments, who live very much like themselves. There is excellent communication between one group and another, with members from different encampments frequently visiting with one another in a highly fluid system of social exchange. As a result of the close associations between these groups, they often have relatives in common.

Each group is territorial, in that they will hunt and gather food in a particular area, but, as often as not, one group's territory overlaps another's, with no serious disputes resulting. Indeed, although tribal territories overlap, neighboring groups live in complete harmony with one another. Their social structures are highly flexible, because of the variation in availability of resources at different times of the year. At times of great rainfall, when food supplies are plentiful, they tend to break off into small groups, spreading out into broader

*The exclamation point indicates a
"click" as the first sound in a
word; such sounds are characteristic of the !Kung language.

*The exclamation point indicates a
"click" as the first sound in a
word; such sounds are characteristic of the !Kung language.

*The hunter-gatherer
community emphasizes
social contact. Most peo-
ple in a village are blood
relations. (San Band at
Temporary Camp in the
Mongo Nut Groves,* by
Richard Lee. Courtesy of
Anthro-Photo.)

and broader territories. At times of low rainfall, the groups gather closely around common
waterholes, pooling their human resources
and sharing scarce food supplies.

The Bush culture's balance with nature is
reflected in everything they do. Their homes
blend into the landscape as subtly as the nests
and burrows of the small animals with whom
they share the savannah. In the words of
Patricia Draper, an anthropologist who lived
with the Bush people, "Standing on the
outskirts of a !Kung* camp for the first time,
one thinks of birds' nests clinging with frail
strength in the branches of bushes. The low,
inconspicuous huts are built of branches and
grass, and are entirely camouflaged."[8]

Each hut takes less than an hour to construct. The basic structure is dome-shaped,

about six feet in height and six feet in diameter.
It is made of bowed branches tied together and
covered with grass, or thatching. The design of
these huts varies according to the weather:
open and airy during the hot, dry seasons of
the year, closed and densely woven during the
rainy season. During the long, hot summer
days, the huts provide shade from the Sun; at
night the people sleep outside, under the stars,
using the huts largely to store personal
belongings. The people sleep in their huts only
during the rainy season.

The Bush people lay out their villages in a
circle. Every hut is built so that the entrance
door faces the center of the circle. In the front
of each hut is a fire hearth, around which the
family gathers to cook and eat, and where, on
evenings when there are no community activi-

ties, members of different families may get together to make clothing, string beads, or make arrowheads—trading stories and gossip as they work. Each family—consisting of husband, wife, and children under the age of fifteen—has a hut and a hearth of its own. The hut and hearth is the family's "private" area, while the space at the center of the village is reserved for community activities, such as meetings and dances.

In an average community there are ten men, ten women, seven boys, and five girls. Each family has blood ties to every other family in the village, though they may be only distant cousins. The community is egalitarian, with women and men having equal status within the social structure, even though jobs are divided according to sex. Women are the gatherers, men the hunters. Children under fifteen years of age have no responsibilities, nor do the adults over 40.

Several times each week, dances are performed at the center of the village. These dances, which last from dusk to dawn, are very important to the people. They are called *!Kia*-healing dances. Everyone participates in these dances: old people, children, men, and women. The women sing songs and clap their hands in ancient rhythms, providing the background for the men, who do the actual dancing. The dancers work themselves into a trance or meditation-like state, called *!Kia*:

!Kia, and its setting of the !Kia dance, serves many functions. It is the !Kung's primary expression of a religious existence and a cosmological perspective. It provides healing and protection, being a magicomedical mode of coping with illness and misfortune. The !Kia at the dance also increases social cohesion and solidarity. It allows individual and communal hostility. Finally, the dance alters the consciousness of many of the members of this community. . . . Also, a !Kung practices extraordinary activities during !Kia. He performs cures, handles and walks on fire, claims x-ray vision, and at times says he sees over great distances.[9]

To an outsider, the land where the Bush people live seems forbidding and inhospitable. It is arid, with an average rainfall that is less than ten inches per year. The summers are long and hot, with a high temperature range of 95 to 115 degrees, whereas winter temperatures fall near freezing. Vegetation consists of grasslands and sparse trees. There are sand dunes all around, and the only water available is contained in five water holes, many of which dry up during the peak of the summer. Looking out over the land, one would see few if any animals. Nevertheless, the Bush people do find game, and their diet is well-balanced between meat and vegetables.

Of the almost 500 species of local plants and animals, known and named by the San [a tribe], some use is found for 150 species of plants and 100 species of animals. By virtue of their extremely extensive knowledge of the environment, the people are self-sufficient, with a single exception: iron for knives, spear blades, arrowheads, and awls must be obtained through trade and exchange.[10]

Work at a bush camp is divided into two basic categories: hunting and gathering. There is no regular schedule; rather, work is based on immediate need. Food is not stockpiled; so hunters and gatherers go out when need arises, usually every two or three days, on a schedule not unlike the urban dweller's regular trips to the market. Whatever food is killed or

gathered is brought back to camp, where it is divided up among every member of the community. The women provide about 80 percent of the food consumed by the group; these foods are staples, available pretty much the year around.

Women go out onto the savannah to do their work in groups, staying within calling distance of each other at all times. The staple they gather year round is called the *mongongo nut*. The mongongo nut makes up about half their daily diet, and has the nutritional value of corn or rice. The plant on which it grows is drought-resistant, and is a far more reliable food source than any crops cultivated by agricultural tribes living adjacent to the Bush people.

In addition to the mongongo nut, the women gather fruits, berries, and melons in the summer, roots and bulbs in the winter, and leafy greens in the spring. They make their choices from 84 species of edible plants, in-

The skills of the gatherers are extensive. They know not only what to gather, but when to gather to enjoy the most succulent offerings. (Filling ostrich eggshells with water. Courtesy of the American Museum of Natural History.)

cluding 29 species of fruits, berries, and melons, and 30 species of roots and bulbs. There is such abundance of these edible plants that most of the time the women bring back to camp only the choicest selections. The skills of the gatherers are extensive; their education includes not only what to pick, but when to pick and how to choose the most succulent offerings.

The men do the hunting, and like the women they go out in groups. They sometimes use snares to trap small animals, such as rabbits, wart hogs, small antelope, and birds, such as guinea fowl and ostrich. The trapping of these smaller animals may be done by individuals, but the hunting of large game, such as antelope or giraffe, is always a group effort, requiring much organization.

important ritual in the Bush culture. The man who shot the killing arrow is given the first meat. He divides this portion among the other hunters with whom he began the hunt. Part of this portion usually goes to the person who made the arrow that was used to kill the animal, and who may not have been among those who actually participated in the hunt. Everyone who receives meat from this original portioning gives meat to others in the community according to a well-established order: wife's parents first, then the hunter's parents, then the hunter's wife and his own children, then his own portion. Each of the people who receives a portion from this division turns around and gives portions to their parents and immediate family. Visitors who happen to be in camp during a kill also receive portions. The

The hunters possess highly sophisticated game-tracking skills. (Bushman archers. Courtesy of the American Museum of Natural History.)

The hunters possess highly sophisticated game-tracking skills. From various signs along the trail, they can identify the species of the game, its size, how long ago it left its tracks, and how fast it is moving. The hunters follow their prey and are able to get within 20 yards of it, due to their knowledge of each animal's behavior patterns. Finally, the killing shot is made with a poison arrow. Since the poison takes some time to kill the animal, the hunters must follow it until it drops. Then, if it is a large animal, the men will butcher it immediately, eating the liver on the spot. They cut up the animal's carcass and carry the meat back to the camp. Nothing of the animal is wasted, and back at the camp the bone, hide, and flesh are shared with other members of the community. (With small animals, it is different; since rabbits and guinea fowl provide only enough meat for a single family, these are kept by the hunter who captures them.)

Sharing the flesh of a large animal is an

end result is that everyone gets a fair share, and there is little if any controversy over dividing up the bounty.

The Bush people are nomadic, following the migrations of the animals they hunt. Their routes are also dictated by water supplies, which change with the seasons. Their movements ensure that their fruit, nut, and vegetable supplies will not be depleted, since they never stay in one region long enough to overpick it. The time spent in one camp can be from two days to two weeks. In his study of the Kalahari Bushmen, John Yellem reported that the group he observed moved 37 times in a six-month period.[11]

Because the hunter-gatherers move so frequently, they have good reason to minimize material possessions. A nonmaterialistic society has thus evolved, not because of anti-materialistic sentiment, but from the direct experience of material goods as a *burden* one must carry. Most families limit their

Bush people are nomadic, their migrations dictated by the animals they hunt and the seasonally changing water supplies. (*San Mother Carrying Possessions on Her Head,* by M. Shostak. Courtesy of Anthro-Photo.)

possessions to what one adult can comfortably carry on his or her back.

Trades such as pottery-making, ironworking, and complex toolmaking are not compatible with this nomadic way of life. Thus, there is no specialization, and each person (except for children and elders) participates equally in the industries of the camp, that is, in hunting or gathering.

Personal gratification is high. Whereas more materialistic societies offer the individual new outlets for self-fulfillment in specialization and in acquiring material wealth or power in the community, the hunter-gatherers find fulfillment in family relationships, in socializing with friends, in dance and religious rites, and in teaching and learning the daily routines of hunting and gathering.

If, as some theorists think, true affluence is measured by the absence of need and the enjoyment of extensive leisure time, then the hunter-gatherers of whom we speak are the original affluent class. Time spent gathering food is minimal: from twelve to nineteen hours per week. In *Man the Hunter,* Richard Lee describes the life style of an average hunter-gatherer woman:

A woman gathers on one day enough food to feed her family for three days, and spends the rest of her time resting in camp, doing embroidery, visiting other camps, or entertaining visitors from other camps. For each day at home, kitchen routines, such as cooking, nut cracking, collecting firewood, and fetching water, occupy one to three hours of her time. This rhythm of steady work and steady leisure is maintained throughout the year.[12]

The man's place in the hunter-gatherer society is somewhat different. As a hunter, his lifestyle is dependent on animals, a less stable food source than the crops gathered by the women. Here Richard Lee describes how the men live:

The hunters tend to work more frequently than the women, but their schedule is uneven. It is not unusual for a man to hunt avidly for a week, and then do no hunting at all for two or three weeks. Since hunting is an unpredictable business and subject to magical control, hunters sometimes experience a run of bad luck and stop hunting for a month or longer. During these periods, visiting, entertaining, and especially dancing are the primary activities of the men.[13]

This view of the hunter-gatherer's life as leisurely and affluent is something new among anthropologists, who until recently painted a picture of a difficult and mean existence for these people. In the past twenty years, however, close-up studies of the hunter-gatherers have revealed coherent cultures in which leisure time far outweighs work time. The stories and actions of these people show that they perceive themselves as happy and fulfilled in their traditional ways of life.

During the great African drought of the mid-1960s, a natural disaster that destroyed millions of acres of cultivated crops and hundreds of thousands of cattle on that continent, the Kalahari hunter-gatherers fared well. They registered little if any change in their lifestyle, even while thousands of people around them were starving. The security demonstrated here, that is, the ability to continue one's traditional lifestyle in the hardest of times, is the product of a social evolution based on a firm understanding of one's dependence on the Earth. The way of life created by the hunter-gatherer seems to derive maximum pleasure with the least effort, using up only the minimum needed out of what the environment has to offer. In contrast, modern city dwellers base their lifestyle on the maximum they can extract from nature, often acquired with an investment of far more hours and energy than the Bushmen could conceive of.

Anthropologists observe that a great sense of personal security is derived by hunter-gatherer peoples who have worked out their balance with nature:

Moreover, hunters seem neither harassed nor anxious. . . . Rather than anxiety, it would seem that the hunters have a confidence born of affluence, of a condition in which all the people's wants (such as they are) are generally easily satisfied.[14]

The children of the hunter-gatherers lead what many modern psychologists would consider idyllic lives. In its first two years of life, the infant is held upright, close to its mother's body, either carried in the mother's arms or in a sling. In these formative years the baby suckles almost constantly, and in its upright position it sees and hears the world the mother experiences. The mother totally indulges the infant's needs, even while she herself socializes and works with other women. Anthropologists believe that because the hunter-gatherer woman shares these early years of motherhood with other adults, she feels neither isolated nor deprived by her responsibility, unlike most modern women. Because the mother is happy, the child is happy, and this becomes the basis for a sense of personal security that most hunter-gatherers carry all through their lives. Because of the nurturing, the social contact, and the constant sensual stimulation of being held close to the mother's body in a vertical position, the hunter-gatherer children develop skills early. They stand, walk, and develop cognitive skills earlier than most modern children from industrial cultures.

At the age of three or four, children are weaned from the breast and join other children, who exist as a group closely supervised by the adults. The group may consist of from nine to twelve children, ranging in ages from three to fifteen. Because these groups are made up of both boys and girls with a wide variety of ages and skill levels, competitive activities are all but impossible. Thus, the activities of the group are, of necessity, cooperative rather than competitive. Older children tend to look after the younger ones, and since there is continuous contact between adults and children, the children learn, not from formal, deliberate lessons, but by watching and imitating the adults.

Children become adults, and take on adult responsibilities, between the ages of fourteen and sixteen. Boys begin going out with the men to hunt; girls start going out with the women to gather. By the time they are old enough to go out with the adults, the children already know a great deal about what they are expected to do, since they have regularly listened to adults discussing their hunting or gathering expeditions, and they have seen and

Children of hunter-gatherers have idyllic existences; in the formative years, the infant suckles almost constantly. (!Kung Mother and Child, by Mel Konner. Courtesy of Anthro-Photo.)

learned the names of many animals and plants that have been brought to the camp.

The populations of the hunter-gatherers remain stable, with a growth rate of less than .5 percent per year. There appears to be some kind of birth-control method at work, but it remains a mystery to anthropologists. Infant mortality is relatively high, but once a child is past the first few years, life expectancy approaches our own. Although there is evidence of some infanticide, it is extremely rare, and doesn't account for the balance maintained between numbers of people and what the land can comfortably support.

Studies of the balance between the Bush people and the environment reveal an amazingly harmonious state. Even though the people kill animals (using only bow and arrow, or snares), the animal populations remain stable. Similarly, gathering fruits and vegetables in no way threatens the natural vegetation. The biggest environmental impact reported is that of deliberately burning the grasses, which the Bush people do in order to encourage the growth of shrubs and trees as ground cover for the animals. Still, even with these burnings, the ecological balance maintained by the hunter-gatherer peoples is admirable.

Anthropologists estimate that the Kalahari Bushmen have lived in this area for at least 11,000 years, and perhaps for as long as 40,000 years. At one time their way of life was the dominant cultural form of the African continent. Prior to the European colonization of Africa, starting with the Dutch in the 1600s, there were as many as 300,000 hunter-gatherers. There are now estimated to be fewer than 1,500. This waning population of hunter-gatherer societies on the African continent is typical of what has occurred wherever

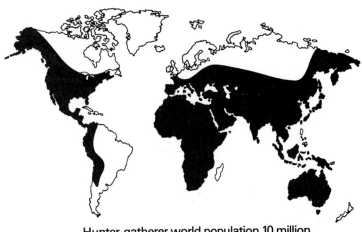

Hunter-gatherer world population 10 million

Studies of the balance between the Bush people and their environment show an amazingly harmonious state. (Bushmen Running from the Rain, 1962, by Joseph Ndandarika. Oil on composition board, 48″ × 48″. Museum of Modern Art, New York. Gift of Mr. and Mrs. Walter Hoschild.)

For hundreds of thousands of years the hunter-gatherer way of life was the main adaptation of human life. When the world population was 10 million, all humans were hunter-gatherers. When the world population was 350 million, 1 percent of mankind were hunter-gatherers. When the world population was 3 billion, .001 percent of mankind were hunter-gatherers.

similar peoples have been assimilated by modern cultures.

Before European colonization, and more recent efforts to "develop" Africa, the Bush people maintained their own lifestyle, even though they were fully aware of other choices and cultural forms. For example, the Kalahari interacted with the Bantu peoples, a society of agriculturalists who planted gardens and herded goats. Although the Kalahari observed and understood the Bantu lifestyle, they did not choose to adopt agriculture instead of their own ways.

In the 1960s, the modern world literally moved in on the Kalahari. This process began with voter registration of the Bush people,

Hunter-gatherer world population 3 billion

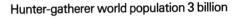

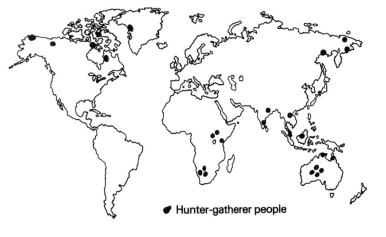

🌑 Hunter-gatherer people

soon followed by the fencing of the Namibia border, an action which restricted the Bush peoples' nomadic way of life. Then came the founding of a store, with modern conveniences and consumer goods on display. The store also sold a form of "home brew," made with imported brown sugar, which introduced the use of alcoholic beverages to the Kalahari. Trucks began bringing products from the modern world for trade, and the same trucks carried Bush people out of their ancient homeland to work on cattle ranches and in gold mines in other parts of the country. Along with these changes came others: Bush people began to adopt agriculture, buying goats, beef cattle, and donkeys for their own use.

For the most part the conditions under which most Kalahari now live are comparable to feudal conditions of medieval Europe. In return for their labors, the Bush people receive meals, a place to live, and from four to seven dollars per month. Occasionally they trade their labor for cattle or other goods. Although there are still a few groups practicing traditional ways, a more common pattern now is seen. Kalahari travel about on donkeys, often loaded down with material possessions. Like gypsies, they live at the edge of modern civilization, occasionally taking jobs at the farms they pass to earn money to buy food or other goods at modern stores.

In the past 20 years the Kalahari, once isolated and autonomous, have become incorporated into the apartheid system of South Africa. Within this rigid caste system, which sets people of European origin against native Africans, the Kalahari are at the bottom of the social order. As Mathias Guenther, an anthropologist, has observed, the Kalahari are "economically exploited; they lack any reliable and nutritionally adequate subsistance base; they are unemployed, underfed, and overcrowded on land that does not belong to them; they are disease-ridden, partly through new organic diseases brought into the area, partly through diseases generated by social conflict."[15]

It is not surprising that even as the Kalahari adopt modern ways—selling their labor, seeking social status by acquiring material possessions, adopting agriculture to replace hunting and gathering—there is expressed a longing for the traditions that have been usurped. Mathais Guenther reports, "The past is held to have been a time of plentiful food and water and minimal disease . . spouses were faithful; the young were respectful to the old; and there was an overall absence of intra- and intergroup conflict."[16]

In exploring the history of the Kalahari, we perhaps catch a glimpse of the history of all hunter-gatherers since the beginning of time. Indeed, it is a pattern expressed in *Genesis* 2, in the myth of the Garden of Eden, where Adam and Eve live in total harmony with nature, free to enjoy all the fruits of the garden, until they disobey their maker and eat from the "tree of the knowledge of good and evil." Banished from the garden for their disobedience, the penitent couple gives birth to Cain and Abel, who are farmers—Abel a shepherd, Cain a "tiller of the soil" (*Genesis* 4:2). In contrast to the hunter-gatherer, these two must, as God warned Adam, "gain your bread by the sweat of your brow" (*Genesis* 3:19).

Agriculture to Urbanization

During the million-year period of the Pleistocene, an era characterized by 15 separate ice

Docile animals moved close to the villages where people were cultivating crops. Observing the animals, people began to see that animals could be used to human advantage.
(Figure of a Bull, sixth Century B.C. Metropolitan Museum of Art. Rogers Fund.)

ages, hunter-gatherers existed in nearly every corner of the globe. Their ability to adapt was largely the result of their big brain. When we consider the dramatic climatic shifts through which humans have lived, with food sources changing in response to the climate, we may well feel awe at the wonderful power of the human brain as an adaptive tool. With this big brain, human beings created their own adaptations to the environment, and took upon themselves the responsibility for adapting to an everchanging environment. Hunter-gatherers during the Pleistocene age invented needles for sewing hides together to make clothes, barbed hooks for catching fish, harpoons for hunting fish and sea-going mammals, boats, sleds, underground houses for protection against the weather, and a variety of weapons and utensils for killing animals and preparing them for human use.

Cultivation of grains and the domestication of animals probably arose naturally out of human ability to observe their surroundings and think of more effective ways to live. One of the most important tools in the development of cultivation was the stone sickle, invented approximately a million years ago. The stone sickle allowed people to harvest large quantities of wild wheat for their food; furthermore, the mass harvesting of this wheat stimulated evolution of a whole new strain of this crop.

The original wheat that humans harvested had only sparse and very small seeds, or grains, and these were difficult to separate from the chaff. The seeds had winglike structures, which allowed them to be carried great distances in the wind, and when they landed the force of their flight planted them in the soil. As the stone sickle came into use, the grain was shaken to the ground in the process of harvesting, and the seeds were easily planted in the soil disturbed by the harvesters' feet. In time the seeds lost their wings, an appendage which harvesting had made no longer necessary to their propagation; as the wings disappeared, the grain itself became fatter and easier to separate from the chaff. This event is perhaps the first example of a human invention that led to a genetic change in nature. In *The Ascent of Man,* Jacob Bronowski reflects that "Suddenly, man and the plant have come together. Man has a wheat that he lives by, but the wheat also thinks that man was made for him, because only so can it be propagated. . . . A happy conjunction of natural and human events created agriculture."[17]

The stone sickle was only a beginning. More nutritious and productive strains of wheat evolved as people selected seeds that gave the best yield for their efforts. In the process of cultivating wheat, other crops benefited from human work; secondary crops, such as barley, millet, rye, and buckwheat, evolved new forms that made them more attractive as human food. Similarly, people began to see that they could increase the yield of various plants by moving them to different elevations or to drier or wetter regions. For example, when flax was moved from the higher elevations, where it naturally grew, to lower elevations, where people could cultivate it, the plants produced large seedpods that, when pressed, produced linseed oil.

Once people had grasped the basic principles of controlling plant life, the domestication of animals soon followed. The animals probably participated in this as much as the humans. We can speculate that docile animals, such as goats and oxen, moved close to the villages where people were cultivating crops; here the animals took advantage of the greater availability of food, nibbling at the farmers' plots and scavenging the scraps. It is generally held that what spurred this development on was the more arid condition of the Earth immediately after the last ice age which forced animals to seek out new food sources.

In observing the animals, people began to see how to use them for human advantage: goats and sheep for wool, milk, and meat; cows for milk and meat; and eventually oxen and burros to help carry heavy loads and pull plows. Once people began to perceive the advantages of having the animals, they began to fence the animals in and train them. Thus humans became an agent of selection, as they chose to breed those specimens that were the most useful: the strongest, the most productive, the most easily trained.

Agriculture brought major lifestyle changes, especially in attitude. People were beginning to see that they could control nature, whereas once they had been at her mercy, having to content themselves with whatever the Earth offered. This change in human perception perhaps corresponds to the loss of innocence as expressed in the story of the Garden of Eden, or in the story of God's displeasure when people attempted to construct the Tower of Babel: "from now on nothing they intend to do will be beyond their reach" (*Genesis* 11:6).

Whereas goatherds remained, like the hunter-gatherers, more or less nomadic, those who planted crops built villages. Gradually the two forms of agriculture merged: those who planted crops fenced in small numbers of cattle for their own use, and pastoralists established regular trade with them.

As human ability to manipulate nature continued to develop, several dramatic cultural changes evolved. The concept of land ownership was born, a concept that would have been difficult for a hunter-gatherer to grasp, since it is totally incompatible with a nomadic way of life. The growing technology of crop cultivation was particularly responsible for this shift in attitude toward land. Tilling the land involved a large investment in time, as did the construction of irrigation systems. People learned how to protect their investments both by threatening violence to those who would take land from them, and by laws of ownership, whereby an investment could be transferred to another person, by sale or trade or inheritance.

Once the concept of land ownership was established, a class structure evolved among the early peoples of the Tigris-Euphrates valley. The highest class, the priests, controlled the irrigation systems, and counseled the people in how to gain favor from the gods. Next highest in the class structure were

for their own use, even when their main source of income was not farming.

Priests dictated rules of behavior for the Sumerians. For the most part, these rules were aimed at "pleasing the gods." There were gods for the irrigation ditches, gods for the plows, and gods of the farms. There were air gods, earth gods, water gods, and gods of the heavens. Humans were clearly subservient to these gods, and to displease any of them was serious.

Early in its history Sumer was governed by a citizen's group; but the larger and wealthier the city became, the clearer became the need for a more structured form of government. The city was frequently raided by nomadic tribes, who swept down out of the hills and took away food and material goods. Even-

Agricultural harvesting and storing ultimately led to hoarding. Such hoarding led to wars and raids, necessitating armies and governments. (Soldier taking captives across a stream, eighth century B.C. Palace of the King of Assyria in Nineveh. Metropolitan Museum of Art. Gift of John D. Rockefeller.)

In the Sumerian village, there were air gods, earth gods, and gods of the farms. To displease any of them was considered a serious matter. (Winged being pollinating the sacred tree: wall panel from the palace of Ashur-nasir-apal II, at Nimrud. 9th century B.C. Metropolitan Museum of Art. Gift of John D. Rockefeller.)

powerful landowners and politicians. Then came the trade and craftspeople, the toolmakers, merchants, pottery-makers, and weavers. At the bottom of the social hierarchy were the slaves, people captured in wars, who had no citizens' rights whatsoever.

The first city was located in the southern part of what is now Iraq. From 4000 to 2500 B.C., the city known as Sumer had a population of up to 50,000 people: fishermen, merchants, craftspeople, priests, and traders. The Sumerians are credited with inventing a sophisticated irrigation system, the wagon wheel, a plow, the potter's wheel, metal casting, the sailboat, a money system, a number system, and a writing system. They processed leather, and manufactured fabric, metal objects, cosmetics, perfumes, and drugs.

The average Sumerian family lived in a one-story, mud-brick house, with several rooms built around a central courtyard. Most families had gardens and a few head of cattle

tually a monarchy was formed, and under the monarch an army was established for protecting the city from invasion.

The combination of a class system and crowding led to increasing tension among the Sumerians. Never before had people faced these particular kinds of pressures, and they had no skills for handling them effectively. Personal power took precedence over all, and power struggles were common between individuals as well as between Sumer and other communities nearby.

In time, Sumer fell, probably because of wars and inner pressures. New cities rose out of the ruins of the old, only to be torn apart by inner conflict with their neighbors. In recent years archaeologists have uncovered layer after layer of new cities, built atop the site that was the original Sumer. It would be interesting to trace the successes and failures of each layer of civilization, to create a picture of human discoveries of increasingly effective ways for living with other people under the complex and often frustrating conditions of the city. From the artifacts that archaeologists have uncovered, we can make our own judgments about how far we have come.

Evolutionary Changes with City Life

The changes that occurred in human beings as they evolved from hunter-gatherer to agriculturalist, and finally to city dweller, were physiological as well as social and psychological. According to Valerius Geist in *Life Strategies, Human Evolution, Environmental Designs,* the changes that took place involved everything from teeth to the shape of the human skull. For example, with the high-carbohydrate diet associated with urban living and agriculture, teeth became smaller and their surfaces less complex, a structure better adapted to grinding, and less prone to decay. Similarly, a diet that included more sugars and alcohol necessitated subtle changes in body chemistry; the hunter-gatherer had no metabolic tolerance for such foods. Although it is not known exactly why, skulls changed from elongated, oval shapes to more spherical forms; perhaps an increase in the size of the verbal centers of the brain—because of greater dependency on the spoken word—brought about the new head shape.

Geist's evaluation of the socio-psychological changes in humans as they became agriculturalists and then city dwellers is not cheerful: "Agriculture brought about selection pressures quite different from those of periglacial society, some antagonistic to human values."[18] According to Geist, the use of animal milk to feed babies, a practice that began with the first pastoralists, had far-reaching consequences for human society. Geist explains that nursing required a calm and anxiety-free setting, and among the hunter-gatherers it was the male's duty to ensure this when his wife had a baby. When women began feeding their children animal milk, the calm setting was no longer essential, and an important part of the male's role vanished. The male soon turned his attention to warfare, forgetting social restraints he probably observed in his role as a nurturing father.

As people came to the cities, the more sedate values of human life were displaced.

Whereas the successful hunter-gatherer had to be calm, observant of nature, reflective, and respectful of all forms of life around him, the male living in the city became loud, flamboyant, and insensitive to others, and was given to bouts of rage and rash action. Geist suggests that women in the city, because they had to compete with many other women for a very small population of dominant males, became aggressive, seductive, and calculating, and in the process of making themselves attractive to males began using cosmetics, jewelry, perfumes, and decorated clothing.

When animal milk replaced breast milk, the birthrate in the cities went up rapidly. While breast-feeding their infants, most women didn't conceive; hence breast-feeding, which the hunter-gatherer woman often continued through the child's third year, acted as an effective birth control. When breast-feeding was discouraged, there was no longer a natural birth-control mechanism at work, and populations skyrocketed. Infant mortality rates were high, but the increased birth rate more than kept pace.

A child growing up in the city received far less early nurturing than the child of a hunter-gatherer. As children grew, they found their way into groups of children their own age. With age and skill levels nearly equal in these groups, children—who were already living in a highly competitive society—developed games of competition, which occupied most of their time and had an important part in shaping their character. Because there was little adult supervision, the gulf between children and parents broadened, and the respect for adults diminished.

One important feature of city living—indeed, one of the innovations that made it possible—was the ability to store large quantities of food. City dwellers, especially the specialists who did not have the direct contact with the Earth that most of the farmers had, became disconnected from the essential source of their well-being, that is, the Earth. Instead of looking at what the land was providing each day, they looked at the quantities of land they possessed and the stores of food, mostly grain, that they had put aside. In time they went a step further, applying mathematics to calculate not only what they had at any given moment, but what they would have in the future, thereby abstracting the essential source even further. Illusions of well-being based on hoarding replaced the immediate recognition of the natural limits of the Earth that would have been an important part of a hunter-gatherer's sensitivity.

As the practice of hoarding, the institution of property ownership, and the possession of luxury goods (gold jewelry, fine fabrics, and pottery) became increasingly important, a new set of values and activities evolved. Personal security was, of course, threatened, because anyone could walk in and carry off personal possessions. This happened to the Sumerians many times over, as tribes of nomads swept down from the hills to ransack the homes of the city dwellers. If a man was to keep his riches, he had to learn how to defend himself, to arm himself against both foreign invaders and avaricious neighbors. Not only nature but other human beings came to be perceived as adversaries, if not enemies, against which one fought an endless battle. These concerns caused individuals to become increasingly alienated from their environment and the people around them.

The increasing separation between people and the Earth allowed our species to evolve a society of rich and varied occupations, with specialists refining their craft, and learning ever more about their chosen field. The drive for excellence, undoubtedly born out of the pressure of competition, the need to make one's product or service more attractive than the next person's, had by now evolved into an ethic of excellence for its own sake. There are, of course, tremendous personal satisfactions in having a wide range of occupations from which to choose, rather than being limited to the routines of food-gathering exclusively. There is little doubt that the urbanization of humanity has encouraged the species to explore certain potentials. But the growing pains as humans moved from a hunting-gathering society to an agricultural society and finally to urban life have been great enough to cause many intelligent people to question if the experiment has even a hope for success.

The problems that plague us in our cities today have their roots in the lives of the first city dwellers thousands of years before us. Between then and now a myriad of institutions have been invented to make the urban experience more comfortable. Public education, for example, seeks to take up the intellectual nurturing of our children, so that the parents can turn their energies elsewhere. And there is Art, Music, Dance, Theater, and a vast array of entertainments, to relieve, or simply take one's mind off, the pressures of urban living. We may even be learning new physiological responses, new ways to deal with our aggressive reflexes. Meanwhile, our exploration of our social evolution takes us from the subject of increased specialization to the Industrial Revolution, because of which we began to recognize and directly confront some of the problems—as well as some of the potential advantages—of urban living.

Social Evolution in the Industrial Revolution

From 4000 B.C. until the mid-1700s, a period of 5,700 years, the cities increased in size and complexity, but animals and humans continued to be the main sources of energy by which social endeavors were carried out. Most crafts—pottery making, metal working, leather processing, weaving, etc.—were "cottage industries"; that is, people made small numbers of items in their homes, both for their own use and for trade with others for goods they might themselves need. Transportation between towns was limited, so trade tended to be limited to the region in which the product was made.

As roads developed, linking one town with another, making it possible to move large quantities of goods, production was encouraged. But it was not until the advent of water power and steam engines that factories began to appear, employing large numbers of people. At about the same time that these developments were taking place, the English were building their central canal system, by which huge quantities of goods could be moved cheaply, efficiently, and with a speed never previously known. These innovations—the machine and efficient transportation—spurred on a new age. Encouraged by the promise of material wealth and excitement, people flocked to the cities. Birthrates soared, and the cities strained at their boundaries.

Along with the development of factories, more intensive farming methods were being created, partly because of the cities' growing demands for food. Fertilizing, the steel-bladed plow, and the steam-powered tractor brought farming in line wih the fast pace and high production principles of the Industrial Revolution. All this occurred in the 1800s.

Early industrial areas had canals for moving goods to and from market. (*Landscape Capriccio With Palace,* 1755, by Canaletto. National Gallery of Art, Washington, D.C.)

Cities increased in size and complexity. Pottery making, leather working, processing, and weaving were cottage industries, with humans and animals providing the main sources of power. (*View Of Munich,* 1750, by Bernardo Bellotto. National Gallery of Art, Washington, D.C.)

Intensive farm methods were created, necessitated by increased demands from the cities. (*The Cornel Farm,* 1800, by Edward Hicks National Gallery of Art, Washington, D.C.)

With the advent of the industrial era, the power of animals and humans was replaced by that of machines. (*Through The Colemma Hollow Up the Allegheny Valley.* Oil on canvas, 30"x38". Museum of Modern Art, New York.)

One of the biggest problems the cities now faced was in sanitation and health. Prior to the growth of the cities, when most people lived in places of low population densities, the disposal of human waste and the purity of drinking water were not seen as important issues. In the early history of even the great cities like Paris and London, human waste, both garbage and sewage, was simply dumped into the streets. Rats scurried around in the refuse, scavenging what they could. The water supplies were open wells, public pumps, or rivers, into which seeped the waste waters of entire populations. From this neglect of sanitation rose the great plagues of Europe, which threatened to destroy entire cities. Then, the moment the problems of sanitation were solved, with sewage disposal and clean water ensured, mortality rates dropped, and population growth soared.

In the medical history books, it is the "removal of the handle of the Broad Street pump," upon the advice of John Snow, a physician, that marked the coming of age of modern sanitation principles. John Snow pioneered the idea that diseases could be water-borne, and in 1824 advised the vestrymen of the St. James parish of London that their epidemic of cholera might be quelled by removing the handle from the public pump, which was apparently supplying the entire community with contaminated drinking water.

The creation of efficient transportation networks, the invention of machines, high-yielding farming methods, and the development of modern sanitation made it possible for large numbers of people to live in relatively small areas. The problems of high density required the evolution of new socio-economic adaptations: political structures to collect taxes for building roads, sewers, and canals; laws to regulate human activities; and the development of new social techniques by which individuals could deal with aggression and frustration, aggravated by crowding and a highly competitive society. People were becoming more and more detached, more and more distant from the Earth, as their daily labors turned from food gathering to tasks that had no direct relationship to food. Within this social framework, it was easy to forget our relationship with the Earth and to evolve an illusion that we were free of nature's bonds.

The Earth's Limits Rediscovered

Nature imposes a system of checks and balances on humans and other creatures who live in the wild. The limits of what the Earth can comfortably support are always at hand. But as we learned to control nature, through the invention of machines, modern farming techniques, food storage, climate control, transportation, medicine, and defense against others of our own species, the illusion that we could create a healthy environmental niche for ourselves anywhere on the face of the Earth was born. Each time a new niche has opened, be it in the jungles of Brazil, the snowy reaches of Alaska, or another suburb of an already vast city, birthrates have soared, just as they do when a species evolves an adaptation to a new niche.

The world population has been rising steadily since the appearance of the first hominids three million years ago. But as new technologies have developed, the growth rate has been astonishing. At the time of Australopithecus, the world population was less than 500,000. By the time *Homo erectus* appeared,

Human population of the world	
3 million years ago	500 thousand
500 thousand years ago	1 million
A.D. 1	250 million
A.D. 1600	500 million
A.D. 1850	1 billion
A.D. 1930	2 billion
A.D. 1980	4 billion
A.D. 2020	8 billion

it had risen to a million, that is, doubled in 2.5 million years. Today the total population has reached 4.5 billion, and by the year 2000 it will have nearly doubled again.

It is easy to forget how short a time we have had to adjust to our technological society and to the problems of high population density that are pressing in on us. Consider, for example, that we were hunter-gatherers for three million years, agriculturists for 6,000, and industrialists for less than 250. As we struggle with the problems of technology and an alarming population growth, we are much like infants thrown into a world we do not have the skills to deal with.

Julian Huxley has reflected that as we have applied ourselves to overcoming the limits of our natural environment, we have become witness to a new phenomenon: "evolution conscious of itself." We can use our minds to create solutions to our immediate problems, and can see the ways in which our efforts to

According to Hopi legend the name of the fourth world is World Complete. It is not all beautiful and easy like the previous ones: it has everything for you to choose from. What you choose will determine if it must in time be destroyed too. (Walpi, 1900. Library of Congress.)

control nature may themselves become environmental problems. The next big step in our evolution may be to apply our knowledge to the conscious creation of a well Earth, but we have only begun to enter this phase of our evolution.

It is interesting to reflect that pretechnological societies have been able to map out both our past and our future. Perhaps in seeking guidelines for this new era in which our efforts will be directed toward creating a healthy Earth, we would do well to study some of their observations. According to Hopi legend, for example, humankind will live through "nine worlds." We are now entering the fifth of these. The first world they describe was a world of bliss, a world of plenty, not unlike the Garden of Eden. Of the worlds that followed, the Hopis say:

In the first world they had lived simply with the animals. In the second world they have developed handicrafts, homes, and villages. Now, in the third world they multiplied in such numbers and advanced so rapidly that they created big cities, countries, a whole civilization.

Now these people started using their powers in wicked ways and flew on hide shields and destroyed each others' cities. That world was destroyed, with the best people emerging into the fourth world.

The name of this fourth world is Tu'waqachi, World Complete. You will find out why. It is not all beautiful and easy like

the previous ones. It has height and depth, heat and cold, beauty and barrenness; it has everything for you to choose from. What you choose will determine if this time you can carry out the plan of Creation on it, or whether it must in time be destroyed too.[19]

The Hopis' image of the fifth world is sketchy, except that it will be created out of the best that has come from the previous four worlds. The legend tells us that:

The emergence of the future Fifth World has begun. You can read this in the Earth itself. Plant forms from previous worlds are beginning to spring up as seeds . . . the same kinds of seeds are being planted in the sky as stars. The same kinds of seeds are being planted in our hearts. All these are the same, depending how you look at them. This is what makes the emergence to the next, Fifth World.[20]

The society we might envision for the future, one that would directly confront the problems we are facing today, would have a powerful technology directed at full cooperation with nature. Whereas societies in the past have focused on what could be reaped from the Earth, sometimes with little thought for the consequences, our coming social evolution will be toward giving to the Earth. To be healthy ourselves we must heal the Earth and create an environment in which the nurture of that which sustains all life is a constant goal.

CHAPTER FOUR

The Living Earth

In the preceding chapters we have spoken of the concept of our planet as a living entity. In this chapter we will explore the ideas of forward-looking scientists like James Lovelock, Lynne Margolin, Carl Sagan, Lewis Thomas, James Miller, and others who have dared to look in a new way at the data collected in their work. From their fields of chemistry, evolutionary biology, astrophysics, medicine, and systems analysis have come evidence strongly suggesting that the Earth is an entity with a life of its own. Although some people would, of course, question whether such hypotheses can be proven, we feel it is important to look at them here, because the idea of a living Earth provides us with guidelines for finding solutions to today's environmental health concerns.

If the Earth is alive, what is the Earth's physiology? How does it nurture itself? How does it heal itself, and maintain a healthy state for the whole including mankind? What are the relationships between the planet and the creatures that live upon it? Does the Earth have a psychology, a set of behavioral principles that characterize it as an individual among the infinite numbers of other heavenly bodies? Once we begin to explore such questions, it becomes very clear that early cultures' views of the Earth as a living thing—as Mother Earth—were less metaphor than insight on reality.

As science learns about the Earth as a living entity, we are drawn into an entirely new relationship with our planet, changing the attitudes we had, for example, at the beginning of the Industrial Revolution, when conquering nature was a major goal. The new, emerging attitude about the Earth we might call *interpersonal*, because it has become increasingly difficult to depersonalize our planet, to be satisfied with an exploitative view of it. Thus, even as science discovers new evidence for our planet's life, we are creating new social values as startling as those our ancestors shaped with the coming of the industrial age.

For health—the central topic of this book—the issues are fairly clear. The Earth nurtures us and keeps us well; in turn, the well-being of our planet must assume a high priority in our lives. Seeing that the Earth is alive and vulnerable, we adopt a gentler, more caring attitude than did, for example, those first men who found ore within her and set out to mine it with little thought for any long-term consequences. Just as we perceive that the well-being of our loved ones—spouse, parents, children, friends—affects our own health, so we begin to perceive that the quality of all our lives is ultimately dependent on the care we bestow on our planet.

In one respect, with our mastery of technology, we are like gods, able to heal many of the diseases feared by humanity for centuries, and able to create an inferno with destructive powers equal to anything created by the cosmos itself. In another respect we are the humblest of creatures, not unlike the staphylococcae, streptococcae, and escherichia coli bacteria that live in and on us. We cannot live without such bacteria, so they must be considered as much a part of us as our heart and lungs. These microorganisms provide us with services as essential to our well-being as breathing and pumping blood through our circulatory systems. We can't be certain that we are as essential to the earth as the helpful bacteria that live on our bodies are to us, but the more that chemists, biologists, and astrophysicists explore this relationship, the more it seems likely that the Earth—at least in its present form—is dependent on us. Although this view of ourselves as tiny microorganisms may be humbling at first, in part it may frighten us by the responsibility it implies.

In their efforts to understand their relationship with the Earth, people have for centuries tried to show the planet as having human qualities and thus requiring the treatment

It becomes clear that early cultures' view of the Earth as a living thing —Mother Earth—was less a metaphor than an insight into reality. (*Mother Earth Sand Painting.* Courtesy of the Museum of the American Indian, Heye Foundation.)

we would each give the ones we love the most. In *The Book of the Hopi,* we learn that the Indians believed that:

The earth was a living entity like themselves. She was their mother; they were made from her flesh, and they suckled at her breast. For her milk was the grass upon which all animals grazed and the corn which had been created especially to supply food for mankind.[1]

For an example of behavior based on perception of the Earth as a mother, turn to the words of Smohalla, a Sioux Indian prophet who believed that cultivation itself was a violation of the Earth:

You ask me to plow the ground? Shall I take a knife and tear my mother's bosom? Then when I die she will not take me to her bosom to rest. You ask me to dig for stone? Shall I dig under her skin for her bones? Then when I die I cannot enter her body to be born again. You ask me to cut grass and make hay and sell it, and be rich like white men! But how do I cut off my mother's hair?[2]

Although science doesn't personify the Earth as much as Smohalla or the Hopis did, the scientific view of the planet is not without human sentiment. To biologist Lewis Thomas, the Earth begins to take on a definite character of its own:

Viewed from the distance of the Moon, the astonishing thing about the Earth, catching the breath, is that it is alive. . . . Aloft, floating free beneath the moist, gleaming membrane of bright blue sky, is the rising Earth, the only exuberant thing in this part of the cosmos. If you could look long enough, you would see the swirling of the great drifts of white cloud, covering and uncovering the half-hidden masses of land. If you had been looking for very long, geologic time, you could have seen the continents themselves in

Viewed from the distance of the Moon, the astonishing thing about the Earth is that it is alive. It has the organized, self-contained look of a live creature. (Earth view, 1977. Courtesy of NASA.)

The Earth was a living entity like themselves. Her milk was the grass upon which all animals grazed, and corn was created especially to provide food for mankind. (*Hopi Corn Fields,* 1982, by Michael Samuels.)

Shall I take a knife and tear my mother's bosom? You ask me to dig for stone? Shall I dig under her skin for her bones? (*Nevada Mining,* 1982, by Michael Samuels.)

motion, drifting apart on their crustal plates, held aloft by the fire beneath. It has the organized, self-contained look of a life creature, full of information, marvelously skilled in handling the Sun.[3]

The very same technologies that allowed us to shoot a rocket into space and send back pictures of our planet that would inspire Lewis Thomas (and others) also gave us the capacity to devastate our planet. In ways that we will explore further in the next few pages, science's newfound appreciation for the Earth as a living entity is a by-product of the space program, our highest technological achievement to date. Out of that same program have come new technologies that hold great promise for providing us with new energy sources (solar col-

which we could be certain there was life. In the process of analyzing the chemistry of our atmosphere, he discovered more than he had expected.

First there were the knowns. Based on his knowledge of plant and animal life, Lovelock could calculate the proportions of gases, such as oxygen and carbon dioxide, that would be in the atmosphere of any planet where these life forms were found. (Oxygen, carbon dioxide, methane, and certain other gases are by-products of life as we know it.) To find these gases in our atmosphere was not surprising. What was surprising was the fact that these and other gases were maintained in exact proportions, which had not varied in millions of years. Certain questions logically followed. What prevented plants from reproducing

Homeostatic functions of earth's gases[a]

Gas	Function
Nitrogen	Maintains pressure and extinguishes fires.
Oxygen	Basis of all energy in chemical reactions.
Carbon dioxide	Used by plants in photosynthesis and insulates the Earth, maintaining stable temperatures.
Methane	Regulates oxygen, and gets rid of natural toxins in anerobic muds and silts.
Nitrous oxide	Regulates oxygen and ozone.
Ammonia	Regulates pH (acid-base balance).
Sulfur gases	Transports gases in the sulfur cycle.
Methyl chloride	Regulates ozone.
Methyl iodide	Transports iodine.

[a]Adapted from Lovelock, p. 68.

Feedback loops allow organisms to monitor themselves and keep their physiological processes within a healthy range. Some of an output or an input changes the flow of a substance (blood, hormones etc.) so the body physiology is altered. When too much of a substance is present, it will feedback and cause less to be made.

lectors), and with extensions of the human brain (subminiature electronics) that come as close as anything we have ever made to mimicking nature. In one stroke we have found ways both to annihilate ourselves and to live on the Earth without endangering her life.

What Is a Living System?

In the new science of the living Earth, we are just beginning to understand how our planet functions. We are now standing where biologists stood before the electron microscope unveiled the complex functions of the cell. We are only beginning to understand our atmosphere, that membrane within which the Earth exists. We are only beginning to ask questions about our relationship to the whole.

One of the most interesting analyses of the living Earth comes from J. E. Lovelock, an English physicist who was hired by NASA to establish a set of criteria for deciding whether or not there was life on any of the planets to which we planned to send space probes. Lovelock began his work by examining our own atmosphere, since ours was the only planet on

wildy and so increasing the amount of oxygen? And what prevented animals from reproducing wildly, generating more and more carbon dioxide, in an upward spiral? The only way the gases in the atmosphere could have maintained their delicate balance was if the Earth itself had a way of monitoring those gases and directing the terrestrial activities that produce them.

The kind of self-monitoring process that Lovelock's findings indicated was strangely like the homeostatic mechanisms of all living things. Just as the temperature of the human body would rise or fall to life-threatening levels if it were not kept stable by the body's homeostatic capacity—an inner director that monitors vital functions and makes physiological changes to keep the temperature of the organism within a healthy range—so there had to be such a director to maintain a healthy Earth. It was Lovelock's belief that most of the regulation took place in the biosphere, that part of the Earth's environment where life is found. He described the biosphere as "a self-regulating entity with the capacity to keep our planet healthy by controlling the chemical and physical environment."[4]

Besides maintaining temperature and the

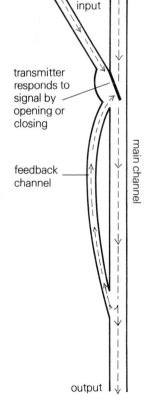

input

transmitter responds to signal by opening or closing

feedback channel

main channel

output

Comparison of gases, pressure, and temperature on planets with and without life.[a]		
Gas	*Without life*	*With life*
Carbon dioxide	98%	.03%
Nitrogen	1.9%	79%
Oxygen	trace	21%
Argon	.1%	1%
Temperature °C.	290 ± 50	13
Pressure (bars)	60	1

[a]Adapted from Lovelock, p. 39.

proportions of gases in the atmosphere within certain ranges, the homeostatic abilities of the Earth must carry out other tasks. For the planet to be healthy, the salinity of the oceans, and acid-base balances on both land and sea, must be kept within certain ranges; otherwise the biosphere will radically change, and the Earth will lose its system for controlling the atmosphere. The same is true in our own bodies; if acid-base balances change too much, bacteria that were once helpful (and a part of us) can begin attacking body cells; unless bacteria populations can be reduced, and acid-base balances reestablished, we will then die.

There can be little doubt that the Earth has homeostatic capacities, but couldn't all this be explained by the fact that species tend to balance each other, and chemicals tend to automatically maintain their stability once certain balances have been attained? Lovelock argues that this can be true only up to a point:

Much of the routine operation of homeostasis, whether it be for the cell, the animal, or the entire biosphere, takes place automat-

ically, and yet it must be recognized that some form of intelligence is required even within an automatic process, to interpret correctly information received about the environment. . . . If Gaia [the living Earth] exists, then she is without doubt intelligent in this limited sense at the least.[5]

In order to better understand why homeostasis is evidence that the Earth is both intelligent and alive, let's look at some specific tasks our planet must undertake to maintain its organic integrity.

Temperature

By examining fossils and rocks, geologists can establish accurate records of the Earth's climate back to its beginnings. They have discovered that the average temperature range of the Earth has not varied more than 10° overall. That is, the seas have never boiled nor have they frozen over (except at the Poles). However, the energy output of the Sun has increased 30 percent since the birth of our planet, and this change presents an interesting puzzle. If the Earth could not regulate the amount of energy coming to it from the Sun, the seas would boil with as little as a 2 percent increase in solar output. (Similarly, the seas would freeze over if temperatures dropped.) How, we must ask, did the Earth maintain its normal temperature range even though the Sun's output had increased fifteen times.

Scientists are not certain of the exact mechanisms that control the Earth's temperature, but there are some interesting speculations. The *albedo* of the Earth, that is, its reflective surface, can vary greatly; and, of course, this determines whether heat from the Sun is reflected or absorbed (dark colors

How, we must ask, has the Earth maintained its normal temperature range even though the Sun's output has increased 30 percent since the birth of our planet? (Sun, 1958. Courtesy of Hale Observatories.)

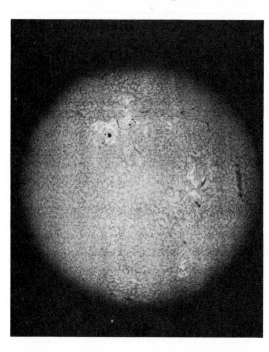

One way in which the Earth may control its temperature is by altering its reflective surface. It can do this by increasing or decreasing cloud, snow, vegetation, or algae growth. (Earth from a quarter of a million milers away. Courtesy of NASA.)

absorb, light colors reflect). The albedo is changed by many factors: white clouds, snow, clear water, and salt marshes, which reflect light; by dark algae growth on bodies of water and salt marshes, which absorbs light; and by the growth of dark vegetation which absorbs heat, and lighter-colored vegetation which reflects it. The tilt of the Earth's axis toward or away from the Sun varies the influence of the polar snowcaps, helping to cool our planet in its annual cycle. There is also the "greenhouse effect," whereby carbon dioxide (and ammonia, in the Earth's earliest history) in the atmosphere forms a roof over our planet, allowing heat to come in, but preventing solar energy reflected back from the Earth's surface from escaping. This greenhouse effect could vary in tiny increments to adjust to solar changes by raising or lowering growth rates of plants and animals.

Taken as a whole, the Earth's mechanisms for controlling temperature would correspond to the mechanisms within our own bodies for raising and lowering body heat: the ability to change blood flow toward skin surfaces to lose body heat, toward inner organs to hold body heat; perspiration and the resultant cooling effects, to lower body heat; the erectile muscles around hair shafts in animals to stand up their fur and produce an insulating air space to hold in the heat in cold weather; and rapid metabolic rates, to raise body heat. But just as we don't know exactly what processes monitor and direct these changes in our bodies, neither do we know exactly how this system operates on the Earth.

Oxygen Content of the Atmosphere

The normal oxygen content of our atmos-phere is 21 percent of the total gases, and the tiny amount that it varies is nearly immeasur-able. Although oxygen is necessary to all animal life on our planet, it could also be immensely destructive if it were to increase. One method by which its proportion is maintained is by production of methane gas, a gas that binds with oxygen. Although it is also a product of animal digestion, most of the methane found in the atmosphere is produced by the fermentation of bacteria in marshes, estuaries, and swamps which are located virtually everywhere on the globe.

If oxygen levels had risen as little as 1 percent every 12,000 years, the world would have turned into a ball of flame, destroying all living things in less than 50,000 years. Precise proportions of oxygen are ultimately maintained by the growth rates of plants (which produce oxygen) and the fermentation of bacteria (which produce methane.) The regulation of these cannot be haphazard. As Lovelock points out, "The constancy of oxygen concentration suggests the presence of an active control system, presumably with a means of sensing and signaling any departure from the optimum oxygen concentration in the air."[6]

Acid-Base Balance

When we speak of acid-base balance, that is, the acidity or alkalinity of a substance, we are actually referring to the concentration of hydrogen ions. Even slight changes in the concentration of hydrogen ions can dramatically disrupt the chemical reactions in the cells of living things, and, of course, these chemical reactions are essential to life.

The symbol pH is used to express the concentration of hydrogen ions in solution; the

Carbon dioxide in the upper atmosphere allows sunlight to enter our gaseous envelope (as short wave radiation) thereby heating the Earth; but carbon dioxide stops the heat from the earth (long wave radiation) from escaping back into space. This is called the "greenhouse" effect.

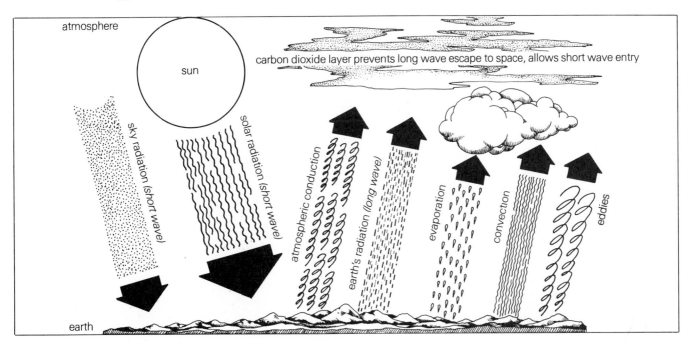

carbon dioxide layer prevents long wave escape to space, allows short wave entry

range of concentration is measured on a scale of 1 to 14. A pH of 1 is the most acid; 7.0 is neutral; and 14 is the most basic. The cellular fluid of different human cells varies in pH from 4.5 to 7.4—and unless this range is maintained, the organism will fail to metabolize properly, will become diseased, and possibly die. The human body is equipped with physiological mechanisms for maintaining its own acid-base balance, but these inner mechanisms could not completely counteract an external environment that was too far out of the range of human tolerance. The same is true for all life forms; so it is essential that the Earth maintain an acid-base balance of its own.

Ammonia in the atmosphere is dispersed by the rain. If there were not a certain amount of ammonia in the atmosphere, we would get

ically release their bicarbonic acid, which in the atmosphere becomes carbon dioxide. In addition to this regulatory mechanism, plants use the carbon in carbon dioxide as part of the process of photosynthesis. Thus the plants help prevent a buildup of carbon dioxide; they constitute one more mechanism by which the Earth maintains homeostasis by its control of the biosphere.

Salinity of the Seas

Over 80 million years, the rain leaches from the land and empties into the seas as much sodium chloride as the seas normally hold. And yet the saline level of the seas does not change. The 3.4 percent salinity has remained the same for thousands of millions of

Every 80 million years the rain leaches from the land as much salt as the seas hold. And yet the ocean's 3.4 percent salinity level has remained the same throughout thousands of millions of years. (Salt Lagoon, 1969, by Michael Samuels.)

acid rains (with a pH in the neighborhood of 3) all the time, which would destroy plant and animal life. The ammonia necessary for a proper acid-base balance is produced by animals, and thus can be controlled by the Earth by regulation of the animal life in the biosphere.

Carbon Dioxide

As we discussed in earlier paragraphs on temperature, carbon dioxide in the atmosphere creates a greenhouse effect, allowing the Sun's rays to enter, but trapping the heat reflected back from the Earth. Normally, the atmosphere contains .03 percent carbon dioxide, and this level must be maintained exactly. Although carbon dioxide is produced by animals, most of the regulation of this gas probably takes place in the oceans.

The seas hold large reserves of bicarbonic acid. When the carbon dioxide in the atmosphere falls to a certain level, the seas automat-

years. If the salinity were to rise, as it has done on certain inland lakes (Salt Lake in Utah, for example), all life within the seas would be extinguished, and the chemistry of the whole planet would be radically altered.

The mechanism that regulates salinity is not fully understood, but we do know that great quantities of salt are trapped in lagoons formed by tremendous coral reefs. The growth rate of coral may be controlled by the Earth's homeostatic mechanism for the purpose of regulating salinity. Sodium is also trapped in the millions of tiny organisms whose skeletons continuously rain downward in the seas. These skeletons are buried in the limestone beds at the bottoms of our oceans, burying whatever sodium they carried along with them.

The problem of how our oceans control salinity remains one of the great unsolved mysteries of oceanography, but Lovelock feels that a mechanism must exist for this process, and that this mechanism is controlled by the Earth.

Iodine

Animals with thyroid glands require iodine to make thyroxin, and they depend on outside sources for this mineral. These hormones are, of course, essential to life, since they control metabolic rates. Traces of iodine can be found in most foods, but in glaciated areas, such as the Great Lakes region, iodine has been leached from the soil; unless people living in the area supplement their diets, they may be deficient in this mineral. Near the oceans, seaweed, notably Laminaria kelp, gathers iodine and produces a gas, methyl iodide, which rises into the air above the oceans. The methyl iodide is eventually picked up in the rains and distributed over the land, where in turn it is assimilated by the plants by which humans and other animals are nourished. The subtle interrelationships between seaweed, the atmosphere, the rains, the plants' use of iodine, and eventual human consumption of the iodine needed to build metabolizing hormones in our bodies becomes awe-inspiring when we consider infinitely complex balances that must be maintained throughout our planet.

These are only a few examples of the ways in which the Earth maintains the homeostasis of the biosphere. Although Earth science has not yet been able to identify the exact system that maintains the homeostasis, the evidence indicates that such a system must exist, and that must be much like the system that exists in all living things, from the simplest cell to the most complex animal.

Comparing the Earth to Other Living Systems

Until recently biologists have found it all but impossible to provide a simple definition of life, a set of criteria for judging whether a thing is alive or not. However, systems analysis has given us a new way of sorting out information about complex organizations.

In his book *Living Systems,* James Miller uses systems analysis to compare cells, organs, organisms, groups, organizations, societies, and supranational systems. He begins with the generalization that all living systems "are made of matter and energy organized by information." In the next few pages, we will see exactly what he means by this, as we explore the categories he establishes for looking at living systems.

One aspect of living systems that Miller's thesis emphasizes is that all systems (cells, organs, organisms, etc.) are made up of parts whose interrelationships contribute to the complete function of the whole. We cannot understand a whole system by studying merely one, or some, of its parts. Thus, we cannot understand the whole system we call life by studying only one species, even though that species we study may be as complex and as precious to us as human beings are. Nor, for that matter, can we understand life by studying only plants and animals. Our knowledge will be incomplete and woefully distorted until we are able to perceive the whole system in which humans, plants, animals, and even chemical phenomena are parts. Usually—and this can certainly be seen for the Earth—the whole system is dependent on the sum total of its parts. The character of the whole would be altered if any of its parts were left out.

We thought it interesting to extend Dr. Miller's analytical system from cells to supranational systems to the Earth itself, and to use that system to compare our planet to other living things. It can be argued, of course, that this is just a way of looking at the Earth, that it establishes no scientific truths about its nature. However, by comparing the Earth to other living systems, using Miller's system, perhaps we can clarify the emerging concept of the Earth as an organism, a living entity like ourselves.

According to Miller's systems analysis, all living systems have certain common characteristics, as follows:

1. *They are open systems.* Even though they have boundaries of their own, living things are able to take in information, matter, and energy, though they may be highly selective about what they accept.

2. *They have negentropy.* This term is derived from the concept of entropy, the second law of thermodynamics. This law, roughly paraphrased, implies that everything in the universe eventually reverts to its simplest form. Thus, an ice cube left in the sun will melt into a pool of water, which will evaporate, dispersing throughout the universe. Negentropy is the force within living things that prevents entropy from taking place.

3. *They are complex.* Systems are made up of numerous parts whose functions interrelate and contribute to the whole.

4. *They contain genetic material.* They have DNA or a "template" of some sort. This could be anything from the nucleus of a cell to a set of instructions for maintaining the organization.

5. *They are composed of protoplasm.* Protoplasm is, of course, a structure composed

of a number of amino acids, water, and other organic materials.

6. *They contain a decider.* This is a subsystem with critical capacities, the ability to monitor and control the whole system and cause its subsystems to work together toward supporting themselves as well as the whole.

7. *They exist in a specific environment.* They depend on environmental variables, such as temperature, air pressure, water, oxygen, intensity of radiation, etc., and variations outside the range to which they are adapted can result in their dissolution or destruction.

These are the generalizations about living systems. Let us now see how cells, humans, and the Earth reflect each of these characteristics.

I. Subsystems that Process Energy and Matter

A. All Living Systems Have Subsystems That Act as Boundaries.

The boundary of the system holds it within itself, protects the system from things outside it, and may selectively admit matter, energy, and information that might be of benefit to the system.

Examples. The cell membrane is the boundary of the cell. The skin is the boundary of a human being. The atmosphere is the boundary of the Earth.

B. All Living Systems Have Subsystems That Act as Ingestors.

The ingestor is a system for allowing energy, matter or information to pass through the system's boundary and enter it.

Examples. The membrane of a cell is porous, to allow selected material and energy to pass through it. Humans ingest foods through the mouth, oxygen through the mouth and nose; the lungs and digestive system select out what is useful. The Earth has a "greenhouse" of carbon dioxide that selectively allows solar energy to enter the system.

C. All Living Systems Have Subsystems That Act as Decomposers.

The decomposer of a system transforms energy and matter into forms that can be used by the whole system, or a subsystem, in a new way.

Examples. The enzymes in a cell break down carbohydrates and turn them into fuels for the cell. The human digestive system breaks down plant and animal matter, and converts it into simple sugars and nutrients that the cells within its boundaries can use directly. The Earth has many decomposers, one of which is the marsh or estuary, where bacteria break down organic matter and create methane gas to bind with oxygen molecules, in order to limit the amount of oxygen in the atmosphere.

D. All Living Systems Have Subsystems That Act as Producers.

The producer makes new things from energy and matter ingested by the living system.

Examples. A cell produces enzymes from protein molecules. The human body produces

All living systems have boundaries. These boundaries are permeable, allowing nutrients to pass through them. (Red blood cell plasma membrane, magnified 415,000 times, 1981. Courtesy of W. Rosenberg.)

All living systems have storage systems for matter and energy. (Villi of the small intestine. R. G. Kessel and R. H. Kardon, *Tissues and Organs.*)

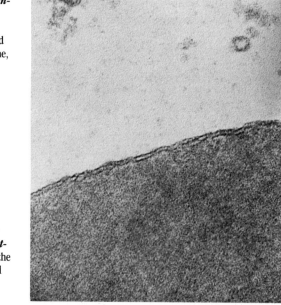

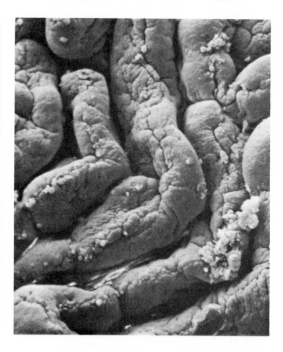

new cells, and through the brain and muscles can produce artifacts. The Earth produces chemical compounds, gases, ores, and heat, and must also be considered to produce all the living systems found within the environment which the planet represents.

E. All Living Systems Have Subsystems That Act as Storage Systems for Matter and Energy.

The storage system accumulates nutrients and releases them as needed.

Examples. Cells store ATP, lipids, and glucose in the cytoplasm, as well as in the membrane. Humans store simple carbohydrates in the liver, fat in fatty tissue, etc. The Earth stores salt and other minerals in the oceans, oxygen and other gases in the atmosphere.

F. All Living Systems Have Subsystems That Act as Extruders.

The extruder gets rid of waste or unwanted matter or energy.

Examples. Permeable cell membranes allow lactic acids and carbon dioxide to be extruded. The human cardiovascular system extrudes carbon dioxide; the kidneys and urinary system extrude urine; and the lower intestine extrudes feces. The Earth extrudes hydrogen and helium atoms through the greenhouse of carbon dioxide forming its boundary.

G. All Living Systems Have Subsystems That Support Them.

Examples. Cell membranes support the cell. The human muscular/skeletal system supports the body. The Earth's mantle/plate system supports the Earth's crust.

H. All Living Systems Have Subsystems That Act as Motors.

The motor is any system or group of systems that moves the whole or any of its parts in relation to the environment, or that moves the environment toward it.

Examples. Microfibers in cells expand and contract, causing the cell to move along in fluids. Humans' legs and arms are necessary for moving around in the environment, and for manipulating things within that environment. The Earth moves its plates, changing relationships between continents, and it rotates on its axis, revolves around the Sun, etc.

II. Subsystems that Process Information

A. All Living Systems Have Subsystems That Act as Input Transducers.

There is a subsystem that receives information from outside the system, and transforms such information into energy or matter transmitted inside the system.

Examples. Cell membranes have receptor sites that receive information, such as pressure and light, from the environment; these are transformed into chemical signals inside the cell, causing that cell to expand and/or contract, moving it either toward the stimulus or away from it, depending on whether that stimulus is identified as harmful or beneficial. Humans receive information in many forms, for example, by a word or phrase that causes

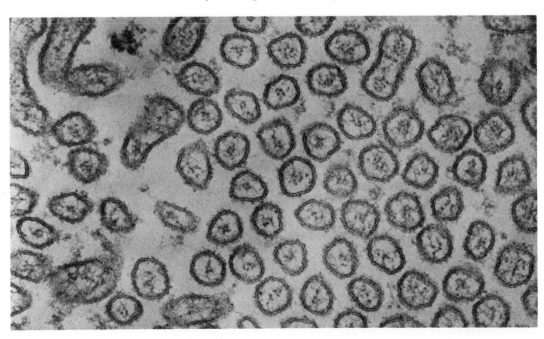

All living systems have "motors" that allow them to move their parts. (Cross section through microvilli, showing microfilaments, magnified 160,000 times. Courtesy of W. Rosenberg.)

discharges of electrical energy in the nervous system, which in turn may be transformed into chemical signals for expanding or contracting muscles. For the Earth, consider how an increase of oxygen content in the atmosphere sends chemical signals to bacteria in marshes, causing them to produce more methane, which binds with and reduces the amount of free oxygen.

B. All Living Systems Have Subsystems that Act as Internal Transducers.

These subsystems receive information about events inside the system, and transform that information so that it can be transmitted to other subsystems that affect the whole.

Examples. A cell produces an overabundance of enzymes; this triggers the production of protein molecules, known as repressor proteins, that inhibit enzyme production. Humans have many internal transducers. One of these is located in the hypothalmus gland, and receives signals about body temperature. When it learns that the body is too hot, it sends out chemical signals to skin surfaces that open capillaries and allow blood to flow toward the surface for cooling. If body temperature drops below the normal range, the subsystem sends signals to the thyroid gland to speed up metabolism and so produce heat. On the Earth, a high salinity in the ocean stimulates coral growth, which creates shallow lagoons that act as solar stills to trap salt.

C. All Living Systems Have Subsystems That Act as a Channel and Net.

The channel and net may be one system

All living systems have subsystems that act as channels for transmitting information. (Nerve fibers, magnified 900 times. R. G. Kessel and R. H. Kardon, *Tissues and Organs.*)

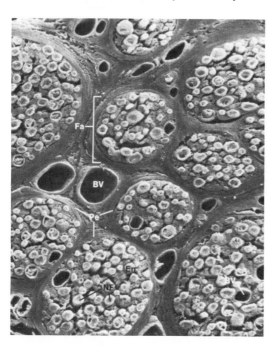

*Interestingly enough, the Earth's north/south polarity reverses about every million years. The most recent reversal occurred about 30,000 years ago, and lasted for 2,000 years.

that transmits information throughout the system.

Examples. A cell has microtubules and microfilaments that act like a central nervous system, transmitting information within the cell. Humans have a nerve net, an electromagnetic field, that receives and sends signals throughout the body. Like humans, the Earth has a magnetic field.* All living things have similar magnetic fields, and experiments have shown that all living systems are affected by the Earth's field, as well as by the fields of organisms nearby them. It can be speculated that the magnetic field of the Earth, like the fields around all living systems, serves as a channel and net through which the Earth communicates.

III. Subsystems that Act as an Intelligence

A. All living systems have subsystems that act as decoders, associators, memory, and deciders.

The purpose of this intelligence is to make sense of information coming in, to ask such questions as "How does this new information affect the whole system?" The intelligence also stores information, integrates new information with old, and finally makes decisions based on its accumulation of knowledge. This intelligence has goals, knows the norms for homeostasis, for example, and can direct new generations in their evolution so that they may be better adapted to a new condition in the environment.

Examples. The behavior of a cell, as it senses food and moves toward it or senses danger and moves away, indicates that it has intelligence, though biologists can't fully identify the subsystem that takes responsibility for these tasks. The human brain and central nervous system process complex information, from signals as simple as the danger of a hot stove to the most complex mathematical abstractions. In the Earth, intelligence is difficult to establish, and Earth scientists have not yet identified a subsystem parallel to the human brain. However, the evidence Lovelock presents for the Earth's ability to sense the subtle variations in gases, mineral contents, temperature, and acid-base balance indicate that such an intelligence must exist. In fact, Lovelock asks, "Do we as a species constitute a Gaian nervous system and a brain which can consciously anticipate environmental changes?"[7] In a similar vein, Lewis Thomas has reflected that, "Joined together, the great mass of human minds around the Earth seems to behave like a coherent, living system."[8]

Human thoughts surround the planet, forming the noosphere, a layer just as extensive as the atmosphere or hydrosphere. (Aerial view of Earth. Courtesy of NASA.)

Both Lovelock and Thomas ask us to entertain the possibility that through human beings, through our possession of a powerful communication network and an almost miraculous grasp of technology, the Earth's range of perception has been expanded. Through humans, who can certainly be viewed as one of the Earth's subsystems, the Earth has become awake and aware of itself. This would be consistent with Miller's statement that, "All systems do not have all possible kinds of subsystems. . . . But all living systems either have a complete complement of the critical subsystems carrying out the functions necessary to life or are intimately associated with and effectively interacting with systems which carry out missing life functions for them."[9]

A Biosphere of Diverse Species Is Essential

Through the centuries we have learned to identify and categorize the species of plants and animals living with us on Earth. Although this has been useful in some ways, it has also dissociated us from other species. It has helped us create artificial barriers between ourselves and other living things, barriers that hinder our exploration of the interrelatedness of humans and other life forms.

On the edge of the African desert, one will find, for example, a modest-looking acacia plant. Environmental studies reveal that this plant has a very special purpose in life. It serves as a border marker for other species of plants and animals that grow on the savannahs outside the desert. The exact mechanism by which it accomplishes its mission is only partially understood, but wherever this plant has been decimated by overzealous woodcutters, the desert has expanded its borders, turning once grassy acres into barren wastelands. What's worse, this plant has been so intensely exploited that it is seriously threatened with extinction—and there appears to be no other species to carry on its mission.

We need not look to other continents for examples of one species guarding the borders of another. In fact, we do not have to look past our own bodies. Staphylococcal bacteria that live on our skin surfaces help guard our bodies from thousands of species of microorganisms that might cause us harm. Staphylococci are so essential we would get infections and die without them. They guard the borders both by creating an acid environment that other species of microorganisms don't like, and by consuming other microorganisms who try to invade this jealously guarded environmental niche. The staphylococci are much like hawks circling over their territories, always on the alert for those who might encroach.

Similarly, there are streptococci living in our upper respiratory systems, and other bacteria living in our intestinal tracts which produce micronutrients we need to maintain our health. These micronutrients include vitamin K, without which our bodies could not produce prothrombin, a substance necessary for blood clotting. Intestinal bacteria also produce B vitamins, most notably B_{12}, which is used for making DNA and promotes the maturation of red blood cells.

On a larger scale there are important relationships between plants, animals, and the atmosphere of our planet. The gases in the atmosphere exist in what sometimes appears to be a precarious balance; serious disruption of that balance could lead to the annihilation of all life. The atmosphere itself contains: 21 percent oxygen, 79 percent nitrogen, 1 percent argon, .03 percent carbon dioxide, and traces of methane, nitrous oxide, ammonia, sulfur, methyl chloride, and methyl iodide. These gases are largely produced by plants and animals: oxygen by plants, carbon dioxide by animals, methane by bacteria breaking down organic materials in marshes, methyl iodide by particular species of seaweed, etc. There are strong indications that a balance among diverse species—from the tiniest microorganisms to the most complex animals—in the biosphere is the key mechanism by which the Earth's homeostatic devices maintain a healthy atmosphere.

We are beginning to understand the full benefits of a biosphere with diverse species. This sort of knowledge first appeared in medicine: in the late 18th century, Edward Jenner, a physician, observed that a microorganism causing cowpox in cattle was passed to humans, causing them to develop antibodies against

smallpox without suffering major disease symptoms. Thus came one of humanity's first observations into the mechanism of vaccination, and an important insight into the subtle benefits of having diverse species. We know that organisms that affect one species of plant or animal can often cross over and affect another species. For example, certain flu viruses that infect man can be carried by migrating ducks. And from this evidence microbiologists speculate that the antibodies produced by one animal may prevent the spread of certain bacteria to other species. If there were no other valid arguments in favor of preserving a diverse biosphere, this alone would be enough.

All too often people jump to impulsive conclusions upon seeing a single act by one member of a particular species. For example, how many farmers, seeing a barn owl carry off a baby chick, have jumped to the conclusion that the owl was a dangerous predator and so declared war on all owls? Had such farmers asked questions, such as how many chicks a barn owl eats in a year, and what benefits owls might offer to offset this sacrifice, they might have come up with some different answers. One Pennsylvania farmer who was interested in ecology collected some 200 pellets of undigested droppings from barn owls on his farm. The pellets were taken to Carnegie Museum and examined. The examination revealed what the owls had eaten: 429 meadow mice; 4 lemming mice; 1 pine mouse; 12 white-footed deer mice; 18 jumping mice; 21 star-nosed moles; 1 Brewer's mole; 95 large short-tailed shrews; 1 least short-tailed shrew; 1 squirrel; 5 cottontail rabbits; 23 unidentified mice; and 5 small birds.[10] Knowing this, farmers might protect rather than destroy their master rodent hunters.

Sometimes the interdependence of species is so subtle that it defies detection except by the most knowledgeable experts. Indeed, what seems to be one thing on cursory examination may, on closer inspection, prove to be something else. For example, when a hermit crab takes up residence in an abandoned snail shell, he shares his home with a marine worm, *Nereis fucata,* who settles in the smallest coils of the shell. When the crab eats, *Nereis fucata* snatches morsels from his host. It is hard to say how the worm benefits his host, but perhaps it is a matter of companionship, for the two seem inseparable throughout their lives.

In Chapter Three we discussed how human cultivation of wheat encouraged the evolution of new species of grain, and how, as a result, there has developed a symbiotic relationship between wheat and humans: the wheat nourishes people, who, in turn, plant the seeds for the wheat, which can no longer germinate except with human help. But humans are not the only cultivating species in the biosphere. There is, for example, a species of ants living in the tropics which systematically cultivates a variety of mushroom. The ants collect circular bits of leaves from favored vegetation, which they bring back to their nest to form a bed of organic material, on which they place spores from the mushrooms. Tiny worker ants then keep this area weeded until the mushrooms have grown to maturity. This fungus constitutes the only source of food for these ants, and this species of mushroom is found nowhere but in the nests of these tiny cultivators. The two species have worked out a perfect symbiotic relationship.

We know only enough about the dynamics of the interdependencies among the Earth's diverse species to recognize how much more we have yet to discover. From the fruit tree's dependence on the bees to carry out pollination, to domesticated animals' dependence on humans to protect and feed them, there are cooperative situations we have barely begun to imagine, much less understand. It is certain that all plants and animals, insofar as they are themselves important elements of the environment, have helped shape the genetic goals of every species around them. In spite of our greatest efforts, we know remarkably little about human evolution, about the kinds of mutations that led to the physical animal we recognize as contemporary *Homo sapiens.* What's more, evolution of our species, and all others, continues; we cannot help but wonder about our future as the diversity of species on our planet narrows, largely because of our own negligence and selfish exploitation.

In 1980, the Eleventh Annual Council on Environmental Quality stated that, "In natural biological diversity, humankind has varied, infinitely renewable supplies of food, energy, industrial chemicals, and medicine."[11] From a selfish point of view, that is, considering only our own survival and comfort, we could find little to argue with in this. But there is more. Though we may sometimes feel superior to other species, we cannot survive without them. Our interdependencies may be far more complex and broad than we can possibly imagine. In the words of Lewis Thomas:

We still argue the details, but it is conceded almost everywhere that we are not the masters of nature that we thought ourselves; we are as dependent on the rest of life as are the leaves or midges or fish. We are part of the system. One way to put it is that the Earth is a loosely formed, spherical organism, with all its working parts linking in symbiosis.[12]

It seems that over and above our scientific reasons for recognizing the purpose and importance of a biosphere made up of diverse species,

there is a moral argument, recently voiced by Paul and Ann Ehrlich in their book *Extinction*, that "other products of evolution have a right to exist."[13]

What Is the Spirit of the Living Earth?

It is difficult in a book of this nature to speak of spirit. Words like *soul* and *spirit* at first seem opposed to our efforts to finely focus our awareness on an issue such as the health of our planet. And yet the spiritual aspects of our living Earth beg our undivided attention as much as the synthesis of chemicals into early life forms or the proportions of gases in our atmosphere.

Because we place so much faith in science

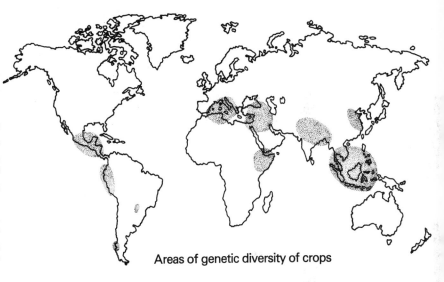

Areas of genetic diversity of crops

and technology, it is difficult for us to entertain the nonrational. As Marilyn Ferguson reflects in her book *The Brain Revolution,* contemporary culture tries to bury the metaphysical side of our nature. She points out that we can compare the "repression of the nonrational core, the spiritual impulse, to the repression of sex."[14] Ferguson quotes several scientists, including the brain physiologist Sir John Eccles, who, with the best modern tools of science at his disposal, confessed, "I believe that there is a fundamental mystery in my existence, transcending any biological account of the development of my body (including my brain) with its genetic inheritance and its evolutionary origin."[15]

We must go a step farther than Eccles, and suggest that not only human beings, but the Earth itself, being a living entity, has a spirit. The spiritual question seems inevitable. There are far too many empty spaces in the puzzle science has handed us. For example, if the sec-

Geographic areas of exceptional genetic diversity for crop plants may be essential for mankind. Monocultures are susceptible to environmental change and illness.

ond law of thermodynamics is true, if all matter and energy, left to their own devices, will evolve toward the simplest form (the state of maximum entropy), why do molecules gather together for a time and organize into plants, animals, and even planets? There is a point at which principles of gravity, genetic codes, and negentropy give way to a concept much harder to grasp: the spirit of life.

Scientists have not been afraid to tackle this question, but their tools and methods have failed to give final answers. Albert Einstein said that the mystical is the sower of all true science: "He to whom this emotion is a stranger, who can no longer wonder and stand rapt in awe, is as good as dead."[16]

The system of Hindu philosophy known as *Samkhya Yoga* postulates that the universe was made up of two elements: the first was *Purusa* (spirit), which had no dimension, neither height, nor width, nor depth, nor weight, nor light, had no finite qualities of any kind, yet was completely autonomous; second, there was *Prakriti*, which was finite. These two, by interacting, became manifest as Intelligence, Energy, and Matter.

Within the Samkhya system of thought, the universe as we know it today grew from a cosmic egg, but the yogins go further back, stating that the cosmic egg passed through an evolutionary stage of its own. The egg began as a mass of pure energy, called *Mahat*, which had taken shape out of the Purusa (spirit). Through a force called *Parinama* (evolution), Mahat developed into its next stage, in which it had *Prakriti*, Intelligence and Matter, in addition to Energy.

When the cosmic egg, or *Ahamkara*, opened up, the force of evolution *(Parinama)* influenced all things in the universe. As matter proceeded to develop increasingly complex forms, so consciousness was also evolving. The universe was unfolding in two different but parallel forms: matter on the one hand, and consciousness on the other. *Purusa* (spirit) meanwhile was everywhere.

The Samkhya yogin believes that human beings have evolved both as matter and as consciousness. We are the most complex animal on Earth, and our consciousness has evolved enough that we can be aware of ourselves and understand our true nature as matter, energy, and intelligence. Moreover, we have developed a spiritual aspect, a mirror in our consciousness which reflects *Purusa*. The yogins describe it as a "mirror reflecting *Purusa*," because *Purusa*, being infinite, without dimension or weight or light, cannot be perceived by our finite perceptual capacities, such as our senses or intelligence. We can use our finite perceptual abilities to become attuned to the mirror that reflects *Purusa*, but we cannot "think" or "rationalize" our way to

this universal spirit.

Interestingly enough, no part of the Samkhya Yoga system contradicts anything in science. In fact, the similarities between modern physics and the yoga system are so great that one might think the physicists had modeled their system after that of the Hindus. The spiritual aspects, though usually avoided by science, are occasionally acknowledged even in the most conservative scientific texts with phrases such as "life force" or even "negentropy," that inexplicable force that causes molecules to move and grow and reproduce and perceive their environment once they have assembled themselves as living entities.

In 1931 the Jesuit palaeontologist Pierre Teilhard de Chardin published an essay entitled "The Spirit of the Earth," in which he presented the belief that just as our body has evolved from chemical matter to its present level of complexity, so our consciousness has been evolving into increasingly complex forms. Consciousness, Teilhard says, is in all things in the universe, and is the singular force that motivates molecular structures to organize into larger and more complex forms. The physical changes that occur as living organisms move up the evolutionary scale are paralleled by equally complex changes in consciousness. Our mind has evolved, Teilhard believes, to a crucial new level marked by our discovery of our own evolution.

The evolution of consciousness is a biological phenomenon. Teilhard's view of the universe is that each particle, no matter how miniscule, possesses consciousness. As tiny particles group together into larger forms, the collective consciousness of the individual particles becomes larger and more complex. The larger the organism, the larger the thought associations that become possible, and the more the organism becomes aware of itself and its own evolution. In humans, those parts of the brain given to thought are larger and more complex than in any other species.

The thoughts generated by individual persons, joining collectively as the thoughts of mankind, literally surround the planet, forming what Teilhard calls the "noosphere." This noosphere is just as extensive and coherent as any other sphere of our planet, be it the atmosphere, the lithosphere, the hydrosphere, or the biosphere. Outside and above the biosphere, the noosphere constitutes the *thinking layer,* which, since its germination at the end of the Tertiary period, has spread over and above the world of plants and animals."[17]

Just as each particle in the universe retains its own individuality as it joins in larger and larger collective structures, so each person retains individuality as his or her thoughts become joined with the collective whole that Teilhard calls the noosphere. This retention of individuality is important, since only if each particle or individual has a separate identity can change (and thus evolution) take place. If each particle or individual were exactly alike, there would be no new associations to be made, and the tension of evolution would cease.

Nevertheless, as separate individuals come together to form a whole, as infinitely complex associations within the whole become possible, the whole itself becomes an individual. This is not an easy concept. We see a single blood cell in our body as being a complex structure made up of millions of molecules, each with its own individuality. The blood cell with its individuality is part of a collective of other cells, each with its own individuality, working together to form a whole person. Similarly, the Earth, containing an atmosphere, a biosphere, a noosphere, and its other spheres, can be seen as having its own life, its own individuality made up of the sum of its equally individualized parts:

The idea is that of the Earth not only becoming covered by myriads of grains of thought, but becoming enclosed in a single thinking envelope, so as to form, functionally, no more than a single vast grain of thought on the sidereal scale, the plurality of individual reflections grouping together and reinforcing one another in the act of a single unanimous reflection.[18]

At this point the planet is not unlike a baby being born, having gestated for a period, first as simple cells joining together to form organs, and finally with the mind developing. During

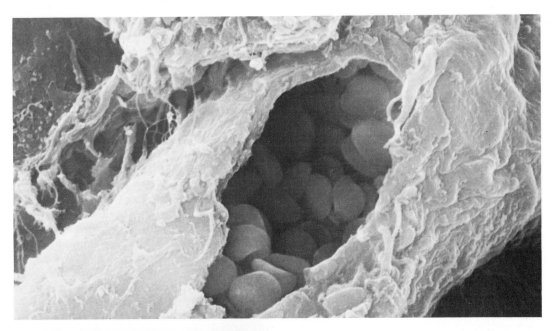

The individual blood cell is part of a collective of other cells, each with its own individuality, working together to form a whole person. (Vein showing red blood cells, magnified 10,000 times. Courtesy of W. Rosenberg.

the long gestation, it is like an organ in the mother's body, nurtured by the same blood that nurtures the mother, not individualizing itself from the rest. Parturition establishes the infant's individuality, of course, but that new individual also resembles and reflects that from which it has come. Teilhard's view is that with the maturation of the noosphere—a fairly recent development on the Earth's evolutionary calendar—the planet is now born; that is, it is emerging as an individual in the universe:

Is this not like some great body which is being born—with its limbs, its nervous system, its perceptive organs, its memory—the body, in fact, of that great Thing which had to come to fulfill the ambitions aroused in the reflective being by the newly acquired consciousness that he was at one with and responsible to an evolutionary All?[19]

Within ourselves we call upon various parts of our beings to solve special problems

At this point, our planet is not unlike a baby being born, emerging as an individual in the universe. (Star Baby, 1975, by Michael Samuels.)

and perform certain tasks. Our mind calls on a part of itself to carry out specific works to which that part is particularly suited. Similarly, Teilhard tells us that the noosphere, or consciousness, of our planet calls upon us, since we are that part of the noosphere that is aware of its own evolution and best suited to the task, to ponder the problems of the Earth: "But is it not precisely the world itself which, culminating in thought, expects us to think out again the instinctive impulses of nature so as to perfect them? Reflective substance requires reflective treatment."[20]

Isn't your reading of this book a response to the Earth's call? Our writing of these pages is clearly a response to the millions of others in the noosphere whose thoughts on this same subject have preceded us. We are all both

The Earth is perhaps preparing to merge with others to form a new, even more complex, and more awe inspiring whole. (The Whirlpool Galaxy in Canes Venatici, NGC 194-5. Courtesy Lick Observatory.)

authors and readers, in a way, and our collective efforts add ever more energy to the challenge of the noosphere.

Even as we become aware of the immensity of associations that are now available in the noosphere, something even larger is occurring. We see that, just as our cells form the whole that is self, so the Earth must be an individual, cell-like structure, perhaps preparing to merge with others to form a new, even more complex, and more awe-inspiring whole. That prospect heightens the importance of our present concerns about the Earth's health. Out of the noosphere comes the thought that there is something beyond us to which we hold a silent allegiance as "the universe ahead of us assumes a face and a heart, and so to speak personifies itself."[21]

The spirit of the living Earth is difficult to define. And the search for words to describe it calls upon each of us to reach deep into the intuitive experiences of our own lives. No

system of thought, no technological tool yet invented, fully circumscribes the truth, but perhaps such delimitation is less important than how the attitudes shaped by our thoughts will be manifest in actions. Will our actions nurture the Earth or make it ill? Teilhard reminds us that "We have as yet no idea of the possible magnitude of the noosphere's effects."[22]

The model we need for using the power of the noosphere to create a system of health for our planet lies in experiencing the spirit of the living Earth. Like the part of our mind that reflects *Purusa*, reason can only help tilt the mirror that reflects that brightest light. The image that will be seen, being infinite, eludes the finite processes to which even the most sophisticated system-building limits us.

Getting in Touch with the Spirit of the Living Earth

Contemporary people spend an extraordinary amount of time in buildings and motor vehicles—in houses, in stores where we shop, at jobs, in cars, buses, trains, and planes. As a result, we rarely touch the Earth with our feet, much less think about our relationship to the Earth except in the most fleeting ways. Moreover, our food comes not from animals we have seen grazing on the same land where we have walked, and whom we once saw as living creatures like ourselves, nor does it come from plants we have sown as seeds and nurtured for months as they grew from the soil. We do, of course, eat plants and animals, but we experience our food as products of supermarkets, neatly packaged and labeled. What effect, if any, does all this have on decision making processes that involve our planet? Would we, for example, drive our cars less or be more careful about where we dumped chemical wastes if we had more regular contact with the Earth? Probably not, unless that contact was experienced in a *ritualized* way that focused our attention on affirming our relationship with the living Earth.

It's not easy for us to entertain the notion of ritualized actions to affirm something that cannot be wholly proven by science. To sophisticated people living in a technological society, such actions seem to fall into the category of superstition, throwbacks to a prescientific age. But like our embarrassment about the metaphysical side of our nature, as Marilyn Ferguson discusses in *Brain Revolution,* we need to look past our prejudices, and establish a new set of attitudes, in order to address today's environmental issues.

There is little in contemporary life to support any form of ritual, either personal or public, to reaffirm our bond with the spirit of the living Earth. For this we must turn to the traditions of ancient cultures, to the social beliefs of a people who considered their relationship to the Earth essential, their traditions having evolved over thousands of years. The Hopis, for example, believe that the Earth and humans each have an axis along which are located vibratory centers which constantly echo the primordial sounds of the life force. They believe that humans, the Earth, and the universe communicate through these vibratory centers.

The Hopis believe that spiritual communication arrives first through a vibratory center located near the fontanel, the so-called *soft spot* that babies have on top of their heads at birth. Second comes intellectual communication through the brain. Third, we communicate with the spirit of the living Earth through the throat, by humming, chanting, and singing. Fourth, we connect with the living Earth through the heart, that is, by entertaining feelings about the Earth, both as a provider of our everyday needs and as an entity we want to protect and love. Fifth, we communicate through the *solar plexus,* the center of the body, by sensing the Earth's energy, in both daily activities and in formalized dance.

Whereas most earlier human beings had complex religious rituals—prayer, tribal councils, songs, meditations, and dances—to affirm their relationship with the Earth, many contemporary people retain only the most sketchy and informal methods for reminding themselves of their relationship to the Earth. Backpacking into remote mountain areas, going to the seashore, and lying under the stars at night

There is little in contemporary life to support any form of ritual to reaffirm our bond with the living Earth. For this we must turn to ancient cultures, to the beliefs of people who considered their relationship to the Earth essential, and who regularly paid homage to it. (The Snake Dance. Library of Congress.)

to contemplate the heavens seem the only ways in which we still respond to our instinctual attraction to nature. Unfortunately, even these activities are usually watered down by the hustle-bustle of taking a two-week vacation on a tight budget, or rushing off on Friday for a weekend in the mountains.

Most of this book so far has been intellectual rather than visceral or musical. In the Hopis' terms, we have focused on the second vibratory center, the brain, although we have tried to touch on visceral, spiritual, and emotional issues. In the following pages, you'll find some exercises you can do to experience the spirit of the living Earth in nonintellectual ways. These are at least as important as the information we communicate through words. As William James said, "The greatest revolution in our generation is that human beings, by changing the inner attitudes of their minds, can change the outer aspects of their lives."[22]

Visualizations of the Living Earth

The practice of visualization, which is an important mental tool for change, has its roots in ancient yoga techniques. (Buddhist image. *Jizo-Bosatso,* eighteenth century, by Hanabusa Itacho. Metropolitan Museum of Art, Rogers Fund.)

The practice of visualization, that is, deliberately using your imagination to focus your attention on a particular goal, is an important mental tool for change. We all use visualization in our everyday lives, whether we're fully aware of it or not, to envision plans for the day, to recall events from the past, to picture solutions to problems in business, science, art, and virtually every area in our lives.

The use of visualization probably dates back to human beginnings, but according to W. A. Jayne, the first important records of its use have been handed down to us from ancient Egypt and Greece. In Greece, for example, when people wanted help in solving difficult problems, they consulted the Oracle at Delphi. At Delphi, incidentally, the priests acknowl-edged a spirit of the living Earth, for which the Greek name was Gaea. Priestesses of Gaea were trained in the art of visualization, and had dedicated their lives to a study of the spirit of the living Earth. When asked to help a person solve a problem—such as when to plant their fields or how to influence the conception of children—the priestess first listened to the person's problem, then imagined herself consulting with Gaea. The answer coming from the visualization of Gaea was the answer the priestess gave the person who had asked for help.

The visualization exercises we describe here are intended to help people focus on the concept of the living Earth. Because most people who live in an urban or suburban setting have little or no daily contact with the Earth, we require something like visualization to help get us in touch with our planet. Just as imagining a trip to the seashore can guide you through all the activities necessary for getting you to

that place, so visualizing the spirit of the living Earth can result in the noosphere changing, rallying the support of millions of people concerned with the Earth's health.

Visualization techniques have been developed in medicine in the past few years, based on data collected from electroencephalograms and other ways of measuring physiological changes, and these techniques are now used in a variety of ways. The basic technique is very simple. First, you put your mind in a relaxed state, by means of the simple exercises we'll be describing. Then you let your mind hear the words that describe the visualization, and let yourself experience as vividly as possible any sensations, such as sight, sound, touch, or smell, that may be suggested in the words.

In all the visualization exercises that follow, the goal is to guide your awareness so that you can benefit the living Earth by taking an active role as homeostatic agent of the noosphere. Choose any of the exercises you find appealing, and if you see ways to change the exercises to better fit your view of the world, feel free to do so.

About the Relaxation Techniques

Medical research has shown that a person's mind is most receptive to visualization when the body is in a relaxed state. If you have ever meditated, done the Jacobson natural childbirth exercises, had any kind of autogenic training to relieve a health problem, or done any yoga, you have had firsthand experience with directed relaxation. If you already have these relaxation skills, use them to establish a quiet place in your mind to receive the visualizations and pass by the following relaxation directions. If you want to learn how to direct your body and mind to relax fully, you'll find the instructions we provide here very helpful.

The Instructions

Usually an instructor will read the directions slowly, allowing the learner to fully respond before going on to the next step. Having a friend with whom you can share instructor and learner roles is a good way to do this at home. Or you can record the instructions on a cassette recorder, and play the tape back to yourself as you do the actual exercise.

We recommend doing the exercises in a comfortable chair. Although they can also be done lying down, you may become too relaxed in that position and fall asleep before you've had a chance to go on to the actual visualization. Later on, you will find that you can do both the relaxation techniques and the visualizations under a variety of circumstances.

Do the relaxation exercise in loose clothing, so that your breathing is unrestricted and your muscles can be relaxed. Remove your shoes, and sit with the soles of both feet firmly planted on the floor. There should be little or no pressure against your thighs from the edge of the chair; such pressure reduces circulation, and can cause unpleasant tingling sensations.

Step One. Seat yourself in a chair, back straight, both feet flat on the floor, hands resting lightly, palms down, on the tops of your thighs. Let your jaw be relaxed. Let your eyes be closed.

Step Two. Take a deep breath. Exhale slowly and smoothly. Take another deep breath. Exhale slowly. Take a third breath. Exhale slowly. Breathe normally.

Step Three. Feel the soles of your feet touch the floor. Let them be heavy. Let every inch of the bottoms of your feet touch the floor. Feel every toe rest gently on the floor. Feel the balls of your feet on the floor. Feel your heels on the floor.

Step Four. Feel your buttocks supported securely by the chair. Let your buttock and thigh muscles be heavy, sinking into the chair.

Step Five. Let your hands rest on the tops of your thighs, palms down, fingers extended. Feel your fingertips resting gently on your thighs. Let your shoulders relax. There is nothing you need to do to support them.

Step Six. Let your neck relax. Imagine that your head is perfectly balanced on top of your spine. Let your jaw droop. Let your face be soft and expressionless.

Step Seven. You are now going to deepen your relaxation. Take a deep breath. As you exhale slowly, say to yourself, "Ten. I am feeling very relaxed." Inhale. Exhale, saying to yourself, "Nine. I am feeling more relaxed." Inhale. Again, exhaling, say, "Eight. More relaxed." Inhale. Exhale, saying, "Seven. More deeply relaxed still." Now, "Six. Deeper." Pause. "Five. Relaxed." Pause. "Four." Pause. "Three. Two. One." Pause. "Zero. I am very, very relaxed."

You are now in a deeply relaxed state, a level of consciousness at which your mind feels peaceful and open. At this level you can be in touch with those forces in the universe that stabilize systems and encourage health and well-being. You can now experience the visualizations vividly and pleasantly. You can stay in this relaxed state for as long as you wish. To return to your normal state of mind, just open your eyes and say to yourself, "I am now coming out." Stretch as you would getting up from a long nap. Get up slowly to avoid becoming lightheaded.

While still in a deeply relaxed state, go on to do one or more of the following visualizations.

Visualizing the Creation of the Universe

In the first chapters of this book, we presented both prescientific and scientific theories about how the universe was created. In the following paragraphs, these theories are presented in a visualization. First go into a relaxed state, then listen to the words of the visualization.

The Visualization

Imagine the void before the creation of the universe. Let your mind entertain the idea of nothingness: no light or dark, no dimension of any kind.

Out of the void, imagine a vast space forming. This space is beyond dimension, has no beginning or end. Let yourself be pure consciousness filling the space. Feel yourself merging with a sense of infinite space.

Imagine a cosmic egg growing out of the void. Imagine the egg dense and smooth, tightly compacted. Sense the egg shrinking as it compresses ever more tightly in on itself. Suddenly it explodes. Darkness is filled with brilliant light. The light fades, brightens again.

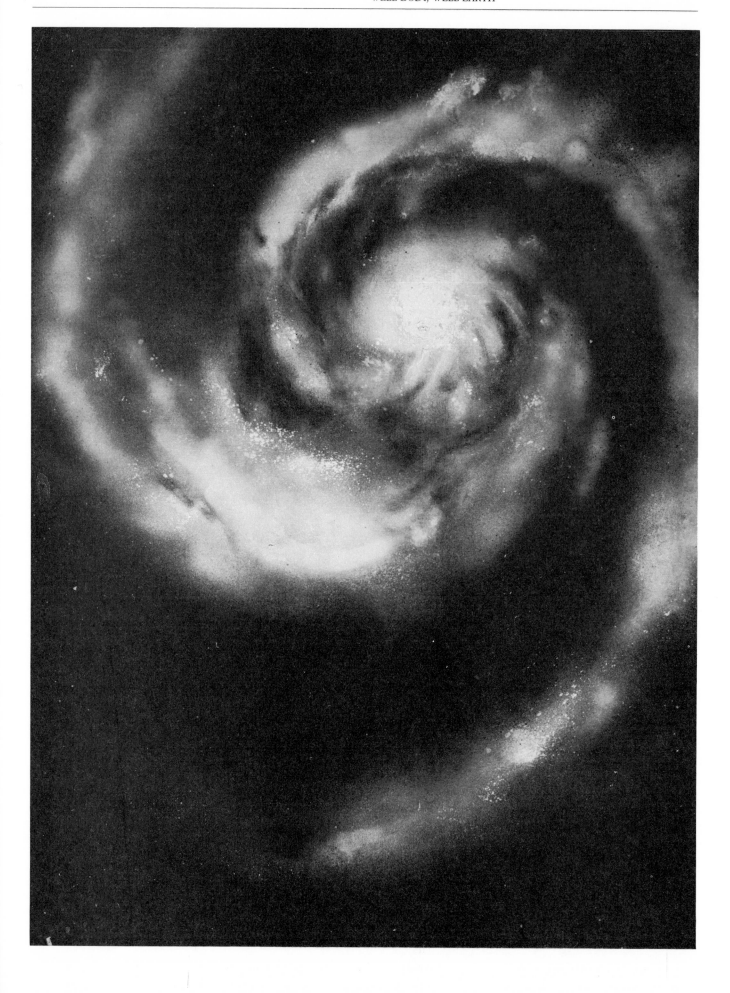

fades, grows brighter still, pulsing as though it is alive.

For a moment the vast light softens. Movement is everywhere. But you cannot see what is causing the movement. Invisible particles are spinning off in all directions at once, expanding outwards. Sometimes particles merge as they collide, forming larger pieces of matter. Sometimes when they collide, one particle annihilates another.

The light extinguishes. A dense, splendid darkness envelopes all. Movement continues, but now it is movement in darkness. The universe fairly bristles with electricity as tiny particles of matter start forming orbits around one another.

In the dark, smooth space, ripples begin to appear. Movement and activity are dense in some places, sparse in others. In the dense places, a vortex of activity begins twisting, an immense swirl of tiny particles in space.

Larger than our present solar system, this vortex winds in on itself ever more tightly. Inside its turbulant form smaller vortexes are forming; each of these twists in on itself ever more tightly, as particles of matter are attracted to one another. Each vortex twists into a ball, and suddenly begins to glow with white light. In this moment of magic, the universe is filled with tiny dots of light, the first stars.

Waves of energy and light shift restlessly in space. Points of light, an infinite number of them, ignite, pierce the darkness with their brilliance, then are extinguished.

For a moment in cosmic time, you focus your attention on a single pulsation of light in the universe. As you watch this light it explodes, scattering intense white sparks everywhere. For awhile this myriad of spinning sparks threatens to disintegrate, but it does not; slowly the sparks begin to move in on themselves, toward an as yet undefined center. As has happened many times before in the cosmos, a great vortex forms, twisting in on itself, tighter and tighter.

The vortex you are watching becomes an immense ball, made up of billions upon billions of tiny particles of matter. As these particles are drawn closer and closer to each other, the ball begins to shrink and becomes increasingly dense and well defined.

This gigantic ball is the embryo of our planet Earth. An immense red sphere, glowing with heat, it fades to a brownish glow, cooling as it hurtles through space. From deep in its core, heat makes its way to the surface. Clouds of steam and gas drift out into space, clinging to the globe. From the clouds come rain, water to fill the indentations that are to become our oceans.

The Earth turns from brown to blue, a lovely sphere of color, pearlized with swirls of crystal-white clouds.

As cosmic hours tick by, you watch in amazement as the Earth seems to sigh, to take a breath. The continents begin shifting about, changing the shapes of the oceans, almost as though the Earth's face is changing expressions.

You focus in on the Earth for a better look. You notice movement in the seas. Molecules are joining into increasingly complex chemical forms. Tiny cells appear in this cosmic stew, and now something more than chemistry is at work in the seas. You cannot say exactly what it means. The cells merge with one another, creating new forms, larger, more complex forms. Amorphous clusters of cells shape themselves into fish and plants.

Along the marshy edges of the seas, fish metamorphose into amphibians, crawling up on land for brief periods, but always returning to the sea. The amphibians give rise to reptiles. In a few isolated places on the globe, reptiles metamorphose into tiny, rodent-like creatures. These animals take up residence in the trees, and metamorphose into monkeys.

There is a moment in cosmic time when monkey-like creatures begin forming societies, making signals to one another that are more complex than the seductive calls at mating time or the shouts of alarm when there is danger. These new sounds are a language, the roots of complex thought. The new creatures are builders, thinkers, organizers. These are the first humans.

At first there are only a few tiny groups of humans, moving about on the planet in search of food. But the groups grow ever larger. Villages of crude huts are seen here and there on the globe. Then some of these villages take on new forms; building materials change, from grass and the supple limbs of trees, to dried mud and sticks. The buildings become increasingly permanent and increasingly symmetrical; hard, square corners replace the round, organic forms of the first huts.

Meandering towns form. The towns develop long roads, joining one group of buildings with another. Towns become cities, then vast metropolises with great ribbons of concrete stretching out across the Earth's surface. Giant metal vehicles race along the concrete ribbons. Metal birds, made by man, shoot across the sky, their contrails leaving behind ribbons of clouds, as though to point the way between cities, mapping out paths in the sky.

You see all this occur within a few short minutes, the process of creation and continuing evolution speeded up to fit into a sphere of consciousness. You allow your thoughts to swirl in on themselves, the images sparkling with their own energy. Like tiny particles of matter, these images are drawn to one another. Like the Earth forming out of a vortex of particles of matter, your separate thoughts and images become one entity, a single thought. It is

*Opposite: **In this moment of magic, the universe is filled with tiny dots of light, the first stars.** (Spiral Galaxy, 1950, by Leo Katz. Oil on canvas, 54" × 42". Collection of the Whitney Museum of American Art, New York. Gift of Dr. and Mrs. Bela Schick.)*

Meandering towns form; towns become cities; then vast metropolises stretch out over the Earth's surface. (North San Francisco Bay. Courtesy of NASA.)

like the single thought in the void that became the seed for our universe.

Feel your own consciousness, your visualization, as a single cell of thought merging with millions of other similar cells of thought that make up the noosphere.

Feel the millions of elementary particles, all born from the cosmic egg, recycled billions of times in the past and destined to be recycled billions of times in the future.

Pause. Enjoy the imagery you have created in your mind. Let yourself feel the kinship between the cosmic material of your own body and the most distant star in the sky. Let yourself feel and enjoy this kinship between your thoughts and the limitless energy of the universe.

Contact the Spirit of the Living Earth

Begin by doing the relaxation exercise at the beginning of this section.

Imagine yourself at a space station ten thousand miles above the Earth. You are safe and secure. You feel the positive forces of healing and growth that you share with the universe. You are in the care of the general goodness of the universe.

You look past the glass and see the Earth: a brilliant blue sphere surrounded by swirling, crystal-white clouds. See the Earth glow in the light of the Sun. Watch the continents shimmer as lacy clouds drift over them. Notice how the planet seems almost to breathe as it slides evenly through space. Clouds and oceans shift restlessly, like expressions changing on a face.

Study the atmosphere, like a silvery membrane embracing the Earth, containing it. Now look closer. It is like the membrane of a cell. Looking through it, you see millions upon millions of organisms, some tiny, some large, swimming in the oceans, moving over the continents, flying through the air above the Earth. The planet vibrates with life.

You listen, hearing the song of the noosphere, a collective humming of millions upon millions of living things, a sound like the symphony of nerve impulses that electrify the human brain. Hear the harmonies of human voices, the cacophony of a billion birds, the howls of monkeys and jungle cats, the croaking of frogs—an immense chorus transmitting the spirit of life through space.

You listen carefully; from deep within the core of the planet, from its cavernous breast, you hear a more sonorous tone. This voice joins the voices of other planets and stars in the universe. Its messages are more like music than words, but part of you, perhaps intuition, hears and understands this inner voice of the planet.

Now let yourself begin a dialogue with the

Earth. Talk to it as you would to another person in the room with you. Begin with an introduction, if you wish:

"Hello, Earth. I am _____."

Pause.

"I want to speak with you, because I am a part of your body, a part of your living being, your noosphere. I am concerned about what I can do in my life to expand the knowledge of the noosphere. I want to know what I can do in my life to ensure your health and mine. I would like to come into this visualization space from time to time and consult with you about how I can take a more active part in your noosphere."

Pause.

Wait for a moment until you feel a response. This may come as words, as ideas that you must shape into words, as feelings, as hunches, as sensations of the Earth's nearness to you.

At this point you may want to ask one specific question about environmental health.

You might, for example, want to ask the Earth about your concern with the water supply or the pollution of the air, and what you can do to make these healthier for everyone concerned. You might ask what you can do to improve the quality of life for the Earth. Ask your questions as clearly and simply as you can. Then wait for a few seconds and allow the Earth's answers to come through you.

Answers come in a variety of ways: as thoughts; as intuitive feelings you have as you go through the normal activities of a day; as an awareness of new possibilities suggested in things you read or see on television, or in something a friend or a teacher has said; as words you hear in your own mind.

When you are done with your conversation with the spirit of the living Earth, say goodbye to it, just as you would say goodbye upon parting from a friend. Then imagine yourself seated in the space station and finally returning to exactly the place you are now.

At first you may feel self-conscious about doing this exercise. You may feel that you are play-acting, as you did when you were a child. This is a perfectly normal response. But you will discover that the more you use your visualization powers in this way, the more meaningful and rich the experience will become in your life.

Recognize that your visualizing the spirit of the living Earth is an action of the noosphere, one that helps build an attitude of caring and concern for the Earth. In this respect it helps us focus our attention on the positive potential in the Earth's homeostasis.

After you have done this exercise, carefully consider the information you have received, with the same critical ear you would use in assessing advice you receive from a friend, a teacher, a book, or the media. If the information you get agrees with the knowledge you have gathered from resources you know you can trust, then accept this new information as a valuable resource in your life. The more you contact the voice of the living Earth, and evaluate what it says, the easier it will become for you to contact it and trust what it provides.

Imagine yourself at a space station a thousand miles from the Earth. You look through the glass and see the Earth, a brilliant, blue sphere. (Apollo 8 Earth view. Courtesy of NASA.)

2

How the Earth's Health and Human Health Are One

All living things are both *in* and *of* the environment; they are both the nurtured and the nurturers. It is an interdependency with no beginning, middle, or end. If any one part of the whole is unhealthy, we must assume that each other part of the whole is in some way affected. With this in mind we must develop a philosophy which fully acknowledges the interrelationships between human beings and the Earth if we are to solve the environmental health problems we face today.

We are not separate from the Earth: we are each as much a part of the planet as every cell in our bodies is a part of us. (*Earth Mother,* 1972, by Michael Samuels.)

We are not separate from the earth; we are as much a part of the planet as each cell in our bodies is a part of us. In a very real way, each cell in our bodies is a part of a continuum that extends from what the yogins called *Purusa,* or spirit, through elementary particles, elementary particles assembled as atoms, atoms assembled as protoplasm, protoplasm assembled as people, people organized as communities, communities organized as biosphere and noosphere, biosphere and noosphere as parts of the Earth, Earth as part of the universe, and so on.

Within the continuum, each unit of life has specific needs. Each cell within the human body has evolved, over perhaps millions of years, to fit that particular environmental niche in which it now lives. Each cell is, in one respect, as individualized and separate as any plant or animal is from its natural environment. The cell membrane, like the animal's skin, delineates the self from the rest of the world, and yet, like the animal, it is dependent on the environment outside itself; the environment provides food and uses the waste byproducts the cell cannot use. The cell is also dependent on the environment to maintain a certain temperature range, a certain acid-base balance, and a certain level of hydration.

When a cell's environment changes radically, the cell will attempt to adapt to the change. It can do so only up to a point. When the environment can no longer provide the food the cell needs, or carry away its wastes, or maintain temperature, acid-base balance, and hydration within tolerable ranges, the cell is in danger, and will rally all its forces to save itself. It is important to recognize how this process occurs, for it may well be the metaphor we need for the environmental problems we face today.

First, the cell recognizes that a change has occurred in its environment by registering discomfort or dis-ease. In a cell this is registered by a deviation from the normal organization of its molecules; molecular damage has already occurred. In order to survive, the cell begins to seek ways to repair that molecular

Each cell within the human body has evolved to fit the environmental niche in which it now lives. (Cells of the lens of the eye, transverse section, left, magnified 810 times, right, magnified 6,955 times. Kessel and Kardon, *Tissues and Organs.*)

 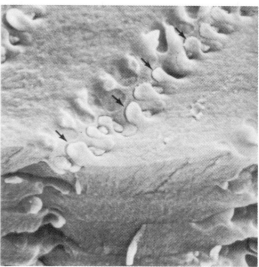

damage, or to return a molecular structure to normal; it also attempts to change or avoid the circumstances that caused the damage. If, for example, the temperature of the body in which it lives has just dropped, the cell can produce more enzymes within its cytoplasm to speed up its metabolism and thus raise its own temperature.

Within the human body, cells seem to recognize their interdependencies and are able to communicate to each other. When the host body's temperature drops, cells in the tissues send out signals to specific cells located in the hypothalamus of the brain. These cells, in turn, cause extensive physiological changes to restore the normal temperature range.

The cell's actions are sophisticated. It both takes care of its most selfish and immediate needs—its own survival—and sends out signals to other cells that are part of its community; these signals prepare the entire community for the changes recognized by the first signal cell, whereupon all members of the community do their parts to restore their environment to a healthy state. In this respect the cell is able to transcend its individual limits of adaptation by contacting other cells living in its community (the human body). All individuals then work together to restore the environment, on which all are dependent.

The adaptive and homeostatic abilities that have evolved in the cell during millions of years have not only ensured the cell's survival, but also enabled the cell to evolve, to become a part of ever more complex life forms, communities of cells with thousands of specializations, such as those we find in the higher animals. As these organisms become more and more complex, they become less and less dependent on the immediate state of their environment. They can move about quickly, finding new environmental niches as old ones cease to serve them. They can build shelters against storms, make tools and weapons to extend the powers of their bodies, and harness energies such as fire to keep themselves warm when the seasons change. Indeed, evolution seems to favor organisms that, by their own will and dexterity, can declare their independence from the environment.

Ironically, our capacities for manipulating the environment, for declaring our independence from it, have led to our increasing alienation from the planet. And this alienation now results in seemingly unlimited exploitation and the creation of many substances that may destroy that environment on which we all depend. Our power is indisputable; our independence, however, isn't.

There are millions of people, working in the noosphere, who are aware of our power to destroy the environment, and who are seeking ways to prevent that; this is also part of our evolution. Power seems always to be most apparent in destruction, but creation from that same base of power seems always subtle, slow, and humble by comparison. The explosion of the cosmic egg is dramatic, whereas the integration of elementary particles into molecules, of molecules into galaxies and life forms, over billions of years, seems almost too subtle to comprehend. We must, of course, be cautious about extrapolations of this kind, for fear that we excuse human destructiveness, forgetting that the tension of our resistance also serves evolution. Even here we must be careful not to let our resistance to destruction hinder our own creative powers, for the freedom of these powers is what ultimately weighs the balance in our favor.

Each one of us, as an integral part of the Earth's homeostatic mechanism, has a relationship to the planet that is not unlike the relationship of each cell to our body. At any given moment, the balance between destruction and creation is delicate. Seeing the power in human destructiveness is only too easy; seeing the power in human creativeness is perhaps too difficult. Creativity is expressed in such acts as your reading this book, or our writing it. It is just as important to see these subtle powers, and believe in them, as it is to see the awesome destructive powers of nuclear weapons.

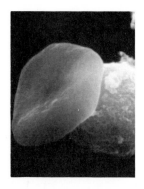

Each one of us as an integral part of the Earth's homeostatic mechanism, has a relationship to the planet that is not unlike the relationship of each one of our cells to our body. (Red Blood Cell and White Blood Cell, 12,500X. Courtesy of Ralph Camiccia.)

That basic unit of life, the cell, is a perfect model from which we can learn how to function as an effective member of the Earth's homeostatic community. First comes awareness. People in industrial societies are suffering from more respiratory illnesses, more cancer and heart disease, and more emotional stress than ever before, and these, without a doubt, are induced by environmental factors of our own creation. The diseases we are creating inevitably threaten not only individuals but the biosphere itself.

The living Earth is as dependent on the biosphere as our bodies are dependent on our cells. And just as the health of each cell is a gauge of our body's health, so the health of each life form in the biosphere is a gauge of the Earth's health. We, then, are truly barometers of the Earth's well-being. Our ability to detect and treat our own diseases enables us to detect change in our environment. As in the cell, our diseases are responses to the condition of the whole outer environment. Survival depends on both repairing damage to ourselves and making changes in the environment to prevent a recurrence of the event that caused the damage.

We have plenty of evidence of human ability to destroy the environment, but we tend to overlook what we have done to restore areas once made uninhabitable. One of the most dramatic examples is found in the history of London, England, where in 1952 thousands of people died of air pollutants generated by mining and burning coal for power and heat. As a result of the great disaster of the London smog, the population lobbied for legislation to clean up both the mining industries and the use of coal. The lobbying effort was successful, as were the reforms. London now has the best air quality of any European city. Not only was human health improved, but birds, insects, and trees returned in vast numbers. Even some species of birds, once described by Shakespeare but thought to be extinct, made their return to the biosphere.

Similarly, there is the reclamation of Jamaica Bay, near New York's Kennedy Airport. For decades garbage and industrial wastes had been dumped into the bay, destroying all forms of life. It was virtually a dead region until a single person, Herbert Johnson, saw what was happening and decided to do something about it. Completely on his own at first, he began planting trees, shrubs, and grasses. Soon he was alerting other people living in the area to what he was doing, and encouraging them to participate in the reclamation process. Today Jamaica Bay has come back to life, and is one of the largest nesting places for migratory birds on their north/south route.

The noosphere required vast numbers of people before it could reach its present power. The population of the globe is, of course, itself a problem at this point in our history. One obvious solution to the population problem is to reduce the birthrate, a solution which has proven more successful in developed nations than in underdeveloped ones. Another, perhaps subtler solution may be found in the example of the cell, which had to develop ways of organizing into communities of ever-increasing size and complexity. In its evolution, the cell had to discover how to protect and heal itself, while signaling others in its vast community to protect and heal themselves or to participate in other ways to keep the environment healthy. The cell might appear to be or to have a separate identity

Jamaica Bay was virtually a dead region until a single person saw what was happening and decided to do something about it. (Jamaica Bay, 1982, by Michael Samuels.)

because of its membrane, but actually the membrane makes possible a profound interdependence. We are able to recognize the grand scale of our global interdependencies, and this awareness will undoubtedly play a major role in our coming to terms with our vast numbers.

In the most optimistic view, the noosphere may mature, in part through population growth, by an evolutionary step that may be as difficult for us to imagine as it would have been for dinosaurs to imagine that there would one day be an organism called *Homo sapiens.* This is the speculation that the Earth is evolving in order to merge with other units of life like itself, just as cells had to evolve to merge with others to make up the community of cells that constitutes each of us.

Among those who have dared speculate on the Earth's future has been Teilhard de Chardin, who, in *The Phenomenon of Man,* asks us to entertain the concept of communication between our noosphere and the noospheres of other planets:

We may begin by asking if life may one day force the bars of its earthly prison, getting in touch with other focal points of consciousness across space. (Crab Nebula in Taurus, NGC 1952. Hale Observatory.)

Under the increasing tension of the mind on the surface of the globe, we may begin by asking seriously whether life will perhaps one day succeed in ingeniously forcing the bars of its earthly prison, either by finding the means to invade other inhabited planets or (a still more giddy perspective) by getting into psychical touch with other focal points of consciousness across the abysses of space. The meeting and mutual fecundation of the two noospheres is a supposition which may seem at first sight crazy, but which after all is merely extending to psychical phenomena a scope no one would think of denying to material phenomena. Consciousness would thus finally construct itself by a synthesis of planetary units. Why not, in a universe whose astral unit is the galaxy?[1]

As we have tried to show throughout this book, we are not, by any means, alone in our perceptions of the interdependencies between the living Earth and ourselves. There can be little doubt that if we are to survive individually, we must acknowledge our dependence on the Earth and our interdependence with every other unit of life on our planet. To accept that you are an integral part of the homeostatic mechanism that ensures the Earth's life is as essential as each cell's acceptance of its homeostatic role in your body.

Levels of living systems

Organelle	Cell	Organ	Organism	Group	Society	Planet	Galaxy
Cilia	Mucosal cell	Lung	Man	Family	Kalahari Bushmen	Earth	Milky Way

In Part One of this book, we explored the creation of the Earth as a living thing. In Part Two we will explore how the Earth—of which each of us is an integral part—will keep itself well. We'll explore its response to change, its capacity for detecting and healing disease, and its capacity for creating health.

Consciousness would finally construct itself by a synthesis of planetary units. Why not, in a universe whose astral unit is the galaxy? (Andromeda Galaxy. Courtesy of Lick Observatory.)

In Part Two we take a second step toward creating a philosophy of environmental disease/health that takes into account the profound interrelationships of Earth and human beings. Part Two builds on Part One, creating a system of environmental health that allows you to effectively appraise an environmental threat that might come to your attention and take responsibility for correcting it.

CHAPTER FIVE

The Manifold Nature of Disease

From the late 1700s, when Edward Jenner initiated the practice of vaccination to prevent smallpox, until the past few decades, the premise of modern medicine was that each disease would eventually be found to have a single cause. Just as smallpox had a single disease agent, the smallpox virus, so would heart disease be found to be caused by fats in the diet, and cancer to be caused by an elusive virus. This single-factor philosophy of disease so dominated medical science and its practice that even today most lay people view it as a basic truth. Moreover, the single-factor philosophy has spread out into virtually every field of health, including the alternative modes of healing that are offered as improvements on mainstream medicine. There are nutritionists claiming that all diseases can be prevented by eating a proper diet, athletic counselors claiming that all diseases can be prevented by a proper exercise regimen, and psychological counselors who are claiming that stress reduction is the way to total health.

Although each approach to health no doubt has some validity, most human diseases are caused not by one, but by a combination of factors. The evidence for this theory of disease comes to us from epidemiological research. Here are some examples to consider:

• Epidemiological studies show that everyone in the United States harbors bacteria that cause meningitis; yet few get sick, and this disease continues to be extremely rare.

• Everyone in the world has staphylococcae bacteria on their skin surfaces, but few get serious staph infections.

• Bacteria that can cause strep throat are found in 40 percent of all people examined, yet this same 40 percent have no symptoms of the disease.

These are examples of infectious disease for which one would fully expect to find single *germs* being the cause of a person's illness. But other types of disease, such as cancer and heart

disease, are rarely found to have anything but multiple causes. There is now a general consensus in the medical community that most cancer and heart disease can be traced to a combination of causes, among them diet, exercise, stress, chemical pollutants, genetics, and microorganisms.

If the mere presence of a disease agent —especially when that agent is a known microorganism—doesn't cause the patient to become ill, what does? The answer is found not in the agent, but in the host. Here we must go back to our earlier discussions about environments and their effects on the life forms they support. The human body provides the environment for the support of millions of microorganisms. There are, in fact, at least a dozen known species of microorganisms that live in and on us in perfect symbiosis, providing services without which we would perish. For example, staphylococcae living on our skin surfaces claim this territory for themselves, and in defending it, they prevent other bacteria from invading the host. Similarly, *E. coli* bacteria in our intestines are necessary for healthy digestion, and without them we would die of malnutrition.

There are circumstances when the host's relationship with the disease agent is temporarily altered, during which time new environmental opportunities are offered, either to the microorganisms usually living there or to microorganisms that normally make their homes outside the human body.

In cold weather, flu viruses—which we must assume are always living somewhere in the biosphere—find a greater opportunity for reproducing in the human upper respiratory tract. What changes occur in the human environment that apparently welcome the virus are not clear, but these changes are apparently significant to the virus. (Because a virus is completely dependent on other cells for its own reproduction, we cannot simply assume the

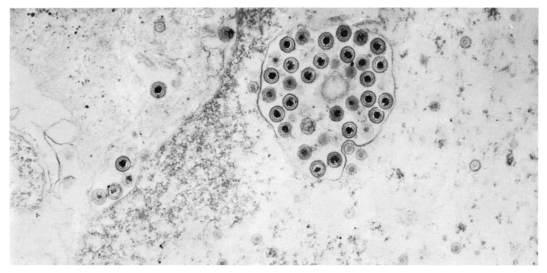

What changes occur in the human environment to welcome the virus is difficult to say, but these changes are apparently important to the virus. (Herpes Simplex virus, magnified 49,200 times. Courtesy of Communicable Disease Center.)

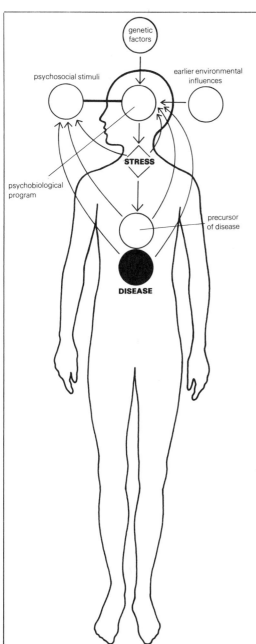

genetic factors

psychosocial stimuli

earlier environmental influences

STRESS

psychobiological program

precursor of disease

DISEASE

cause to be a higher viral population prior to human infection.)

Why does the environment of the human body change so that it offers a new opportunity for either outside disease agents or normal microorganisms to become disease agents? What, in other words, accounts for human resistance to disease? The explanations are not simple. In fact, when epidemiologists study various factors—age, ethnic background, genetics, socio-economics, educational levels, pregnancy, emotional stress, diet, exercise, geographic location, climate, and environmental pollution—they find that each and every factor studied has an effect on the host's resistance to disease.

Summing up the multiple-factor theory of disease, an epidemiologist from the Harvard School of Public Health has stated that:

We have come to recognize that the one cause—one disease model is too simple. Illness in an individual is the result of a multitude of prior circumstances—including those multiple, independent, minor circumstances that we call chance—and causal circumstances differ from one individual to another, even when the manifestations of their illness are indistinguishable. Seemingly minor differences in diet or in physical or chemical environment determine the reaction of a person to a given microbial or genetic stimulus, and vice versa. Indeed, the causal antecedents of illness in any individual comprise a web of intertwined circumstances that in their full breadth and complexity lie quite beyond our understanding.[1]

This sounds rather formidable. Must we explore every conceivable factor, and the interrelationships of these factors, before we can understand a disease or our resistance to it? We need not do so. In reality, the multiple-factor view of disease means that we have many ways to prevent disease, heal it, or simply understand it, as we will see.

Illness is caused by multiple factors in the environment. Every factor affects the condition of the organism. First genetic factors control the initial makeup of the body. Then psychosocial stimuli and the psychobiological program interact and the person perceives stress. This may cause precursors of disease, and if continued, disease. (Adapted from Kagan in Henry.)

All Diseases Are
Environmental Diseases

Bearing in mind that humans and the environment are intimately interrelated, and that we are all both *in* and *of* the environment, we inevitably see that all disease must of necessity be environmental. Everything affects us, either positively or negatively. Just as viruses are a part of our environment, so are factors such as chemicals in the workplace, or the lack of nutritional food or a quiet place at home where we can rest at the end of the day. If the chemicals in our workplace were eliminated, our diet improved, and our home made more restful, our bodies would be more resistant to disease, and the virus would have less opportunity to find a niche there. Our bodies are permeable; they are constantly changed by our interactions with the environment, however subtle those interactions might seem.

In observing these interrelationships, Rene Dubos, the noted microbiologist and environmentalist, has stated that:

Any event in the outer world which impinges on an individual modifies, however indirectly and slightly, the balance between his various organs and functions. In reality, therefore, the internal environment should not be considered apart from the external environment. Shivering or pallor brought about either by exposure to cold or by a sudden fear is but the outward manifestation of a physiological disturbance which may alter indirectly the performance of many essential body mechanisms. . . . thus, the internal environment is constantly responding to the external environment, and history—racial, social, as well as individual—conditions the manner of responses just as much as does the intrinsic nature of the stimulus.[2]

The study of cancer research provides an excellent opportunity for exploring the principle of multiple disease factors, and this knowledge ultimately provides a wide range of choices in preventing this disease. The medical literature divides the factors that cause cancer into two interrelated groups: causes in the outer environment, and causes within the host.

Recently, many external environmental factors have been established by linking them with people who have cancer or have been cured of it. They include polycyclic hydrocarbons (benzine, alkylating agents, aminoazo dyes, carbon tetrachloride), asbestos, pesticides, home and industrial paints, cleaners, prescription and over-the-counter drugs, insulating materials, and radiation such as sunlight and x-rays.

The mere presence of one or more of these substances in your environment does not immediately cause cancer. There is no one-to-one relationship between these disease agents and the disease. The process by which cancer is created is complex, but it is important to understand the process if we're to come to terms with the subject of environmental health.

The creation of cancer in healthy tissue is a two-part process. First, there is the *initiation* stage. In this stage the DNA of a particular cell, or group of cells, in the body is in some way altered by a disease agent. The mutation happens suddenly, and is not reversible. But the change in the DNA doesn't immediately cause cancer. On the contrary, it is quite

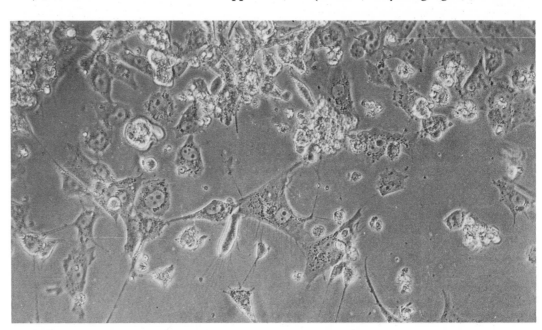

In exploring how the condition of the host relates to the vulnerability to disease, we find that virtually every factor one might imagine has an effect, that is, increases the chances of getting a disease such as cancer. (Sarcoma cells in culture. Courtesy of B. I. Sikic, M.D., Stanford University School of Medicine.)

possible that cancer may never result from this initial mutation, even though DNA damage has occurred.

In the second phase, called the *promotion* phase, continuous exposure to either the original agent or to other disease agents causes further changes in the affected cells. This promotion phase takes place over a long period of time, and it is, unlike the initiation stage, reversible.

To summarize, the cell's DNA is altered by the carcinogen, not immediately making it cancerous, but making it vulnerable to further change by prolonged exposure either to the initial agent or to other environmental disease factors. Continued exposure to disease agents causes further damage to the DNA, so that eventually new generations of the affected

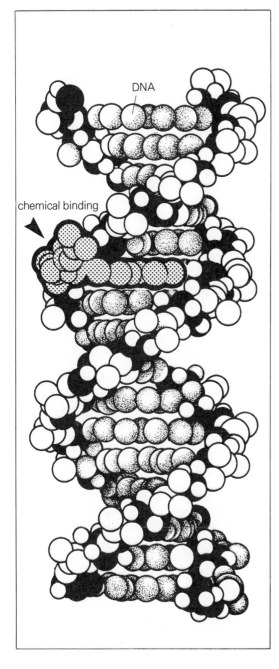

DNA

chemical binding

cells have a genetic makeup that causes them to be malignant. Thus, through the two-part process of initiation and promotion, healthy cells can experience a radical set of changes in their genetic makeup that transforms them from healthy tissue cells into malignant cells that reproduce but make no contribution to the total organism. We can say that environmental influences such as carcinogens transform healthy cells from symbiotic to parasitic relationships with the body.

In the laboratory, animals subjected to heavy doses of a carcinogen invariably contract the disease, and in the beginning of cancer research this fact led many experts to jump to the conclusion that the mere presence of a carcinogen would result in a malignancy. Disease research has progressed a long way since then. We now know that the condition of the host, or potential host, makes a big difference in determining whether or not the *initiating substance* or an associated *promoting substance* causes cellular damage. For example, an agent that can theoretically initiate or promote lung cancer may be present in the environment, but be incapable of reaching healthy lung tissue, because the mucosal blanket and the cilia in the upper respiratory tract of the person subjected to these threats prevent the agents from entering. On the other hand, if the mucosal blanket or cilia are damaged—as happens with most people who smoke—the carcinogenic agents have little or no trouble reaching the lung tissue. In this case, smoking is like opening a door for the disease agent to enter.

Many substances that cause cancer in laboratory animals are detoxified by enzymes in normal human cells. These substances, called *induced enzymes,* because they are produced by host cells whenever the disease agent is present, alter the chemical makeup of the carcinogen and render it harmless. The host's ability to produce these enzymes varies according to the host's general physiological condition, which is affected either positively or negatively by nutrition, hormonal balance, age, and even psychological outlook.

We also know that chemicals used in the environment can interact with one another: sometimes they intensify one another; sometimes a relatively innocuous substance will thus become toxic. For example, the pesticide malathion, which is ordinarily a minimal threat to humans, since it passes through the body in an inert state, can become dangerous to human health in the presence of an organophosphate, EPN, which inhibits the human body's ability to produce an enzyme that renders malathion harmless. When EPN is present in the environment, it allows the human body to assimilate and store malathion, which then becomes toxic.

The first step in chemical carcinogenesis, called the initiation stage, *occurs when a chemical binds to the DNA of a cell. This alters the cell's genetic material so that it can no longer reproduce normally.*

The body has an amazing ability to repair DNA damaged by chemicals or radiation. An enzyme cuts out the damaged area, leaving the space open for the creation of new DNA.

damage

enzyme cuts out damaged area

damaged area repaired with new DNA

In exploring how the condition of the host relates to vulnerability to disease, we find that every factor one might imagine has an effect, increasing or decreasing the chances of getting a disease such as cancer. For example, a man who is under great stress in his workplace, drinks several martinis a day, smokes a pack of cigarettes a day, and has a high-calorie diet, will be much more susceptible to carcinogenic materials than a person who is relaxed in his workplace, has only a glass of wine with dinner, doesn't smoke at all, and has a low-calorie diet. The end result is that, all else being equal, the man who takes good care of himself will be less vulnerable to a carcinogen in his environment than the man who neglects his health in more general ways.

According to Bernard Fox, M.D., a re-

Although it may seem very different from pesticides and viruses, stress is a major environmental disease factor.
(*Saint George and the Dragon,* by Rogier Van der Weyden. National Gallery of Art, Washington, D.C.)

Personal and environmental factors that influence a person's risk of cancer

1. Genetics and life events
Age; sex; income level; race; religion; marital status; geographic location; life stress; personality; attitudes; body type; obesity; complexion, eye color, and hair color; age at menarche and menopause; family history of cancer; cancer-associated diseases, eg., skin keratoses.

2. Lifestyle and habits
Smoking; alcohol; caffeine; sunbathing; number of sexual partners; circumcision; age at first intercourse; age at birth of first child; hygiene; amount of food eaten; cholesterol, fats; vitamin and mineral intake; amount of refined foods, bulk; water purity.

3. Environmental factors
Radiation; chemicals; water pollution; air pollution; occupation, especially x-ray, uranium, asbestos, arsenic, polyvinylchloride, benzene; drugs.

Adapted from Weiss, p. 103.

---

searcher at the National Cancer Institute, there are some very specific areas where personal choices and habits can definitely lessen your chances of getting cancer. They are: reducing the consumption of alcoholic beverages, stopping smoking, reducing exposure to the sun for long periods of time, stopping the use of prescription drugs containing known carcinogens, learning effective ways to handle stress, cutting out foods with additives (preservatives, artificial flavorings and colorings) known or suspected to be carcinogenic, reducing the consumption of fats in the diet, cutting down on exposure to occupational carcinogens, and making certain you have a fully nutritional diet.[3]

With these points in mind, we begin to see that we can do many things to reduce our risk of contracting diseases that are ordinarily considered to be caused by environmental hazards beyond the control of the individual. Even when we cannot immediately change something threatening in the environment, we are not helpless victims. We can take action in our personal lives to reduce the risk of disease for ourselves, and undertake longer-term plans to change conditions in the environment. Statistically, the more you can do to create a generally healthy lifestyle for yourself, the less will be your chances of getting a major illness.

Emotional Stress As An Environmental Disease Factor

Although it may seem very different from pesticides and food additives, stress is a major environmental disease factor. Our best research on this subject is found in the field of heart disease. Like cancer, heart disease is considered to have multiple causal factors. The factors causing or contributing to heart disease can, like the causes of cancer, be divided between inner and outer sources, that is, between the condition of the host and the condition of the environment in which the host lives. But for heart disease the lines between inner and outer are less clear. For example, the food we take in comes from the outside, but it is a personal choice, that is, an inner factor, that determines what we include in our diet. Similarly, the choice to get more exercise involves a personal decision that results in dramatic inner changes from doing something in the outer environment. It is no wonder that health experts have created the category of "lifestyle changes" to describe such things as diet and exercise.

According to the Framingham study, which was one of the first large research projects undertaken on the subject, the four most important interrelated conditions present in people with heart disease are: high blood-cholesterol levels, high blood pressure, obesity, and smoking.[4] The Framingham work was the first medical research to establish the contribution of these multiple factors in heart disease. The list of causal factors now includes at least 35 known categories of substances: exercise (lack of it), soft water (low mineral content), excess salt in the diet, certain prescription drugs (such as some commonly used hypoglycemic medicines), and high-caloric and high-fat diets.

Whereas the chemicals we ingest or the exercise we get represent physical factors, there are social and psychological factors to consider as well. Most medical authorities now list social and behavioral patterns among the multiple causal factors contributing to heart attacks. According to C. David Jenkins, a behavioral epidemiologist at the University of Texas School of Medicine at Austin,

Several families of social and behavioral variables have been implicated in the scientific literature as being risk factors for ASHD (atherosclerotic heart disease). The following categories, while somewhat arbitrary in definition, have proved useful in summarizing the literature: (a) indices of social position and social change; (b) environmental stressors such as work overload, chronic conflict situations, and life changes; (c) personal responses to external or internal circumstances, including life dissatisfactions, anxiety, depression, neuroticism, emotional drain, and sleep disturbances; and, finally, (d) a personal style of outward action (as contrasted to inner feeling) in response to the environment —the aggressive, competitive, irritable, Type-A, coronary-prone behavioral pattern.[5]

There are certainly environmental circumstances that are stressful, but in the final analysis it is the individual's inner response to the external event that contributes to heart disease. The individual's perception of the event is often more important to explore than the event itself. Because of acquired (that is, *learned*) responses, one person may become anxious and depressed by the same event that another person, with a different set of responses, might find exciting, and be stimulated into a course of action that is ultimately satisfying and relaxing. Thus, the way we think and feel about the world around us is as much a potential disease factor as obesity, lack of exercise, smoking, or poor nutrition.

Although mental factors may at first seem ethereal or even imaginary, they are no less real than a chemical's capacity for altering the DNA of a cell. Diseases created in this way, by our learned responses, our individualized perceptions of the environment, are not "imagined" diseases. They can result in molecular changes in our bodies that are just as profound as any created by chemicals.

We can trace how a mental perception of an external event is transformed into a physiological change in the human body. As an example, let's look at a man whose work load has been suddenly and unexpectedly increased. He doesn't know how he can possibly accomplish everything that needs to be done. Moreover, he perceives that the future of the company, a great deal of money, and his own professional status depends on his ability to produce. It is easy to see how all this information might add up, in his mind, to a threat, one as real to him as

any chemical.

The perception of the demands being made on him, and the consequences for him if he fails, all come together in the cerebrum. Almost instantly, the central nervous system alerts the sympathetic nervous system, which sends out signals to all parts of the body. One of the organs signaled is the adrenal gland. The adrenal gland responds by secreting a hormone called epinephrine, which is sent out to every organ in the body through the bloodstream. Signals from the sympathetic nervous system, combined with hormones from the adrenal glands, profoundly affect the functions of a number of organs: the heart pumps faster, with higher pressures; muscle cells of the heart take in more oxygen; and the kidneys retain fluid in the body to keep the blood pressure high.

At this point, whether or not any damage is done by the increased heart rate depends on the condition of the host. For example, most

Most medical authorities now list social and behavioral patterns among the multiple causal factors contributing to heart attacks. (Violencia, 1980, by Ed Paschke. Oil, 74" × 96". Collection of the Whitney Museum of American Art, New York.)

Sympathetic nerves to:
A. head, eyes, saliva glands
B. lungs
C. heart
D. stomach muscles, liver
E. kidneys, adrenals
F. pancreas
G. intestines
H. bladder, rectum, genitals

Parasympathetic nerves to:
1. eyes, nose, palate, saliva glands
2. heart, lungs
3. colon, stomach
4. intestines, liver, kidneys
5. bladder, rectum, genitals

——————— sympathetic nerves

- - - - - - - parasympathetic nerves

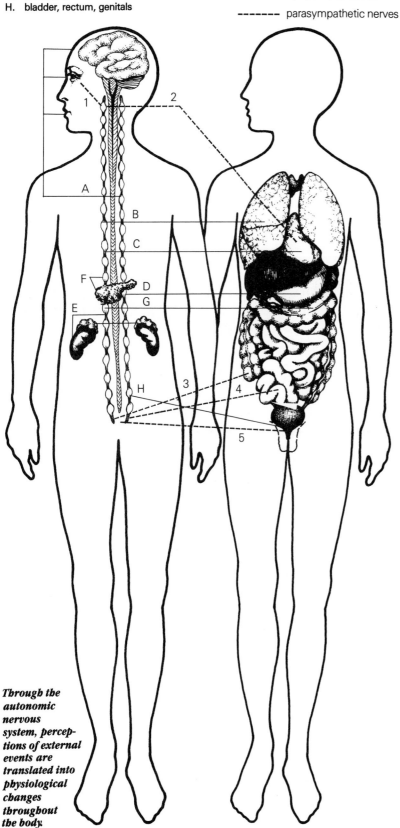

Through the autonomic nervous system, perceptions of external events are translated into physiological changes throughout the body.

physicians now argue that a person whose cardiovascular system is well-conditioned by aerobic exercise will probably not be threatened by the additional stress, because his blood vessels are more elastic and can expand more than those of people who get little or no aerobic exercise. For the latter group, increased blood pressure, with more blood surging through narrow passages, with increased turbulence throughout, causes tiny tears and abrasions in the walls of the capillaries.

Along with hormonal changes that occur under stress, free fatty acids are released from fat cells to give the body instant energy. These fatty acids circulate through the bloodstream until they reach the liver, where they are transformed into low-density lipoproteins. These lipoproteins cling to the smooth-muscle cells in the walls of the blood vessels, causing them to thicken, which results in a narrowing of the passage through which blood is meant to be carried. Free fatty acids circulating in the blood cause *platelets*, normally helpful in healing cuts and abrasions, to clump together wherever there has been damage to the vessel walls. Free fatty acids now stick to both the platelets and the damaged vessel walls. As the passage through which blood normally passes grows narrower and narrower, more pressure is needed to carry the volume of blood demanded by the extra stress the person is feeling.

Increased blood pressure, now caused by two problems—the environmental demands on the host and the narrowed passages of the blood vessels—causes even more damage to the cardiovascular system, with further build-up of fatty acids and narrowing of the blood vessels. The condition that has been created in the host is called *atherosclerotic heart disease,* which means, in everyday terms, a narrowing and hardening of the blood vessels. Atherosclerotic heart disease does not occur overnight or as the result of a few isolated experiences of stress. On the contrary, it takes years to develop, and there are many opportunities, including diet, exercise, and relaxation techniques, for either preventing or reversing it. When the condition is allowed to progress, the result is that narrowed and weak blood vessels must try to supply vital organs, such as the heart, brain, and kidneys, with enough blood to meet their needs. Obviously, when the vessels finally get to the point that they can no longer supply the needed blood, cells in the heart, brain, and kidney die, and the organs cease to function.

Although we can trace the development of heart disease in the laboratory, it is large epidemiological studies of people that provide us with the most dramatic and useful information about the relationships between environments, emotions, and health. Epidemiological studies at the Kennedy Space Center prior to the 1969 Moon launch provide us with some particularly interesting figures. For example, among the people working at the Space Center at that time, there was a 50 percent higher sudden-death rate, due to heart disease, than there was among people working at similar occupations in other industries. In addition, the workers at the Space Center had significantly higher rates of abnormal EKGs, higher divorce rates, higher levels of anxiety, and more incidence of depression and alcoholism than comparable workers outside the space program.

Objective work loads were not necessarily to blame for the high stress levels at the Kennedy Space Center, but workers' perceptions of the consequences of their performance put them under stress in ways that workers outside this industry could only imagine. High on the

nate animals expressed great anxiety. When the stress situation was prolonged, the subordinate animals eventually produced physical symptoms. Many animals died of kidney failure (a vascular disease) within two to sixteen days.[7]

In another experiment, baboons were subjected to the extreme stress of love triangles. This form of social stress was chosen because baboons are normally monogamous animals, and males establish very close bonds with their mates. Thus, when their relationships are threatened, the baboons suffer deeply. One experimenter separated male baboons from their mates of long-standing, and put rival males in their place. The displaced male was then put in an adjacent cage, where he could see his ex-mate and her new suitor. The

Workers at the Kennedy Space Center had 50 percent greater sudden-death rates than workers in comparable occupations in other industries. Stress levels had more to do with the workers' perceptions of stress than the actual stress to which they were exposed. (Mission Operations Control Room. Courtesy of NASA.)

list of influences affecting people's perceptions were: national visibility, the recognition that "the eyes of the nation are upon us," and a continous threat of budget cuts from the government. Following these were: urgency of meeting deadlines, genuinely difficult tasks, and the fear of not being able to perform satisfactorily.[6]

Although animal experiments don't necessarily translate directly to humans, it is interesting to speculate on some of the work that has been done in this field. It has been found, for example, that animals who normally live in groups, and who are considered to have social abilities at least in some ways similar to those of humans, manifest heart disease when placed in socially stressful situations.

In one animal experiment, subordinate males were put in cages next to dominant, especially aggressive males of their own species. Even though the cages were separated by a glass wall, making it impossible for the two animals to have physical contact, the subordi-

isolated male invariably developed atherosclerosis and high blood pressure within a few months.[8]

The baboon experiments were originally conceived as a way to study psychoneurotic disease. What was surprising was that the animals' ordeals revealed at least as much about stress as a factor in organic disease as they did about the animals' psychology. The experiments established that the perception of a threat or the experience of a profound loss— even though it was an *internal* or *mental* experience—could cause life-threatening damage to the organism.

Most people have experienced how stress manifests itself in organic malfunctions, even if it has been something as obvious as feeling sick to their stomach after a particularly unpleasant experience. But we don't often think of how stress affects infectious disease. However, stress and infection are interrelated, and the physiological mechanisms that link them are worth exploring.

The autonomic nervous system sends messages to the adrenal glands whose hormones affect heart rates, muscle tension, and blood pressure. This allows the body to mobilize against perceived threats from the environment.

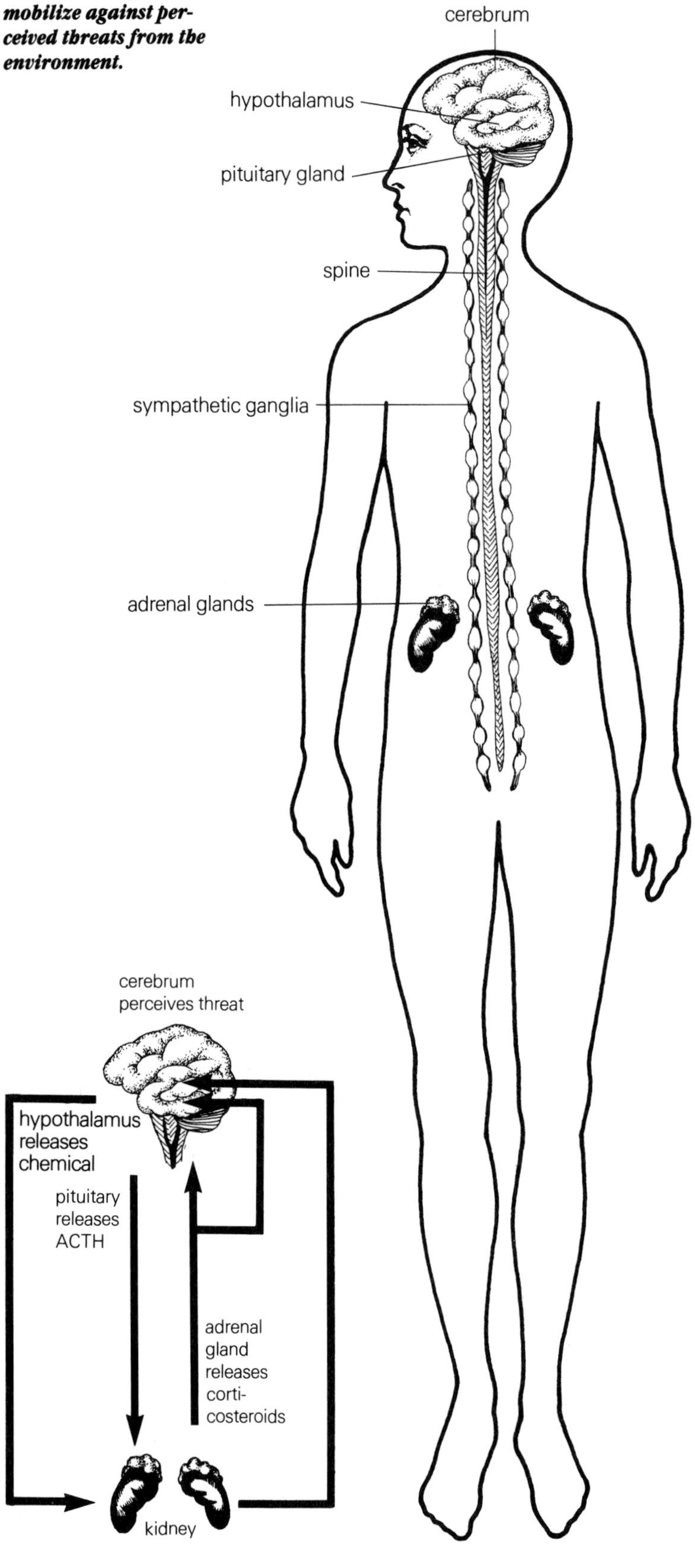

cerebrum

hypothalamus

pituitary gland

spine

sympathetic ganglia

adrenal glands

cerebrum perceives threat

hypothalamus releases chemical

pituitary releases ACTH

adrenal gland releases corti- costeroids

kidney

Emotions and Infectious Disease

Perceptions of environmental stress can impede the body's normal defenses against infectious disease. In addition, stress can have dramatic physiological effects on the human body, significantly altering temperature, acid-base balance, and hormone levels. The end result is the creation of new opportunities, that is, the opening of new environmental niches, for microorganisms that normally live in limited numbers in the body or that discover the new opportunities more fortuitously.

The hypothalamus of the human brain is responsible for transmitting signals to all parts of the body, controlling heart rate, blood flow, glandular secretions, and even the production of antibodies for fighting infection. The hypothalamus receives its signals, in part, from the cerebral cortex, wherein we shape our perceptions of our relationships with the environment. When, for example, ancient man was confronted by a threat (such as a bear) as he walked through the woods, he first *perceived* that threat in his cerebral cortex, which sorts out the meaning of the sensory material coming in through the eyes, ears, and other sense receptors.

The perception of danger triggers certain events in the hypothalamus, which, in turn, signals muscles and organs throughout the body. The hypothalamus causes blood flow to be diverted from less important organs to the heart, lungs, and large muscles needed for *fight* or *flight*. Similarly, the adrenal glands are stimulated to secrete hormones for increasing heart and respiration rates and for putting large muscles into action. Thus, major physiological changes are brought about by a mental perception of danger.

Although most people who have studied basic physiology know something about these links between perception and action, few understand the relationships between threats —both imagined and real—and the immune system. A number of interesting studies have helped medical science put together the pieces of this puzzle.

Damage to the hypothalamus in animals causes complete suppression of antibody production, even though the rest of the immune system responsible for this production is left fully intact. Whereas stimulation of the hypothalamus by a mild electric charge in a normal animal will increase antibody production.[9] These experiments clearly establish the importance of the hypothalamus in normal immune responses.

In several experiments, animals were subjected to a variety of stress situations, ranging from changes in social systems (ratios of male to female, overcrowding, isolation from the group, and breaking up of families) to sensory stimuli, such as noise and electric shock. Animals subjected to these stresses for prolonged periods showed significant changes in their levels of antibody production. When they were injected with antigens that caused normal, unstressed animals to instantly produce antibodies, the stressed animals produced extremely small amounts of antibodies or none.[10] Although these experiments did not reveal the mechanisms by which antibody production is affected by stress, they did establish the fact that most forms of stress reduce an animal's ability to defend itself against infection.

Many studies demonstrate that even a learned perception of stress, that is, an experience in which there is no real threat, can affect immune responses. In one such experiment, mice were conditioned to escape from an electric shock that was always foretold by a loud buzzing sound. After being taught to associate the buzzing with the electric shock, the mice were then subjected to the sound only, and *no* electric shock being given.

Mice living under the stress of the buzzing sound were matched against mice who had received no stress conditioning but who were otherwise exactly like their conditioned brothers and sisters. During a period of 14 days, both groups of mice were infected with a Herpes virus. At the end of this period, 60 percent of the stressed mice had succumbed to the infection, compared with only 40 percent among the control group. After 28 days, the mortality rate remained the same for the unstressed mice, but it climbed to 75 percent among the stressed mice.[11] Clearly, this established that perceptions of danger can affect an organism's response to infection as profoundly as the pressure of an external threat.

In a similar experiment, animals were exposed to a mild virus, first under normal conditions and then in the presence of a stress factor. Under normal conditions the animals suffered no symptoms from either the virus alone or the stress alone. However, when the animals were subjected to the stress and the virus simultaneously, there was a measurable loss of body weight and a number of deaths.[12] This experiment demonstrated how multiple factors contribute to disease and how resistance to disease can be affected by a variety of seemingly dissimilar stressors.

In one very surprising experiment, it was discovered that animals could be taught to suppress antibody production. They were given a shot of a drug which suppressed their immune systems, and at the same time they were given drinking water with a distinct flavor. After a period of being conditioned in this way, the animals' immune systems were suppressed simply when they drank the flavored water,

without the administration of the immunosuppressant drug. Somehow the animals had learned to associate the flavored water with the immunosuppressant; drinking the flavored water alone had the same effect as getting a shot of the immunosuppressant drug.[13]

Medical studies establishing relationships between stress and infection are not limited to animal experiments. In a study published in the journal *Pediatrics*, R. J. Mayer and R. J. Haggerty observed sixteen families, testing for correlations between stress and the presence of streptococcus bacteria in their upper respiratory tracts. Multiple variables were involved in this study: a high rate of infection because of the season of the year (winter); close contact between family members, offering good opportunities for the infection to spread from one person to another; and the potential for high stress within a number of the families being tested.

It was found that families judged to be highly stressed—as measured by a stress test—had four times as many infections of all kinds as those families who were not under stress. Similarly, people with high stress scores were found to be carrying strep germs (even when they did not have symptoms), and to have antibodies against strep (indicating that they had contracted the infection on a subclinical level), much more often than those with low stress scores.

In a study published in the *Annals of Internal Medicine,* G. G. Jackson reported on the reactions of Army volunteers to cold viruses. Subjects taking part in this study were given nose drops containing the virus; of these only 40 percent got colds or reported any symptoms as a result of the drops. A second test group, made up of people who said they normally had five or more colds per year, was given nose drops which were sterile, but the subjects were told that they contained cold viruses. Of this group, 26 percent manifested cold symptoms soon after taking the drops.

One of the best known studies of the relationships between emotions and infection was done by Lawrence Hinckle, an epidemiologist at Cornell University, on a group of 1,000 telephone operators. Within the total group one-third of the people accounted for two-thirds of all the illness reported. The group that got sick most frequently described themselves as "dissatisfied, discontented, unhappy, and resentful at their lot in life, and that throughout their working lives they were loaded with outside responsibilities, worries, and frustrations." This group reported twelve times as many colds as the group that was happy with their life, and they had a high incidence of symptoms such as stomach pains, menstrual cramps, and menopausal discomfort.

When we examine the complex interactions between ourselves and our environment, and the vast number of variables involved, from genetic differences in the organism to stress to the presence of microorganisms and pollutants, it becomes clear why we must establish a theory of disease and health based on multiple, rather than single, causes. This is especially important when we are considering prevention; when multiple disease factors are involved, there will normally be some factors over which we have complete and immediate control, whereas our control over other factors may be elusive or distant. Thus we can choose to work on the factors we can most effectively change, and thus gain immediate benefits in terms of our own health and the health of our families. For example, we can immediately avoid foods containing suspected carcinogens, and avoid the use of insecticides or certain cleaning compounds in our homes, reducing the number and variety of suspected pollutants affecting our bodies; meanwhile, though we may not be able to immediately improve the quality of air in the neighborhoods where we live, we can support political-action groups whose long-range goals aim toward these ends.

Atoms, animals, stars, and solar systems have their cycles of birth, maturity, and death. (The Spiral Galaxy NCG 4303 and its 1961 Supernova. Courtesy Lick Observatory.)

Systems Theory and Environmental Health

General systems theory looks upon everything in the universe as a system of matter, energy, and information. The success or failure, the life or death of each system, from the tiniest molecule to the largest star, depends on its ability to keep a particular balance of these three universal ingredients.

Each system in the universe, with its own individual integrity, has a mechanism for maintaining itself in a more or less steady state. In animals and plants we call this *homeostasis*, the system's capacity for keeping an orderly balance of matter, energy, and information. It is homeostasis that maintains a dog as a dog, a man as a man, a planet as a planet, and a solar system as a solar system.

Each individual system must be able to maintain its internal integrity and monitor the external environment. In order for the individual system to remain healthy, it must be capable of detecting environmental changes and making adjustments in itself to compensate for the changes it detects outside itself. Disease in any system occurs when the ideal balance of matter, energy, and information is disrupted. This can happen either because the homeostatic mechanism fails or because the changes that occur in the environment are of a magnitude greater than the systems can compensate for. All homeostatic mechanisms of all known systems have finite limits, and it is the nature of

those limits that we must carefully consider in addressing today's environmental issues.

All systems in the universe are constantly changing, rearranging their organizations of matter, energy, and information. Atoms, animals, stars, and solar systems have their cycles of birth, maturity, and death, forever arranging and rearranging all the elementary particles in the universe. We accept these cycles of change as necessary to a universal order that may forever remain a mystery to us. At the same time, we respect the existence of the millions of systems, be they molecules, animals, or stars, that have evolved and that maintain their individual identities for however brief a time.

In today's world, more than ever before, we cannot afford to look upon any disease as

an isolated event. What happens to any one organism or system has consequences for the whole. Approaching the problems of environmental health in this way, we break the bonds of the one-cause/one-disease system of thinking that has served medicine up to now; we reach toward a holistic view of environmental health, that is, a theory of disease and health that acknowledges the relationships of all parts to the whole.

This broader view of environmental health is far more complex than seeking single causes, but the task is not as difficult as one might think. The following principles, drawn from James J. Miller's work on living systems, provides a framework for evaluating a wide range of environmental problems.

Principle 1. All systems have a particular range of stability determined by the capacities of their homeostatic mechanisms. If a system is placed in an environment that pushes it beyond its homeostatic capacities, that system is strained to its outer limits and is in danger of breaking down.

Principle 2. Pathology is the breakdown of a system that has been pushed beyond its range of stability.

Principle 3. Unusual demands due to an imbalance of matter, energy and/or information can cause pathology. Such imbalances include:

(a) lack of matter-energy input (example: if plant cells do not get enough sunlight, they cannot photosynthesize);

(b) excess of matter-energy input (example: extreme heat changes the chemical bonds inside cells and kills them);

(c) inappropriate forms of matter-energy input (example: smallpox bacteria enter human cells and cause infection);

(d) lack of information input (example: monkeys separated from mothers at birth fail to develop adequate social skills);

(e) excess of information input (example: a young child is subjected to an experience which it does not have adequate information to cope with, and is traumatized as a result);

(f) abnormal internal matter-energy processes (example: the DNA of a cell is damaged by radiation and the cell then cannot metabolize carbohydrates properly);

(g) abnormal internal information processes (example: a busy executive, overloaded with work and highly stressed, misinterprets an employee's report and makes an inappropriate decision).

In the broadest sense these three principles provide an important key for assessing the multiple factors of environmental disease. Rather than seeing each system as a separate entity, and every disease as an isolated event, systems analysis directs attention to the complex interrelationships between all living things. As an evaluative tool, such analysis allows us to maintain a vision of all living things as being both in and of the environment.

Excess information input is one of the factors that disrupts homeostasis in any living system. (Republican Automatons, 1920, by George Grosz. Watercolor, 23″ × 18″. Museum of Modern Art, New York.)

CHAPTER SIX

Human Health as a Barometer of the Earth's Health

The cosmologies of both modern science and prescientific peoples paint a convincing portrait of humanity's kinship with the universe. The basic components of life appear timeless, moving through us and through all we see around us, maintaining kinship regardless of how their manifestations might seem to be separated. Bell's theorem, that "a change in the spin of one particle in a two-particle system would affect its twin simultaneously, even if the two had been widely separated in the meantime," causes us to reflect on the breadth and depth of our kinship.

Regardless of how we incorporate the concept into our thinking, whether through scientific symbols, poetic imagery, or religious visions, the central idea of interconnectedness—with our present world, with worlds before us, and with worlds yet to come—influences the formation of new criteria for evaluating the actions of contemporary people.

There is evidence that the basic components of life are timeless, maintaining kinship regardless of separation in time and space. (Polar star trails. Courtesy of Lick Observatory.)

In a sense, the growing cancer rates, the increased incidence of illness related to stress, and the much elevated risk of upper respiratory disease are all signals that we have violated certain laws of the natural world, throwing off the delicate balances of matter, energy, and information that all living systems require. We have yet to learn how to bring our technologies into harmony with nature, fully respecting the importance of our kinship and interconnectness, and until we do, disease will undoubtedly be one of the products of our efforts, as well as the valuable ores we mine or the chemicals we create or the great cities we build.

As we reflect on our universal kinship, we see ever more clearly that the diseases of mankind are not simply isolated events or the personal misfortunes of a few individuals. Rather, the human diseases we face today mark a turning point. Since life began, disease has been the bellwether of evolution, the signal for life to change, to develop new forms and new adaptations to the environment. Our present awareness of environmental health, of the impact of modern technology on our lives, is as much a part of the evolutionary process as the blue-green algae's adaptations to increased oxygen in the Earth's atmosphere.

However we cannot expect a quick emergence of a new species, able to thrive on the toxins we have created. The changes our technologies press upon the world are far too swift for such physiological adaptations. Rather, the evolutionary process we must look to is intellectual, beginning with the collection and evaluation of information about the universe and our relationship to it, moving on to the creation of compatible technologies.

The best measure we have for designing our future technologies is human health. There is nothing that seems more immediate and important than personal health, our own and that of our loved ones. It is here that we feel the greatest urgency to solve problems of environmental pollution, and it is here that the consequences of our actions are most dramatically demonstrated. But there is a larger picture.

Because of the interconnectedness between ourselves and the Earth, our own bodies become barometers of the Earth's health. The dynamic of human health, human technology, and the Earth's health places at our disposal an instrument of evaluation somewhat like that which Horacio Fabrega, a medical anthropologist, noted among the Zinacanton people of southern Mexico: "The individual himself, his worldly contemporaries, and the gods are locked in a triple web of relationships; and a frequent expression of disarticulation of this web is illness."[1]

Until very recently, life has been nudged toward change by external causes, that is, by geological events causing shifts in the climate or by new species of plants and animals moving in to share a particular environmental niche. Not until *Homo sapiens,* however, were such vast changes imposed on the Earth by the deliberate and conscious efforts of a single species. This places the human race in a unique position: we have created many threatening environmental changes that can be met only by means of the same innovative spirit—though with different priorities—which created those changes in the first place.

It can be argued that before about 10,000 years ago, changes were brought about by natural forces that, because they were symbiotic, stayed within the homeostatic limits of

The best measure we have for designing our future is human health. It is here that we feel the greatest urgency to solve problems of environmental pollution, and it is here that the consequences of our actions are most dramatically demonstrated. (Blue Morning, 1909, by George Bellows. National Gallery of Art, Washington, D.C.)

Throughout history disease has signaled the need for change. The first appearance of oxygen on this planet—ironically created by the natural evolution of plant life—was a mortal threat to the anaerobic life forms that had previously dominated. And the only survivors of that change were those who could make the shift from an anerobic to an oxygen-rich environment. Similarly, the diseases of malnutrition, as the result of a drought, force a herd of deer to find new food sources, either by moving to greener pastures or by evolving enzymes, tooth patterns, and musculature that enable them to eat new forms of vegetation that took root in their native grazing territories following the drought.

the Earth. In other words, the dis-eases they created were self-limiting. We are tempted to place the human race outside this natural order, to say that the threats we create are not self-limiting, because we enjoy an exhalted position that no other species before us has ever enjoyed. However, this is clearly not the case. The self-limiting factor is our potential for annihilating ourselves, which could happen long before the universe is pressed to its homeostatic limits. We can push the Earth beyond its homeostatic limits, but not the universe.

The diseases of the Earth are our diseases. There is no difference in who suffers them, because the Earth is a single living cell and we

We respond to disease as a signal for change. (*Self-Improvement,* 1969, by William Allan. Synthetic polymer, 79″ × 113″. Collection of the Whitney Museum of American Art, New York.)

are like organelles within it. As the creators and sufferers of our own diseases, we are faced with a challenge no other species has ever known.

At our most optimistic, we respond to disease as a signal for change, seeking adaptations not only to prevent our suffering, but also to participate in a larger issue, the evolutionary flow of our species and our planet.

In *The Well Body Book,* we explored the relationships between lifestyle and disease. From this point of view, feeling tired becomes a signal to rest. Indigestion becomes a signal to change the diet. At a more complex level, high blood pressure becomes a signal for a business person to develop new problem-solving techniques, delegate authority, and develop new attitudes about competition and winning. In the narrower perspective of personal health, instituting positive change can enrich daily life, increase comfort (the opposite of disease), and even make a person more effective in achieving professional goals. Changing our lifestyle in response to disease need not be a deprivation; on the contrary, as we respond to our limits (as signaled by dis-ease), we can bring into balance the matter, energy, and information that are the basis of our existence.

Like radio buoys guiding a ship at sea, disease and health can guide our lives. Steering our course by these signals not only leads to a life relatively free of disease, it can also guide us to the upper limits of personal fulfillment. Again, because of our interconnectedness, the fulfillment of any single individual or system ultimately benefits all systems around it. Guided by disease and health, Gaea, the living Earth, benefits from every person's human fulfillment.

CHAPTER SEVEN

The Power to Create a Healthy World

Our power to change the environment, to reshape the face of the Earth for buildings and roads, to harness the energies of atoms, great rivers, and oceans, to control insect populations and the growth patterns of plants and animals, to send spaceships to other planets, is indeed awesome. To ancient people we would seem to be alchemists, creatures who look like humans but have the powers of the gods, the power to challenge and in many cases subdue Nature.

Looking out over the Earth, we can see that our powers have created at least as many problems as they have solved. Although we no longer fear plague, smallpox, and polio, never before in history have we faced the specter of human suffering caused by toxic chemicals, nuclear radiation, and the destructive capacities to obliterate the planet itself. In view of all this, we might be tempted to embrace a simplistic answer, to advocate an end to modern technology. But as many writers before us have asserted, human history shows that having power means it must be used in some form. We have never been able to turn back.

The solution lies not in denying our power, but, on the contrary, in embracing it. Only by embracing it can we hope to understand it fully, and learn to use it to benefit the greatest number of people. It is not, after all, power itself that creates problems; it is the way we have chosen to use that power.

The power we have at our disposal has grown out of the noosphere, that is, out of human innovation and creativity as resources of the living Earth. The real power we have lies there, in the network of pure thought, not in the objects manifest in the physical world as an end product of that thought. We must recognize that the noosphere itself is (at the very least) benign, a resource that can be shaped into unlimited forms, destructive or construc-

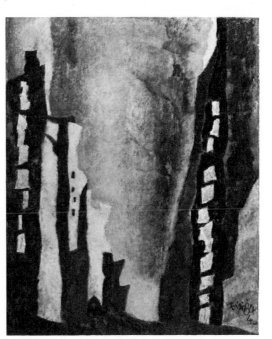

To ancient peoples we would seem to be alchemists, creatures with the power to challenge, and in many cases subdue Nature. (The Alchemist, 1661. From Henrici Regii's Philosophia Naturalis.)

The solution lies not in denying our power but in embracing it. (Manhattan I, 1940, by Lyonel Feininger. Oil on canvas, 39″ × 31″. Collection of the Museum of Modern Art, New York. Gift of Julia Feininger,)

tive, life-threatening or life-enhancing, according to the user's intent.

It is interesting to reflect on the evolution of the noosphere in just the past few decades, since out of this comes the vision of a newly emerging way of life. During the first part of the industrial revolution, new inventions, new forms of hardware, seemed to grow from the creative efforts of individuals working more or less in isolation. Thus, the invention of the cotton gin was attributed to Whitney, the electric light to Edison, and the assembly line to Henry Ford. Actually, these men built on ideas that had been in existence for hundreds or even thousands of years. Still, they were the greatest inventors of their day: if not the first to think of the idea, they were the first to make it a physical reality.

Most major inventions today, however, are not the products of single people working in isolation. The concept of a noosphere is revealed even in our largest corporations. The inventions of recent generations—nuclear power, the space program, and the computer—have all involved hundreds, if not thousands, of people, working jointly or in parallel, with common goals in mind. Moreover, the knowledge from which they have drawn, and on which they have built, extends over space and time, seemingly not limited by geography or national boundaries, reaching back over the ages even as it grows into the future. Whether openly shared or dispersed by electronic eavesdropping equipment, knowledge is breaking free of the ego. No single person can any longer take credit for an invention.

There can be little doubt that the boundaries of the ego are being torn down, even in the technological world, and as people begin to appreciate the fact that thoughts and ideas—

Using the image of the living Earth as a model, we can see that all living things that take part in the biosphere are like organelles in a single living cell. (*Song,* 1958, by Kenneth Noland. Synthetic polymer, 65″ × 65″. Collection of Whitney Museum of American Art. Gift of The Friends of the Whitney Museum of American Art.)

all that is contained in the noosphere—are natural resources as much as coal and oil, those boundaries will dissolve even more. The noosphere is a broad and open resource, one that cannot be claimed like a piece of property. Moreover, like other hard resources (ores, minerals, etc.), information and knowledge can either raise our quality of life or lower it, depending how we choose to use them.

Until recently, invention has been staked out as a personal possession, an extension of the ego, which is that aspect of every system which strives to maintain its separateness and individual integrity. Although ego is essential, it is also transitory and, in many respects, illusory. It is ego that maintains the elementary particles' separateness even as those particles join others to form an atom. And although it seems like a contradiction, the atom's integrity would not become possible unless each particle maintained its own integrity. The atom's ego likewise allows it to join with other atoms to form molecules. The same patterns are repeated again and again as we move up the evolutionary ladder, up to the largest, most complex known structure, the universe itself.

Higher, more complex structures become possible only if less complex structures are able to relinquish some of their interest in maintaining their separateness. There seems to be a time in the life of every separate entity, from elementary particles to humans, when ego is translated into an interest in oneself as an integral part of a larger system. Using the image of the living Earth as a model, we can see that all living things that take part in the biosphere, from viruses to birds to humans, are like the organelles in a single living cell. And every human idea, from the wheel to agriculture to spaceships, contributes to the power of the noosphere, the mind and soul of the living Earth. Herein lies the organizing visualization for our next evolutionary step, one being thrust upon the Earth by the threat of an environmental holocaust.

William Irwin Thompson's statement, in *Darkness and Scattered Light,* that we are moving from a hardware-oriented culture to an information-oriented culture provides a signpost for the new age. He says,

As we shift from hardware to information in ecology, architecture, and medicine, we shift from viewing the world as arranged in categories protected by iron walls to seeing it as a living organism in which permeable membranes allow information to pass through while still respecting the integrity of the cell. [2]

Being aware of human interconnectedness with the universe, of a relationship among all living systems that transcends the ego, sets the stage for a transition from an exploitative to an integrative use of all natural resources. The end of the old model, which depended on the exploitation of natural resources, is marked by human suffering caused by environmental pollution. The new model begins in the search for an end to that suffering. Old questions such as "How can I use the Earth's resources to make myself wealthy?" are being replaced by questions such as, "What is that larger, more important whole, that system of which I'm a part, evolving toward? What can I do to help it attain that goal? What can I do to keep the noosphere and the *organelles* that are my progeny alive and well long after I am gone?" This interest in a transition from an exploitative to an integrative pattern in the human condition is not so much philosophical as biological, a response to the age-old evolutionary mechanism of disease.

We need not doubt that we could use the resources of the Earth (from other species in the biosphere to ideas in the noosphere) to benefit not just a few at the expense of many, but everyone and everything only at the expense of our creative energies, which in itself leads to personal fulfillment. We need only acknowledge the immensity of the power in the relationship between the Earth and humanity to set our imaginations in motion toward achieving the broadest goals of environmental health.

As we set out to create a new human condition based on integrative rather than exploitative systems of thought, the task may seem far too large for any one person to affect. But this is not the case. The Earth itself communicates its needs through human disease and health, those measures of relative well-being that no one can refute. The noosphere contains the mental tools necessary for solving all environmental problems, and the voice of that sphere speaks to all persons through their own creative acts. This book and others like it, as well as every reader's search for solutions to current environmental problems, are the elements of the noosphere; they suggest just a few of the paths people can follow to create health for themselves and their families, and consequently benefit the living Earth.

Healing is never an isolated event. Healing ourselves, we help heal the environment. Healing the environment, we help heal ourselves.

Visualization Exercises

Because human life is essential to the Earth, our well-being must be perceived as an important indicator of the Earth's health, in much the same way that the health of your heart or lungs or stomach is to your body. By means of our own awareness and our own potential for making rather immediate changes to create health, we can and do play an important role in the Earth's homeostatic processes. We are all *sensors* in an immensely complex biofeedback loop, monitoring the Earth's condition for any damaging deviation from the ideal homeostatic range. Each person in his or her own way can communicate that information to those parts of the Earth—often ourselves—that can most immediately act to help the whole system survive.

The first of the exercises that follow is called the *Ease/Dis-ease Scale.* It is a mental tool for sharpening your awareness of relative states of illness and well-being, so that you can act to seek change, for yourself as well as for the Earth, at an early stage. As homeostatic sensors for the Earth, we are each, in a very real sense, connected to the noosphere and able to communicate with the voice of the living Earth.

The Ease/Dis-ease Scale

Most people have been taught to respond to disease at the point when they feel enough pain, fever, and/or lethargy that they cannot carry out their normal routines. However, those symptoms are not the first signals of disease. Before that are much subtler symptoms, such as restlessness, irritability, vague anxiety, or a feeling that things just aren't going as well as they might.

The goal in this exercise is to scale down your definition of disease, to fine-tune your receptors, so that you can become aware of areas that need to be changed long before they become the source of serious diseases. This is particularly important in environmental health, where it is sometimes too late to make changes once actual diseases are manifest.

To begin this exercise, imagine a scale like this:

Dis-ease   0 1 2 3 4 5 6 7 8 9 10   Ease

The right side of the scale (10) represents how you feel at your very best, for instance, following an important personal accomplishment, or after an invigorating athletic experience. The left side of the scale (0) represents how you feel at your worst, for example, when you are quite ill or have had a serious emotional setback. The center of the scale, from 4 to 7, is how the majority of us feel most of the time.

Whereas a cold or flu would obviously be rated at the lower end of the dis-ease side of the scale, say, around 2 or 3, it might not be so obvious how to rate environmental diseases. For one thing, we tend to numb ourselves to environmental issues, creating shields against what may seem beyond our immediate control. We accept the problems as normal conditions of everyday life, since, after all, they aren't causing enough pain, fever, or lethargy to prevent us from working or playing.

Environmental disease, such as air pollution in the cities, has some recognizable symptoms that we would probably rate in the 3–4 range of the ease/dis-ease scale. These are eye irritation, mild upper respiratory congestion, and low-level sinus infections from living in the city. Most of the time these symptoms range around the tolerable levels on the table, though occasionally they do drop down to 1, when many people become ill enough to stay home from work or cancel plans for recreation.

Still more subtle than air pollution can be the symptoms of eating manufactured foods, which are often high in calories and low in nu-

received as forms of stress focused on a particular subject, can go as low as 0 on the ease/dis-ease scale; for others they range around 3 or 4.

As we have said, dis-ease has always been a signal for change, the voice of the living Earth telling an organism to seek alternatives to its present way of life. In the same way, ease is the voice of the living Earth telling the organism that it is in harmony with its environment.

To use the ease/dis-ease scale, go into a deeply relaxed state (see page 000) and ask how you feel about your relationship with the living Earth in any of the basic categories of environmental issues. For example, you might ask yourself the following:

• How do you feel about radiation?

• How do you feel about food additives and the quality of the food in your diet?

Ease is the voice of the living Earth telling an organism that it is in harmony with its environment. (Mother Earth, 1975, by Michael Samuels.)

Cycles emerge: a story; cosmos in chaos—order surfaces, rhythm, sequence, pattern, repetition; Earth revealed, rotation, rise and fall, day into night; Life emerges, growth and decay, wake and sleep, birth and death; Life is given choice, good or evil, hope or despair, nurture or ignore?; the hands, the eyes, the hearts, serve those choices . . . in . . . the creative cycle, inspiration, persistence, completion, release. (Haystack Celebration, 1982, by Florence Samuels.)

trition, and have added "flavor enhancers" and preservatives to prolong shelf life. The symptoms of dis-ease experienced here can range from mild indigestion to lethargy, irritability, fluctuating energy levels throughout the day, and the overstimulation of taste buds from too much sugar, salt, and other flavorings. To a person eating sweets, these sensations can seem quite pleasurable at the time, though the end result can be placed around 2 or 3 on the dis-ease side of the scale.

Issues such as nuclear radiation are another matter altogether. We don't experience pain, fever, or lethargy because of radiation until it is too late to do much about it. From day to day, however, we experience the global concerns about radiation, as anxiety, anger, fear, confusion, a sense of being at the mercy of forces outside our control and being ignorant about where to turn for dependable information on radiation and health. For some persons, these forms of dis-ease, understood or

• How do you feel about the quality of the water you are drinking?

• How do you feel about toxic chemicals in your environment? At work? At home? Where you vacation?

• How do you feel about stress at your job, in your family, between you and your friends? usually felt as sensations in your body or as emotions. How you rate your own feelings is, of course, purely subjective; how you feel about it is exactly what you'll want to measure on this scale. Rate your responses to several different environmental problems, then use these ratings to establish priorities for change.

PART

3

The Sourcebook

I n this part of the book we present the basic source material for understanding, evaluating, and seeking solutions to current environmental problems.

The material contained here can be both frightening and discouraging. There is, perhaps, a very human tendency to feel overwhelmed and defeated by the number and extent of the problems we face today, and so to tell ourselves that nothing a single person does could possibly matter. However, a great deal has been accomplished by individuals, in the past decade alone, to solve pollution problems. The reclamation of New York's Jamaica Bay and a successful program to clean up the air in national parks were both initiated by individuals.

Having the facts at one's disposal—regardless of how distressing those facts may be—is the first step toward positive change. The diseases that now threaten the living Earth are, for the most part, our own creations. And as their creators, we are now in the process of learning to control our creations. That's what this part of the book is all about.

In this section we discuss radiation and chemical pollution, the two main sources of human pollution in our food, water, and air. Each pollution source is examined in terms of how it causes disease, the scientific evidence as to the type and extent of the threat, where it is found, and what you can do to avoid exposure. In addition, our research sources are noted, and lists of books and other materials for further reading are given.

You will also find, for the chemicals, a category called "bioaccumulation factor." This needs a special explanation. Some chemicals bond to the molecules of fatty tissue in animals and fish, instead of being metabolized and passing through. The bioaccumulation factor is a scale for measuring how many parts per million of a chemical can accumulate in living tissues. For example, if a fish is living in a body of water where there is generally one part of DDT in an area equal to the amount of water displaced by the fish, that fish can (because of the constitution of the chemical) accumulate up to 2 million parts of DDT in its body. This factor is important to human health, because we could consume high concentrations of a chemical in the flesh of animals. The implications are broad. First, cattle that drink water contaminated with chemicals store those chemicals, at the rate of the bioaccumulation factor, in their fat, and in their milk (dairy cows). Certain grains may also take up large quantities of a chemical from the air,

The reclamation of Jamaica Bay and the program to clean up the National Parks were initiated by individuals, not groups. (*Zion National Park,* 1982, by Michael Samuels.)

the land itself, or the water. And finally, fish used for human consumption or for fertilizers on crops may contain high concentrations of chemicals in their body fat, even though they were caught in water that is relatively safe for human consumption.

We would like to make two comments about our working methods. First, in most categories we have drawn information from a broad spectrum of scientific sources. Doing so is especially important for subjects such as radiation, where there is considerable controversy over how much radiation is dangerous. Thus, you will find we have presented a range of opinion, so that readers may draw their own conclusions. Second, we wanted to make this information, which is often highly technical, available to the broadest cross section of the population. In order to accomplish this, we have minimized our use of technical terms, though without compromising the material itself. For this reason we feel this part of the book will be as useful to the environmental professional as it is to the lay reader.

CHAPTER EIGHT

Radiation

Radiation is vibrating electromagnetic energy moving at the speed of light. This phenomenon can be envisioned as packets of energy vibrating up and down in a sawtooth pattern while they race along a given path. To illustrate this, imagine that you and a friend are holding onto opposite ends of an elastic cord about the length of a jump rope. If you jiggle your end up and down, you will see your energy transmitted to the other end of the cord in waves until it comes to your friend's hand. Depending on how hard you jiggle the cord, your friend will simply feel the energy you have projected to him, or his hand may even be jiggled by it. Every source of radiation, be it uranium, sunlight, or microwaves, can be identified by its characteristic wave length or pattern of vibration (see Table 8.1).

When vibrating packets of energy strike matter, that matter is set in motion in a pattern corresponding to the radiation. This motion can be violent enough to disintegrate or permanently alter the matter affected. Radiation is important to human health, because the human body, being made up of matter, is altered by radiation. What makes it particularly significant to human health is that radiation affects us at a molecular level, not simply by killing cells, the way trauma or infection does, but more insidiously by altering DNA molecules. Such radiation damage can be transmitted to subsequent generations of cells. We'll discuss this fact in greater detail in each of the subcategories that follow.

Atomic (Ionizing) Radiation

What It Is

Atomic or nuclear radiation are popular terms for *ionizing* radiation. Ions are created when electrons are removed from an atom, re-

Radiation can be envisioned as vibrating packets of energy. (*Untitled*, 1968, by Lawrence Stafford. Synthetic polymer, 72″ by 96.″ Collection of The Whitney Museum of American Art, New York.)

To envision the way in which radiation transmits energy, imagine a cord is held between two people and one end is jiggled up and down. Energy, that is movement, is transmitted to the stationary end of the cord in waves.

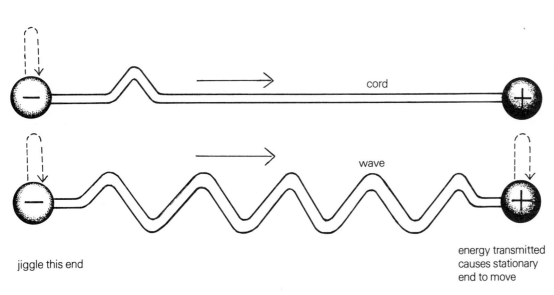

cord

wave

jiggle this end

energy transmitted causes stationary end to move

Table 8.1: Types of radiation

Type	Source	Wavelength (nanometers)
Gamma rays	Radioactive minerals and cosmic rays	.001 – .14
X-rays	Sun, x-ray machines	.005 – 20
Ultraviolet (UV-C)	Sun	40 – 286
Ultraviolet (UV-B)	Sun	286 – 320
Ultraviolet (UV-A)	Sun	320 – 390
Visible light	Sun (violet-to-red spectrum)	390 – 780
Infrared light	Sun	$780 – 4 \times 10^5$
Electromagnetic waves	Electrical devices	10^{15}
Microwaves	Sun, radio, radar, tv	$10^5 – 10^{11}$

sulting in a positive electrical charge rather than the normal neutral state. Ionizing radiation occurs naturally in the decay of uranium and other radioactive elements, and is produced by x-ray tubes. Of all forms of radiation, it produces the highest energy, an energy sufficient to strip electrons from an atom.

How It Causes Disease

Traveling at the speed of light, ionizing radiation can pass directly through human tissue, missing all matter. Its ability to pass through in this way allows us to make x-ray films. On the rare occasion when an x-ray does strike a molecule that is a part of the body, it can set in motion a whole series of events. Let's say, for example, that it knocks one electron off an atom that is part of the DNA of a muscle cell. The displaced electron, vibrating like the x-ray that struck it, begins bouncing around,

striking other electrons. The DNA in the immediate area is literally shaken to pieces.

Most of the bonds that maintain the stability of the atoms in human tissue have between five and seven electron volts of energy. X-rays, by contrast, have hundreds of thousands of volts, and gamma rays are measured in millions of volts. There is no chemical bond in living tissue that can resist the damage of a direct hit from such radiation. It is estimated that somewhere between 14,000 and 20,000 chemical bonds in the human body can be broken by such a hit from a single x-ray energy packet.

Protein molecules hit by an x-ray packet are shattered into millions of electrons, which run wild, scattering in all directions and wreaking havoc. Chaos is created where once there was balance and order. Since we are dealing with atoms, the damage occurs on an infinitesimally small scale, and at first glance the disease potential might seem correspondingly

Ionizing radiation can displace electrons that are part of the DNA of a cell. These electrons then bounce around, displacing other electrons and altering the genetic pattern of the cell.

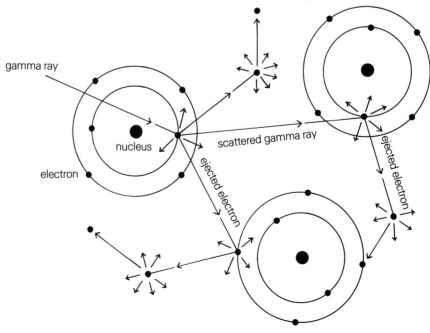

small. However, it is that smallness itself that poses the biggest health problem.

Working at submicroscopic levels, radiation can alter the genetic material inside any living cell. Once altered, the affected gene can pass along inappropriate information to every generation of cells that it propagates. Since all the cells of our bodies are in a continuous state of reproducing themselves, the consequences of DNA affected in this way (mutation) can be substantial.

Mutation is a normal occurrence in nature, being responsible for most evolutionary change. However, for every positive change that results from radiation, there are millions, or perhaps even billions, of either useless or disease-causing mutations. By far the greatest number of mutations weaken rather than strengthen the organism.

Although there is no scientific doubt that radiation-altered DNA causes cells to go wild and to create tumors, not all genetic material struck by radiation goes on to create these anomalies. Almost always the affected cell simply dies or fails to reproduce. Moreover, the homeostatic mechanisms of the body are quite powerful, and can seek out and dismantle cells that are destructive members of the cellular community. But as we have said, the homeostatic capacity of any system can be pushed past its limits, resulting in disease. Thus, if the amount of radiation increases, so does the number of hits in the human body, and the damage done may surpass what the body's homeostatic mechanisms can do to right the damage. We must also assume that the multiple-factor principle of disease can be applied here, with the result that radiation levels not damaging to a person in good health might cause significant damage in a person who was

very young, very old, or already sick.

One significant characteristic of chromosomal damage resulting from radiation is that there can be a latency period of as long as forty years between initial exposure and the manifestation of a tumor. Because so much time may pass between exposure to radiation and the appearance of any disease symptoms, the task of compiling accurate epidemiological data is especially complicated. Records must be maintained for at least the duration of the latency period; interpreting data for shorter periods can be misleading. In a graph drawn to study correlations between exposure to radiation and disease resulting from a particular industrial accident, it could very well appear that no disease occurred for as long as three decades after exposure. From this, observers

Because so much time may pass between exposure to radiation and the appearance of any disease symptoms, the task of compiling accurate epidemiological data is especially complicated. (*Ark. Nuc. One,* 1982, by Michael Samuels.)

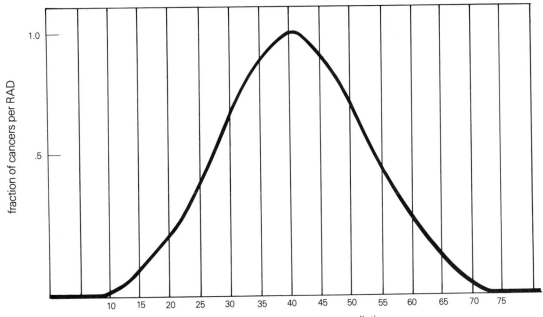

The greatest manifestation of cancer as the result of radiation does not peak until forty years after exposure.

fraction of cancers per RAD

1.0

.5

10 15 20 25 30 35 40 45 50 55 60 65 70 75

time in years after exposure to radiation

Linear, no threshold

excess cancers / *dose*

Linear, with threshold

excess cancers / *dose*

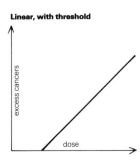

excess cancers / *dose*

Supra-linear

excess cancers / *dose*

There are four common formulas for estimating the number of expected cancers following very low doses of radiation or chemical exposure. Investigators' projections will vary greatly, depending on which method or curve they choose.

* *"Person year" is a statistical term used to record the number of people studied times the number of years they were studied.*

might wrongly draw the conclusion that the accident in question caused no disease. However, extended one decade past this time frame, the picture might very well be altered, showing a dramatic increase in tumors as the people exposed moved out of the latency period.

Although most people are well aware of relationships between radiation and cancer, cancer is not the only hazard of this environmental disease factor. Radiation can also cause birth defects and can reduce fertility. In the same way that radiation can alter the DNA of cells, it can alter the genetic material contained in an egg or a sperm, resulting in mutations which show up in babies of the next generation. Altered eggs and sperm tend to die before they can produce a child with birth defects, but it does happen, even if only rarely.

Radiation during pregnancy is especially hazardous. Within the uterus the developing infant is particularly vulnerable to ionizing radiation. For this reason, x-rays and exposure to even low levels of radioactive material should be avoided from conception to birth. Damage to the infant in utero includes mental retardation, small head size, stillbirth, childhood leukemia, and anomalies of the central nervous system.

Evidence of Its Danger

There is no disagreement in the scientific community that ionizing radiation causes cancer as well as genetic mutation. Evidence of the health hazard to humans comes from both animal and human studies. Human studies are of immense scale, including intricate, detailed follow-up of Hiroshima and Nagasaki survivors, as well as continuing follow-up of thou-

sands of patients who received x-ray treatments for medical purposes, most of which were ill-advised. In other experiments animals have been deliberately radiated with ionizing materials in order to measure both short-term and long-term effects after a variety of doses, exposure rates, etc.

The most famous human study is one called "The Life Span Study," a long-range follow-up of 109,000 survivors of Hiroshima and Nagasaki.[1] This study demonstrated that in a group of people *not* exposed to artificial radiation there were 8 cancers per 158,000 *person years,** equivalent to 50 cases of cancer per million person years. In the group exposed to nuclear radiation from the Hiroshima and Nagasaki bombings, there were 18 cancers per 200,000 person years, or 88 cases per million

person years. Hence there were 76 percent more cancers in the exposed group.

Another famous study of the effects of radiation on human health is known as the "Ankylosing Spondilitis Series," a study of 6,800 patients over almost two decades, following their treatment (by x-ray) for the spinal disease of the study's title.[2] Among this group there were: 45 percent more lung cancers than in a control group not receiving these treatments; 37 percent more cancer of the large intestine; 60 percent more cancer of the pancreas; 43 percent more cancer of the stomach; 109 percent more cancer of the esophagus; 97 percent more lymphoma; 124 percent more cancer of the kidney; and 34 percent more urinary/bladder cancer.

There are literally hundreds of studies similar to these in the medical literature. A variety of radiation sources and radioactive substances

Table 8.2: Birth defects caused by radiation of laboratory animals

Exposure levels (rads)	Effects
5	Increased natural abortions, retarded growth, excess fingers and toes, skeletal malformations, reduced tail lengths
10–40	Alterations of brain architecture
15–20	Brain malformations
25	Malformations of spinal cord and skull
50	Eye defects
100	Malformations of heart, face, and urinary tract

Table 8.3: Risk of cancer caused by radiation[a]

Age of exposure	Amount of rads necessary to cause cancer		Years of life lost from cancer deaths	
	Male	Female	Male	Female
1	64.5	70	21.9	28.4
5	70.8	79.6	20.1	26.3
10	87.8	103.6	17.9	23.6
15	178.1	217.2	15.9	21.0
20	200.1	248.5	14.2	18.6
30	234.2	284.6	11.6	14.8
40	537.5	636.1	9.6	11.5
50	13,434.0	14,615.0	8.0	9.3

[a]Adapted from Goffman, pages 285–288. To use this chart, find out how many rads of radiation the person received, at a certain age. For example, if a 20-year-old man received 100 rads of radiation to his whole body, you would divide 100 by 200.1; so he would have a 50 percent chance of getting cancer from this dose.

have been studied in depth by the scientific community, and have been scrutinized for their specific short-term and long-range effects on humans. Although cancer rates are well-known, scientists are only beginning to understand the extent of the effects of artificial radiation on the living Earth.

Extent of the Threat

Whereas scientists agree that radiation causes cancer, they do not agree about *how much* radiation causes it. To try to provide a fair picture of differing viewpoints, we have drawn upon three basic collections of information: the BEIR report, from the National Academy of Sciences; the UNSCEAR report, from the United Nations Scientific Committee on the Effects of Atomic Radiation; and the book *Radiation and Human Health,* by John W. Gofman.

Four principal problems in evaluating the effects of radiation on humans create the controversy surrounding the interpretation of data. The first issue is measuring how many rads* of exposure a person actually received, a factor that is certainly in question with such studies as the Hiroshima and Nagasaki reports, because there was little chance to find out exactly how far the survivors were from the center of the explosion, whether or not they were shielded by a building or other obstacle, and how much radiation was actually produced on the ground.

Second, we know that in tracing medical records such as those used in the "Ankylosing Spondylitis Series," we cannot fully depend on the accuracy of records. Moreover, it is known in the medical community that malfunctions in x-ray machines, as the result of poor maintenance, mean there are probably discrepancies between how many rads a person got and how many rads the records say that he or she got. Often radiologists themselves don't know this.

Third, children are far more sensitive to radiation than adults. The younger the child, the higher will be its cancer rates per rad. Thus, unless age groups are carefully separated, statistics showing relationships between radiation exposure and excess cancers will be significantly skewed.

Fourth, when interpreting information on people exposed to radiation, one must take into account a latency period of up to 40 years between the time of exposure and the peak period when disease symptoms can be expected to show up. Obviously, if data is compiled for only 20 or 30 years, still within the latency period, the incidence of disease will be lower than if the same study extended past the latency period.

One of the most important variables in predicting disease from exposure to radiation is a statistical technicality. This becomes particularly important in estimating excess cancer deaths from industrial accidents, in which radiation levels are usually very low, and there is little or no history available to plot the exposed people through the 40-year latency period. To predict cancer deaths, statisticians produce a graph which begins with a known figure on the higher radiation levels. Then, using one or more statistical curves, they trace a line downward to establish a theoretical picture of what happens at the lower radiation levels. Differences of interpretation, skewed one way or another because of the shape of the statistical curve, can be observed in Figure 8.2.

Because of the wide range of choices available for interpreting data, it is important to fully assess the biases of the investigators

Table 8.4: Genetic risk in exposure to radiation[a]

Type of Disease	Estimated number of cases per million live births, with one rad exposure per person per generation
Dominant gene types: eye malformations, extra fingers and toes, skull and bone disorders, hemophilia	40–400
Recessive gene types: Phenylketonuria (PKU), cystic fibrosis, muscular dystrophy, deafness, cystic kidney disease, etc.	4–44
Chromosomal types: Downs syndrome (Mongolism), mental retardation, small head, etc.	27–many thousands
Irregularly inherited types: mental retardation, congenital heart disease, etc.	120–18,000
Totals	191–many thousands

*Rad is a term used to describe how much radiation a person actually absorbed per unit of body weight.

whenever the affects of radiation on human health are being presented in statistical form. For example, in estimating excess cancer deaths caused by one rad of radiation exposure, the three major sources arrive at three different predictions:

(1) The BEIR report estimates from 177 to 353 excess cancer deaths per million people as the result of that population receiving one rad.[3]

(2) The UNSCEAR report estimates there will be only 100 excess cancer deaths for the same group.[4]

(3) Gofman, meanwhile, predicts 3,771 excess cancer deaths for this group, in part because he takes into account many more variables than do the first two studies.[5]

Where It Is Found

Ionizing radiation that affects human health comes from four basic sources:

1. Natural sources (also known as "background radiation"). Natural radiation must be traced to the formation of the Galaxy itself, and to the explosion of a supernova as much as 33×10^6 years ago. Natural radiation comes from uranium and ^{40}potassium, elements that have been a part of the living Earth since the beginning of time.

2. Consumer products. Artificial products with radiation sources, such as luminous dials on clocks and other instruments, television sets, record cleaning and other antistatic devices, smoke detectors, glassware and ceramics, as well as cement and other building products made from earth.

3. Medical sources. Modern medicine is currently the largest source of radiation that affects humans. It is now responsible for more excess cancer than any other artificial radiation source. From medical diagnosis and treatment procedures, humans receive higher organ doses of radiation than from any other source except rare industrial accidents. The main examples of this radiation are x-ray diagnosis, radiation treatment, and radioactive pharmaceuticals.

4. Nuclear fuel and weaponry. Radiation exposure from nuclear industries includes loss of radioactive materials during mining, milling, fuel fabrication, reactor operation, fuel reprocessing, waste disposal, and transportation of radioactive fuels and wastes, as well as fallout from nuclear weapons testing.

Natural radiation

Natural radiation has existed for at least a billion years. In fact, human evolution is at least in part dependent on genetic change produced by this energy. Although an essential part of the living Earth, natural radiation is the source of much illness in humans. The Gofman data provides us with a calculation showing that natural radiation causes about 8 percent of all cancer deaths; UNSCEAR gives a figure of about .3 percent.[6]

The Earth's homeostatic capacities have evolved in the presence of a radiation level that has varied only a small amount during millions of years. The natural radiation level is a human health hazard, but it may not be a threat to the whole system we envision as the living Earth. In fact, it is probably correct to assume that it is beneficial. Although these issues may remain a part of the puzzle of the universe, it is clear that the Earth has evolved to live in homeostatic balance with natural radiation levels. We ask ourselves: how close to the limits of our planet's homeostatic capacities artificial radiation may be pushing us?

In truth, we who live in the biosphere are sandwiched between two sources of natural radiation: radiation from the soil and radiation from outer space (cosmic radiation). The hazards of natural radiation vary with geography.

Table 8.5: Radiation from natural sources[a]

Source	Dose (millirems per year)
Cosmic rays	28
Radionuclides in the body, such as tritium, carbon-14, sodium-22, potassium-40, rubidium-87	28
Earth, such as soil, rock, building materials	26
Total	82

[a]Adapted from BEIR, p. 125

Exposure to cosmic radiation, for example, is greatest at highest elevations. There is considerable controversy over how important elevation may be in terms of human health, with estimates ranging from 40 to 1,200 cancer deaths per year, worldwide, as a result of this geographic variable. Gofman estimates that airline crews flying 1,000 hours per year increase their risk of cancer by a factor of one death per thousand population. Gofman also says that Denver, Colorado, with the highest elevation of any city in the United States, has 81 more cancer deaths per million population per year than cities at lower elevations.*

The argument is often put forth that the levels of radiation produced by a single nuclear power plant, or the testing of a nuclear weapon, are "safe" because they produce radiation no higher than what we already receive from natural sources. There is, however, a serious flaw in this line of reasoning. Radiation created by humans does not stand separate and alone; if it is *equal* to natural radiation, we are doubling the amount of radiation in the environment. From this increased radiation we can expect corresponding increases in cancer

*To put this in proportion, 24,075 cancer deaths per million population would be expected at lower elevations. Denver, then, would be expected to have 24,156 cancer deaths per million population.

When assessing human health hazards from nuclear power, we also have to assess the reprocessing of nuclear waste. In nearly every step of the nuclear-power industry, some radioactivity leaks into the environment. (*Hudson Valley Nuclear-Reprocessing Plant at Sunset,* 1982, by Michael Samuels.

deaths. As a preventive measure, we can do little to control radiation from natural sources, but we can do much to control radiation that we ourselves produce.

Modern building materials such as concrete and stone, because they are extracted from the earth, carry with them the natural radiation levels characteristic of the land from which they come. Thus, in a cement building we are not only standing on a source of radiation, but are surrounded on all sides by it. On the other hand, even though such a building subjects the inhabitants to more radiation than, say, a wooden building does, it also shields them from cosmic rays. In any case, the doses are very low, and the hazards tend to be counteracted by the shielding advantages. Wooden structures do little to shield the inhabitants from either cosmic rays or soil radiation, but don't subject people to radiation concentrated in building materials from the earth.

Our bodies normally contain radioactive

materials in the form of ^{40}potassium and rubidium. We ingest these through the food chain, and since these levels are fairly uniform from one person to another, we must assume that our homeostatic capacities are balanced to accomodate them.

Coal-powered electrical generators release natural radiation, since coal, like all other ores, contains ^{238}uranium. When it is burned, ^{238}uranium produces a certain amount of radiation, though it is still 35 times less than the radiation produced by a nuclear power plant for the same wattage hours.

As uranium breaks down in the earth, a radioactive gas called *radon* is released. This gas is inhaled by humans and other animals. Concrete and brick buildings, which contain radioactive materials, release small quanitites of radon, and therefore need a system of ventilation providing a constant flow of fresh air. To establish a perspective on the hazards of radon for humans, Gofman estimates that a male living and working in concrete structures, who also smokes, increases his risk of lung cancer by 1,700 per 100,000 population compared with the same group inhabiting wood structures.[7] Since it comes from the earth, natural gas is also a source of radon. This same radioactive gas is found in phosphate rock fertilizers, and in gypsum board made from the waste products of these fertilizers.

Radioactive consumer products

Several factors need to be taken into account with radioactive consumer products. These products affect more than the initial owner. Because the radioactive elements are extremely long-lived, they may affect many generations to come. The damage is passed from one generation to another in two ways: first, through genetic damage suffered by factory workers who produced the product; second, by the accumulation of such products

NL Industries, in Albany, New York, has been cited by New York State for radioactive spill from their stacks, and for dumping waste, uranium-238 in a field where children play. (*House and Garden with NL Stacks in Distance,* 1982, by Michael Samuels.)

dumped at any of a million disposal sites around the world. As long as these consumer items are produced, the dump sites and their corresponding radiation levels will grow.

Is the tiny risk of a clock with an irradiated dial worth worrying about? Don't its benefits clearly outweigh its dangers? What most people don't take into account is that they make choices not just for one product of this kind, but many: luminous dials on the instrument panels of cars; smoke alarms in homes, restaurants, public buildings, and work places; and nuclear power plants hundreds of miles from their own homes.

For consumer products, isolated choices have a cumulative effect. We must look not at the amount of radiation emitted by single consumer products, each one of which is safe by

---

Table 8.6: Radiation from consumer products[a]

Product	Nuclide	Radioactivity level
Radiated watch faces	^{3}H	1–25 μCi
	^{147}Pm	65–200 μCi
	^{226}Ra	.1–3 μCi
Cathode-ray tubes (tv)	various	1–1,000 μCi
Antistatic devices for cleaning records and photographic equipment	^{210}Po	.05–.5 μCi
	^{241}Am	2–25 μCi
Smoke and fire detectors	^{241}Am	1–100 μCi
Chinaware	Natural uranium, thorium	10–.001 μCi per .01 square centimeters

[a]Adapted from UNSCEAR, p. 95.

---

itself, but at those amounts multiplied by the number of similar products being produced. It is important to estimate how many such products will be made during the lifetime of the radioactive material each product contains; if the lifetime of a radioactive element is 20 or 30 years, the accumulation of such items could present a significant health hazard.

It has been recently discovered that some eyeglasses and false teeth emit radiation. Eyeglasses, made of highly refined glass, have thorium and uranium in the glass itself—as much as 30 percent by weight. From this the eyes may receive as much as one millirad of radiation per hour. Some dental porcelains used in false teeth contain uranium to give teeth a pearly natural sheen. A full set of dentures can produce as much as 3 rads of radiation per year, a rather significant dose. Recently the United Kingdom banned the use of uranium

for dental porcelains; in the United States uranium for this purpose is limited to .05 percent per weight.

Color televisions produce radiation using the same electronic principles as the x-ray machine. The earliest sets, using vacuum tubes, can emit radiation in excess of present safety standards unless kept in good repair. The safety limits set by the International Atomic Energy Safety Series, Number Nine, say that at 2 inches from the set the radiation should not exceed .5 milliroentgens* per hour. New sets with transistors (solid state) emit radiation far below the safety standards when properly working. In one study researchers examined 28 new television sets of different makes and models sold in Taiwan; they found these emited between .01 and .07 milliroentgens per hour.[8] Gofman calculates that a person sitting six feet from a color television set, and watching it 12 hours a day, would receive .25 millirads of radiation per year. Statistically, this increases the average television watcher's risk of cancer by .1 percent.

Medical radiation

Modern medicine is the largest source of artificial radiation. It is second only to natural sources. Ironically, the health industry is responsible for increasing the amount of worldwide radiation more than any other technology, including weapons testing and the nuclear industry. According to the UNSCEAR report, the radiation used by the healing industry in one year is more than twice the amount from fallout during the peak years of nuclear weapons testing. Modern medicine produces a hundred times more radiation than the present nuclear-power industry. The UNSCEAR report states that reduction in the use of medical x-rays would significantly reduce human cancer deaths, with no loss of benefits, since many diagnostic x-rays are not medically necessary.

Authorities agree that physicians themselves can rarely predict the actual radiation a patient will receive from an x-ray, because x-ray machines are not always kept in good repair; so the patient might be getting far more than is safe. One study showed that the amount of radiation that patients received for the same diagnostic procedure varied from 1.6 to an astounding 90 roentgens. Among the machines the researchers discovered one that was pouring out a constant 12 rads *per minute* as the result of an improperly installed electrical contact.[9]

Calculating radiation levels from x-rays is not an easy task for the individual patient. Several factors must be considered. Most x-ray diagnosis is directed at a single organ, and the organs around it will receive less radiation. Hence only the specific organs being x-rayed

---

*Roentgen is an older unit of measurement used in measuring radiation from x-rays. It is approximately the same as *rad*.

Table 8.7: Skin doses from typical x-rays[a]

Dose group	Rads per exposure		Rads per examination	
	Median value	Range of average values	Median value	Range of average values
High skin dose				
Barium swallow R			1.4	
Barium swallow F	6.4		8.5	
Barium meal R	0.9	0.09 – 2.2	1.7	
Barium meal F	4.4		2.1	6 – 25
Barium enema R	0.7	0.4 – 1.0	1.5	
Barium enema F	4.9		20	5 – 26
Whole chest R	0.02	0.006 – 0.09	0.14	0.07 – 0.15
Whole chest F	2.0		12	3 – 22
Mammography			6	0.2 – 7.8
Pelvimetry	2	0.8 – 3.8	8	6 – 10
Lumbosacral spine	2.7	0.5 – 2.9	5	5 – 6
Lumbar spine	1.5	0.7 – 2.9	4.5	
Cardiac catheterization			47	
Medium skin dose				
Head	0.4	0.3 – 1.5	1.5	1.4 – 1.9
Cervical spine	0.3	0.03 – 0.8	1.5	0.6 – 1.9
Clavicle and shoulder	0.9		0.3	0.3 – 0.4
Dorsal spine	1.8		2.8	2.0 – 4.7
Thorax	0.4		0.8	0.6 – 0.9
Cholecystography	0.8	0.2 – 1.2	2.2	1.5 – 2.8
Abdomen	0.2	0.15 – 1.3	1.2	1.0 – 1.4
Abdomen (obstetric)	2.0	0.4 – 3.9	3.2	2.7 – 3.8
Urography (descending)	1.2		3.2	1.7 – 5.0
Urography (retrograde)			2.9	1.4 – 2.4
Salpingography R			1.2	
Salpingography F			3.4	
Placentography			3.0	
Cystography	0.2		3.1	
Pelvis	1.4	0.4 – 1.7	3.3	2.1 – 4.5
Hip and upper femur	1.1	0.4 – 1.7	1.4	1.1 – 3.0
Dental	0.4		2.5	1.6 – 3.4
Angiography (head)			1.0	
Angiography (abdomen)			3.3	
Tomography (chest)			1.1	0.8 – 1.4
Mass survey chest	0.9		1.0	0.6 – 1.4
Low skin dose				
Arm and hand	0.1		0.3	0.1 – 1.7
Chest	0.02	0.006 – 0.09	0.14	0.07 – 0.15
Femur (lower two thirds)	0.03		0.4	
Leg and foot	0.1		0.4	0.3 – 0.4

[a]R, radiography; F, fluoroscopy. Adapted from UNSCEAR, p. 330.

are at risk—assuming x-rays are taken correctly and the machines used are in excellent condition. Gofman suggests the following way to calculate the effects of x-rays:

Assume that one-fourth of the radiation that theoretically should be projected from the x-ray machine, as measured at the skin surface, will actually get to the targeted organ. Because machines are rarely in perfect condition, multiply the theoretical dose to the targeted organ by a factor of ten.

Dental x-rays are done repeatedly in children. Not only the teeth and gums but the whole head and neck regions receive this radi-ation. In addition, children are more vulnerable to radiation than adults.

Diagnostic x-rays constitute only one source of radiation in medicine. Although increasing restrictions are being placed on the indiscriminate use of x-ray treatment, it has been used by uninformed physicians to treat ringworm, acne, arthritis, the common cold, enlarged thymus glands (rarely now, though it was once done to thousands of infants), deafness, menopause, and hyperthyroidism. Today the most common use of radiation is in the treatment of cancer.

Radiopharmaceuticals, that is, radioactive drugs, are another important source of radiation. A drug called [131]iodine, used in treating hyperthyroidism and cancer of the thyroid, has itself been found to be an important cause of cancer. Gofman estimates that as many as 25 percent of the people receiving this drug will get cancer from it.[10] His figures show that the average dose for hyperthyroidism results in 5 excess cancers per 100 among the group receiving that treatment at the age of 25. There are other effective forms of treatment for this disease that do not involve radiation.

A fourth source of radiation from medical procedures is the ingestion of radioactive material for diagnosing various organs and organ systems. These diagnostic measures, called *scans*, are used increasingly in the medical community. They produce radiation comparable to standard x-rays for the same diagnosis.

troversial findings should be given careful consideration.

In 1972 there were 188 nuclear reactors worldwide. Located in 19 countries they produced 80 GWs.† Their projected output for the year 2,000 is 2,000 GWs, or 25 times as much as now.

In 1980, in the United States alone, there were 72 nuclear reactors producing a total of 50 GWs. Gofman states that in spite of social protest and unfavorable publicity for the industry following the Three Mile Island accident, nuclear-power planners still look forward to having 1,000 nuclear installations producing a total of 1,000 GWs in the United States alone. However, escalating costs due to safety problems have slowed building and expansion since 1981.

Table 8.8: Organs affected by x-rays[a]

X-ray procedure	Organs at risk
Dental	Skin, thyroid gland, hypothalamus, lens of the eye
Chest	Lung, heart, thyroid, bone marrow
Mammography	Breast—important for people with high risk of breast cancer
Barium: upper gastrointestinal tract	Stomach, small intestine, pancreas, bone marrow
Barium: lower gastrointestinal tract	Large intestine, colon
Kidney (IVP)	Kidney
Pregnancy	Whole body of the fetus

[a]Adapted from UNSCEAR, p. 329.

Table 8.9: Organs affected in dental x-rays[a]

Organ	Upper jaw, molar, and premolar x-ray (average exposure in millirads for tube voltage of 60 kV)
Eye	118
Thyroid	3.5
Testes	.21
Ovary	.0007

[a]Adapted from UNSCEAR, p. 331.

Table 8.10: Doses to organs from medical scans[a]

Name of exam	Nuclide	Organ at risk	Dose (millirads)
Thyroid scan	[131]I (Iodine)	Thyroid	101,500
		Gonads	5
		Skeleton	10
Brain scan	[99m]Tc (Pertechnate)	Lower intestine	1,350
		Thyroid	6,000
		Gonads	200
		Skeleton	200
Liver scan	[131]I (Iodine)	Spleen	7,500
		Liver	296
		Gonads	45
		Skeleton	75
Thyroid function	[131]I (Iodine)	Thyroid	750
		Gonads	2.5
		Skeleton	2.5

[a]Adapted from UNSCEAR, p. 332.

The age of the person getting x-rays is important in estimating health risks. Young children are far more likely to be adversely affected than older people. For example, it takes only 64 rads of radiation to cause one excess cancer per 100,000 males when the person radiated is one year of age. It takes more than eight times as much (537 rads) to cause one excess cancer per 100,000 males radiated at 40 years of age. People who get cancer as a result of radiation at one year of age will lose an average of 22 years of life. By contrast, people radiated at 40 years of age will have their average life expectancy reduced by ten years.

Nuclear fuel and weaponry

The authorities disagree about long-term risks of radiation from the nuclear-power industry, but the industry is growing so rapidly, and the radioactive materials used or produced have such long lives*, that even the most con-

When assessing human health hazards from nuclear power, we need to assess several areas in addition to the power plants themselves. The production of nuclear power involves many steps: mining, milling, conversion of fissionable materials to fuel, fabrication of fuel elements into rods, trans-

*Radioactivity may last from a few moments to thousands of years, depending on the particular material in question.

†GW means Gigawatts: 1,000 megawatts, or one million watts.

portation of radioactive fuel, storage of fuel, reprocessing of radioactive waste (through breeder plants), packaging radioactive wastes that are not recyclable, transporting radioactive wastes, and disposing of these wastes. In nearly every step of this complex operation, at least some radioactivity leaks into the environment, even under the most ideal conditions.

Four groups of people are exposed to radiation in the nuclear industry:

(1) *workers,* people employed in any of the phases of the industry, from mining through the disposal of wastes;

(2) *local populations,* people living directly adjacent to uranium mines, processing plants, power plants, waste-handling installations, etc.;

(3) *regional populations,* people living

which provides the energy used by the industry. Even the most avid supporters of nuclear energy predict that certain amounts of these radioactive materials will leak into the environment at every step along the way. We know that radioactive material is released, how it is released, and the exact identity of each source. But because of the profoundly complex nature of the environment, there is currently no accurate way to measure or predict the long-term effects of leaked radioactive materials on the living Earth.

Let's take an example. While a reactor is operating, waste radioactive materials are released into the liquid coolants required by the power plant: the material leaks through microscopic defects in the alloy shroud that envelopes the radioactive fuel rods. Atoms identi-

Table 8.11: Populations affected by radioactivity leaked into environment by nuclear industry[a]

Process	People affected
Mining, milling, fuel fabrication	Workers
Reactor operation	Workers and local populations
Reprocessing	Workers Local and regional populations Global populations
Research and development	Workers

[a]Adapted from UNSCEAR, p. 14.

Table 8.12: Radionuclides released by reactors worldwide

In Air	
Ribium-88	Iron-59
Cesium-137	Strontium-89
Manganese-54	Strontium-90
Cobalt-58	Cesium-138
Cobalt-60	Chromium-51
Cesium-134	Barium-140

In Water	
Iodine-131	Cobalt-58
Iodine-132	Cobalt-60
Iodine-133	Chromium-51
Cesium-134	Manganese-54
Cesium-137	Antimony-124
Strontium-89	Ruthenium-103
Strontium-90	Silver-110
Nobium-95	Zirconium-95

Adapted from UNSCLEAR, p. 172

near but not directly next to nuclear facilities; and

(4) *global populations,* people living throughout the world who are exposed through the food chain, air, and water.

The reason these groups are considered separately is that radioactive materials, and their effects on humans, vary tremendously; a material that affects workers or local populations may have little if any effect on regional or global populations. Similarly, materials that have no immediate or direct effects on workers or local populations can be dispersed in the air or the waterways, eventually making their way into the human food chain to affect the global population.

In this complex industry there are hundreds of different kinds of radioactive materials, all products of decaying uranium or byproducts of the industry at any one of its several processing levels. The very nature of nuclear technology means that large numbers of people will be dealing with materials that are extremely unstable. They are working with materials whose atoms are continuously pulling apart, producing the ionizing radiation

fied as [137]cesium account for somewhere between 30 and 50 percent of the radioactivity in the effluent of the reactors. (Other radioactive materials are also found in the effluent; see Table 8.12.)

Effluents from the reactors are discharged into nearby bodies of water: rivers, lakes, oceans, etc. The [137]cesium ends up in drinking water, since the effluent makes its way through waterways into the water table of the Earth. Having entered the water table, the radioactive materials are later found in the irrigation systems used in the cultivation of grain crops. Grain crops fed to animals take up the radioactivity, which is then transferred to cows (and eventually to milk drunk by humans), beef cattle, pigs, sheep, etc. The food chain is affected by the effluent at all levels from fish and sealife to human water supplies, grain crops, and cattle.

The lifespan of radioactive materials poses a special problem. For example, [137]cesium is said to have a half-life* of 30.2 years. Atoms of [137]cesium are therefore active in the food chain for hundreds of years. And every day, from every nuclear reactor, immense quantities of new [137]cesium atoms are being released. Because of their extremely long life, the radioactive materials accumulate on an inverse pyramiding scale.

In defense of the nuclear industry, it is sometimes argued that nuclear-power plants produce only insignificant amounts of radioactivity, in fact, far less than the nuclear-weapons tests of the 1950s and 1960s produced. According to the UNSCEAR report, the statement is true, as far as it goes; all the nuclear-power plants now in existence worldwide produce only 1/50th of the global radiation produced by one year of those weapons tests. However,

---

Table 8.13: Estimated annual cancer deaths in United States according to degrees of containment of wastes in a nuclear-powered economy

Percent of containment	Cancer deaths from:	
	Cesium	Plutonium
99	1,560,000	6,630,000
99.99	15,600	66,300
99.9999	156	663

Adapted from Goffman, pp. 526, 551.

---

for a true picture, we must remember that radioactive materials have extremely long lives: the radioactivity produced by bomb testing is still with us, and whatever is produced by power plants must be added to that.

A scientific understanding of how radioactivity affects the human food chain grew out of studies of nuclear-weapons testing. It is known, for example, that during a bomb test tremendously high temperatures are generated; the soil is literally atomized, rising into the sky as an immense fireball. Hundreds of different kinds of radioactive atoms are released, just as they are in a nuclear reactor. In a bomb test, these radioactive materials rise and condense, becoming an aerosol that enters the troposphere and the stratosphere. Winds disperse the radioactive materials throughout the northern (or southern) hemisphere, until it eventually rains down onto the earth and the oceans. Like the [137]cesium we discussed earlier, the radioactive by-products of the bomb are

taken up by fish and other sealife, grain crops, and livestock, thus ending up in higher concentrations in foods consumed by humans.

Having once entered the human body, different types of radioactive materials tend to make their way to different organs. That is, each material tends to be organ-specific: [90]strontium goes to bone; [131]iodine goes to the thyroid gland; [137]cesium makes its way to muscle tissue.

The new nuclear-power technology includes plans for *breeder plants* that reprocess spent fuel and radioactive wastes on site. Among the materials produced by reprocessing is [239]plutonium, which has a half-life of 24,400 years. This material became famous during the early years of atomic weapons testing, when its global dispersion patterns were extensively studied. Humans and other animals inhale [239]plutonium. Although the cilia, the body's homeostatic mechanism for expelling foreign objects, can expel plutonium fairly quickly, it takes 500 days for the body to expel [239]plutonium from nonciliated tissue deep in the lungs themselves. Throughout the time [239]plutonium is in the lungs, it is radiating the tissue around it.

Gofman predicts that there will be 950,000 excess lung-cancer deaths throughout the world as a result of [239]plutonium fallout from weapons testing of 1963. These excess deaths are calculated for smokers, who are at much greater risk than nonsmokers because their cilia are crippled or destroyed. According to Gofman's figures, 152,000 male smokers will die for every 764 nonsmokers.[11] Because [239]plutonium will be produced by breeder reactors, we need to consider these projections carefully.

In 1980, Gofman stated that in the projected nuclear economy—1,000 nuclear-power plants with breeder plants—a million kilograms of [239]plutonium will be processed each year. By comparison, all the nuclear-weapons tests up to 1972 produced a total of only 328 kilograms of [239]plutonium. Gofman estimates that 663 excess lung cancers will be produced by every single kilogram of [239]plutonium released into the environment.[12]

The big question that needs to be asked is, how much of the million kilograms of [239]plutonium produced each year by the nuclear industry will leak into the environment? From an engineering standpoint, we might calculate that leakage will be minimal. However, technology is only one part of the picture; history shows that human error must be figured into the safety equation.

In 1969 there was a fire at the Rocky Flats plutonium plant, after which the authorities reported that less than one milligram of [239]plutonium had escaped into the environment. The figures looked good, and it appeared that the monitoring and containment system then

*Half-life is a term used to statistically calculate the lifespans of radioactive materials. The definition of this term isn't simple. Each atom of [90]Strontium has a half-life of 28.5 years. If you had a block of material containing 100 Strontium atoms, half of them would have decayed (producing radioactivity as they did so) after 28.5 years. Another 28.5 years later, half of that remaining block would be gone, leaving a smaller block which nevertheless would still have a half-life of 28.5 years. This process continues until there are no atoms remaining.

in operation was doing the job for which it was designed. In 1970 a follow-up study by the Colorado Committee for Environmental Information discovered that the previous figures were wrong; in fact, somewhere between a quarter and a half pound of ^{239}plutonium had escaped into the environment. In tracing the error, they discovered that the Rocky Flats plant's monitoring system had failed to detect leakage from storage barrels.

The military handles more radioactive material than any other single industry or institution. Since they have the latest and best technology at their disposal, we might expect the military to have a good record in handling ^{239}plutonium. In fact, they have never been able to account for more than 98 to 99 percent

these estimates, we begin to see how even the smallest errors in monitoring ^{239}plutonium can have drastic effects on human health.

The estimates of excess human deaths from lung cancer as a result of leakages of ^{239}plutonium, whether estimates are based on the industry's most optimistic figures or Gofman's more pessimistic ones, provide us with a broad scale for weighing benefits against risks in the future of nuclear power in this country. Other radioactive materials, such as ^{237}cesium, will be making their way into the environment, but the containment and accurate monitoring of ^{239}plutonium provides one of the clearest pictures we can have of the broad scope of the risks presented by nuclear power.

Table 8.14: How radioactive materials get into the food chain from nuclear reactors[a]

| Nuclide | Element | Half-life | Concentration in: | | Water | Part of body at risk |
			Fish	Shellfish		
^{3}H	Hydrogen	12.26 yrs	1	1	.0071	Total body
^{14}C	Carbon	5,730 days	1	1	.057	Total body
^{32}P	Potassium	14.3 days	10,000	10,000	.011	Bone
^{51}Cr	Chromium	27.7 days	100	1,000	.0012	Colon
^{60}Co	Cobalt	5.26 days	100	10,000	.37	Colon
^{65}Zn	Zinc	244 days	5,000	50,000	.029	Bone
^{90}Sr	Strontium	28.5 yrs	1	1	29	Bone
^{95}Zr	Zirconium	63 days	30	100	.0083	Colon
^{103}Ru	Rutheneum	41 days	3	100	.0046	Colon
^{110m}Ag	Silver	270 days	1,000	5,000	.41	Colon
^{125}Sb	Antimony	2.7 yrs	1,000	1,000	.37	Colon
^{129}I	Iodine	1.7×10^7 yrs	20	100	1,050	Thyroid
^{137}Cs	Cesium	30.2 yrs	30	50	.27	Total body
^{239}Pu	Plutonium	24,400 yrs	3	300	.25	Bone

[a]Adapted from UNSCEAR, pp. 120–150.

of the ^{239}plutonium in their care. That lost 1 to 2 percent can be significant for human health.

Spokespeople for the nuclear industry claim they can do much better than the armed forces, estimating 99.999 percent containment of ^{239}plutonium. Even granting these optimistic figures, Gofman believes there will be 6,630 lung-cancer deaths per year in the United States alone, if the nuclear industry fulfills the plans for the future. These deaths will be the result of only the ^{239}plutonium leakage. Judging from history, Gofman believes that the industry will be able to contain only 99.0 percent of the ^{239}plutonium they handle; with this level of containment, there will be about 6,630,000 lung-cancer deaths per year (see Table 8.15). That is, for every decimal place in the percentage of containment, deaths go up by a factor of ten.[13] Given

What You Can Do

The most immediate way you can reduce ionizing radiation in your life is to limit your exposure to x-rays and other radioactive materials that may be prescribed for either diagnosis or treatment by the medical community.

(1) Avoid all so-called "precautionary" x-rays, that is, x-rays prescribed for annual routine checkups. This means turning down *routine* chest x-rays, barium x-rays of the lower gastrointestinal tract, routine dental x-rays (especially full mouth), and mammography (particularly women under 50 years of age). Refusing these diagnosis procedures need not, in any way, be a sacrifice. Alternatives to x-rays for these tests include the following: TB-skin test in place of chest x-rays; manual examination, with sigmoidoscopic exam, by a

physician, to replace barium x-rays; breast self-exam by women to replace mammography (the National Cancer Institute recommends mammography only for women under 50 who already have a history of breast cancer or a strong family history of this disease); and manual dental exam in the place of annual dental x-rays. (The American Dental Association recommends full-mouth x-rays no more than once every 3 to 5 years. Many dentists recommend full-mouth x-rays only every 6 to 10 years.)

(2) Except for medical emergencies, women should refuse to be x-rayed during pregnancy.

(3) Women of childbearing age should avoid x-rays except during the ten days following the onset of each monthly menstrual period. In this way, x-rays will not be given during ovulation or during the period of potential fertilization.

(4) Avoid x-rays for young children. The younger the child, the more susceptible he or she is to radiation of this kind. Agree to x-rays only if you are convinced that there is solid medical evidence that the risk of x-raying is outweighed by the potential benefits.

(5) Whenever a physician recommends high-radiation x-rays for you or a member of your family, insist that he or she sit down with you and discuss, to your *complete* satisfaction, the risk of the x-rays versus the risk of what would happen if you didn't get the x-ray. If you fail to get a satisfactory response, do not feel badly about refusing the x-ray and seeking out a new doctor. (Although you can roughly calculate cancer risks of x-rays from Table 8.8, only you and your physician can weigh risks against benefits for your particular case.)

(6) Whenever you have x-rays done, understand that you have a right to transfer them to other physicians if you change doctors. Most physicians cooperate gladly in forwarding your diagnostic tests to other physicians, and as increasing information is made available on the health hazards of x-rays, more and more doctors are making the forwarding of diagnostic information a matter of policy. (The forwarding of x-rays is especially important in insurance cases, where the defense may want a separate set of x-rays from those ordered by the prosecution. However, the practice of providing two sets of x-rays should definitely be discouraged.)

(7) Avoid x-rays ordered to protect doctors from malpractice suits. Ask your physician frankly if the diagnostic procedures he or she has ordered have a solid medical purpose. Most physicians are well aware of this issue, and will discuss it openly with the patient.

(8) Any time you must get x-rays, make certain the radiologist uses a lead shield, usually a lead apron, to protect your gonads. This is as important in dental x-rays as elsewhere. If the radiologist fails to provide you with such a shield, be assertive about refusing the x-ray.

(9) If at all possible, choose a radiologist with the very latest, newest equipment to do any necessary x-rays for you. Ask if the laboratory is using fast films with low exposure levels, image intensifiers, automatic photo exposure controls, pulsed fluoroscopy, and careful, accurate monitoring of the output of every machine.

(10) Refuse treatment from chiropractors who recommend full-body x-rays.

Radioactive Consumer Products

Consumer products may contain radioactive materials, and even though the ionizing radiation from these items is extremely low, you may wish to choose alternative products that don't radiate. When choosing such items, consider not only the radiation of the single item you may be purchasing, but the cumulative effects of other items like it, both in your home and in the environment outside:

(1) "Luminous" dials and other products that glow in the dark: clocks, wristwatches, instrument panels on automobiles, chemical flashlights, luminous switchplates, etc.

(2) Smoke detectors equipped with radioactive cells. Note that detectors are available that use the photoelectric cells, which don't contain radioactive material. (Nonradioactive smoke detectors will be so noted on the box.)

(3) Eyeglasses. You can have prescriptions filled using new plastic lenses which are lighter than glass and optically equal.

(4) Natural gas. If you cook or heat with natural gas, a certain amount of radon gas will be released into your home. To minimize radiation from this source, ventilate the area, providing a good source of fresh air.

(5) Concrete, stone, and earthen buildings: ventilation of such buildings, along with a constant flowthrough of fresh air, reduces the effects of radon.

(6) High-altitude professions: people who fly frequently, as either passengers or crew members, will be getting slightly higher radiation than people who don't fly. If you find yourself in these groups, take special care to minimize x-rays, radiating consumer products, etc.

Nuclear-Power Industry

In terms of the nuclear-power industry, increasing numbers of people concerned about radioactive health hazards are faced with deciding whether or not to continue living near or working in nuclear-power plants.

People who are working in the nuclear industry, and who are concerned about the

There is a definite amount of leakage measurable from the effluents of all nuclear power stations. (*Arc, Nuc. One,* 1982, by Michael Samuels.)

health hazards, should not depend entirely on safety information distributed by the industry itself. In addition to anything they might learn through these channels, they should also study research prepared by government and private sources who do not have a vested interest in keeping people on the job. (Examples of such research are cited in *Further Reading* below.)

Radiologists and other people working in occupations where radiation badges are required will know how much radiation their bodies are receiving each year, and can roughly calculate their risks of cancer from Table 8.4. Objective choices about changing occupations, or reducing radiation levels on the job by the purchase of new equipment or adjustment of old, can be based on such calculations.

Furthermore, change can be brought about by political action, which is often the only way to bring attention to the construction of nuclear-power plants, weapons testing, or the overuse of x-rays in medicine. Since we are faced with environmental risks of radiation from these and other sources, political action can be the most direct and important *preventive medicine* we have.

Further Reading

1. United Nations Scientific Committee on the Effects of Atomic Radiation (UNSCEAR). *Sources and Effects of Ionizing Radiation:* 1977 Report to the General Assembly, with Annexes. United Nations, 1977.

A 725-page book filled with charts and text explaining levels of radiation, where it is, how it gets there, and its effects on human health. An excellent introductory resource, accessible to the layperson. However, we think the cancer rates predicted seem extremely low, compared with other information, and may well be inaccurate.

2. Advisory Committee on the Biological Effects of Ionizing Radiation (BEIR), Division of Medical Sciences, National Academy of Sciences. *The Effects on Populations of Exposure to Low Levels of Ionizing Radiation.* National Research Council, Washington, D.C.

A more technical report than UNSCEAR, but with excellent descriptions of cancer causation. Probably underestimates the effects of doses. Authorities writing reports herein present opposing views and opinions on dosages.

3. John W. Gofman. *Radiation and Human Health.* Sierra Club Books, 1981.

A superb, painstaking analysis of the sources of radiation and their effects on health, with complete charts that allow the serious layperson to calculate risks and radiation levels from a wide variety of sources. The figures he cites for excess cancer deaths in relation to radiation are higher than others, but Gofman backs up all his conclusions with excellent data. This is very important reading for the serious student of this subject and for people working in the nuclear industry.

Sunlight

What It Is

Most of the natural radiation we receive on Earth comes from the Sun. The Sun burns 564 million tons of hydrogen, transforming it into 560 million tons of helium, each second. The four million tons of matter lost in this transformation are converted into radiation; that is, four million tons of atoms are pulled apart to create the energy of radiation. This energy of radiation comes to us as 60 percent infrared (heat), 37 percent visible light, and 3 percent ultraviolet (nonvisible) light. Ultraviolet radiation is second only to gamma rays in intensity (see Table 8.1). Ultraviolet radiation produced by the Sun is the most important health factor related to sunlight. Physicists divide ultraviolet into three classifications: UV-A is the lowest-energy form of ultraviolet, with a wavelength close to visible light, and is the least threat to health; UV-B has more energy than UV-A, has a shorter wavelength, and significantly affects human health by causing sunburn, aging the skin prematurely, and causing skin cancer; UV-C puts out the highest energy, and its wavelengths even overlap into the spectrum of x-rays. If UV-C were to reach the Earth in large amounts, it would destroy almost all life on the planet. It is prevented from doing this by the ozone layer (ozone is produced when oxygen is split by UV-C), a factor that becomes extremely important when we consider the effects of certain artificial chemicals that threaten the ozone layer (see "Air Pollution," page 170).

In a normal, balanced state, UV-A and UV-B are our main concerns in human health.

How It Causes Disease

Being a lower-energy form of radiation than gamma rays, UV-A and UV-B cause damage on skin surfaces, including the cells on the outer layers of the eyes. Ultraviolet radiation can transform the DNA of skin cells, either altering the normal functions of the cells or killing them, but its effects do not extend deeper into the body.

Sunburn is brought about not by the heat of the Sun, but by its radiation, largely in the form of UV-B. The UV-B rays break chemical bonds in the DNA of outer skin cells, killing them or injuring them badly. The symptoms characteristic of sunburn are actually the body's normal response to any damage from trauma or infection. The body releases fluids into the injured area, sends white blood cells to clean away cellular debris, and increases blood flow, bringing nutrients for creating new cells. This multifaceted healing process is what causes the pain, redness, heat, and swelling associated with sunburn. The redness phase of sunburn begins in from 4 to 14 hours after initial exposure, peaking in from 10 to 24 hours. Severity depends on degree of exposure. Skiers, people who live in snow-covered regions, and (to a lesser degree) fishermen and others who work long hours on the water may suffer from another form of sunburn, which affects the eyes. The most common term for this is *snow blindness,* and it is caused by ultraviolet rays reflected from the snow or water surface. Cells in the cornea of the eyes are damaged or killed by excess exposure to ultraviolet radiation.* The cornea then becomes opaque, making the person partially blind. The dead cells slough off, and while this process is occurring the eyes can be extremely painful. In time the cornea regenerates, and the person's sight is restored, the total process from first exposure to complete healing being from two days to a week.

With more prolonged exposures to ultraviolet radiation from both natural and artificial sources, there is an increased risk of cataracts, that is, permanent damage to the lens of the eye. This is a special consideration for people living in the equatorial latitudes and for those using ultraviolet radiation commercially.

Tanning, the natural process by which the skin creates its own filter against ultraviolet radiation, is triggered by the radiation of sunlight itself. Special cells in the skin, called melanocytes, synthesize the pigment melanin when exposed to ultraviolet radiation. The pigment produced is taken up by normal skin cells, which, once "dyed" in this way, are protected from damage by ultraviolet rays. A suntan reduces the amount of ultraviolet radiation coming through the skin by as much as 90 percent. Tanning begins approximately ten hours following exposure, and reaches its peak after approximately ten days of exposure.

Even though tanning protects the skin from burning, it cannot protect it from "premature aging" caused by radiation from the Sun. Continuous exposure to ultraviolet rays for many years actually causes the skin to thin, so that it appears profoundly wrinkled and creased. Elastic tissues in lower skin layers are damaged, causing the skin to sag. Sweat and oil glands are damaged, so that the skin looks leathery and dry. Blood vessels are damaged, becoming dilated, so that the skin looks permanently pink. Melanocytes are damaged, so that the pigmentation process is no longer possible, and the skin appears blotchy and white.

Common skin cancer, called *basal cell carcinoma,* occurs when ultraviolet radiation

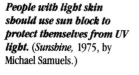

People with light skin should use sun block to protect themselves from UV light. (*Sunshine,* 1975, by Michael Samuels.)

*At high elevations skiers without adequate eye protection can suffer snow blindness in three to four hours.

Table 8.15: Skin protection factors of suntanning creams and lotions

Skin protection factor	Degree of protection
15 or greater	No suntanning or burning
8-15	Little or no suntanning
4-6	Limited suntanning
2-4	Little protection, deep suntanning, possible sun burn hazard for fair to medium skin

Adapted from Parish, p. 244.

damages the basal cells of the skin. Basal cells are skin cells in the lower part of the outer skin layer. Sometimes when radiation alters the DNA of these cells, new cells reproduced from them fail to mature. These defective cells grow as a lump, and although they are malignant, they generally don't metastasize or spread. The cure rate is extremely high with early treatment.

Our bodies have a miraculous ability to repair DNA damaged by radiation from the Sun. Each cell can actually rebuild damaged areas of DNA, or excise the damaged area and create a new part to replace it. Without this

Table 8.16: How UV-B affects human skin.[a]

Symptoms

Minimal dose	Medium dose	Exposure over years
Temporary reddening or tanning	Deep coloration, blistering, sunburn pain	Permanently pinkish skin, spotty tanned areas surrounded by pale areas Loose skin with leathery and dry surfaces Deep wrinkles or creases Thinning of skin

Physiological changes

Injury to skin cells, temporary enlargement of blood vessels	Numerous cells killed, blistering, peeling of dead skin layers, stimulation of melanocytes, and tanning, stimulation of cell division, causing thickening of skin	Destruction of some cells and organelles, damage to blood vessels, melanocytes killed, altered sweat glands in skin

[a]Adapted from Giese, p. 88.

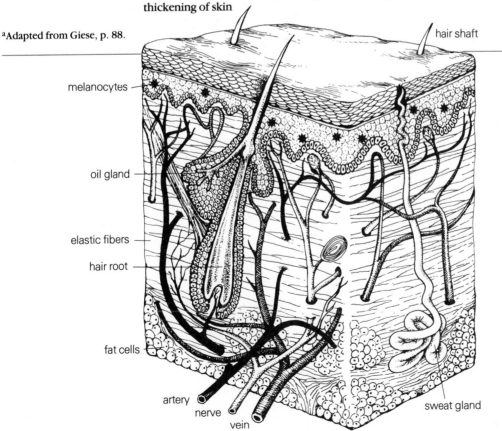

melanocytes

oil gland

elastic fibers

hair root

fat cells

artery

nerve

vein

hair shaft

sweat gland

This drawing shows the structures of the skin which are damaged by ultraviolet rays: sweat and oil glands, elastic tissues, blood vessels, and melanocytes.

inner healing ability, all animals would have extremely high rates of death from skin cancer.

Basal skin carcinomas are distinctively different from malignant melanomas. The latter are the offspring of melanocytes whose DNA has been altered by ultraviolet radiation from the Sun. Melanomas metastasize and can grow in other sites throughout the body. Although melanoma is a dangerous form of skin cancer, it is extremely rare, making up less than 10 percent of all skin tumors.

Evidence of Its Danger

Physicians have long observed that skin cancers occur most frequently in the areas of the body that have the greatest exposure to sunlight: head, neck and arms. Moreover, it is more common near the equator and among populations who spent much time in the Sun. Out of 840 skin tumors studied, 91 percent were located on the head and neck. Most of these were found on or near the nose, and the fewest tumors were found on people's abdomens and buttocks. In people compared by occupations, the highest incidence of skin cancer was found among sailors, farmers, and outdoor constructions workers, the lowest incidence among office workers, store clerks, and others who work inside. In the United States, people in southern latitudes, with the highest exposure to the Sun, have significantly higher incidents of skin cancer than people living in northern latitudes. For example, skin cancer in the Dallas-Fort Worth area, at a latitude of 32.8 degrees, is 2.5 times more common than in the Minneapolis-St. Paul area, at 44.9 degrees latitude.

For one type of skin cancer, the incidence doubles with each eight to eleven degrees toward the equator. Light-skinned people are, of course, much more susceptible to skin cancer than people with dark skins. In animal studies, sunlight has been shown to cause skin cancer in albino rats and in hairless skin areas of albino mice. The amount of skin cancer is proportional to the intensity and duration of exposure to the Sun.

Extent of the Risk

According to the National Cancer Institute's epidemiological figures for 1979, there were 300,000 cases of all kinds of skin cancer in the U.S. as a result of overexposure to the Sun. These resulted in 7,500 deaths. The incidence for nonmelanoma skin cancers in the U.S. is 165 per 100,000 people. This amounted to one-third to one-half of all kinds of cancer.

There are four skin types, each with a slightly different vulnerability to the Sun.

(1) *Light skin.* People who have very light skin, who burn in 10 to 15 minutes when exposed to the Sun, and who can't tan. Ireland, which is located in a northern latitude, has the world's third highest rate of skin-cancer deaths, presumably because the Irish are a light-skinned people.

(2) *Fair skin.* People who have moderately light skin, but who usually get sunburned and rarely get a tan.

(3) *Medium fair skin.* People who usually tan and who rarely burn.

(4) *Dark skin.* People of Hawaiian, African, Mexican and Mediterranean descent, who rarely if ever burn.

Ultimately, the danger of getting cancer depends on at least three factors: skin type, geographic location, and the amount of time spent in the Sun.

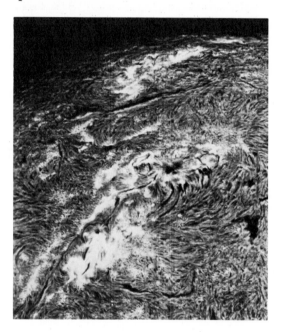

Because of the high incidence of skin cancer among people living in the British Isles, some medical researchers use a scale called *Celticity* to measure a person's natural susceptibility to skin cancer. Those with the greatest number of Celtic grandparents are presumed to be the most vulnerable to skin cancer. Similarly, people who stay red two to three weeks after a single moderate exposure to the Sun have a higher risk of skin cancer.

Multiple factors contribute to skin cancer. Heat, wind, humidity, and chemicals increase the health risk as they are added to ultraviolet radiation. Human skin becomes increasingly photosensitized (sensitive to ultraviolet rays) when exposed to smog, industrial chemicals, and certain medicines.

Scientists predict there would be a 2 percent increase in skin cancer for each 1 percent decrease in the ozone layer. A 5 percent decrease in the ozone layer would result in a 20 percent increase in skin cancer, with unknown

According to the National Cancer Institute, there are 300,000 cases of skin cancer per year as a result of overexposure to the sun. (Sun-Spectroheliogram in red light of hydrogen. Hale Observatories.)

damage to other forms of life on Earth. There is already speculation that shrimp and crab larvae are being killed by reductions of ozone that allow increased exposure to ultraviolet radiation in the oceans. For these reasons it is important to avoid the use of chloroflourocarbons that threaten to reduce the ozone layer. Chlorofluorocarbons (CFCs) are a class of chemicals used as refrigerants, aerosol propellants, and blowing agents for foam. Studies by the National Academy of Sciences "confirm earlier reports that continued release of CFCs will significantly decrease the Earth's protective layer of ozone."[14] If CFCs continue to be released at 1977 rates, the ozone layer will deplete 8 percent by the year 2030.

Atomic weapons are undoubtedly the most dramatic threat to the ozone layer of our planet.

Substances that increase sensitivity to the sun's rays[a]

Industrial effluents, smog
riboflavin (B vitamin)
diethyl stilbestrol (female hormone)
a variety of antibiotics
quinine
chlorothiazide (a diuretic)
barbiturates
some antibacterials in soaps, detergents, and cosmetics
dyes in some lipsticks and makeup
psoralens in perfumes
various coal-tar products (pyridine, acridine)

[a]Adapted from Giese, p. 122.

If half the bombs now stockpiled by the U.S. and Russia were detonated, it would destroy somewhere between 50 and 75 percent of the ozone layer. The resulting destruction would be as vast as that caused directly by the atomic explosions themselves.

Where It Is Found

Although the Sun is the main source of ultraviolet radiation on Earth, the amount getting through to the earth varies greatly with time of day, season, and latitude. Radiation is highest when the Sun is directly overhead (when the distance from Earth to Sun is shortest), and diminishes as the Sun's angle becomes more acute.

Ultraviolet radiation can also be artificial. It is found in special lighting fixtures, such as mercury discharge, quartz, xenon arc, and fluorescent lights, and in lasers used in medicine, research, and industry. Artificial ultraviolet light has recently come into popular use in "tanning parlors."

Ultraviolet technology is rapidly changing, and although there are government standards established for its commercial use, not everyone subjected to this form of radiation is aware of its health hazards. Anyone subjected to "special light rays" used in medicine, industry, or tanning should be aware of the health hazards of ultraviolet light, and investigate the amounts of this radiation they might be receiving.

What You Can Do

On a day-to-day basis, you can lower the risk of disease from ultraviolet radiation by understanding the multiple disease factors contributing to skin cancer and taking precautions accordingly. For example, estimate your particular risks: skin type, geographic location, and degree of exposure. Also, consider chemicals in the air, any medication you are taking that could cause you to be photosensitive, and the weather (heat, wind, and humidity). Ultraviolet radiation (UV-B) is greatest from 10 A.M. to 3 P.M.

Do not depend on cloud cover, cool temperatures, or the water when you are swimming to protect you from UV-B. About 80 percent of the ultraviolet radiation still penetrates. Ultraviolet rays reflected from sand, snow, or other surfaces can be as intense as direct rays from the Sun; so don't depend wholly on hats, umbrellas, or overhanging roofs to protect you.

Sunscreens, that is, lotions and creams that contain chemicals to absorb ultraviolet rays, are recommended by most dermatologists to protect the skin of people working or playing in the Sun. Many dermatologists recommend that people, especially if light-skinned, should avoid the Sun entirely between the hours of 10 A.M. and 3 P.M., even with a sunscreen, if at all possible.

Sunscreens are rated by the FDA on a numerical scale: the higher the number, the greater the sun protection factor.
Most of the sunscreens commercially available contain PABA (para-amino-benzoic acid), which extends tenfold the time you can be exposed to the sun without reddening. This chemical actually binds with the oils in the top layers of the skin; so it must be applied 30 to 45 minutes before Sun exposure, to allow the chemical reaction to take place. Sweating and swimming tend to remove the PABA; so it needs to be reapplied every few hours.

Other sunscreens, such as zinc oxide, titanium oxide, clay, chalk, or pigments in clay or mud don't bind with the natural oils of the skin, but do their work by scattering or reflecting ultraviolet rays before they can penetrate the skin.

People who spend a lot of time in the Sun, especially around snow, water, or highly reflective earth surfaces, should take special care to wear eyeglasses designed to give maximum protection. Eye protection is similarly important for people using tanning lights, or receiving or administering ultraviolet treatments for medical reasons. Arc welders and glass blowers working with quartz need special eye protection to prevent temporary blindness, cataracts, and other eye damage from UV-B light.

If eye protection is important to you because of your occupation or recreational preferences, make certain you get sunglasses that actually filter out ultraviolet light. Just because they block visible light, don't assume they block ultraviolet radiation. Sometimes only the manufacturer can supply this information.

In terms of long-range protection of the ozone layer, avoid purchasing or using chemicals that affect this important part of the living earth. Support political action groups seeking to end the use of nuclear weapons, and to protect the atmosphere against chemical pollutants and other human actions that threaten the ozone layer.

Further Reading

ARTHUR GIESE. *Living With the Sun's Ultraviolet Rays.* Plenum Press, 1976.

A readable book for the layperson on all aspects of the Sun's effects on human health. Although technical, the information it contains is quite accessible to the average reader.

CHARLES PANATI AND MICHAEL HUDSON. *The Silent Intruder: Surviving the Radiation Age.* Houghton Miflin, 1981.

Using a question and answer form, the authors alert people to the health hazards of all types of radiation: x-rays, sunlight, microwaves, nuclear, etc.

Microwave Radiation

What It Is

Microwaves are near the low end of the radiation spectrum in the energy they put out, and are less energetic than visible light (see Table 8.1). Although microwaves do exist in the natural world, artificial devices such as radar, radiocommunication systems, television transmitters, and microwave ovens are the main sources that affect human health. Such sources can produce large amounts of microwaves.

We might postulate that microwaves enable chemicals to cross the barrier and enter brain tissue, with unknown effects on human health. (Suburban Cable TV Tower, 1982, by Michael Samuels.)

How It Causes Disease

Microwaves are absorbed by the body, but whereas the energy of ionizing radiation can actually knock particles off atoms, the lower energy of microwaves simply starts the molecules vibrating. The vibration can cause symptoms ranging from emotional stress to actual burning of tissue. Microwaves affect different organs in different ways; the more dense or solid the tissue, the less it is affected. Interestingly enough, the tissue with the highest water content is the most susceptible to microwaves. Surrounded by water, molecules have room to vibrate or shake, causing friction and heat.

Animals are affected by high doses of microwaves in the same way they are affected by any heat source. That is, microwaves beamed in on their bodies can cause temperature increases past the limits of their homeostatic abilities. This is known as the "thermal effect" of microwaves.

Researchers in recent years have become increasingly interested in nonthermal effects of microwaves. It has been demonstrated that even when temperatures are not measurably raised, cell structures and functions can be significantly altered. Functions such as mitosis (cell division) and permeability of cell membranes can be disrupted.

Evidence of Its Danger

Research on the health hazards of microwaves comes from two sources: studies of humans injured by microwaves in their occupations, and experiments with animals being deliberately radiated. Most of the microwave research has been done in Russia, and the studies available to scientists in the U.S. have been the source of considerable controversy.

Russian researchers have studied thousands of people, since 1948, who have been subjected to microwave radiation in their jobs. The "microwave syndrome," as they define it, includes a long list of subjective complaints: headaches, fatigue, irritability, sleep disturbances, weakness, a higher incidence of viral infections, and general feelings of malaise. The medical symptoms included slow heart rates, changed EEGs, and increased thyroid functions. All these are symptoms ordinarily associated with stress; so we may suspect that microwaves can create stress just as overwork, worry, and conflict can.

An American research ophthalmologist at New York University School of Medicine, Milton Zaret, discovered a definite increase in cataracts among people working in industries where microwaves were used. Another American researcher, Alan Frey, a biophysicist, discovered that people can "hear" microwaves. What is fascinating about this is that they "heard" the microwaves not through their ears, but directly in the auditory centers of their brains, which were being vibrated. The implications of this study are vast. Frey found that just as the brain could be vibrated by microwaves to stimulate the auditory center, so microwaves could also stimulate the hypothalamus, the center that controls the so-called autonomic functions of the human body. Moreover, Frey found that microwaves change the permeability of the blood-brain barrier which normally prevents certain chemicals from entering the brain from the bloodstream. Frey was able to alter the permeability of this barrier in animals by subjecting them to microwaves. From these experiments, we might suspect that microwaves can allow chemicals, both natural and artificial (such as food

research should be done in this area.

Extent of the Threat

Present government safety standards for microwave devices in the United States are based on theoretical research by H. Schwan done in 1953. Looking only at temperature increases in living tissue caused by microwaves, he advised the government that at ten milliwatts per square centimeter (10 mW/cm^2) there was no temperature rise. This essentially means that living tissue is not in danger of burning at these levels. The same researcher showed that, at an exposure level of 50 to 100 milliwatts per square centimeter, bone marrow can be damaged and cataracts can be formed. This is interpreted by much of the in-

Table 8.17: How microwaves affect people[a]

System level	Primary effects	End results
Molecular	Heating, rotates water molecules in the body	Temperature rise, biochemical reactions, alterations of DNA, mitochondria, cell membranes.
Cellular	Interfaces with membranes	Mitosis disturbances, possibly causing carcinogenicity.
Organs	Heat	Specific organ or area of the body damaged. Cardiovascular, nervous, endocrine system are the areas most often affected.
Whole body	Disturbs electromagnetic wave transmissions throughout the body	Stress, disadaptations, interference with biorhythms.

[a]Adapted from Baranski, p. 77

Table 8.18: Human symptoms from microwave exposure[a]

Percentage of exposed workers who report:

	Headaches	Fatigue	Sleep disturbances	Irritability	Abnormal sweating
(1)	58	53	47	—	—
(2)	37	31	29	9	7
(3)	42	3	44	9	0

[a]Adapted from Baranski, p. 159, reporting on studies by (1) Klimkova (1963), (2) Uspenskuja (1963), and (3) Serel (1959).

preservatives), to cross the barrier and enter brain tissue, with unknown effects on human health.

There is some concern that microwaves may cause birth defects. Although the studies on humans are inconclusive, mutations have definitely been observed in fruit flies subjected to microwaves. Similarly, research has shown that the chromosomes of human cells outside the body can be damaged by microwaves; so we can't overlook the possibility that microwaves may cause not only birth defects but human cancers. Although the current evidence is inconclusive, it clearly suggests that more

dustry, as well as the Army and Navy in their radar and radiocommunications programs, to mean that 10 milliwatts of exposure is completely safe, and exposures up to 100 milliwatts are safe for short periods.

Bell Telephone Laboratories have established tighter safety standards than the U.S. government, based on animal studies of real temperature increases caused by microwave exposure. They say that *any* microwave exposure above 10 milliwatts is dangerous and should never be allowed. They recommend only "incidental exposure" of from 1 to 10 milliwatts, and that regular exposure should not exceed one milliwatt.

Whereas safety regulations in the United States are based only on the thermal effects of microwaves, regulations of microwave exposure in some other countries are based on behavior changes observed in both animal and human studies. For example, in Russia, researchers have shown that animal behavior is affected after microwave exposure of one milliwatt per centimeter of tissue for one hour. From this they have derived the following safety guidelines, which are strictly enforced.

(1) Exposure of one milliwatt should be allowed for no more than one minute, and then only with goggles to protect the eyes.

(2) Exposure of .1 milliwatt is allowed for no more than two hours of any working day.

(3) For an entire working day (10 hours), a

wave technology by the general public, including television/radio-communication, microwave ovens, CB radios, electronic "frisking" systems in stores, radar in boats, police radar, two-way radios in taxis and police cars, as well as numerous technical devices in medicine and industry.

The most popular source of microwave radiation in the home is the microwave oven. Present government safety standards require that there be no more than 1 mW/cm² at 5 cm from the door, at the time the oven is sold. During use, up to 5 mW/cm² at 5 cm from the device is allowed. Since the radiation levels drop at distances more than 5 cm from the device, the exposures within the room where such a device is operating are probably within the Russian guidelines for exposure to the gen-

Table 8.19: Sources of microwaves[a]

Source	People affected	Power levels
Radar installations*	Workers and nearby residents	High
Missile guidance facilities	Workers and nearby residents	High
Radio and television transmitters*	Workers and nearby residents	High
Cable tv transmitters*	Workers and nearby residents	High
Microwave devices in food industry	Workers	High
Radionavigation equipment	Workers and others aboard ship or airplanes	Med
CB and other two-way communication systems in cars, trucks, etc.	Operators and passengers in vehicles so equipped	Med
Microwave ovens for home use	Housewives and children	Med to Low

[a]Adapted from Baranski, p. 16.

*Radar, television and radio transmitters may be operated at either high or low levels. Their effects on human populations will vary accordingly.

person should receive no more than 0.1 mW/cm².

(4) Exposure to the general public should never exceed .001 mW/cm².

In spite of differences of opinion on safe exposure levels, there was an international conference in 1973 ("The Biologic Effects and Health Hazards of Microwave Radiation," held in Warsaw) at which the Russians and Americans agreed to the following:

(1) Above 10 mW/cm² there are definite thermal effects on living tissue.

(2) Below 1 mW/cm² there are unlikely to be thermal effects.

(3) Between 1 and 10 mW/cm² there are both thermal and nonthermal effects, which are as yet unclarified.

Where It Is Found

There is a rapidly increasing use of microwave technology by the general public, includ-

eral public.

The highest levels of regular exposure to microwaves, other than in industry or medicine, are in large buildings where microwaves are being used for radiocommunications and in neighborhoods located near microwave broadcast facilities. EPA-measured levels in a sampling of these facilities—including such buildings as the Sears Tower in Chicago, and the Pan Am Building and World Trade Center in New York—place microwave exposure from .01 to .03 mW/cm².

Exposure to microwaves from handheld walkie-talkies and CB radios can be as high as 10 mW/cm² at 5 inches from the device. There are future plans for inexpensive microwave telephones for cars, large radar-landing systems at airports, and, most dramatically, solar collectors in space that will beam energy down to the Earth as microwaves. Although no one has predicted how much more microwave radiation these new technologies will produce, their development will clearly mean a slow global increase of background radiation of this kind.

What You Can Do

If you are working in an industry where microwaves are used—radar, telecommunications, electronic sealing, medical applications—check out the levels of radiation to which you are exposed. How you can do so will depend on your particular situation. Some industries have instruments for monitoring microwave exposure levels; some do not. If these instruments are not available, you may have to write to the manufacturers of the microwave device you're using and ask them for figures. You may find that the labor union to which you belong can provide data that will help you evaluate the radiation levels to which you are exposed. Your findings can then be checked against the safety standards we have given.

In other countries such as Russia and Poland, multiple disease factors are seriously considered for people working in microwave industries. For example, people with any neurological disease, any blood disease, cancer, or ulcers are considered to be at greater risk than people without such health problems, and they are not allowed to work around microwaves.

If you are working in a microwave industry, and you are suffering any of the symptoms of the "microwave syndrome," defined by the Russians, you should be aware that these symptoms may be job-related. Protective goggles and shielded clothing are recommended in many industrial situations where microwaves are used. If these are recommended in the industry where you are employed, don't underestimate their importance to your health.

If you live near a large radar installation, radio or TV station, or satellite communications antenna, or in higher floors of large city buildings with transmitting towers, check on microwave levels in the general environment. Such facilities must keep records and, depending on the facility, may be required to monitor the levels of radiation daily.

Consumer products, such as microwave ovens, CB radios, car telephones, and hand-held walkie-talkies, have varying levels of radiation. The major consideration with all of these is careful maintenance. When working improperly, they can give off extremely high levels of microwave radiation. CB radios, car telephones, and walkie-talkies, although they can give off high levels, do so only in brief spurts. These have not been shown to present health hazards.

Community problems, such as radiation from large radar installations near residential areas or the installation of radar reflectors for beaming energy from outer space, need to be approached on a political basis.

Further Reading

STANISLAW BARANSKI. *Biological Effects of Microwaves.* Dowden, Hutchinson, and Ross, 1976.

A technical summary of microwaves, including microwave research from other countries. Supports the view that microwaves at low doses have multiple biological effects.

Electromagnetic Fields (ELF Waves)

What It Is

Electromagnetic radiation is produced by high-tension power lines, and is the lowest-energy wave in the radiation spectrum (see Table 8.1), but it can be dangerous because so much radiation is produced.

How It Causes Disease

Being of low energy and long wavelength, electromagnetic radiation cannot do the damage that ionizing radiation can. Whereas an x-ray can knock an electron off course, thus destroying the integrity of an atom, and microwaves can set up a vibration that disrupts molecules in living tissue, the effects of longwave electromagnetic radiation are more subtle. All living tissue has an intimate relationship with natural electromagnetic fields around the Earth, and biologists speculate that these fields made possible the evolution of amino acids by helping to align the molecules in space. Similarly, living cells produce detectable electrical fields that medical instruments can measure to diagnose diseases of the nervous system (EEG), the heart (EKG), and the muscles (EMG). Each cell has its own electromagnetic force field, which is an integral part of its functions, including its ability to communicate with other cells. Consider, too, that electromagnetic fields of the Earth have frequencies in the range of 1 to 30 cycles per second. That of the human heart muscle is 60 cycles per second. Artificial electromagnetic fields fall within these ranges, and there is scientific speculation that because artificial electromagnetic fields are so close to the natural ones, they may have a disorienting effect on living things. This disorientation may be a form of stress. Remember, life evolved in an environment that included a certain level of electromagnetic radiation, and is homeostatically equipped to live in harmony with it. Migrating animals are known to depend on the Earth's natural electromagnetic fields. For example, migratory fowl become disoriented when these fields are disrupted along migration routes. But when much new electromagnetic radiation is introduced, as it has been in the twentieth century, homeostatic capacities are pressed to the limit. In addition, studies have shown that electromagnetic fields change the permeability of cells and alter the flow of calcium across cell membranes, perhaps because electromagnetic fields influence the alignment of molecules that make up the structure of the cell membrane.[15]

Evidence of Its Danger

There are well-documented studies of the effects of electromagnetic radiation at all

mice living in an electromagnetic field had lower resistance to infection and less white-blood-cell activity than the mice in a normal setting.[17]

• Experimenters broke small bones in the legs of rats, choosing a bone that would not affect the rats' normal activity. The rats living in electromagnetic fields healed poorly compared to rats living in control environments.[18]

• Learning responses were slowed in both humans and monkeys placed in electromagnetic fields.[19]

As a result of scientific research on the effects of electromagnetic radiation, most European countries have strict guidelines for people working in or living near electrical fields. In the United States there are no guidelines, in part because American scientists feel the scien-

There is scientific speculation that, because artificial electromagnetic fields are so similar to the natural ones, they may have a disorienting effect on living things because of overstimulation. (High Men and Hogans, Arizona, 1982, by Michael Samuels.)

wavelengths, but because of the pervasiveness of such radiation from high-tension wires, we'll limit our discussion to radiation from 60-cycle per second alternating current, which is the wavelength of electricity used in homes and most work places.

Studies of both animals and humans have shown behavior changes and changes in healing rates.

• Honeybees put under high-tension power lines exhibited hyperactivity, increasing honey production, but loss of body weight. Bees located in experimental electromagnetic fields built flawed hives, destroyed or abandoned hives, ate their own honey instead of storing it, and sometimes even sealed themselves up inside the hives and died.[16]

• Two groups of mice injected with bacteria were set in two different environments:

tific information about the effects of electromagnetic fields on humans is inconclusive.

Extent of the Threat

American scientists, even while acknowledging the validity of the animal studies, disagree about the importance of these findings for humans. One group believes that animal experiments don't carry over to humans, and that only clear and immediate symptoms of disease would indicate a danger. A second group of American scientists, although convinced that electromagnetic fields do affect human cells, feel that further study is needed and that caution should be exercised until more conclusive evidence of the danger to human health is established. The Russians, however, are convinced by the evidence that there are effects on humans, and have established rigorous guidelines for people working and living in and around electric power lines and other sources of electromagnetic fields. The Russian safety regulations establish that people should stay at least 20 meters (60 feet) away from 400-kV lines or 30 meters (90 feet) from 750-kV lines.

Herbert Konig, a West German researcher on the effects of electromagnetic fields, has established his own set of criteria for safe human exposure to this form of radiation (see Table 8.21).

In 1978, the Public Service Commission of the State of New York held a series of very emotional public hearings on the plan of the Power Authority of New York to build 750-kV lines from Canada to New York, in order to

Table 8.20: Safety standards for electromagnetic fields *

Electric field intensity	Maximum allowable daily exposure (minutes)
5	unlimited
10	180
15	90
20	10
25	5

*The above are USSR standards, allowable exposure for 50-H$_z$ transmission systems. (Kurobkova, 1971, 1972), sited in Kronig, p. 257.

Table 8.21: Minimum safe distance from high-voltage lines [a]

Line Voltage	Distance from right-of-way		
	Undoubtedly safe	Probably safe	Probably dangerous
380kV	600 feet	350 feet	60 feet
220 kV	450 feet	240 feet	30 feet
100 kV	300 feet	150 feet	— —
50 kV	180 feet	120 feet	— —

[a]Adapted from Konig, page 263.

prevent blackouts in the city. The outcome was that the Public Service Commission, although allowing the construction of lines, placed great safety restrictions on the project.

Where It Is Found

There are three sources of electromagnetic radiation. In the order of their potential importance as health hazards, these are: (1) high-tension, high-voltage power lines, such as those seen through the countryside strung between high metal towers; (2) electric railways, subways, and buses; (3) electrical wires and telephone lines in houses and residential areas. (When shielded with metal conduit in homes, the electromagnetic fields in buildings are greatly reduced.)

What You Can Do

If you work in and around electromagnetic fields, and if you have been having any symptoms of stress, they may be related to your exposure to this kind of radiation. You may want to explore techniques for shielding the sources of radiation or limiting duration of exposure. Do not depend on information supplied by the industry; under *Further Reading* we cite two works that provide a broad picture

Rulings by the Public Service Commission of the State of New York on 760-kV transmission lines [a]

1. The utility company is to acquire right of way sufficient to exclude existing residences in an area extending 175 feet on each side of the centerline of the certified route.

2. The utility company must acquire permanent rights to bar future residential development within a zone extending 125 feet on each side of the centerline of the certified route.

3. The utility company will report to the Commission and attempt to resolve all complaints concerning audible noise produced by the lines. In the event such a complaint is made by the owner of a house located within a zone extending from the edge of the right of way to a point 600 feet from the centerline of the certified route and cannot be satisfactorily resolved by other means, the Commission may require the utility company to offer to purchase or move that house.

[a]From the Public Service Commission of the State of New York's Opinion #78–13, 1974; cited by Konig *et al.*, p. 294.

If you live or work around electromagnetic fields, certain physical and mental symptoms you may have might be due to this kind of radiation. (High Tension, 1953, by Lucille Blanch. Oil on canvas, 50″ by 36.″ Collection of the Whitney Museum of American Art, New York.)

of the research done on this subject in both Europe and the United States.

Further Reading

H. KONIG *et al. Biological Effects of Environmental Electromagnetism.* Springer-Verlag, 1981.

A highly technical handbook for physicians and scientists interested in the health effects of electromagnetic fields. A European view, the book advises caution in human exposure to this form of radiation.

Hanford Life Sciences Symposium. *Biological Effects of Extremely Low Frequency Electromagnetic Fields.* Technical Information Center, U.S. Department of Energy, 1978.

Papers from a conference sponsored by the U.S. Department of Energy, Pacific Northwest Laboratories, and Battelle Memorial Institute in cooperation with the Electric Power Research Institute, chosen to support the view that electromagnetic radiation is completely safe. An interesting example of how the "objectivity" of science can be used to support a particular viewpoint by careful selection from available material. This technique is called "special pleading," and is considered both unscientific and unscholarly in all academic fields.

CHAPTER NINE

Chemicals

When people learned to manipulate molecules to form new chemical structures, the ageless and universal balance of chemistry and life was broken, introducing new forms of stress into the natural order. Stress has always been imposed on the animal world as the chemistry of the biosphere has been changed by such naturally occurring events as electrical storms, volcanic eruptions, changes in climate, and evolution of new life forms. But these changes often spanned tens of thousands of years; so the living Earth had time to find ways to adapt to, and finally reap benefits from, these changes. Indeed, from the broadest vantage point, we see that the living Earth has created its own chemistry of change from the beginning of time and is continuing to do so even now.

Although it can be argued that the science of chemistry is a product of the living Earth, that is, a creation of the noosphere, we are still struggling with our new found power to manipulate the chemical world; the outcome of this struggle is by no means predictable. We are creating substances that push our homeostatic capacities far past their limits; and, as a result, we know we must seek ways to limit our own inventions. Optimistically, we can say that the recognition of self-created disease and the search for ways to balance our environment are basic homeostatic responses, evidence of the eternal drive for ease and health, and that one day, if our search succeeds, we will learn to live harmoniously with our technology.

What It Is

In recent years we have synthesized chemicals that exist nowhere else in nature. An example of this is the *organochlorine* family of chemicals, often found in pesticides.* These chemicals are made by joining atoms of carbon, hydrogen, and chlorine in a combination that did not—in billions of years of natural evolution—come into being until we created it.

When we consider the effects of our chemical inventions on the environment, it is easy to lose perspective. As consumers of chemical products, we may see no harm in using a small spray can of pesticide for killing insects around the house, and for the farmer the benefits of more abundant crops seem to far outweigh the dangers of spraying a few acres. But the reality of the issue goes far beyond individual use. In 1966, for example, Shell Chemical, just one

*Organochlorine pesticides include Aldrin and Dieldrin.

Figure 9.1: Growth of chemical production in the U.S. from 1915–1975[a]

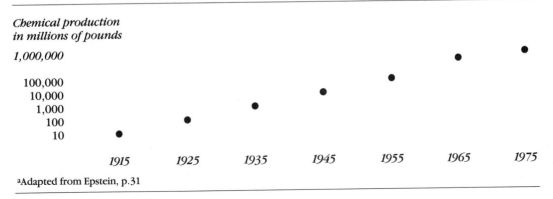

Chemical production
in millions of pounds

[a]Adapted from Epstein, p.31

producer, made 22 million pounds of the organochlorines Aldrin and Dieldrin!

The rate of growth in the chemical industry, both in new chemicals being invented and in pounds produced each year, has been phenomenal. In 1940 one billion pounds of organic chemicals were produced; in 1976 this figure had risen to 300 billion. The Environmental Protection Agency recently estimated that 33,000 chemical compounds are now in common use; as of 1977 there were 6,000 new chemicals registered each week, and although not all of these are commonly used, at least 700 new chemicals enter the marketplace each year.

Chemicals cause disease in one of two ways: by causing *immediate cellular changes* in organisms, either aggravating an existing disease or creating a new one; or by *damaging DNA molecules,* eventually creating birth defects or cancer. That is, chemicals can both poison us and cause mutations.

The EPA lists 65 priority pollutants that present human health hazards. Of these, 32 are indisputably carcinogenic; 33 are poisonous, and *may* also be carcinogenic. Most carcinogens are petrochemicals from three chemical families: aromatic amines (dyes and epoxies); chlorinated olefins (plastics and pesticides); and alkyl halides (solvents). The poisons group includes some of these plus heavy metals: lead, mercury, zinc, etc.

How It Causes Disease

All chemicals cause cancer in basically the same way. It is a two-part process. In the first

The living Earth has created its own chemistry of change, from the beginning of time. That process continues even now. (*Shadow,* 1977, Neil Williver. Oil on canvas, 8′ × 8′. Museum of Modern Art, New York. Gift of Katherine Lustman-Findling.)

part, the *initiation* stage, the chemical is metabolized by the body, breaking down into smaller and smaller pieces. In this process, a compound that appears to be innocuous outside the body becomes a carcinogen as it is broken down by the metabolic processes. Chemically, a molecule is created that is deficient in electrons; because of its deficiency, it seeks out other molecules with which it can share electrons. DNA and RNA, the substances that guide the reproduction of cells and organisms, have plenty of electrons that are accessible to the electron-deficient chemical; so the electron-deficient molecule joins with the DNA. Out of this union comes a DNA molecule quite different from one with normal structure; its code for reproducing a new protein or cell has been altered.* This entire initiation

phase occurs rapidly, and possibly after only a single exposure.

Up to this point cells or proteins are altered, but they have not yet become cancerous. They may remain this way forever, never causing any health problem, or they may go into the second stage, called *promotion*.

Promotion may not happen for months or even years, and then only with repeated exposure, either to the initiating chemical or to a new chemical, which does not have to be a carcinogen. The promoting chemical is thought to increase enzyme activity inside the affected cell. The cell now has two major sources of imbalance: altered DNA, plus a change in its enzyme-protein relationships. Although the exact mechanisms are not yet understood, the cell is now cancerous: it can reproduce, but

*In biological terms, an example of this would be ethylation of guanine residues of the DNA, resulting in base-substitution mutations.

Chemical carcinogens are deficient in electrons, therefore they seek out other molecules that have more electrons to share. DNA has plenty of accessible electrons, so carcinogens easily join with DNA, creating a mutation.

65 priority chemicals

Carcinogens, or suspected carcinogens

Acrylonitrile
Aldrin/Dieldrin
Arsenic
Asbestos

Benzene

Benzidine
Beryllium
Cadmium
Carbon
  tetrachloride
Chlordane
Chlorinated ethanes
Chloroalkyl ethers
  (BCIE, BCEE)
Chloroform
Chromium
DDT
Dichlorobenzadine

Dichloroethylenes
2,4-Dimethylphenol
Dinitrotoluene
Diphenylhydrazines
Halomethane
Heptachlor
Hexachloro-
  butadiene
Hexachlorocyclo-
  hexane (BHC)
Nitrosamines
Polychlorobi-
  phenyls (PCB)
Polynuclear aromatics
Tetrachlorodibenzo-
  p-dioxin
Tetrachloroethylene
Toxaphene
Trichloroethylene
Vinyl chloride

Toxins

Acenaphthene
Acrolein
Antimony
Chloronated
  napthalenes
Chloronated
  phenols
2-Chlorophenol
Copper
Cyanide
Dichlorobenzene

2,4-Dichlorophenol
Dichloropropane
Endosulfan

Endrin
Ethylbenzene
Fluoranthene
Hexachlorocyclo-
  pentadiene
Isophorone
Lead
Mercury
Naphthalene
Nickel
Nitrobenzene
Nitrophenol

Pentachlorophenol

Phenol
Phthalate esters

Selenium

Silver

Thallium
Toluene
Zinc

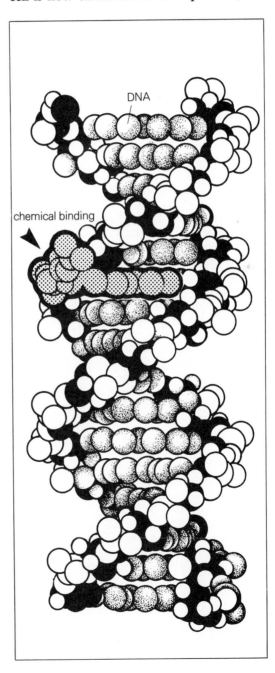

DNA

chemical binding

Even a very small dose of a chemical can create a parent cell that produces a whole colony of abnormal cells, a tumor.
(Tumor cell entering a vein. Courtesy of Peter De Bruyn and Yongock Cho, University of Chicago.)

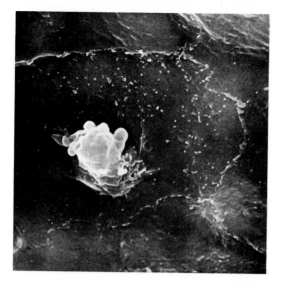

has no guidelines for specializing and becoming a contributing member of the whole organism.

The important thing to recognize in the relationship between cancer and chemicals is that a tumor can grow from a single cell. Even a very small dose of a chemical can help create a parent cell that produces a whole colony of cells, a tumor. Of course, the greater a person's exposure to the chemical carcinogen, the greater are the risks of disease. Yet it is false to assume that the smallest doses, especially in the initiation stage, can't lead to a disease-causing mutation. In addition, just as for ionizing radiation, there is a latency period between exposure to a chemical and the appearance of a tumor; this latency period is estimated to be somewhere between 25 and 35 years (see Figure 8.1). These factors make it extremely difficult to estimate safe levels of exposure or the general hazard of any new chemical substance. Furthermore, unless a chemical has been studied for its full latency period, any claim about its safety has to be considered invalid.

Evidence of Its Danger

Until the 1960s, cancer was thought to be a complete mystery, a disease of aging or perhaps an elusive virus. However, even as early as the 1700s there was evidence that cancer had chemical causes: in 1775 Percival Pott, a London surgeon, published a paper linking the high incidence of scrotal cancer among chimney sweeps to soot. Later, a follow-up study in Germany showed a much lower rate of cancer among chimney sweeps in that country. The difference, it was finally shown, was that London chimney sweeps seldom bathed, whereas German chimney sweeps, with a higher social status and more self-esteem, had better personal hygiene. In effect, the chimney sweeps of London were receiving constant exposure to

the soot, whereas their German counterparts had reduced their exposure by regular bathing.

Research on these studies continued. In the 1920s scientists extracted the chemical benzopyrene from soot and, after applying it to the skin of mice, concluded that this specific substance was the agent causing scrotal cancer in chimney sweeps.

The studies of scrotal cancer in chimney sweeps were only a beginning. By the mid-1900s there were thousands of studies linking cancer to environmental substances, most of which derived from petrochemicals, but which also included other agents: tobacco, betel nuts (in Asia), aflatoxin (in Africa), asbestos, alcohol among heavy drinkers, and even vitamin deficiencies. At this point cancer researchers had established that most cancer could be linked to substances in the environment.

Epidemiologists began plotting the incidence of cancer on maps. Comparing geographic areas, they found the incidence of cancer varied by as much as 2,000 percent. Moreover, certain types of cancer were identified with particular geographic regions. Using areas of lowest cancer rates as the baseline, they found cancer of the esophagus was 300 times higher in Iran; cancer of the liver 70 times higher in Mozambique; cancer of the prostate 30 times higher in the U.S.; and cancer of the lungs 35 times higher in London. From extensive environmental studies, epidemiologists theorized that the areas with lowest cancer rates reflected the disease rates that would normally occur from natural causes, such as mutations caused by background radiation. Cancer rates above those levels were usually caused by substances unique to a specific geographic location.

Because not everyone who was exposed to a substance identified as a carcinogen got cancer, epidemiologists began to perceive that multiple disease factors might be important. For example, in the U.S., cancer of the esophagus is not significantly higher for people who drink large quanitities of alcohol or are heavy smokers, but the incidence is much higher among people who drink *and* smoke.

Epidemiologists observed that when people moved from one area to another, they tended to exhibit cancer rates of the new area. For example, people moving from London to Connecticut tended to get bladder cancer at the rate associated with Connecticut, not lung cancer at the rate identified with London. Age made a difference in these patterns, however; if an older person who had lived in London most of his or her life moved to Connecticut and got cancer, it would most often be lung cancer, reflecting the carcinogenic substances to which the person had been exposed for the greater length of time. Such observations made

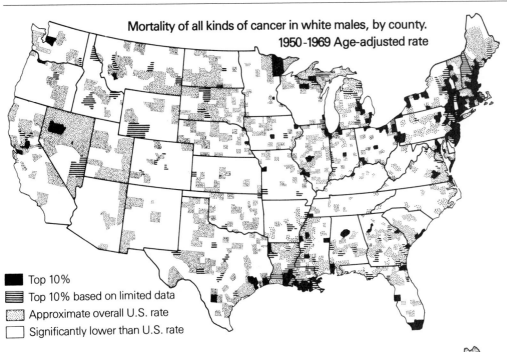

Mortality of all kinds of cancer in white males, by county.
1950-1969 Age-adjusted rate

Epidemiologists learned much about the environmental causes of cancer by studying the incidences of cancer in different areas of the world. Cancer maps show the incidences of specific cancers in particular geographic regions.

■ Top 10%
▤ Top 10% based on limited data
▨ Approximate overall U.S. rate
□ Significantly lower than U.S. rate

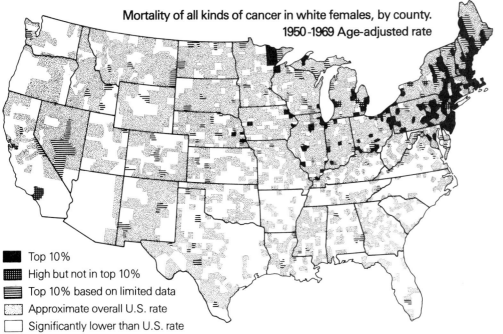

Mortality of all kinds of cancer in white females, by county.
1950-1969 Age-adjusted rate

■ Top 10%
▦ High but not in top 10%
▤ Top 10% based on limited data
▨ Approximate overall U.S. rate
□ Significantly lower than U.S. rate

Adapted from Atlas of Cancer Mortality for U.S. Counties: 1950-1969, DHEW Publication #75-780.

Table 9.1: Comparative incidence of cancer from various areas throughout the world[a]

Type of cancer	High incidence area	(times)	Low incidence area
Skin	Queensland, Australia	200 ×	Bombay, India
Lung	England	35 ×	Nigeria
Stomach	Japan	25 ×	Uganda
Prostate	United States (blacks)	30 ×	Japan
Breast	Connecticut, U.S.	5 ×	Uganda
Colon	Connecticut, U.S.	10 ×	Nigeria
Bladder	Connecticut, U.S.	4 ×	Japan
Uterus	Connecticut, U.S.	10 ×	Japan

[a]Adapted from Hiatt, p. 2.

it increasingly clear that specific substances in the environment caused cancer.

In maps produced by the National Cancer Institute, cancer rates were plotted county by county throughout the United States. Cancer rates were found to be highest in urban areas and areas where paper was manufactured or petroleum products refined. For example, one rural county in Maryland had a 62 percent lower cancer rate than heavily industrialized counties in the same state. Similarly, certain districts in Los Angeles, California, which have high levels of benzopyrene in the air and soil from the petrochemical industry, have 40 percent higher lung-cancer rates in white males than do areas where these conditions don't exist.

The evidence that specific chemical substances cause cancer comes from two types of research: short- and long-term studies of human populations, and animal studies. Human population studies are difficult to do, for several reasons. First, in order to have meaningful figures, extremely large numbers of people must be studied for many years, partly because of the relatively small cancer ratios. For example, among people 35 to 65 years old, there are 2 to 5 cancers per year per 1,000 people. Obviously, to find significant differences in cancer rates as the result of exposures to particular environmental carcinogens, many hundreds of thousands of people would have to be studied. And, once again, long latency periods between exposure to a carcinogen and the manifestation of disease make short-term studies, especially those showing no relationship between an environmental substance and disease, highly suspect. The exception to this is very rare tumors, such as mesothelioma tumors of the lung, which occur at high rates in the asbestos industry. In an average population of 500 people, the statistical prediction would be no mesotheliomas; by comparison, the rate among asbestos workers has been found to be 10 mesotheliomas per 500 workers.

Animal studies present some of the same problems as human studies, in that large numbers of animals must be observed to get dependable figures on common exposure levels of a carcinogen. In order to establish the potency of a carcinogenic material, researchers often increase exposure rates tremendously. Critics of such research argue that any substance, even the most innocuous material, would cause cancer at the rates of exposure to which some research animals are subjected. But as one writer has put it, "you can drown an animal in a pool of some substance, suffocate an animal under a heap of it, or beat an animal to death with a sock full of it, but if it isn't carcinogenic you can't give an animal cancer with it."[1] Cancer researchers use high rates of exposure in animal studies not in order to distort the picture, but because the cost of studying thousands or hundreds of thousands of animals would be prohibitive. To give some perspective on this, a typical cancer study using 50 animals of each sex, in 1978, would have cost $300,000.

Although we cannot always claim that substances that cause cancer in an animal will also cause it in humans, research shows amazingly close correlations. We know, for example, that all the substances known to cause cancer in humans also cause it in rats. And many substances first found to cause cancer in rats later were shown to cause the same cancers in humans.

In recent years scientists, having recognized that the chief mechanism of carcinogenic chemicals is damage to the DNA, devised new

Table 9.2: Occupational hazards for women of childbearing age[a]

Occupation	Hazardous substances
Textile and garment workers	Cotton and fiber dusts, noise, formaldehyde, dyes, heat, asbestos, solvents, flame retardants
Health personnel	Anesthetic gases, x-rays, alcohol, noise, laboratory chemicals
Electronic assemblers	Lead, tin, antimony, trichloroethylene, methylene chloride, resins
Hair dressers/ cosmetologists	Hair-spray resins, aerosol propellants, solvents, and dyes
Cleaning personnel	Soaps, detergents, heat, enzymes, solvents
Launderers of industrially-contaminated clothing	Various industrial chemicals
Photographic processors	Caustics, bromides, iodides, silver nitrate
Plastic workers	Acrylonitrile, formaldehyde, vinyl chloride
Transportation personnel	Carbon monoxide, polynucleararomatics, lead, vibration, microwaves
Painters	Lead, titanium, toluene
Clerks/ clerical workers	Trichloroethylene, carbon tetrachloride, formaldehyde, asbestos, cigarette smoke
Printing personnel	Ink mists, methanol, carbon tetrachloride, lead, noise, solvents, trichloroethylene

[a]Adapted from HEW, *Guidelines on Pregnancy and Work*, p. 65.

tests using bacteria instead of animals for their experiments. These methods greatly reduce the costs of cancer research. A widely used test of this kind is the Ames Test. In assessing the dependability of this new method of research, scientists found that 90 percent of known carcinogens caused mutations in bacteria. Although the Ames Test is not conclusive, it is an excellent indicator for at least the first assessment of potentially carcinogenic materials.

There is also increasing fear that toxic chemicals may, at extremely low doses, cause birth defects and gene mutations. The Banbury Report, *Assessing Chemical Mutagens* (1979), estimates that "ten percent of all live born will manifest a wide variety of genetic diseases." Other research (Neel, University of Michigan, 1979) suggests that this figure may be as high as

Table 9.3: Environmental chemicals and drugs affecting male reproduction[a]

Chemical	Effect
Anesthetic gases	Congenital anomalies in offspring
Carbon disulfide	Impotence, loss of sex drive
Chloroprene	Decreased sperm count and motility, increased miscarriages among wives
Cigarette smoke	Abnormally shaped sperm
Dibromochloropropane	Decreased sperm count and infertility
Hydrocarbons	Offspring with higher cancer risk
Kepone	Decreased fertility
Lead	Decreased sperm count and motility, abnormally shaped sperm
Vinyl chloride	Excess fetal loss
Alcohol	Abnormal testes
Anti-amoeba drugs	Decreased motility of sperm, abnormally shaped sperm
Anti-convulsants	Developmental disabilities in offspring
Iodine	Atrophy of testes
Testosterone enanthate	Sterility

[a]Adapted from Hunt, p. 158.

16 percent.

Although it was once believed that the fetus was protected, there is now solid evidence that a variety of chemicals cross the placental barrier; these include benzene, carbon tetrachloride, chloroform, hydrocarbons, plastic polymers and food preservatives (Dowty 1976). Moreover, a study of human sperm in healthy college students (Dougherty 1980) revealed that more than half the sperm contained

quantities of trichlorophenol, a metabolite of dioxin.

It is now believed that chemicals affect the ability to conceive by causing infertility and sterility, that they can cause fetal death, and that they cause low birth weight in babies, reducing these babies' survival rates. One researcher (Abramson 1973) states that up to 20 percent of all pregnancies end with fetal deaths as a result of chemicals; most of these occur before the fourth week of pregnancy, and so go undetected.

Women of childbearing age are exposed to chemicals in the workplace. As a consequence, exposure of the fetus to chemicals before the woman knows she is pregnant is becoming commonplace. Studies have shown that pregnant women exposed to PCBs had low-birth-weight babies with mottled skin (Thomas 1975). Women exposed to lead had an increased incidence of spontaneous abortion (Hunt 1979).

Extent of the Threat

As in assessing the dangers of radiation, assessing the extent of the threat of chemicals can be a complicated process. In industry and agriculture, where the exposure of workers to extremely high doses is possible, toxicity, and often even carcinogenic potential, can be easily established. But for the general public these high levels of exposure are not usual; on the contrary, the general public's exposure to carcinogenic chemicals is very low. Establishing a safe level of exposure is complicated by latency periods between exposure and disease manifestation, the number of people who would have to be studied, the number of years that would need to be covered to establish depend-

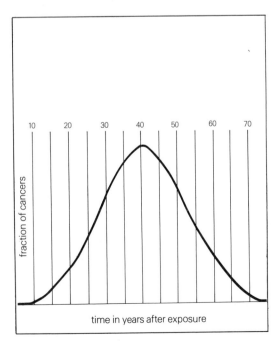

Long latency periods between exposure to a chemical carcinogen and the manifestation of the disease make short term studies inaccurate.

able figures, the extremely high cost of animal studies, and the existence of multiple disease factors in all cancer. To calculate the effects of low doses of chemicals, scientists must construct graphs based on high dosages and project the results for lower dosages. This becomes a statistical procedure (see Figure 8.2), which may or may not provide us with a realistic picture of the human health hazards of chemicals.

In trying to plot graphs of safe radiation levels, scientists get a linear nonthreshold curve, suggesting that there are *no* safe levels of exposure (see page 106). Even the smallest exposures will have some effect on human health. Using other statistical methods, we could take the same figures and show that there is no effect on human health until

At this point in our history, we must assume that all government safety standards in the chemical industry grow out of compromises between economic pressures and human health requirements. (*University City, Cancer Research Institute,* 1937, by Lewis Quintanilla. Pen and ink, 16″ by 12″. The Museum of Modern Art, New York. Gift of the artist.)

exposures reach quite a high level.

Based on animal studies of powerful carcinogenic materials, the linear, nonthreshold curve appears to be the most accurate statistical method, showing that the health of animals is affected by exposure to carcinogens even at the lowest exposures. This has led the EPA, whose statements are ordinarily quite conservative, to say that the safe level of any carcinogenic chemical, for maximum protection of human health, is absolute zero. Obviously, since we are living at a time when chemicals are used to produce everything from high-performance fuels to prescription drugs, the problem of establishing safe levels of exposure becomes a complex and heated socioeconomic issue. For now we must assume that all government safety standards in the chemical industry grow out of compromises between economic pressures and human health requirements.

In the United States, industry has consis-

*At the time these standards were imposed, animal studies had shown that five parts per million of vinyl chloride caused cancer. Since then, animal studies have shown that one part per million causes increased cancer.

tently fought public agencies that are seeking exposure standards, presenting figures from their own chemists and statisticians to "prove" the safety of exposure levels that were often hundreds of times higher than the findings of less-biased laboratories. Furthermore, lobbyists sponsored by chemical industries have consistently threatened that the the cost of installing industry safeguards would close down the factories and cause vast economic hardships.

In spite of a history of conflict, many large chemical industries have cooperated with public agencies, and have installed safeguards without experiencing the predicted economic disasters. For example, vinyl chloride, a basic chemical in the plastics industry, was shown, in the early 1970s, to be responsible for a significantly increased incidence of a previously rare form of liver cancer. For several years the plastics industry kept this information quiet. In spite of efforts to suppress this data, it came to the attention of the scientific community, and after congressional hearings on the matter, the Occupational Health and Safety Administration (OSHA) lowered the levels of safe exposure in 1974, from 500 parts per million to 50. Labor and independent scientists urged OSHA to drop the permissible exposure levels to zero. Industry responded by threatening huge financial losses and unemployment if they were forced to meet such "unreasonable" standards. After four years of struggle, OSHA demanded a one part per million standard.*

In spite of their bleak predictions, large manufacturers began to comply with OSHA standards. They found it surprisingly easy to bring their plants in line with these standards, and, in fact, were able to cut production costs as a result of the new machinery that had to be installed. B. F. Goodrich, one of the world's largest synthetic rubber manufacturers, was able to comply with OSHA regulations for $34 million, a relatively small amount of money for a company of its size. Similar discoveries were made by Union Carbide.

What must be kept in perspective when considering industry standards is that it is not just the worker—who presumably can choose whether or not to take a hazardous job—who is at risk. The real problem is global. Before standards were established by OSHA, the EPA was able to measure 2.8 parts per million of vinyl chloride in a classroom located near the Keysor-Century Corporation in Saugus, California, a manufacturer of phonograph records. Similarly, the EPA found that one out of ten of the communities they investigated had vinyl chloride levels of 33 parts per million a third of a mile from the vinyl chloride plant.

In the Surgeon General's Report entitled "Evaluation of Environmental Carcinogens," the following recommendations were made concerning the safety of low levels of chemicals.

1. Any substance that is shown to cause cancer in animals should be considered a potential cancer hazard for man.

2. No level of exposure to carcinogenic chemicals is to be considered "insignificant" or "safe."

3. No chemical substance should be assumed safe without controlled animal studies.

4. Any study showing a chemical to be carcinogenic preempts any other study showing it not to be carcinogenic.

5. Any chemical that produces tumors, even though those tumors are considered benign, must be considered carcinogenic.

6. Permissible exposure levels of zero should be maintained unless such maintenance

points out, first of all, that information about the safety of chemicals is generally submitted to the government either by the industry manufacturing the chemical or by an industry interested in using it. This information is compiled by scientists employed by or under contract to the industry, that is, by either private laboratories or universities who are receiving compensation from the industry.

In evaluating the scientific integrity of such reports, Epstein found the following: experiments were poorly designed, using too small a number of animals or killing the animals with toxic doses before they got cancer—giving the impression, therefore, that none died of cancer. In addition, he found that animals exposed to carcinogenic materials were destroyed before they could manifest cancer, or

Wastes don't just go away. For years, General Electric dumped 30 pounds of PCBs per day from their Fort Edward capacitor plant into the Hudson River. From there it entered the human food chain through fish. (Man and Boy Fishing On the Bank Across from the Fort Edward PCB Plant, 1982, by Michael Samuels.)

can be proven impossible.

7. Carcinogenic materials may be used in industry only if the exposure to the general public remains at zero.

These guidelines indicate that chemicals must be treated with respect, and they provide us with a set of criteria for evaluating reports we might read in the newspaper or see on television about chemicals in the environment. In his book *The Politics of Cancer,* Samuel Epstein, M.D., gives us another set of criteria for evaluating newspaper accounts of the safety of chemicals in the environment. Epstein

the wrong organs were examined in autopsy. Finally, Epstein states that cases of "alteration, falsification, and even destruction of records" were numerous.

With 6,000 new chemicals being invented each week, and 700 new chemicals going into common use each year, we each need a way to evaluate their effects on our lives. The preceding material can be helpful in assessing safety reports released by the chemical industry through the media, and for making decisions about the wisdom of governmental controls for these substances.

Where It Is Found

We use products in our homes, or on the job, that are made with chemicals that are either toxic or carcinogenic, but these are only one part of the picture. In the production of these chemicals, certain amounts of the hazardous substances make their way into the environment: through venting systems and smokestacks, and most importantly in disposal of wastes. The latter has been the source of much controversy in recent years, largely because as the production of chemical wastes increased, it became clearer and clearer that wastes didn't "go away" just because they were trucked away from the factory. Though removed from sight, they were not removed from the environment. If they didn't escape into the air, they escaped into the earth and the waterways, and eventually made their way into the food chain to humans.

An excellent example of a chemical's effect on the food chain is found in the history of the Housatonic River in Pittsfield, Massachusetts. In the 1970s it was discovered that General Electric was dumping PCBs into the river from a transformer plant. The records show they were dumping only .1 pounds of PCBs per day. (At about the same time G.E. was dumping 30 pounds of PCBs per day into the Hudson River from their Fort Edward capacitor plant and 17 pounds per day from their Hudson Falls plant.) At the rate of .1 pounds per day, water near the

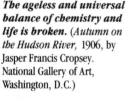

The ageless and universal balance of chemistry and life is broken. (*Autumn on the Hudson River,* 1906, by Jasper Francis Cropsey. National Gallery of Art, Washington, D.C.)

dump site contained only 1 to 3 parts per billion of PCB. Sediment in the bottom of the river 6 miles away, where there were no detectable PCBs in the water, contained 30 to 60 parts per billion PCBs.

In the food chain, PCBs (and all other chemicals) are taken up by plant life in minuscule amounts. Then small fish, eating large amounts of this plant life, take up the chemicals and store them in their fat cells in relatively high concentrations. Large fish eat the small fish, and they, in turn, take up and store even higher concentrations in their tissue. Eventually, of course, people eat the larger fish, ingesting large quantities of chemicals along with the fish.

Whereas the parts per million of chemicals in the water may be "safe," the mechanism by which animals ingest and concentrate these substances in their flesh can result in astonishing concentrations in the human food chain. For example, in less than a month some species of fish can store up to 9 million times the PCB levels found in surrounding waters. Many species of fish also migrate, thus carrying PCBs out into the oceans. In addition, catching tons of fish, drying them, and grinding them up to be fed to poultry and cattle, brings the chemicals we produce into our own food chain.

The EPA estimates that 10 million pounds of PCBs come into the environment every year through spills, leaks, and vaporization. As a result, human fat now contains relatively high

levels of PCBs: 40 percent of Americans have levels greater than 1 part per million; in Israel the average person has levels of 2.75 per million; and in Germany the average person has levels of 6.8. In America the average level of PCBs in mother's milk is 1.8 parts* per million; this is 7 times the level allowed by the FDA in cow's milk.

In 1979 the manufacture and sale of PCBs was banned in the United States. However, this chemical is extremely stable, and persists in the environment for many years. At present, even with the banning of PCBs, there are still 758 million pounds in use in transformers and other products, 290 million pounds in dump sites, and 150 million pounds in the soil, air, and water. In Michigan and New York, PCB transformers were routinely drained, mixed with drain oil, and spread on rural gravel roads to keep the dust down.

Chemical pollution begins in the industry in which the substances are produced,* but it by no means ends there. Once produced, these chemicals are used in a variety of other industries. They are also used by consumers and in agriculture. In industry there are nearly a million workers constantly exposed to carcinogenic substances or toxic substances regulated by OSHA. In general these workers know very little about the chemicals with which they're working, and there is often little or no effort by manufacturers to inform the workers of the health hazards of their jobs.

Exposure levels to the consumer may be higher than those allowed for factory workers. Ironically, a paint, dye, or solvent containing carcinogens might have very strict regulations for its production, but once in the hands of the consumer the carcinogen can be used freely. For example, vinyl chlorides were used in hair sprays until the mid-1970s. In 1974 OSHA allowed 50 parts per million for vinyl chlorides. In 1978 the level was reduced to 1 part per million. A person using the vinyl chloride hair sprays received between 100 and 400 parts per million per usage.

Similarly, consumers can buy solvents for stripping paint from furniture that contain high levels of benzene. OSHA now allows one part per million for regular exposure in factories, with occasional "peaks" of up to 5 parts per million. A homeowner using a benzene solvent to strip paint from a chair can be receiving as much as 225 parts per million.

Production and consumer use of carcinogenic substances are the more obvious exposure routes in the human population. A third source of exposure comes from chemicals such as pesticides that are ingested with food (see Chapter 13). The normal discharge and escape of chemicals from factories into the environment accounts for a fourth source of exposure, that is, global pollution. For exam-

ple, in the making of benzene 2.5 percent of the total annual production of 260 million pounds goes "up the stack," evaporating into the atmosphere. This 2.5 percent entering the environment means that tens of thousands of people get exposure levels close to the OSHA limits* set for workers, and millions get constant, low-level exposures. Outside large benzene plants, refineries, and dye factories that use benzene, pollution levels are .1 to 3 parts per million. People living in the general vicinity of benzene plants get 2 parts per billion, and even 12 miles from the plant there will be exposure levels of several parts per billion. Since benzene is a common gasoline additive, put in gasoline after the ban on ethyl additives, cities like Los Angeles, Dallas, Chicago, and New York have exposure levels of 1 to 4 parts per

Table 9.4: Occupations with higher risks of cancer[a]

Occupation	Hazardous chemical	Type of Cancer
Miners, textile workers, insulation workers, glass and pottery workers, chemical workers, radiologists, steel workers	Arsenic, asbestos, chromium, petroleum products, radiation	Lung
Tanners, smelters, vineyard workers, plastic workers	Arsenic, vinyl chloride	Liver
Coal and pitch workers, die users, textile workers, paint workers, leather workers	Petroleum products, coal products	Bladder
Explosives workers, rubber cement workers, painters, radiologists	Benzene, radiation	Bone marrow
Smelters, wood, leather, glass and pottery workers	Chromium, nickel, dust	Nasal cavity

[a]Epstein, p. 78.

billion in downtown areas coming from gasoline filling stations. It is estimated that 16 million people are exposed to low levels of benzene around factories where it is produced, and another 118 million people living near gasoline filling stations get exposure levels between .1 and 2 parts per billion. These levels of exposure are for a single chemical amidst many; more than half the population is being

*One mother tested in Michigan had over 10 parts per million PCBs, a level high enough to cause learning disabilities in monkeys.

*Chemicals are produced in the billions of pounds; benzene production in 1977 was 11 billion pounds in the U.S. alone.

*The OSHA levels of 1 part per million allowable for factory workers are not *safe* levels; they are *allowable* levels, in OSHA's opinion.

Table 9.5: Benzene exposure[a]

Industry	Total number of people exposed
Petroleum refineries	6,597,000
Chemical manufacturing	9,883,000
Solvent operations	215,000
Coke ovens	16,299,000
Gasoline stations	
Self-service	37,000,000
People living nearby	118,000,000
Auto exhausts in city air	113,690,000

[a]Adapted from Epstein, p. 128.

exposed to this single chemical at levels sometimes higher than those recommended for factory workers.

What You Can Do

There has been a tendency, in recent years, to think of prevention of cancer and birth defects that result from manmade environmental health hazards as strictly a community-action issue. However, individual efforts, that is, changes in lifestyle, are an essential part of any prevention program. According to John Higginson, director of the International Agency for Research on Cancer, a two-part program is necessary for prevention: (1) a community plan, and (2) a personal plan. He believes that by following simple rules of life, including the avoidance of smoking and of heavy alcohol consumption, a low intake of animal fat, dietary moderation to avoid obesity, and reasonable exposure to sunlight, we can each reduce our risk of getting cancer by 30 to 40 percent. This relatively simple set of changes could extend the average life expectancy of a 45-year-old male approximately 11 years. Doctor Higginson states that "the greatest benefits will depend on personal action, whereby a person controls his personal environment and that of his family." But he also emphasizes that individual responsibility does not reduce the "requirement by governments, legislators, employers, etc. to ensure that the present environment be made as safe as possible."

A general plan for preventing disease created by toxic chemicals should include the following ten points.

(1) Stop smoking, and avoid being in rooms with smokers. Smoking increases your chances of getting lung cancer 10 times; it increases the chances of an asbestos worker getting cancer 92 times. One out of 10 smokers, smoking more than a pack a day, will develop lung can-

cer. The smoker is creating a chemical environment in the lungs and upper respiratory system that not only sets the stage for more severe damage by other environmental pollutants, but in itself is creating a greater health hazard than any other environmental pollutant confronted by the average person.

(2) Avoid heavy drinking, particularly of hard liquor. Although researchers feel that alcohol does not itself cause cancer, there is evidence that it makes normal cells more susceptible to carcinogenic materials ingested or inhaled by the drinker.

(3) Reduce the intake of foods on the high end of the food chain, that is, animal fats (which have high concentrations of chemical pollutants). Don't eat freshwater fish. Avoid organ meats because chemicals tend to con-

---

A personal cancer plan[a]

Most important: stop smoking (40 percent of all cancers).

Avoid heavy alcohol drinking (5 percent of all cancers).

Avoid heavy exposure to sunlight in summer.

Avoid x-rays.

Avoid animal fats and decrease red meats (carcinogens accumulate as you go up the food chain).

Wash fruits and vegetables before eating.

Avoid organ meats, especially liver.

Avoid foods high in preservatives, chemicals, or colorings, especially red dye #40 and saccharin.

Beware of your drinking water; use a filter if necessary.

If possible, do not live near a chemical plant, refinery, asbestos plant, or waste-disposal site.

Educate yourself if you work with any chemicals.

Avoid pesticides and chemicals at home.

Avoid drugs if not absolutely necessary, especially Flagyl, Griseofulvin, Lindane (Kwell), and estrogen.

Avoid cosmetic products with warning labels.

[a]Adapted from Epstein, pp. 472–495.

centrate in them in high amounts. Emphasize high-fiber foods: grains, fresh fruits, and vegetables. Reduce the use of dairy products. (Also see pages 210 to 215.)

(4) Avoid processed foods containing chemicals in the form of artificial coloring, preservatives, and flavor enhancers.

(5) Avoid drinking water with chemical contaminants. The EPA or local Public Interest Research Group (PIRG)—not the water department in your district—can inform you of the chemical content of the tap water on your area. (Also see pages 210 to 215.)

(6) Be informed about medicines. Both over-the-counter and prescription drugs may contain carcinogens or suspected carcinogens. The most common drugs that contain chemicals known to cause cancer are: griseofulvin

Table 9.6: Carcinogenic and toxic substances in cigarette smoke[a]

Substance	Concentration in cigarettes (ug/cigarette)	Concentration allowable in the work place (parts per million)	Disease factor[b]
Acetaldehyde	770.	100	CI
Acrolein	578.	.1	CI
Benzene	67.	. . . .	CA
Dimethyl-nitros-amine	.08	. . . .	CA
Formalde-hyde	90.	2	P
Hydrazine	.03	. . . .	CA
Hydrogen cyanide	240.	10	CI
Nitrosopi-peridine	.01	. . . .	CA
Nitrosopyr-rolidine	.1	. . . .	CA
Vinyl chloride	.01	1	CA

[a]Adapted from Wynder, 1976.
[b]Code: CA, carcinogen; CI, kills cilia; P, promotes carcinogenicity.

(for ringworm), lindane (for head lice and crab lice), flagyl (for trichomonas), and estrogen (for menopausal discomfort and birth control pills). All medicines have side effects and can be toxic. For detailed analyses of all drugs, see the *Physician's Desk Reference,* available in book stores and many public libraries.

(7) Be informed about consumer products. Many consumer chemicals, such as pesticides, aerosol sprays, and solvents (paint thinners, strippers, and cleaning preparations) are used by consumers in potencies that would never

Table 9.7: Carcinogens in arts and crafts supplies[a]

Type of cancer	Hazardous chemical	Source
Lung	Beryllium, cadmium, chromium, nickel, asbestos, arsenic	Sculpture and ceramic dust, soldering, painting, welding, etching
Liver	Beryllium, carbon tetrachloride, trichloroethylene, tetrachloroethylene	Sculpture and ceramic dust, solvents, painting, cleaning
Skin	Arsenic, arsene	Printing, etching
Nasal	Wood dust	Woodwork, sculpture
Leukemia	Benzene	Use of solvents in painting and cleaning

[a]Epstein, p. 497.

be allowed in industry (see Tables 9.4 and 9.5). Cosmetics, hair dyes, plastic containers made with PCBs, arts and crafts materials, and home-improvement products may also contain carcinogenic or toxic substances.

(8) If you are moving or can choose where you live, investigate neighborhoods carefully, avoiding environments close to chemical plants, refineries, asbestos plants, metal mills and hazardous-waste disposal sites. Remember, also, that downtown urban areas and neighborhoods close to major expressways are high in chemical pollutants, and have higher cancer rates than other areas. Rural areas and forests routinely sprayed with herbicides and pesticides may pose even greater health risks than the inner city.

(9) In choosing an occupation, consider the

People living adjacent to large refineries are often exposed to higher levels of benzene than is allowed for workers inside the plants. (Sandlot Baseball Next to Oil Refinery, 1982, by Michael Samuels.)

If you are moving or can choose where you live, investigate new neighborhoods carefully. Avoid environments close to chemical plants, refineries, and hazardous waste-disposal sites.
(a, *Bulldozer Burying Houses at Love Canal,* 1982, by Michael Samuels.
b, *Admittance by Permit Only,* 1982, by Michael Samuels. c, *Abandoned and Boarded-Up Housing at Love Canal,* 1982, by Michael Samuels. d, *The American Dream, Caputo PCB Dump,* 1982, by Michael Samuels.
e, *The American Dream, Love Canal,* 1982, by Michael Samuels.)

risks from chemical pollutants in the work-place. Investigate safety records of any company you might work for. Do not depend on the management of that company or that company's physicians to provide you with dependable information about health risks in the workplace. Investigate risks on your own; OSHA, labor unions, and books such as this can be important resources.

(10) Join or in other ways support local public-interest groups specializing in protecting the environment. Make it a point to bring environmental health information to the attention of any groups to which you belong: business or professional organizations, church groups, PTA, athletic clubs, labor unions, political parties, etc. (See also pages 232 to 233.)

Further Reading

H. HIATT, ed. *Origins of Human Cancer.* The Cold Spring Harbor Conferences on Cell Proliferation. Cold Spring Harbor Laboratory, 3 vols., 1977.

Transcripts of a conference held in 1977, bringing together information on the effects of location, occupation, drugs, chemicals in the air, water, and food chain, the types of animal tests used in research, etc. This three-volume collection is an important scientific document on the subject of chemicals and cancer. Oriented toward safety, it nevertheless presents diverse points of view. Available in medical school libraries.

T. J. MASON. *Atlas of Cancer Mortality for U.S. Counties: 1950–1969.* Government Printing Office, 1975.

Maps showing incidence of cancer and types of cancer, organized according to geographic location. The graphic presentation shows the effects of environmental health hazards on human populations in a dramatic way.

JOSEPH FRAMENI, JR. *Persons at High Risk of Cancer.* Academic Press, 1975.

From an American Cancer Society Conference of 1975, this is an excellent source for people seeking specific ways to prevent environmental health hazards.

U. SAFFIOTTI, ed. *Occupational Carcinogenesis. Annals of the New York Academy of Sciences,* Volume 271, 1976.

A technical presentation of the occupational causes of cancer and their physiological mechanisms. Available through medical school libraries.

SAMUEL S. EPSTEIN. *Politics of Cancer.* Doubleday/Sierra Club Books, 1978.

Studies and case histories of industry's participation in the chemical pollution of the human environment, providing a clear picture of how and why government regulation became necessary. Although this book is fairly technical, it is very readable and arousing for the general public. Important reading for anyone working in the chemical industry or involved in political activity focused on the issue of chemicals in the environment.

JOSEPH HIGHLAND. *Malignant Neglect.* Random House, 1980.

This short book is well-researched and well-written, making the complex information from the Environmental Defense Fund available to the general reader.

Poisons List A

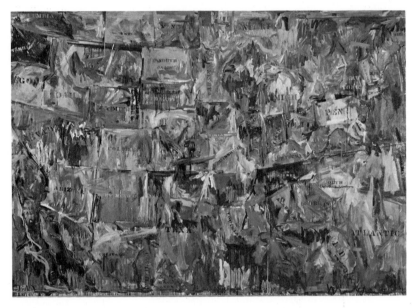

Each year more than 3,000 new chemicals are invented. Our nation has been called "the land of the poisoned" for good reason. (Map, 1961, by Jasper Johns. Oil on canvas, 8' by 125.' Museum of Modern Art, New York,. Fractional gift of Mr. and Mrs. Robert C. Scull.)

I n this list of chemicals, and in Poisons List B, page 185, we discuss chemicals now considered to be among the most common substances dangerous to human health. Obviously, with 3,000 new chemicals being invented each year, we cannot list all chemicals, but the chemicals we do list are representative.

This material will enable you to critically approach discussions of chemicals in the media, to evaluate substances containing these chemicals, and to present informed opinions in discussions of chemical pollution problems with friends or in public meetings.

The chemicals in these lists are arranged alphabetically. Then each discussion is organized in the following way.

Name of the substance: includes both the name and the chemical formula.

What It Is: a short description of the chemical's use, such as pesticide, herbicide, plastics production, etc.

Major Health Concerns: first you will notice one, two, or three symbols: CA, indicating carcinogenicity; BD, indicating that the substance may cause birth defects; and TX, indicating that the chemical is toxic and can cause immediate poisoning or can aggravate an existing chronic disease in humans. Following these symbols you'll find discussions of the research that has shown the substance to be hazardous to health.

Exposure Levels/Standards: outlines monitoring standards by public and private agencies. One standard we cite is based on proposed "safe" levels established by the Environmental Protection Agency. We quote their estimates for the amounts of carcinogenic materials in water that would cause one death per 100,000 lifetimes.

Where Found/What to Avoid: lists of products or procedures in agriculture or industry where the chemical is commonly used.

Bioaccumulation Factor: we previously discussed this on page 101, at the beginning of Section 3. To review, fatty tissue stores chemicals at different rates that depend on the makeup of the chemical. A bioaccumulation factor of 100, for example, would mean that if there was 1 part per million of a chemical in water, an animal would store up to 100 parts per million of that chemical in its tissues.

Acrylonitrile
Formula: $CH_2 = CHCN$

What It Is: a liquid found in the production of plastics, widely used in consumer products ranging from food-packaging materials to fabrics and contact lenses. Dupont, American Cyanamide, Monsanto, and Standard Oil produced 1.6 billion pounds in 1976.

Major Health Concerns (CA, BD, TX): after being fed water with 35 parts acrylonitrile per million parts of water, research animals have manifested cancers in the nervous system, breasts, ear canal, and stomach. Similar results occurred when the animals breathed the fumes of this chemical.

In human studies, Dupont workers in Camden, South Carolina (1977), had nearly twice the incidence of lung and colon cancer as people not exposed to this substance.

Bacteriological tests showed significant mutations after exposure to acrylonitrile.

Toxic effects included difficulty in breathing, vomiting, diarrhea, nausea, weakness, headache, and fatigue in humans. Toxic doses caused deaths of embryos in animals.

Exposure Levels/Standards: the EPA has established that .0008 nanograms per liter will cause one excess cancer per 100,000 lives.

OSHA allows exposure levels of 2 parts per million for factory workers. Russia's stricter standards limit exposure to .2 parts per million.

Where Found/What to Avoid: great amounts of this chemical are used in industries producing synthetic fibers and plastics, such as Acrylon, Creslan, Orlon, Zefran, Elura, Sef, Verel, ABS, and SAN resins.

Acrylic or modacrylic materials are made by: American Cyanamid, Milton, Fla.; Dow Badish Company, Williamsburg, Va.; E.I. Dupont de Nemours and Company, Inc., Camden, S.C., and Waynesboro, Va.; Eastman Kodak Company, Kingsport, Tenn.; and Monsanto, Decatur, Ala.

Products manufactured with these materials include clothing, carpeting, blankets, draperies and upholstery, synthetic furs and wigs.

Acrylonitriles are also used in the production of materials for furniture, food wrappers, acrylic dentures, contact lenses, and pesticides.

People not working in industries producing such materials are exposed to this chemical by breathing contaminated air, drinking contaminated water, eating fish living in contaminated waterways, or eating foods either sprayed by acrylonitrile pesticides or packaged in acrylic food wrappers; also, by wearing underclothes, diapers, and sanitary napkins containing these materials. People who smoke actually have measurable amounts of acrylonitriles in their blood.

Bioaccumulation Factor: 110 measured in bluegill sunfish.

Aldrin/Dieldrin
Formula: 1,2,3,4,10, 10-hexachloro-1,4,4a,5,8,8a-hexahydro-1,4:5,8-hexodimethanonaphthalene; Aldrin metabolized in the human body becomes dieldrin.

What It Is: An organochlorine pesticide made up of hydrogen, carbon, and chlorine. Up until 1974, this chemical was used as a pesticide for protecting corn crops. At its peak, 22 million pounds were used per year. In 1974 it was banned by the EPA for food crops, but is still in use for killing termites, protecting nonfood seeds, and protecting plants during their transportation. Being an extremely stable chemical (lasting from 5 to 25 years in the soil), it persists in the environment even though no longer used as a pesticide in corn crops. Like many other chemicals, it accumulates in animal fats. EPA tests found traces of this chemical (average of 3 parts

In 1974, Aldrin was banned by the EPA for food crops. An extremely stable chemical, it persists in the environment and continues to accumulate in animal fats. (Insects, 1919, by Paul Klee. Lithograph, 8″ by 6.″ Museum of Moern Art, New York. Gift of Mr. and Mrs. Walter Bareiss.)

per million) in all human fat samples taken in 1974.

Major Health Concerns (CA, TX): 24 out of 90 research animals manifest cancer of the liver after exposures of .1 parts per million.

Low exposure levels cause reduced growth rates and reduced reproductive performance in fish.

Exposure Levels/Standards: in 1976 the EPA found traces of aldrin in 85 percent of air samples taken throughout the U.S. In the air, aldrin travels globally. Levels of aldrin in the air were as high as 2.8 nanograms per cubic meter. Water tested in the U.S. showed aldrin levels as high as .05 micrograms per liter. And the standard middle class diet in the U.S. contains 43 nanograms of aldrin per gram.

EPA limits for water are 4.6×10^{-2} ng per liter.

Where Found/What to Avoid: this chemical is now found in all parts of the environment, and in the food chain globally. Two years following the banning of this chemical, tests of the Great Lakes waters (Michigan) showed 1 to 3 nanograms per liter; in fish, lake herring had .23 parts per million, and Kiyi had .28 parts per million.

To minimize ingestion of aldrin, choose a diet low on the food chain.

Bioaccumulation Factor: average of 4,500 and up to 100,000 in fish.

Arsenic

What It Is: arsenic is a *metalloid*, a shiny, gray, brittle element, possessing both metallic and nonmetallic properties. It occurs in nature, and as an environmental hazard we are most concerned with the vast amounts of it released into the atmosphere by burning coal.

Major Health Concerns (CA, TX, BD): residents of Antofagasta, Chile, S.A., showed a high incidence of lung and heart disease, as well as a high incidence of both premalignant and

malignant skin cancers. Investigators discovered that their drinking water contained .8 mg of arsenic per liter.

Similarly, in Taiwan there was found to be .6 mg of arsenic per liter of drinking water. The Taiwanese had a high incidence of "Blackfoot" disease, a vascular disease in which circulation is impeded or blocked to the outer extremities, such as fingers and toes, eventually leading to gangrene. The same population had a high incidence of skin cancer.

Studies of human populations in industry and agriculture, where large amounts of this chemical are used, have linked increased lung and skin cancers with arsenic.

Although arsenic is strongly associated with human cancers, laboratory experiments have failed to demonstrate that it is carcinogenic for animals.

Arsenic is, of course, one of the more famous poisons, immortalized by detective novels and by the play *Arsenic and Old Lace.*

Acute toxic symptoms caused by eating are: abdominal pain and vomiting. Poisoning by inhalation produces dizziness, headache, weakness, and finally nausea and vomiting. Death occurs with high doses.

Chronic toxic symptoms: low doses taken for a long period of time can cause freckling and darkening of nipples, redness and puffiness around the eyes, thickening of the skin of the hands and soles of feet and, in later stages, weakness and numbness in hands.

Birth defects: experiments have demonstrated birth defects in chicks, hamsters, rats, and mice exposed to arsenic in utero.

In a report entitled "Estimates of the Fraction of Cancer in the United States Related to Occupational Factors" (1978), HEW says the use of arsenic in agriculture and industry may, in the next decades, account for 10 to 20 percent of all human cancers. It is listed as one of the six leading causes of future human cancers.

Exposure Levels/Standards: fatal dose is .76 to 1.95 mg of arsenic per kilogram of body weight. Chronic symptoms can

occur in adults with doses of 3 to 6 mg per day.

Standard of safety set by EPA is 50 micrograms per liter of water; standard for air, set by OSHA, is 10 micrograms per cubic liter in any eight-hour work day. EPA is considering setting a safety guideline of .02 micrograms per liter (water), which they estimate will cause one case of cancer per 100,000 people exposed during their lifetimes.

Arsenic, it should be recognized, is actually a dietary requirement in humans. Nutritionists estimate that adult humans require about .025 mg per day. Since most foods contain at least traces of arsenic, a good diet will easily supply these requirements.

Where Found/What to Avoid: major sources of arsenic pollution are coal-fueled power plants, copper, lead, and zinc smelters, and cotton gins. Manufacturers use arsenic in the production of glass, cloth, semiconductors, fungicides, wood preservatives, pesticides, and veterinary drugs.

Six million pounds of arsenic are sent out into the atmosphere each year by coal-fueled power plants, and 75 million pounds are used in manufacturing each year.

Arsenic is also found in cigarette smoke, adding still another argument against smoking.

Consumer products, such as some paints and dyes (primarily greens) contain arsenic, usually at low levels.

Bioaccumulation Factor: 2.3 in fish.

Asbestos
Formula: $Mg_3Si_2O(OH)_4$

What It Is: a mineral made of silicon, oxygen, hydrogen, and metals such as sodium, magnesium, and calcium. The most commonly used asbestos is *chrysotile*. Mined from the Earth, asbestos was first used in Finland 4,500 years ago for making pottery. It is virtually indestructible, being highly resistant to fire, and has more than 3,000 uses in industry, and more than 300 uses in household and consumer products. Capable of being spun into fi-

of brake linings. A person living in such an area will take .1 micrograms of asbestos into his or her body each day.

OSHA standards for preventing pulmonary asbestosis in workers is 2 million fibers per cubic meter of air during an eight-hour work day. This means a worker will inhale 16 million asbestos fibers in a work day. To prevent cancer, OSHA has proposed a safety standard of 500,000 fibers per cubic meter of air during an eight-hour day. NIOSH has proposed a safety standard of 100,000 fibers.

EPA is considering a safety standard of 300,000 fibers per liter of water, which they estimate will cause one cancer per 100,000 people.

In his book *Politics of Cancer,* Samuel Epstein estimates that asbestos is responsible for 50,000 cancer deaths per year.

In its report "Estimates of the Fraction of Cancer in the United States Related to Occupational Factors," HEW says that asbestos will result in up to 2 million excess cancer deaths as the result of past exposures. This will represent from 13 to 18 percent of all cancers for those years in the next several decades.

Where Found/What to Avoid: approximately 4.3 million tons of asbestos are produced each year worldwide; 243,000 tons are released into the environment each year, much of it through solid waste disposal by consumers. Industries have also been responsible for dumping large quantities of asbestos waste into waterways and landfills. One example of this was in Duluth, Minnesota, where the Reserve Mining Company was dumping 67,000 tons of taconite (a kind of asbestos) into Lake Superior. This asbestos made its way into the drinking water of hundreds of thousands of people; it also affected air quality. This dumping practice was ended in March 1980 as a result of environmental action groups working through the courts.

Wherever there is an asbestos industry, be it a mine, a mill, or a fabrication plant, there will be high levels of asbestos in both the air and the water unless the company has taken special meas-

Industries dump large quantities of asbestos waste into waterways and landfills. In Duluth, Minnesota, Reserve Mining dumped 67,000 tons into Lake Superior, affecting the drinking-water supplies of hundreds of thousands of people. (*The Magician,* 1954, by Jean Dubuffet. Slag and roots, 43 inches high. Museum of Modern Art, New York. Gift of Mr. and Mrs. Richard Miller.)

bers, it can be woven into fabric. It can also be mixed with binders, such as plaster and cement. Asbestos is still in wide use in industry and household products, and some restrictions are now being imposed where asbestos fibers are released into the water and air. Johns-Manville is the world's largest asbestos company.

Major Health Concerns (CA, TX): laboratory experiments have shown that rats, rabbits, mice, and hamsters have all developed cancer from all types of asbestos fibers (there are five main types).

Numerous studies of workers in the asbestos industry—mining, milling, and manufacturing—have shown increased incidence of a rare lung cancer (mesotheliomas) and gastrointestinal cancers.

Toxic effects include a lung

disease called *pulmonary asbestosis* caused by particles scarring the lungs; it is similar to black lung disease. Severe cases can lead to extreme debilitation and even death.

A study of workers from the New York and New Jersey International Association of Heat and Frost Insulators and Asbestos Workers revealed that out of 444 deaths from all causes, 89 died of lung cancer. In a normal population 11 deaths from lung cancer would have been expected. In the same group of workers, 10 died of mesothelioma where none would have been expected, and 40 died of gastrointestinal cancers where 13 would have been expected.

Exposure Levels/Standards: metropolitan areas have concentrations of from .5 to 5 ng of asbestos per cubic meter of air, primarily from wearing

ures to filter or otherwise contain this substance.

Asbestos is often used in the production of cement, cement products, wallboard, pipes, and brake linings for cars and trucks. Over the years there have been many consumer products made with asbestos insulation, including hair dryers, toasters, aprons, blankets, insulated electrical cables, filters, gaskets, insulation (attics and walls), ironing board covers, pot holders, siding, stove linings, textiles, twine, and yarns. Although restrictions have recently been imposed on the use of asbestos in some of those products, many people may still have such items in their homes.

Bioaccumulation Factor: not available.

Benzene
Formula: C_6H_6

What It Is: a liquid byproduct of the petroleum and coke-steel industries, it is highly volatile and is used in the manufacture of numerous pesticides, inks, paints, plastics, and other products. Because benzene has a basic ring structure, it is used in the synthesis of many chemicals, including pharmaceuticals and home care products. It is widely used as an industrial solvent and as an octane booster in gasoline.

Benzene levels outside plants producing petroleum products have been shown to be far higher than OSHA levels allowed for workers. (Petroleum Plant with New York Skyline Behind, 1982, by Michael Samuels.)

Major Health Concerns (CA, BD, TX): in laboratory tests, benzene fumes breathed by animals five hours per day, four days per week, for six weeks, at levels of 61 parts per million, resulted in significantly reduced production of white blood cells. It has also been shown to cause chromosome damage to bone cells in rats. Until recently it was thought that benzene did not cause cancer in animals, but two new studies (Maltoni 1977, and New York University 1978) have shown that ear tumors, skin tumors, and leukemia can be caused in rats and mice exposed to 100 parts per million (when ingested).

In humans the blood is affected in various ways: production of both red and white blood cells is reduced, and leukemia may occur. Benzene probably does its damage in the bone marrow, where blood cells are produced.

In humans benzene has been shown to cause chromosome damage to bone cells.

Benzene is used in the tire industry. In Akron, Ohio, in a study (Infante 1977) of the Goodyear tire plant making *pliofilm,* it was found that workers were exposed to benzene at levels up to 10 parts per million; this group of people had ten times as much leukemia as the general population.

Birth defects and chromosome damage have been demonstrated in experiments with rats.

Benzene causes a toxic syndrome which industrial workers call the "benzol jag": drunken behavior, lightheadedness, and disorientation.

Long-term, low-dose exposures cause tiredness and loss of appetite, symptoms characteristic of anemia.

Exposure Levels/Standards: the existing air standards are 10 parts per million, established in 1974. In 1977 OSHA alerted the industry of the need to reduce exposure to one part per million.

The EPA is considering setting a standard of 15 micrograms per liter for water, which would cause an estimated one excess cancer death per 100,000 people.

The annual average exposure of the general population is .001 part benzene per million parts air.

Drinking water in the United States has been found to have from .1 to 10 micrograms per liter, and 250 micrograms per liter have been found in our food.

Most people take more than 1 milligram of benzene into their bodies each day: 1.4 percent from water, 17.7 percent from food, and 80.9 percent from air.

Benzene levels outside plants producing tires, petroleum products, etc., have been shown to be as high as 3 parts per million immediately outside, with levels as high as .7 parts per

million a quarter mile from the plant. Benzene levels originating from industrial plants have been measured at "a few" parts per billion at up to twelve miles away. Also, 250 parts per billion have been measured next to gasoline pumps in filling stations, and 2 parts per billion "near" these businesses.

Benzene levels have been measured at 1 to 4 parts per billion in urban centers.

Where Found/What to Avoid: gasoline refineries are the main source of benzene in the environment. Most of these are located in California, Texas, Louisiana, and Illinois. Smaller but still significant numbers of refineries are located in Pennsylvania and New Jersey.

As a solvent, benzene is used in tire and rubber manufacturing, adhesives, and paints, and in floor coverings, such as vinyl tiles.

The burning of blast-furnace coke in smelter processes in Pennsylvania, Indiana, Ohio, and Alabama releases large amounts of benzene into the air.

When ethyl was banned from automobile gasoline, it was replaced by benzene as an octane booster. As a result, each automobile now dispenses some benzene into the atmosphere, and pumping gas releases some benzene from the tanks.

Consumer products containing benzene include paint solvents, furniture strippers, glues, cleaning fluids, some paint thinners, and hobby and art products. It is also found in cigarette smoke.

Bioaccumulation Factor: 6.9 in fish.

Beryllium

What It Is: a dark gray metal used in the production of light alloys, and an air and water pollutant that comes from burning fossil fuels. It is one of the four substances (beryllium, mercury, asbestos, and benzene) covered under the EPA emissions standards.

Major Health Concerns: (CA, BD, TX): extremely low doses of this chemical have been found to cause bone cancer and leukemia in laboratory animals, by both ingestion and inhalation.

Evidence is accumulating that inhalation of beryllium may cause lung cancer in humans.[1] It has been suspected as a human carcinogen since the early 1970s.

Toxic effects: irritation of the skin and mucous membrane; inflammation of the lungs; cough or shortness of breath; fatigue.

Causes mutations in bacteria.

Exposure Levels/Standards: found in 5 percent of the surface water (lakes and rivers) in the U.S. At these sites concentrations of .01 to 1.22 micrograms per liter were found.

Average concentration in air in the United States: .0005 micrograms per cubic meter.

OSHA safety guidelines: 2 micrograms per cubic meter for an eight-hour workday. (Projected recommendation, 1 microgram per cubic meter for an eight-hour workday.)

EPA national emission standards for hazardous air pollutants: 10 grams in 24 hours, resulting in maximum concentration outside the plant of .01 micrograms per cubic meter of air.

EPA is considering setting levels of .087 micrograms per liter of water, producing an estimated one case of cancer per 100,000 lives.

Where Found/What to Avoid: the major source of this chemical as an air and water pollutant is the burning of fossil fuels.

It is used in the manufacture of ceramic materials (used for spark plugs and other insulators), electronic tubes, space industry metals (alloys), and mantles for gasoline lanterns; in the latter, beryllium is burned off in the first fifteen minutes after installation of a new mantle, and these fumes should be avoided.

It is found in vapors and dusts of metal sculpture and ceramics.

Bioaccumulation Factor: from 20 to 1,000.

Cadmium

What It Is: a soft white metal resembling zinc or lead, used primarily for electroplating and making paints, and as a stabilizer in plastics.

Major Health Concerns (CA, BD, TX): causes cancer of soft tissue and testes in mice and rats. There is conjectural evidence that it causes prostate, lung, and kidney cancer in humans (Leman 1976 and Kolonel 1976).

Causes birth defects in rodents.

Toxicity: causes vomiting

and diarrhea. In the Jintsu River region of Japan, a disease called Itai-Itai is found among people eating rice that contains high levels of cadmium. Symptoms include bone pain caused by demineralization of the bone. Among 200 cases in 1970, half the people with this disease died.

With high doses, as in industry, cadmium causes lung and kidney disease.

Exposure Levels/Standards: OSHA recommends 100 micrograms per cubic meter of air. EPA recommends 10 micrograms per milliliter of water. FDA recommends .5 micrograms per milliliter of food.

Average air samples: .03 micrograms of cadmium per cubic meter.

Gasoline refineries are the main source of benzene. Benzene levels outside plants can be as high as 3 parts per million. (Refinery, 1982, by Michael Samuels.)

Average water sample: 1.3 micrograms per liter.

Average amount of cadmium in American diet: 30 micrograms per day.

Total average intake per day from all sources: 36.2 micrograms per day.

The toxic threshold for cadmium intake is estimated at about 200 micrograms per day. Carcinogenic thresholds are unknown.

Where Found/What to Avoid: industries where cadmium is used in large amounts include: electroplating, paint manufacturing (pigments), plastics, and metal alloy production; also welding alloy metals, battery production, photoelectric-cell production, and nuclear reactors. Also, one pack of cigarettes has 2–4 micrograms.

Avoid cadmium-plated cooking and serving utensils.

Bioaccumulation Factor: 1,000 measured in fish.

Carbon Tetrachloride
Formula: CCl_4

What It Is: The simplest organic chloride, used as a solvent, now being replaced as a pesticide for grain, used in fire extinguishers, and once as a propellant chemical for aerosols. Although it is no longer widely used, and has been removed from the consumer market, this chemical is important because, as a result of its widespread past use, it is still in the environment, and will need approximately 70,000 years to break down.

Major Health Concerns (CA, TX): causes cancer of the liver in hamsters and various tumors in fish.

One of the most toxic of all solvents, this chemical causes kidney and liver disease in all animals, including humans. Toxic symptoms include nausea, vomiting, and cramps.

Exposure Levels/Standards: Although there are no legislated standards for this chemical, the U.S. Department of Labor's recommendation for air is 10 milligrams per cubic meter per eight-hour workday; the EPA is

considering setting standards for water of 2.6 micrograms per liter, resulting in one case of cancer per 100,000 lives.

EPA has revealed that 10 percent of the drinking water sampled in the United States had levels of 2.4 to 6.4 micrograms per liter, caused by industrial spills.

Average levels in the air are .0008 milligrams per cubic meter. This chemical is dispersed throughout the Earth's atmosphere more or less uniformly, largely because carbon tetrachloride has been used so widely through the years.

The National Research Council estimates that the average person takes in 7.7 milligrams of carbon tetrachloride per year: 62 percent from the air, 23 percent from the water, and up to 15 percent in food (bread made from fumigated wheat contains up to .2 milligrams of carbon tetrachloride per kilogram of bread).

Where Found/What to Avoid: carbon tetrachloride has been removed from most consumer products because of its high toxicity. If you have bottles of this chemical in your home or workshop, do not use them.

This chemical is still used in refrigerants and limited industrial applications as a solvent. Industrial spills are a main source of exposure. In February 1977, 63 metric tons of this chemical were spilled into the Ohio River. Surface concentrations were as high as 340 micrograms per liter.

Bioaccumulation Factor: 69 measured in fish.

Chlordane/Heptachlor
Formula: $C_{10}H_6Cl_8$ or $C_{10}H_5Cl_7$

What It Is: Organochloride pesticides, once used for corn, termites, and general home use, were suspended from use in food and consumer products in 1975 by the manufacturer, and restricted in 1976 by the EPA.

Major Health Concerns (CA, TX): causes a high incidence of liver cancer in rats and mice; 25 parts per million resulted in liver cancers in 41 of 52 mice. Levels as low as .5 parts per million

have been shown to cause cancer.

According to Samuel Epstein, in *Politics of Cancer,* there are "scattered reports" of aplastic anemia caused in humans by this chemical. He also says there are "recent reports of cancer and leukemia in infants and young children born to mothers exposed to chlordane during pregnancy, following house-proofing for termites."[2]

Highly toxic to wildlife: birds die in five days after ingesting .22 parts per million in body weight.

Highly toxic for humans.

Exposure Levels/Standards: the American Conference of Governmental Industrial Hygienists has established an air standard of .5 milligrams per cubic meter.

In 1975 the EPA proposed a water standard of 3.0 micrograms per liter; it was not adopted. The EPA is considering a standard of 1.2 nanograms per liter, resulting in one case of cancer per 100,000 lives.

It is estimated that the average daily intake from all sources is 9 micrograms per person.

Where Found/What to Avoid: residues of this chemical have been found in the soil as much as 10 years after an application. These residues are highest in corn-growing areas and in residential areas where it has been applied to lawns.

Studies have shown that this chemical travels in dust; levels of 135 parts per million in the air were found in pesticide workers' homes, and 40 parts per million in average homes located in the corn-belt regions of the U.S.

Stream sediments in corn-belt regions have shown levels of 800 parts per billion. The flesh of fish contains 24 parts per million.

This chemical moves swiftly up the food chain, affecting dairy, meat, poultry, and freshwater fish. Chlordane is found in virtually all human body fat samples, umbilical cord blood, and mother's milk.

This chemical was made entirely by Velsicol Chemical Corporation, Marshall, Illinois, and Memphis, Tennessee. In 1972, the company hired two independent laboratories (one a university laboratory, Kettering Laboratory of the University of Cincinnati) to test these pesticides. Both laboratories reported the chemicals to be noncarcinogenic, and the chemicals continued to be used in large amounts. The EPA asked for a reexamination of laboratory slides from these studies, and discovered that they clearly revealed cancer. In 1977 Velsicol was indicted by the Federal Court of Chicago for withholding findings of carcinogenicity, and conspiring to defraud the United States and conceal material facts from the EPA.[3]

Bioaccumulation Factor: 18,000 in oysters, 5,500 in fish.

Chloroalkylethers
Formula: $ClCH_2OCH_2Cl$ (BCME)

What It Is: a family of chemicals, including BCEE, BCME, CMME, and BCIE, all used in the manufacture of plastic, rubber, and insecticides.

Major Health Concerns (CA): in studies, BCME —bis(chloro-methyl) ether— caused lung cancer in rats exposed to .01 parts per million inhaled for six hours per day, five days per week; twelve of twenty rats exposed developed lung cancer.

In studies, BCEE —bis(2-chloroethyl) ether—caused liver tumors in mice exposed to 300 parts per million in food; fourteen of sixteen mice developed tumors.

One study (Figueroa 1973) of Rohm Haas Plastics in Pennsylvania revealed extremely high lung-cancer rates among workers exposed to BCME. At the time of this study, four out of 44 employees exposed to BCME in their work had died of lung cancer. By 1978, 54 workers from this plant had died.

Exposure Levels/Standards: both BCME and CMME have been listed as human carcinogens and restricted by the federal government since 1974. Regulations decree that the use, storage, handling, and waste disposal of these chemicals must be rigidly controlled to avoid exposure to humans.

Exposure to BCME must be limited to 1 part per billion in air for an eight-hour day (American Conference of Governmental and Industrial Hygienists).

EPA is considering a standard of .00002 micrograms of BCME per liter of water, producing one case of cancer per 100,000 lives.

Exposure to BCEE must be limited to 15 parts per million in air for an eight-hour day (ACGIH).

EPA is considering a standard of .42 micrograms of BCEE per liter of water, producing one case of cancer per 100,000 lives.

The highest concentration of

these chemicals in drinking water, reported by the EPA, was .5 micrograms per liter.

Where Found/What to Avoid: BCME is used in the production of plastics and resins. In research laboratories where this chemical is handled, workers may be exposed to unsafe levels because of the lack of adequate restrictions and safeguards in the work environment.

Recently there has been general concern with the discovery that BCME is formed spontaneously in the presence of formaldehyde and hydrochloric acid vapors. Any industries where these two chemicals are used together may be exposing their workers to BCME. These industries include textile production, particle-board and paper pro-

duction, and biological and chemical laboratories.

BCEE is a solvent used by dry cleaners, textile workers, and paint producers.

High levels of BCEE have been found in drinking water because of spills and waste from chemical plants and industries involved with BCEE.

Bioaccumulation Factor: 106 in fish.

Chromium

What It Is: chromium is an element, a heavy metal, used for finishing metals and for stabilizing dyes in the fabric industry.

Major Health Concerns (CA, TX): chromium is an important human carcinogen, causing both lung and gastrointestinal cancers in workers exposed to it. Air levels of .1 milligram per cubic meter caused "significant" cancer rates (Mancuso 1951; Taylor 1966).

An extremely toxic element, it causes a skin rash ("chrome holes"), nasal ulcers, and bronchitis.

Lethal dose for an average fish is 7.4 milligrams per liter of water.

Exposure Levels/Standards: standards for drinking water, as formulated by EPA, are 50 micrograms per liter.

NIOSH standard for air in the workplace is 1 microgram per cubic meter.

Chrome causes both lung and gastrointestinal cancers in workers exposed to it. (*Untitled,* 1963, by John Chamberlain. Steel automobile parts, 31″ by 37.″ Collection of the Whitney Museum of American Art, New York.)

EPA is considering a standard of 8 nanograms per liter of water, resulting in one case of cancer per 100,000 lives.

In air samples it has been found that, in 59 out of 186 urban areas tested, the air contained .01 micrograms per cubic meter.

The EPA found that 25 percent of the water tested had as much as 50 micrograms of chromium per liter.

Where Found/What to Avoid: used in electroplating, leather tanning, dying fabrics, magnesium alloy production, the treatment of lumber for

Although DDT was banned in the U.S. in 1972, it continues to come back to us in foods from other countries, since our chemical companies still produce and sell it abroad. Its bioaccumulation factor is up to two million in fish. (*Around the Fish,* 1926, by Paul Klee. Oil on canvas, 18" × 25". Museum of Modern Art, New York. Abby Aldrich Rockefeller Fund.)

special weathering applications, pigments, and primers in paints.

Bioaccumulation Factor: 1 in fish.

DDT
Formula: 1,1'-(2,2,2-Trichloroethylidene)-bis (4-chorobenzene)

What It Is: a broad-spectrum, low-cost pesticide, banned in 1972 because of its persistence in the environment and its broad effect on the human food chain.

Major Health Concerns (CA, TX): induces liver tumors in mice; also suspected of causing mutations. In one study (Turusov 1973), DDT levels of 2

parts per million, in food, caused 179 liver tumors in 354 animals.

Toxicity is high. Tests on crayfish caused 50 percent of them to die within 96 hours, at exposure levels of .24 micrograms per liter, and 2 micrograms per liter, over 96 hours, resulted in the deaths of 50 percent of bass, one of the hardiest of fish.

Exposure Levels/Standards: by EPA standards, DDT should never exceed .41 micrograms per liter of water. Average content in water should not exceed .00024 parts per million.

By OSHA standards, exposure to skin surfaces should never exceed 1 milligram per kilogram of body weight.

WHO (World Health Organization) sets a food standard of .005 milligrams per kilogram of body weight.

EPA is considering a standard of .98 nanograms per liter, estimated to result in one cancer per 100,000 lives.

Content in air (1972): .1 nanogram per cubic meter.

Content in water (1972): .001 to .2 micrograms per liter in water.

It is estimated that the average person ingests .0001 milligrams of DDT per kilogram of food. In 1972, measurements of a large sampling showed that the average person had 6 parts per million DDT in body cells.

The history of DDT is con-

troversial. Although highly carcinogenic in animals, it has not been shown to cause human cancer in countries where it continues to be used. It was banned from the U.S. because the amounts of DDT in soil, water, and human body tissue were accumulating at an alarming rate. The biggest danger with this chemical is its extremely high bioaccumulation factor.

Where Found/What to Avoid: although DDT is banned in the United States and other countries, there are still world agricultural producers who use this pesticide. Current restrictions are changing the world over, so it is difficult to name accurately countries whose use of this chemical continues.

DDT may still be high in soils where this pesticide was once extensively sprayed, since it is a very long-lasting chemical.

Since DDT is stored in dairy products, animal fats, and fish, you could reduce your intake of DDT by lowering your ingestion of these foods, especially if they are from regions of the world where DDT *was* once used or is still being used as a pesticide.

Bioaccumulation Factor: from 40,000 to 2 million.

Dioxin
Formula: TCDD, or 2,3,7,8-Tetrachlorodibenzo-p-dioxin

What It Is: a chemical contaminant formed during the synthesis of herbicides such as 2,4,5-T and 2,4-D, dioxin is carried with these herbicides wherever they are applied. During the Vietnam conflict, a mixture of these chemicals, known as "Agent Orange," was sprayed by the Air Force over thousands of acres to destroy crops and expose enemy supply lines.

Major Health Concerns (CA, BD, TX): causes liver cancers in rats (Kociba 1979); animals affected had ingested 5 parts per billion in one study, and as little as .001 micrograms of dioxin per kilogram of animal's weight.

In pregnant rats ingesting .125 micrograms of dioxin per kilogram of body weight per day, fetuses had intestinal bleeding, died, or were resorbed.

Pregnant rats ingesting 1.0 microgram of dioxin per kilogram of body weight produced infants with an increased incidence of cleft palate.

Dioxin has been shown to be mutagenic in bacteria.

In humans exposed to dioxin, there has been reported an increased incidence of birth defects, including cleft palate, hare lip, and malformed limbs. These have been seen in Vietnamese women exposed to Agent Orange during pregnancy and in Humboldt County, California, where pregnant women were exposed to 2,4,5-T and 2,4-D sprayed by the U.S. Forest Service.

Dioxin is highly toxic, causing skin rash, weight loss, shrinking of the thymus gland, and liver damage. Because it can kill white blood cells and reduce the effectiveness of the immune system, dioxin ingested at toxic levels can cause death.

Exposure Levels/Standards: in 1979, because of protests in Humboldt County led by women whose children had been born with birth defects, the EPA gained a temporary suspension of 2,4,5,-T and 2,4-D spraying around highway right-of-ways and forests.

EPA is considering a standard of .00000045 micrograms of dixoin per liter in water, producing an estimated one case of cancer per 100,000 lives.

Approximately 46,000 Vietnam veterans have been exposed to Agent Orange; in 1980, reflecting this, 1,200 veterans filed a class-action suit with the Veterans Administration, a suit which promises to be the largest of its kind in history.

Where Found/What to Avoid: herbicides containing dioxin are sprayed over forests, rice fields, range land, and highway and electrical company right-of-ways.

Dioxin is contained in more than 400 consumer products, including 2,4,5-T, Silvex, Kuron, Weed-be-gone, and similar "weedkillers."

Dioxin may be high in water supplies around areas sprayed with herbicides, and in fish caught in lakes and rivers around such areas.

Bioaccumulation Factor: 6,000 in fish.

Halomethane

What It Is: a general category of methanes including chloroform ($CHCl_3$); TBM or tribromomethanes ($CHBr_3$); trichlorofluoro-methane (CCl_3F), etc. Although these chemicals have industrial applications, our main interest in them as an environmental disease factor is that large quantities are by-products of chlorination of drinking water nationwide, affecting both water and the ozone layer.

Major Health Concerns (CA, BD): chloroform administered by mouth to mice (National Cancer Institute Bioassay, 1976) produced 36 liver cancers out of 45 animals.

Dichloromethane caused mutations in salmonella bacteria and mice (Simmon 1977).

Trichlorofluoromethane caused mutations in yeast (Stephens 1971.)

In the air, halomethane rises up into the stratosphere and ionosphere, where it combines with the ozone and depletes it.

Exposure Levels/Standards: EPA standards for total halomethanes, including chloroform, is 100 micrograms per liter of water. These standards were a compromise between "economic necessity" and "public safety;" initially they affect water supplies only for communities greater than 75,000 people.

EPA estimates that each person ingests between .73 milligrams and 343 milligrams per year from drinking water.

EPA estimates that 2.1 micrograms of halomethanes per liter of water will cause one case of cancer per 100,000 lives.

Where Found/What to Avoid: halomethanes are ubiquitous as a result of chlorinating water. This means they are in most drinking water in the United States.

Halomethanes are also released into the air by water-chlorination plants.

Bioaccumulation Factor: 14 in fish.

Lead

What It Is: a soft, gray metal used in storage batteries, gasoline additives, and paint pigments. Lead has become a major health concern because it is highly toxic and is now found throughout the environment as a result of our extensive use of it in gasoline and house paints. It has recently been postulated that lead poisoning from eating utensils was in large part responsible for the decline of the Roman Empire. If verified, this will be the first example of pollution bringing down an entire civilization.

Major Health Concerns (BD, TX): pediatricians have long been aware of the dangers of lead poisoning in children. Symptoms include loss of appetite, listlessness, irritability, clumsiness, and loss of recently acquired developmental skills. High doses can produce convulsions.

Adults who have ingested toxic levels of lead suffer gastrointestinal upset, joint and muscle pain, headache and sleep disturbances, and sometimes tremors. With high doses they may experience sharp intestinal pain.

Biochemical studies show that lead poisoning can reduce production of red blood cells, and disrupt the biochemistry of blood cells.

Lead has been shown to cause birth defects and death of fetuses in rodents (McLain and Baker 1975).

Decreased reproductive ability has been reported in both men and women exposed to toxic levels of lead (Lancranjan 1975).

Exposure Levels/Standards: lead is now so ubiquitous in our environment that efforts are being made to regulate it in all products where humans might be affected or where it might enter the air and water.

The *Consumer Product Safety Commission* limits the use of lead in paint to not more than .06 percent.

The OSHA industrial standard is .1 milligram of lead per cubic meter of air. By 1988 the industry must have reduced lead content in their factories to .05 milligrams per cubic meter of air.

The EPA standard is 50 micrograms of lead per liter of water.

Surface waters measured along the Pacific Coast contain .35 milligrams of lead per liter of water, approximately ten times the level prior to the Industrial Revolution.

Concentration of lead in the air of urban centers can be as high as 10 micrograms per cubic meter.

Average U.S. diet can have as much as 200 micrograms of lead per day.

Where Found/What to Avoid: large quantities of lead are found in lead smelting. Lead is used in the production of batteries, alloys, paint pigments, solder, gasoline additives, ceramic glazes, and metal cans.

From industrial sources, lead enters the environment through dust, rain, and waste discharges. Each year approximately 5,000 tons of lead enter the ocean as runoff from these channels.

Before lead was restricted in automobile fuels, the EPA estimated that 90 percent of the lead in the general environment came from the exhaust of internal combustion engines.

Dust and dirt around homes have been found to have a lead content as high as .1 percent, which translates to 1,000 parts per million.

Some paints produced before 1940 were 50 percent lead. Lead content in house paints was reduced, but was still relatively high through the 1960s. Safe levels were not really established until the 1970s. As a result, when people are restoring older homes, scraping and sanding of paint can cause lead content in the home to become high enough to cause major health problems; so homeowners or restorers should take special precautions, such as using respirators, vacating the house during restoration (especially if children are involved), and protecting food and water from contamination.

Lead is also found in the yellow lacquer of some pencils and in cigarette smoke.

If you are living in an older home, be particularly careful to prevent children from ingesting paint or chips peeling from the walls, both inside and outside the house. Repaint old flaking surfaces, and if flaking occurs indoors, sweep up or vacuum paint particles daily, so that children won't eat them.

Bioaccumulation Factor: not available.

Lindane
Formula: γ-1,2,3,4,5,6-hexachlorocyclohexane, $C_6H_6Cl_6$

What It Is: a broad-spectrum insecticide and organochloride, used in a variety of applications, including the treatment of animals and humans for lice and other parasites.

Major Health Concerns (CA, TX): mice were fed 400 parts per million in their diet for 110 weeks; 27 out of 28 animals got liver cancer.

In Japanese factories producing lindane, convulsions were experienced by workers receiving 23 milligrams of this chemical per cubic meter of air.

Toxic effects include skin rash, headache, irritability, and digestive problems.

Exposure Levels/Standards: although not made in the United States, lindane is imported for a number of applications. For this reason there are no U.S. standards on production.

World Health Organization has set an "allowable daily intake" of 1.0 microgram per kilogram of body weight per day.

EPA standards: for air, .5 milligrams per cubic meter; for drinking water, .004 parts per million; for animal fat, 7 parts per million; for milk, .3 parts per million; for fruits and vegetables, 1 part per million.

In 1969 the average daily intake for U.S. citizens was .002 micrograms per kilogram of body weight per day from air, and .07 micrograms per kilogram of body weight from food.

The EPA is considering a standard of 54 nanograms per liter in water as causing an estimated one case of cancer per 100,000 lives.

Where Found/What to Avoid: used as a fumigant for protecting seeds. Workers processing and packaging seeds treated with lindane, as well as agricultural workers handling seeds, may be exposed to high levels of this chemical.

Lindane is widely used for the treatment of animal parasites and other insects. It is the active ingredient in *medicated shampoos* (Kwell Shampoo) prescribed by doctors for the treatment of head lice and scabies in children, and of pubic and body lice in adults, and in the treatment of pets for lice and fleas. It is contained in flea "bombs" used to fumigate homes to kill fleas, and in some flea powders and shampoos used for animals.

People using shampoos and other lindane products are exposed to this chemical both by breathing it and by absorbing it through the skin.

(Two other shampoos, *Rid* and *A-200*, do not contain Lindane and therefore present lower health hazards to humans and are nearly as effective as Kwell.)

Bioaccumulation Factor: 780 in fish.

Mercury

What It Is: a silvery white metal, liquid at room temperature; 30 percent is used in industry for processing chemicals (chlorine and caustic soda), the remainder is used in electrical devices, such as lamps, batteries, and switches, and in thermometers and barometers.

Major Health Concerns (TX, BD): it has been discovered (Jensen and Jernelov 1969) that certain microorganisms convert mercury into a highly toxic chemical called methyl mercury. The microorganisms containing methyl mercury generally live in the sediment of bays, streams, and rivers, and are eaten by fish. When humans eat the fish, they ingest methyl mercury.

Mercury is one of the oldest known industrial pollutants. Its history of toxicity dates back to Roman times, when one of the worst fates for a slave was to be sent out to mine it.

In the early 1900s, mercury was used for making hats, and caused a variety of symptoms in workers: irritability, involving timidity and fear; tremors; inflammation of the gums, and sometimes increased salivation. (Low-level exposure can cause spongy gums and a variety of vague complaints.) The expression "mad as a hatter" arose from this use of mercury.

In the late 1960s, the famous photographer W. Eugene Smith produced a photo account of Minamata, Japan, where hundreds of people's lives were ruined by the careless dumping of mercury into Minamata Bay. The course of the disease caused by methyl mercury poisoning was numbness, slurred speech, aggression, and tunnel vision, followed by deformation of limbs, memory loss, and finally death. In Minamata the people ate fish containing large amounts of methyl mercury, and the health problems that ensued involved everything from crippling tremors, psychological disturbances, and mental retardation to birth defects and physical deformities.

Exposure Levels/Standards: the EPA standard for drinking water is .2 micrograms per liter.

The EPA has also set a standard for bodies of fresh water because of the effects of mercury on fish. The *mercury* standard is .065 micrograms per liter. Similarly, the EPA standard for salt water is .19 micrograms per liter.

The EPA standard for *methyl mercury* in fresh water is .016 micrograms per liter and in salt water .025. The reason for setting these low levels is because

fish take up large quantities of methyl mercury, passing it up the food chain to humans.

In 1970 the Department of the Interior tested industrial waste water for mercury content: 30 percent contained more than 10 micrograms per liter, and 4 percent of the waste water contained more than 1,000 micrograms per liter. According to the EPA, most of the very high mercury levels were found in small streams. The same survey found that half the samples of Mississippi River water contained less than .1 micrograms of mercury per liter. Miscellaneous lakes and reservoirs contained .1 to 1.8 micrograms of mercury per liter.

A recent study by the EPA found that 11 of 273 drinking-water supplies tested in the U.S. contained from 1.0 to 4.8 micrograms of mercury per liter of water. Minamata Bay measured 1.6 to 3.6 micrograms per liter; that is, drinking-water levels of mercury are higher than mercury levels at Minamata Bay. The only reason more people don't show symptoms from the drinking water is that they are not eating fish or microorganisms raised in it, and so are not ingesting methyl mercury.

Where Found/What to Avoid: industrial uses are 33 percent for the preparation of chlorine and caustic soda, 27 percent for such devices as lamps, switches, batteries, and ther-

mometers, and 12 percent in paints to prevent the growth of bacteria and mildew; the remainder is used in a variety of laboratory and industrial applications.

Some outdoor house paints may contain as much as 35 percent mercury; others may contain none at all. (Sherwin Williams and Sears Exterior paints contained no mercury in 1982.)

When you are painting, mercury content in the air may be in the range of the NIOSH levels for industrial air: .05 milligrams per cubic meter.

Bioaccumulation Factor: 63,000 in freshwater fish, 10,000 in saltwater fish.

PCBs
Formula:
$Cl_{2-5}H_{0-3}C_6H_{0-3}Cl_{2-5}$

What It Is: stable organic compounds used extensively in transformers and capacitors as insulators, as well as in other products. Production was banned in the United States in 1979 as a result of their threat to the environment.

Major Health Concerns (TX, CA): Kimbrough (1975) found a significant increase of liver cancer in rats exposed to PCBs. In this study 26 rats in a group of 184, exposed to 100 parts per million, developed liver cancer. Several other studies using rodents failed to show an in-

In 1974, studies showed that there are PCBs in the fat of more than a third of the people in the United States. Although banned, PCBs persist in the environment, mostly in fresh water. (General Electric on the Hudson River, 1982, by Michael Samuels.)

crease in cancer, but did reveal an increased incidence of "precancerous" tumors.

Toxic levels of exposure produce "chlor acne," fatigue, loss of appetite, and diminished sexual drive.

Birth defects included cases of spontaneous abortion, stillbirths, undersized infants, and survivors with behavioral problems and learning deficiencies. This experiment (James R. Allen 1975) was done with monkeys that were given 5 parts of PCBs per million in food.

Exposure Levels/Standards: because PCBs are persistent in the environment and there is a

Mother's milk contains significant concentrations of toxic chemicals including PCBs. (*Madonna and Child,* 1938, by Andrea de Bartolo. National Gallery of Art, Washington, D.C.)

Bioaccumulation factors of PCBs in various sea life

Animal	Bioaccumulation Factor
Oyster	100,000
Crab	4,000
Shrimp	3,200 up to 11,000
Pinfish	11,000 up to 24,000
Minnow	2,500 up to 8,000

high concentration of them in the food chain, a large percentage of the world's human population is exposed to this chemical. A study done in 1974 found PCBs in the fat of 30 to 40 percent of people in the U.S. It is in 43 percent of blood plasma studied, and in a significant amount of mother's milk.

EPA is considering standards for water of .26 nanograms per liter; this would produce one cancer per 100,000 lives.

In Canada it was found that the average person had 1 part PCB per million in body fat.

U.S. tests found that mother's milk contained 1.8 parts PCBs per million.

In samples of drinking water tested in the U.S., 20 percent showed an average of .2 micrograms of PCBs per liter.

Average air samples contained 100 nanograms of PCBs per cubic meter of air.

The average intake of PCBs in food is approximately 9 micrograms per day.

Where Found/What to Avoid: although PCBs have been

banned, they persist in the environment, mostly in fresh water and in the body fat of animals and humans. As a result, nursing infants and sportsmen eating freshwater game fish are more at risk than other members of the population.

Disposal of PCB transformers and capacitors presents a special problem, since these chemicals, unless permanently contained, will leak out into the environment.

Although a relatively weak carcinogen, the environmental impact of PCBs is important because of its incredibly high bioaccumulation factor.

Bioaccumulation Factor: average of 46,000, with a high of 100,000 in oysters.

TCE or Trichloroethylene
Formula: $Cl_2C = Ch\ Cl$

What It Is: a solvent with numerous medical, industrial, and home applications, ranging from degreasing machinery to decaffeinating coffee.

Major Health Concerns (CA, TX): 26 out of 50 mice ingesting 1,169 milligrams of TCE per kilogram of body weight for eighty weeks got liver cancer (National Cancer Institute 1977).

A study done by the Manufacturing Chemists Association (1977), with mice inhaling 600 parts TCE per million, showed a "modest increase" of liver cancer.

TCE has been shown to cause mutations in yeasts and bacteria, and changes in the protein structure (microsomes) of rodent liver cells.

Toxic effects include gastrointestinal upsets, depression of the central nervous system, narcosis, and heart and liver malfunctions.

Exposure Levels/Standards: NIOSH standard is 25 parts per million in air during an eight-hour work day.

EPA is considering a standard of 25 micrograms per liter of water as producing an estimated one case of cancer per 100,000 lives.

The American Conference of Governmental Industrial Hygienists has not yet established recommendations about TCE's

carcinogenicity; their standards, based on toxicity, are now 3,820 milligrams per day.

In Russia, the governmental health standards are 7 milligrams per day.

The USFDA has established limits of 10 milligrams per kilogram in spices and coffee.

Where Found/What to Avoid: TCE is highly volatile, and escapes into the air during manufacture and use. As a result large quantities make their way into the environment, distributed globally through air, oceans, rivers, drinking-water supplies, food, and human tissue.

It is used extensively as a solvent by caffeine processors, dry cleaners, machinery and electronics degreasers/cleaners, oil processors, printers, perfume makers, resin workers, rubber cementers, shoe makers, soap makers, textile cleaners, tobacco denicotinizers, varnish workers, drug makers, and fat processors.

NIOSH (1978) estimates that over 3.5 million workers are exposed to this chemical.

Consumer products containing TCE include cleaning fluids, decaffeinated coffee, varnishes, paints, and degreasers. In areas near industries using TCE, consumers may find this chemical in their drinking water.

Bioaccumulation Factor: 39 in fish.

Toluene
Formula: $C_6H_5CH_3$

What It Is: an organic chemical in the benzene family. 694 million gallons were produced in the U.S. in 1970. Of this, 75 percent was converted to benzene, 15 percent was used in the production of other chemicals, and the remainder was used as solvents or gasoline additives.

Major Health Concerns (TX, BD): the chemical has been tested by several sources, and has not been found to be cancerous or mutagenic in animals.

Toxic effects in humans (from inhalation) include nervous system and mental changes, irritability, and disorientation; it acts as a depressant, and can cause heart, liver, and kidney damage.

In rats, 4,000 parts per million inhaled cause learning defects.

Some tests (Lyapkalo 1973) showed chromosome damage to bone cells of rats given extremely high doses.

One test (Hudak 1978) showed embryo death in rats given 600 milligrams per cubic meter of air.

Women who used toluene in varnishing work during pregnancy (Syrovadko 1977) showed lowered blood cell production, and reported premature babies, babies who had difficulty breathing and acted drugged, and babies who were late in expressing sucking instincts. The women also reported menstrual disorders.

Exposure Levels/Standards: toluene has been found in the drinking water of several major cities in the U.S.; hence standards for toluene in water are important. For example, it has been found that the drinking water in New Orleans had toluene levels of 11 micrograms per liter.

EPA standards for water are 12.4 milligrams per liter, and 375 milligrams per cubic meter for air.

Because this chemical has not been proven to be a carcinogen, tremendously high levels are allowed in the workplace.

Where Found/What to Avoid: used primarily as a spot remover and dry-cleaning agent in consumer products.

Toluene is found in levels of 108 micrograms per cigarette.

Bioaccumulation Factor: 20 in fish.

Vinyl Chloride
Formula: $CH_2 = CHCl$

What It Is: derived from petrochemicals and chlorine, it is widely used in the production of plastics. This chemical is a *monomer,* that is, a molecular unit which functions as a basic building block for common plastics such as polyvinyl chloride (PVC). It is the most widely used material in the plastics industry: 18 billion pounds were produced worldwide in 1972.

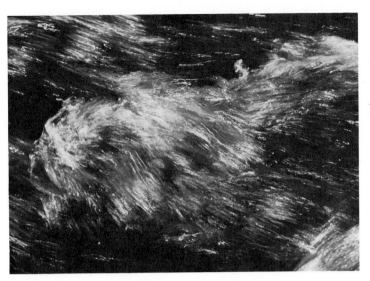

Major Health Concerns (CA, TX): this chemical is known to cause liver cancer in rats (Maltoni 1972*). The specific type of liver cancer it causes—angiosarcoma—is rare, and it was this rarity that led scientists to discover the correlation with exposure to vinyl chloride. In addition to angiosarcomas, it also causes more common forms of liver cancer, as well as kidney, brain, breast, and lung cancer. The Maltoni research in 1972, establishing that as little as 50 parts per million in air cause angiosarcomas in animals, as well as a previous study by Viola in 1970, were kept secret by the plastics industry until 1974. The information became public only after PVC workers at B.F. Goodrich in Louisville, Kentucky, were found to have an extraordinarily high incidence of the rare angiosarcoma.

Epidemiological studies of vinyl chloride workers show an increased incidence of rare liver cancers and all other cancers. The cancer rate is directly related to the number of years a worker spends in the industry.

As a toxin, vinyl chloride causes skin rashes and numbness to the fingers, kills blood cells, and causes liver malfunctions.

Exposure Levels/Standards: EPA standards for air at factory sites are 10 parts per million.

EPA standards for water are 517 micrograms per liter; at this level it is estimated that there will be one case of cancer per 100,000 lives.

OSHA standard for air in the workplace is one part per million during an eight-hour period.

In 1974 the EPA banned the use of vinyl chlorides in aerosol propellants.

In 1975 it was found that more than 4.5 million people lived within five miles of vinyl chloride industries, and that their average exposure to this chemical was 17 parts per million; within a half mile of these sites, exposure rates were as high as 323 parts per million.

The EPA estimates that continuous exposure to levels of 1 part per million doubles the probability of getting all types of cancers, and that such an exposure level would produce 71 cases of angiosarcoma per million people per year.

Where Found/What to Avoid: levels of vinyl chlorides in the air are highest around vinyl chloride and polyvinyl chloride plants.

Factories producing the following goods also account for high exposure levels for the general population: phonographs, electric wire, floor tile, furniture, vinyl fabrics, food wrappers, children's toys, PVC pipe, inside trim for automobiles, garbage cans, and other containers. Butchers wrapping meat in heat-sealed vinyl are subjected to high levels of vinyl chloride.

Vinyl chloride is found in levels of .01 micrograms per cigarette.

Bioaccumulation Factor: 2 in fish.

Toluene has been found in the drinking water of several major U.S. cities. Drinking water in New Orleans had toluene levels of 11 micrograms per liter. (*Surface Water Source,* 1982, by Michael Samuels.)

*Maltoni found that as little as 1 part per million caused breast cancer in rodents.

CHAPTER TEN

Water Pollution

Water is the circulatory system of the living Earth. It is the common link between all life forms. Early people treated water resources with the highest reverence, and their cultures were often organized around a water source; the city of Jericho, for example, began to grow 10,000 years ago around a spring that had been used by humans for millennia and is still in use now.

We depend on water no less now than we did hundreds of thousands of years ago, and yet we have lost touch with the significance of this resource to all life. In his book *Patterns in Comparative Religion,* Mircea Eliade describes how water "precedes all forms and upholds all creations." Throughout history, he says, people have paid homage to water. Indeed, it is at the basis of many religious rituals, including baptism, wherein "immersion in water symbolizes a return to the pre-formal, a total regeneration, a new birth, for immersion means a dissolution of forms, a reintegration into the formlessness of pre-existence; and emerging from the water is a repetition of the act of creation in which form was first expressed." Water purifies and regenerates "because it nullifies the past, and restores—even if only for a moment—the integrity of the dawn of things."[1]

What It Is

From a scientific point of view, water is the most important chemical compound known. The atoms that make up water—hydrogen and oxygen—have existed since nearly the beginning of time, with hydrogen being the first substance formed after creation. Water makes up three-quarters of the Earth's surface and two-thirds of the human body. It is the most essential single component of living mat-

Water is the circulatory system of the living Earth. (*Water Painting No. 5,* 1973, by Joseph Raffael. Oil on canvas, 78″ × 114″. Collection of the Whitney Museum of American Art, New York.)

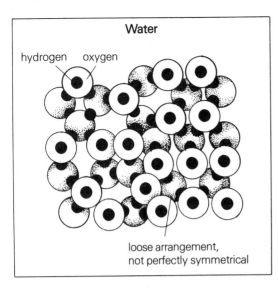

Water

hydrogen   oxygen

loose arrangement,
not perfectly symmetrical

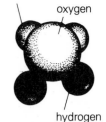

oxygen's electron

oxygen

hydrogen

Water is the single most important part of life because it is a medium in which molecules can combine, and because it is a source of hydrogen. Liquid water has oxygen atoms surrounded tetrahedrally by four hydrogen atoms in random and changing arrangements.

ter, because of two properties: (1) it is a medium in which all atoms can combine and recombine into new and more complex molecules; and (2) it is the basic source of all hydrogen and oxygen, the chemical foundation of all energy and life.

To pollute such a basic life source is more than an act of negligence; it is a clear signal that we have lost touch with the physical and spiritual roots that nurture us. The evidence that we need to once again embrace our essential resources is nowhere more in evidence than in the diseases we are now suffering because we have allowed our water resources to be destroyed by the chemicals of industry.

Water does have homeostatic capacities, just as cells, animals, and the living Earth do. But the fact that our water is ceasing to provide health for humans and all other living things shows that we have overloaded it with inappropriate forms of matter, energy, and information. When water ceases to be able to purify itself, to reestablish its integrity after being violated by human excess, it ceases to serve humanity.

There are two forms of water resources we need to consider in the problem of pollution: first, *surface water,* that is, lakes, rivers, streams, and wetlands; and second, *groundwater,* that is, underground streams and the water table, which we tap for wells.

When people first began polluting their water resources by dumping human wastes into them, the main concern was bacteria. Disease-causing bacteria entering the water supplies quickly spread infection throughout large communities. After sewage and sanitation methods were invented and applied, both to disposal of human wastes and to purifying water, human infection from bacterial pollu-

Water is important to many religions; in Christian baptism, it symbolizes rebirth. (The Baptism of Christ, by the Master of the Life of St. John the Baptist, fourteenth century. National Gallery of Art, Washington, D.C.)

To pollute such a basic life source as water is more than an act of negligence; it is a clear signal that we have lost touch with the physical and spiritual roots that nurture us. (Nine Coves and Three Bends in the River, 1953, by Sokyo Ueda. Brush and ink, 26" by 50." Museum of Modern Art, New York. Japanese house fund.)

tion ceased to be the major health hazard it once had been.

Even when people were polluting surface waters with their wastes, they still had a source of pure water in groundwater. This water was unique in that bacteria from human wastes were filtered out or broken down by minerals and bacteria in the Earth itself. However, when people began manipulating molecules to create new chemicals, the problem of maintaining pure water supplies was complicated a hundredfold. Technologies could be created for filtering effluent from factories and sewage-processing plants before it entered both surface and groundwater resources, but the problem didn't end there.

Massive quantities of chemicals are sprayed over the Earth as pesticides, herbicides, and fertilizers, and these, too, seep through to the groundwater, or wash away into streams, rivers, lakes, and oceans. Chemicals easily make their way into groundwater. For the most part, they are not broken down by microorganisms or filtered out by minerals in the soil, and once in the groundwater they are dispersed throughout the millions of

Water is not static, it moves through the complex circulatory system of the living earth.

streams in the complex circulatory system lying beneath the Earth's crust. Added to this is the fact that chemicals which are dispersed in the air above the Earth's surface, are then carried back to Earth in the rains. These chemical-rich rains then seep into the Earth, entering both groundwater and surface waters.

Chemical wastes in solid form likewise can make their way into groundwater. Although such wastes are originally dumped as solids, rains dissolve these chemicals, however slowly, and they eventually form a plume, or channel, through the Earth into the groundwater. In time solid contaminants can move great distances, averaging tens of feet per year. Because of varying characteristics of the soil, how and where solid chemical wastes will affect water supplies is completely unpredictable.

How It Causes Disease

Until the Industrial Revolution the main issue in water pollution was microorganism content. Since drinking water was often drawn from shallow wells or surface waters, it was easily polluted by human sewage and garbage disposal. Infections such as salmonella, enterobacteria, pseudomonas, typhoid, enteroviruses (causing eye, ear, nose, and throat infections),

Table 10.1: Chemicals found in hazardous waste dumps[a]

Name of chemical	How chemical is used	Health hazard
Trichloroethylene	Degreaser	CA, TX
PCB	Insulators	CA, TX
Benzene	Solvent	CA, BD, TX
Vinyl chloride	Plastics manufacture	CA, TX
Mercury	Various uses	BD, TX
Lead	Various uses	BD, TX
Carbon tetrachloride	Solvent	CA, TX
DDT	Pesticide	CA, TX
Tris	Fire retardent	CA
Curene 442	Plastics manufacture	CA

[a]Adapted from *Environmental Quality*, 1980.

and even polio can be spread by unclean drinking and/or bathing water. When fish living in polluted waters are eaten by humans, bacterial infections have a second route to the human digestive system. Fish, especially shellfish, can accumulate rather high concentrations of bacteria and viruses. Bioaccumulation factors range from 33 to 2,200 to hundreds of thousands.

In developed countries where water purification is employed, filtering and processing

Industrial plants along rivers pollute the drinking water and irrigation supplies. (River Rouge Plant, 1932, by Charles Sheeler. Oil on canvas, 20" by 24." Collection of Whitney Museum of American Art, New York.)

of this important resource are aimed almost exclusively at bacteria and virus contents. Most modern water-cleansing systems have no effect on chemical pollution from pesticides, dumping of chemical wastes, or leakage of dangerous chemicals from industry into both surface water and groundwater. Ironically, the purification processes themselves introduce chemicals, both into the water and into the air, which can be hazardous to humans.

Of course, there are still problems with bacterial pollution in many parts of the world, but the main concern today is how carcinogenic chemicals make their way into human water supplies. Carcinogens can and are contaminating our water supplies: throughout the United States the EPA has found more than 700 agricultural and industial chemicals routinely

Between Baton Rouge and New Orleans, on the Mississippi River, there are more than 50 major chemical plants. In 1972, the EPA found chloroform, benzene, and BCEE in the drinking water of New Orleans. The benzene and BCEE originated from the chemical industry, but it was later found that the chloroform resulted from the treatment of drinking water with chlorine. These findings led to a study, in 1974, by the Environmental Defense Fund. The EDF found, in comparing similar groups of people, that those living in New Orleans, and drinking water contaminated with substances from the chemical plants, had significantly higher incidences of genitourinary and gastrointestinal cancers than did people from southern communities who used water from other sources.

Chemicals in the drinking water cannot be ignored as a disease factor in cancer. These chemicals come from agriculture (pesticides), industry, consumer products (septic tanks), auto emissions (hydrocarbons), mining, and leakage from petroleum wells. (*Painted Water Glasses,* 1974, by Janet Fish. Oil on canvas, 53″ × 60″. Collection of the Whitney Museum of American Art, New York.)

The most prevalent dangerous chemicals in drinking water

Chloroform (TCM)	PCBs
Benzene	Toluene
BCEE	Toxaphene (pesticide)
Carbon tetrachloride	Methoxychlor (pesticide)
Nitrosamines	Endrine (pesticide)
Polynuclear aromatic hydrocarbon (PAH)	Lindane (pesticide)
	2,4-D (herbicide)
Trichloroethylene (TCE)	2,4,5-T (herbicide)
Xylene	Vinyl chloride
Selenium	Mercury
Arsenic	Lead
Cyanide	DDT

making their way into the drinking water. Of these, at least 22 are known or proven carcinogens. We cannot yet be certain how many substances in our water are carcinogenic, because as yet very few of them have been tested. What is perhaps even more alarming is that the 700 chemicals thus far identified may represent as little as 10 percent of the chemicals actually in the water, because we cannot yet detect all the chemicals that may be making their way into the water. Although it would be a slight exaggeration, it is fair to say that nearly every time a new test is invented, it reveals a new chemical in our water supplies.

Evidence of Its Danger

The health hazards of each chemical are different, of course. In Poisons List A (pages 144 to 157) we tell how each chemical has been shown to cause cancer in humans, animals, or both. Epidemiological studies suggest strong associations between cancer and the human ingestion of water with high chemical content. Consider the following.

Studies of the Ohio River (Kuzma and Kuzma 1977; Buncher 1975; Environmental Defense Fund 1977), where water is contaminated by industrial dumping, agricultural (pesticide) runoff, and forestry (pesticide and herbicide) operations, two groups of people were compared. Those who received their water from surface water had significantly higher rates of stomach, bladder, liver, and breast cancer than people who received their water from deep wells (groundwater).

In upstate New York, Alavanja and Goldstein (1977) studied people drinking chlorinated versus nonchlorinated water. Mortality studies showed significantly higher death rates from gastrointestinal and urinary-tract cancer among people drinking chlorinated water than among people drinking nonchlorinated water.

Similar studies done in: Washington County, Maryland (Kruse 1977); the Ohio River Basin (Salg 1977); Pittsburg, Pennsylvania (Carlson and Andoman 1977); and in New Jersey

(Vasilenko 1975) have shown definite correlations between chemical contaminants in the water supplies and increased cancer rates.

In two studies of EPA Region Five (Illinois, Indiana, Michigan, Minnesota, Ohio, and Wisconsin), the correlations between cancer and chlorinated drinking water were studied. The first study (Cantor 1977) showed that the incidence of death from cancer of the bladder increased as the amounts of trihalomethanes (other than chloroform) in the drinking water went up. The second study (Hogan 1978) showed that the incidence of death from cancer of the bladder, rectum, and possibly large intestine increased as the amounts of chloroform in the drinking water went up.

At least seventeen studies have shown strong correlations between cancer and chemicals in the drinking water.

Extent of the Threat

The amounts of chemicals in drinking water supplies are extremely low, making it difficult to establish exact correlations between disease and chemical content or to predict cancer deaths from their presence. However, studies such as those described in the preceding paragraphs suggest associations between chemical content and cancer that cannot be ignored. As in most cancers, multiple factors are usually involved, and although contaminated water is clearly one factor, it is by no means the single cause. In other words, drinking contaminated water may, along with other factors, increase your risk of getting cancer. How much it increases that risk is controversial.

Solid-waste disposal sites are the single most important source of groundwater contamination. There are 75,000 active industrial dumps in the United States. (Peacock Gap, 1970, by William Wiley. Watercolor, pen and ink, 29″ × 21″. Museum of Modern Art, New York. Larry Aldrich Foundation Fund.)

Peacock Gap

The plumage was varied enough. The incredible range of colors, textures and shapes as always were beyond amazing. It was perfect in all visual aspects. But the smell. The smell was impossible. There was just no way to feel right about it.

Wm. T. Wiley 1970

One study (Hogan 1978), of chloroform in drinking water, estimated that for every increase of 100 micrograms of chloroform per liter of water, there will be an increase of .3 deaths per million people per year. This represents an increase of 4.4 percent over normally expected cancer rates.

Another study (Alavanja and Goldstein 1977) found a 177 percent increase in genitourinary and gastrointestinal cancers in chlorinated over nonchlorinated regions. This represents an excess 300 cancers per year per million people.

In 1978, the EPA proposed to restricting halomethanes (THMs) to 100 parts per billion parts of water, in water systems supplying 75,000 or more people. The EPA estimates that if these restrictions were *enforced*, the THMs would still account for approximately 200 excess cancer deaths per year in the United States. Other researchers, using the same data but interpreting it differently, estimate that this amount of THM exposure would account for up to 3,000 cancer deaths annually.

Such estimates are for extremely low levels of chemical exposure in drinking water, and only take into account the effects of a single chemical, not the multiple chemicals contained in most water. Moreover, they do not estimate health effects from industrial accidents, such as spills, careless monitoring of effluent, or the disposal of chemical wastes.

Where It Is Found

Our water supplies are contaminated from several sources: agriculture (pesticides, herbicides, and soil runoff); industry (waste disposal, spills, and leaks); consumers (sewage and septic tanks, auto emissions, use and disposal of toxic substances, such as aerosols, paints, and solvents); mining (waste disposal of toxic byproducts, the leakage of chemicals used in processing slag); and leakage from petroleum and natural gas wells and processing.

The problems in groundwater and surface-water contamination are quite different. Let's consider the groundwater issues, keeping in mind that this source supplies approximately 25 percent of the nation's water resources, 13 percent of which is used as drinking water, the remainder in agriculture and industry.

Solid-waste disposal sites are the single most important source of groundwater contamination. There are 75,000 active industrial dumps, 50,000 of which are handling potentially dangerous wastes. For 95 percent of these, there exists no system for monitoring how groundwater is being affected. An EPA evaluation of 50 industrial disposal sites in 1977 found contaminated groundwater at 40 sites, and migration of chemical contaminants at 27. In addition, they found water contaminated with heavy metals at 49 of these 50 sites. Prior to this study no contamination had been reported from any of these sites.

In areas where there is no industry chemical dumps, but where there are large populations, septic tanks are the major cause of groundwater contamination. There are an estimated 19 million septic tanks in the United States, discharging a trillion gallons of waste water into the ground each year. What is alarming about this is that, although septic-tank runoff can present a bacterial threat to groundwater, the main concern now is the contamination by toxic chemicals. For exam-

Toxic chemicals that are dumped are dissolved by rains and percolate into the ground. Plumes are then formed in ground water that bring these chemicals up in wells that tap the water sources. Septic tanks, sewers, toxic waste dumps, waste pits, and disposal wells all send toxic chemicals into the streams and fresh water wells.

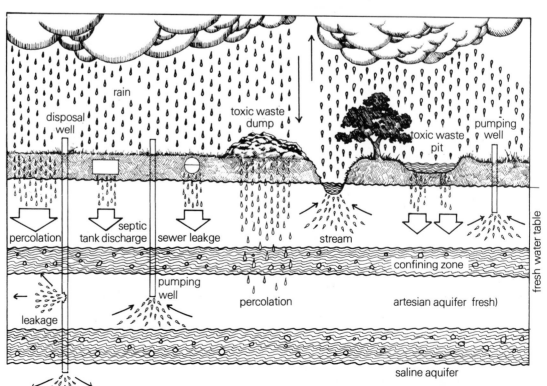

ple, most septic tank "cleaners" contain high levels of trichlorethylene (TCE).* It is virtually impossible to estimate the quantities of solvents, cleaning preparations, paints, and other toxic consumer products that also make their way into the groundwater through septic-tank fields.

The following statements provide a picture of the seriousness of contaminating groundwater with chemicals. In 1979 the Massachusetts Legislative Commission on Water Supply closed or restricted the use of water in 22 towns, after a study in which they found that a third of the 350 communities in the state had drinking-water supplies contaminated with chemicals. In 1980 the California Public Health Department closed 37 wells in 13 cities of the San Gabriel Valley, following the discovery of TCE in these water supplies, affecting more than 400,000 people. In 1980 the New York Public Interest Research Group showed that "all three major aquifers under Long Island are seriously contaminated with effluent from industrial wastes, discharges from municipal treatment plants, and runoff from highways." In 1978, New York State shut down 36 wells in Long Island, affecting 2 million people, because of high TCE and other chemicals in the water. In 1978 Bedford, Massachusetts, closed four of its municipal wells, which had been supplying 80 percent of its water, after a resident engineer found that the town's water contained 2,100 parts per billion of dioxin and 500 parts per billion of trichloroethylene; Bedford then bought water from a neighboring community until that community had to close

Table 10.2: Hazardous substances found in ground water

Substance	Number of cities sampled	Percentage of cities with chemical present
Trichloroethylene	25	36
Carbon tetrachloride	39	28.2
Tetrachloroethylene	36	22
1,1,1-Trichloroethane	23	21.7
1,1-Dichloroethane	13	23.1
1,2-Dichloroethane	25	4
Trans-dichoroethylene	13	15.4
Cis-dichloroethylene	13	30.8
1,1-Dichloroethylene	13	7.7
Methylene chloride	38	2.6
Vinyl chloride	25	4.0

Many major aquifers under Long Island, New York, are seriously contaminated by effluents from industrial wastes. In 1978, New York State shut down wells in Long Island affecting two million people, because of chemical contamination. (top: Glen Cove, 1982. Bottom: Hooker Chemical Plant, 1982, by Michael Samuels.)

*In 1979 400,000 gallons of TCEs were dumped into septic tanks in Long Island alone, resulting in the closure of all local water supplies.

its well because of contamination with TCE.

Such stories describe only the tip of the iceberg. Dozens of similar reports are on file throughout the United States.

Approximately 75 percent of all the water used in this country is surface water. Of that, 80 percent is used by agriculture and industry, the remaining 20 percent being used as drinking water.

Until very recently, surface waters in this country were used indiscriminately as dumping grounds for liquid wastes from factories and sewage-treatment plants. In the 1970s great efforts were made to regulate this kind of (point source) dumping, requiring filtering systems, and in some cases prohibiting dumping altogether. Although the progress has been significant in this area, the gains have allowed us only to keep up with the problem, not to conquer it. Because of the growth of industry, contamination levels in most surface waters have been kept fairly constant, but only because of government restrictions on dumping.

Another serious (nonpoint) source of surface-water contamination is the runoff from agriculture, which contains pesticides, herbicides, fertilizers, and animal waste products.

The chemicals used to make pesticides and herbicides often have extremely high bioaccumulation factors. Fish and other sea life accumulate and store vast quantities of such chemicals, not only passing them up the food chain, but concentrating them in the silt at the bottoms of rivers and lakes when these organisms die.

In the late 1960s and early 1970s, it was discovered that huge quantities of DDT and al-

Table 10.3: Chemicals found in Long Island water[a]

Chemical	Number of wells found with chemical
Tetrachloroethylene	57
1,1,2-Trichloroethylene	50
Chloroform	41
1,1,1-Trichloroethane	33
Carbon tetrachloride	20
Trifluorotrichloroethane	4

[a]Figures are for 372 wells tested in 1978.

drin were building up in surface waters throughout the United States. When these chemicals were banned by the EPA in the mid-1970s, this particular problem began to subside. But the quantities of these chemicals remaining in the silt of our lakes and rivers will take many decades to clear. In the meantime, much caution must be exercised in the use of new agricultural chemicals that might create new sets of similar problems.

Chemical fertilizers pose a problem of their own. It has been estimated that 51 million tons of chemical fertilizers are used in this country each year. From these fertilizers, 7.5 million tons of nitrogen and 600,000 tons of phosphorus run into the surface water annually. Phosphorus is a serious problem, triggering algae blooms that completely disrupt the

Each year 181 million tons of topsoil are silted into the waterways, representing two bushels of lost topsoil for every bushel of corn. (Brummitts Cornfield, 1939, by Roff Berman. Oil on canvas, 24″ × 36″. Museum of Modern Art, New York. On loan from WPA Art Program.)

ecological balance of waterways.

Grazing animals and stockyards in the U.S. each account for 600 million tons of waste that run into surface water each year. These materials contain chemicals ingested by the animals as well as bacteria from feces.

Silting, that is, erosion of topsoil, in this country presents a particularly grim picture. Cultivation of the land in ways that cause soil erosion has been so severe that, in many agricultural areas of our nation, lakes and rivers are being seriously threatened. For example, the backwater lakes and rivers along the Illinois River have half-filled with silt during just the past fifteen years. Each year 181 million tons of topsoil silts off into waterways, representing two bushels of lost topsoil for every bushel of corn produced in that area.

dards; 6.8 percent violated standards for *turbidity*;* and 10 percent violated standards for chemical content.

In addition to the preceding problems of water pollution, pipes carrying water are frequently made of materials that corrode or leach chemicals into the water. There are three types of pipes: metal pipes can leach cadmium, copper, iron, lead, or zinc; AC (asbestos cement) pipe can leach asbestos fibers; PVC (polyvinyl chloride) pipe can leach many chemicals, including emulsifiers, catalysts, glues, stabilizers, vinyl chlorides, and solvents, used in production and installation of the pipe.

Moreover, storage tanks for municipal water systems are periodically cleaned and coated with coal tar. As a result, a mixture of polynuclear aromatic hydrocarbons and other

*The percent of suspended particles in the water.

Urban runoff after rains contains heavy metals, bacteria, asbestos, oil, and grease. (*Rain,* 1933, by Per Krogh. Gouache, 11" × 15". Museum of Modern Art, New York.)

Urban runoff is one of the major causes of surface water contamination. Every time it rains, the contents of streets and gutters run off into our lakes and rivers. This runoff contains heavy metals, bacteria, asbestos, oil and grease, soil, etc. One dramatic example of contamination from this source is the discovery in 1979 by the EPA that lead in the runoff from streets in Washington, D.C., was a thousand times greater than what comes out from sewage-treatment plants.

To what extent are the water resources of this country affected by these contamination processes? In 1980 the EPA studied 62,000 community water systems. Of these, 10.9 percent were in violation of bacteriological standards; 6.8 percent violated standards for *turbidity*;* and 10 percent violated standards for chemical content.

organic chemicals, which are both mutagenic and carcinogenic, are found in the water.

What You Can Do

Most people in this country receive their water from a community water supply. Those with their own wells may discover that the groundwater from which they draw their water is contaminated by either industry or agriculture. Whether you get your water from a community water supply or from your own well, the issue of pure water is a political one and requires political awareness and responsibility. Begin by contacting your local EPA

***Our drinking water
requires testing. Political
action is necessary if toxic
chemicals are found.***
(*Drinking Fountain,* 1972, by
Michael Samuels.)

office and requesting all the information available on your local water supplies. You can ask your local water district for this information as well, but do not be satisfied with "assurances" that the water is "safe." Ask for test results and the names of testing laboratories that performed the tests.

The average citizen can join in collective action as well: either form or join a political action group to improve local drinking-water quality; investigate your local water system (meetings are open to the public), asking for tests of both organic and nonorganic contents of the water; explore whether or not your water supply is drawn from an area downstream from agricultural areas, chemical or processing plants, industries that are dumping wastes, etc.; and investigate the local watersheds for how much runoff they may be receiving from city drainage systems, forestry and agricultural sources, etc. If there is not a clear set of guidelines for such activities in your area, consult with the political action groups listed in the back of this book.

Your own tap water can be tested for contamination. Well-drilling companies have information about whom you can contact for tests of bacterial content, minerals, suspended particles, and odor. Sometimes these tests are administered by county health departments. Both well drillers and the county may also be able to tell you where to get tests for organic chemical contamination.

The EPA has tested commercially bottled water, and has found some to be contaminated with heavy metals and bacteria. They have not tested for organic chemicals. If you are considering buying bottled water as an alternative to your tap water, ask the company from which you plan to buy for test results of bacterial, chemical, and heavy-metal contents.

If you plan to use your local tap water for drinking, use the cold rather than the hot tap. Hot water tends to have slightly more contaminants, since the heat dissolves chemicals and heavy metals that may be in your hot-water tank and in the pipes themselves. If you have PVC (plastic) pipes in your home, the California Department of Consumer Affairs advises running water for a minute or so before using it.

Further Reading

National Academy of Sciences. *Drinking Water and Health*. Washington, D.C., 1977, 1980.

A rather technical report on water in the United States, with complete data on all chemicals affecting water quality. Available in medical libraries or from the U.S. Government Printing Office. Presents a moderate view of the dangers of contaminants in drinking water.

United States Environmental Protection Agency. *Quality Criteria for Water*. Washington, D.C., 1976.

A list of chemicals in water, with complete information on the effects of these contaminants on fish and other wildlife. In the field, this is called the "Red Book," because it spells out the criteria for each chemical in drinking water, streams, and salt water. Available from the U.S. Government Printing Office.

Environmental Quality 1980: The Eleventh Annual Report of the Council on Environmental Quality. Washington, D.C., 1980.

A report to the President on the condition of the global environment, as of 1980, including ecology, water quality, air quality, toxic substances, energy, natural resources, and land use. Available from the U.S. Government Printing Office.

The Environmental Defense Fund. *Malignant Neglect*. Vintage Books, 1979.

An excellent discussion on carcinogenic materials in the environment. Written for the layperson, it contains sections on water, air, and diet.

RALPH NADER, RONALD BROWNSTEIN, AND JOHN RICHARD. *Who's Poisoning America: Corporate Polluters and Their Victims in the Chemical Age*. Sierra Club Books, 1981.

Alarming disclosure of pollution by industry and an explanation of how they have affected both our natural resources and human health.

CHAPTER ELEVEN

Air Pollution

For ancient people the air surrounding the Earth, and all the heavens beyond, were the source and the power of all. For the Andamans, the most primitive of peoples still in existence in Asia, "the Supreme Being . . . dwells in the sky and his voice is the thunder, the wind his breath; hurricanes are the sign of his anger."[1] For the Ewe tribes of West Africa the sky itself is their supreme being; their name for their god is Mawu, which means "to spread or cover all." Indeed, the most common prayer in the Judaeo-Christian tradition begins "Our Father, who art in heaven . . ."

Most of us seem to have lost touch with how much we depend on the air. We're aware of the skies darkening over our cities from industrial and automobile pollution, of our eyes smarting on high pollution days, even of some irritation of our respiratory systems when we breathe. But in many respects these complaints are only superficial. The air provides all living things with the exact chemicals needed for life. Those chemicals are the vital raw materials that originally made life possible and that continue to nurture the biosphere. Atmospheric carbon dioxide is the main source of carbon for building all living tissue. Atmospheric oxygen is the main atom used in the release and transfer of energy. And atmospheric nitrogen is the main source of nitrogen for creating amino acids. (Remember that DNA is a carbon/nitrogen structure.) In a very real way, then, we are made of air. Air literally is the creator of all, the father in heaven.

What It Is

Although we think of our atmosphere as an ethereal space above the land upon which we live, it is actually very much a part of the living

Our Father Who Art In Heaven . . . (*God the Father Surrounded by Angels and Cherubim,* fourteenth century, by Francisco di Giorgio. National Gallery of Art, Washington, D.C.)

For ancient people the air surrounding the Earth was the source of all power. (*Father Sky,* 1970, by John Lee Begay. Sand painting, 12″ × 12″. Museum of the American Indian, Heye Foundation.)

Most of us have lost touch with the extent of our dependence on the air. We are only aware of the skies darkening over our cities. (a, *The Black Rainbow,* 1959, by Jim Dine. Oil on cardboard, 39″ × 59″. Collection of the Whitney Museum of American Art, New York; b, *New York Skyline at Noon,* 1982, by Michael Samuels.)

Earth, and is, in a real sense, as alive and as essential to the Earth as our lungs are to our bodies. The natural interactions of chemicals in the troposphere, that part of the atmosphere in which we breathe, and in which plants photosynthesize, make possible the new formations of everything needed to create and nurture life. This lively interaction depends on an unlikely and fragile combination of gases and elements. However, in the past few hundred years we have introduced chemicals to this fragile living structure that early humans could never even have imagined. At this point in our history, this fragile living structure barely resembles its original makeup.

It is important to understand that the essential chemicals carried by the air are not inert or static. They are constantly moving, con-

---

Gaseous composition of our air

nitrogen	acetylene
oxygen	nitric oxide
argon	propene
carbon dioxide	isobutane
neon	sulfur dioxide
carbon monoxide	ozone
krypton	ammonia
methane	formaldehyde
nitrous oxide	trans-2-butene
helium	cis-2-butene
hydrogen	methylacetylene
xenon	dichlorofluoromethane
butane	dichlorodifluoromethane
ethane	methyl chloride
propane	fluorotrichloromethane
ethylene	hydrogen sulfide
nitrogen dioxide	vinyl chloride

---

stantly changing, always undergoing complex cycles of synthesis and resynthesis. For example, carbon dioxide in the air is taken in by plants through photosynthesis. The plants are then eaten by animals, and finally, upon the deaths of the animals, the carbon is once again given back to the air. Similarly, oxygen is taken up by plants and animals in their respiratory processes, and is metabolized, at which time it joins with hydrogen molecules to form water; the water is released by plants and animals, and is taken up by them once again in that form. Finally, when plants photosynthesize, they release oxygen atoms once again into the air.

By introducing new chemicals into the atmosphere, we alter the cycles of carbon, oxygen, and many other chemicals. How could we expect to do otherwise when, as J. E. Lovelock points out in *Gaia*, we have "increased the carbon cycle by twenty percent, the nitrogen cycle by fifty percent, and the sulfur cycle by over one hundred percent."[2] In addition, the

presence of other chemicals, such as the vinyl chlorides, fluorotrichloromethanes, formaldehydes, and methyl chlorides used by industry, presents potentials for new chemical reactions in the air, many with unknown results. One example of this phenomenon is *acid rain,* which we'll be discussing in greater detail later in this section.

There are two major health concerns with air pollution. First, there are the short-range effects on human health, such as emphysema, bronchitis, asthma, and increased incidence of upper respiratory disease and heart disease, caused or aggravated by sulfur oxides, nitrogen dioxide, carbon monoxide, ozone, and suspended particles. Until the past decade, these respiratory problems caused thousands of deaths, making this form of pollution a top priority in the public mind. Over the years government regulation and the cooperation of industry have greatly reduced levels of pollution, so deaths from these causes have decreased in modern cities. But we still have to face the second major health concern with air pollution, namely, that it is a source of human cancer. Health officials estimate that general air pollution in the United States alone is responsible for 53,000 deaths annually.[3]

How It Causes Disease

Air pollution affects us in three major ways: by damaging tissue of the respiratory system, by entering the bloodstream to poison the blood, and by altering the DNA to cause cancer and/or birth defects.

The history of air pollution is rather astounding. In 1952 a temperature inversion trapped the air of the entire Thames Valley, in England, which was highly polluted by fossil fuels, causing an estimated 3,500 to 4,000 excess deaths, manifested as a variety of heart and lung diseases. Before the problem of pollution from fossil fuels was finally solved in the 1960s, ten similar episodes occurred in this region. In 1953, when the entire air mass in the eastern United States became stagnant, there were an estimated 24 excess deaths per day for a ten-day period. In October 1948, in Donora, Pennsylvania, the site of both steel and sulfuric acid manufacturing, the smog became so thick you could not see across the street. In a population of 14,000 people, 7,000 became ill, 1,400 became severely ill, and 20 died. Interestingly enough, in a ten-year follow-up study it was discovered that those who had been ill had significantly higher death rates in subsequent years than the general population. Perhaps the most spectacular case of air pollution was a global occurrence in 1962, caused by unusual meteorological events, and resulting in excess deaths in London, the eastern United States, the Netherlands, Germany, and Japan.

Oxygen is not static. It moves throughout the biosphere.

hydrogen escape

atmosphere
3.8×10^7T moles O_2

photosynthesis

methane oxidation

weathering of rocks

respiration

aerobic biosphere

anaerobic biosphere

burial

atmospheric carbon dioxide

The carbon cycle shows how carbon moves between the air, plants, and animals.

animal protoplasm

plant protoplasm

plant photosynthesis

animal respiration

decay

organic carbon

Because of the response of government and industry to public protest, episodes of this dramatic kind have increasingly become more rare. However, episodes in which people's health is affected more subtly—eyes tearing, difficulty breathing, more frequent upper respiratory disease, aggravation of chronic heart and lung disease—are still occurring almost daily. Between 1976 and 1978, New York and Los Angeles have each registered an average of 200 unhealthy days annually, and 118 hazardous per year. But even if we had fully conquered the problem of air pollution and respiratory disease, we would not have yet addressed ourselves to cancer and birth defects.

Seven air-pollution substances have been identified as mutagenic and listed as hazardous

In this way either the same substances that broke down the homeostatic mechanisms, or other carcinogenic materials in the air, both initiate and promote changes in the DNA molecules of lung cells, contributing to the production of cancer.

Evidence of Its Danger

In addition to the epidemiological histories described earlier, there are many research studies revealing how air pollution adversely affects human health. For example, people exposed to air pollution show marked decreases in their immunological responses; there is reduced lymphocyte and antibody production.

In Japanese children exposed to air pollu-

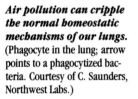

Air pollution can cripple the normal homeostatic mechanisms of our lungs. (Phagocyte in the lung; arrow points to a phagocytized bacteria. Courtesy of C. Saunders, Northwest Labs.)

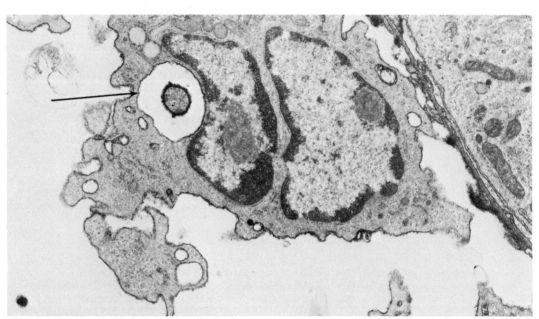

to human health, under Section 112 of the "Clean Air Act." These substances are asbestos, mercury, beryllium, vinyl chloride, benzene, radon, and arsenic. Several others are being considered for hazardous labeling, including cadmium, acrylonitrile, methyl chloroform, toluene, and trichloroethylene. Because we have described in Poisons List A (pages 144-157) how each of these substances can cause cancer, we will not repeat that specific information here.

In air pollution the route of exposure to carcinogenic substances is slightly different from that for the same chemicals in water. Air containing toxic substances fills the lungs, and in the process, cells lining the air passages to the lungs are injured. The normal homeostatic mechanisms of the respiratory system, such as cilia activity and mucosal flow, are overloaded and then crippled. As a result, carcinogenic substances easily make their way to the lungs, where they may remain undisturbed for years.

tion, breathing was inhibited, and the frequency of bronchitis and pneumonia was increased (Toyama 1967).

In studies of children in the United States, air pollution has been linked to an increased incidence of croup, asthma, and bronchitis (Hammer 1976).

In studies of athletes in the United States, it has been shown that the performance of cross-country runners is impaired by air pollution (Wayne 1967).

In studies of healthy nurses living in Los Angeles, it was found that air pollution caused headache, cough, and chest discomfort (Hammer 1976).

Families living near air-polluting industries in Chattanooga, Tennessee, were found to have an excess of upper respiratory infection, and breathing difficulties in children (Shy 1970).

In studies of angina patients, it was found that even relatively small amounts of carbon

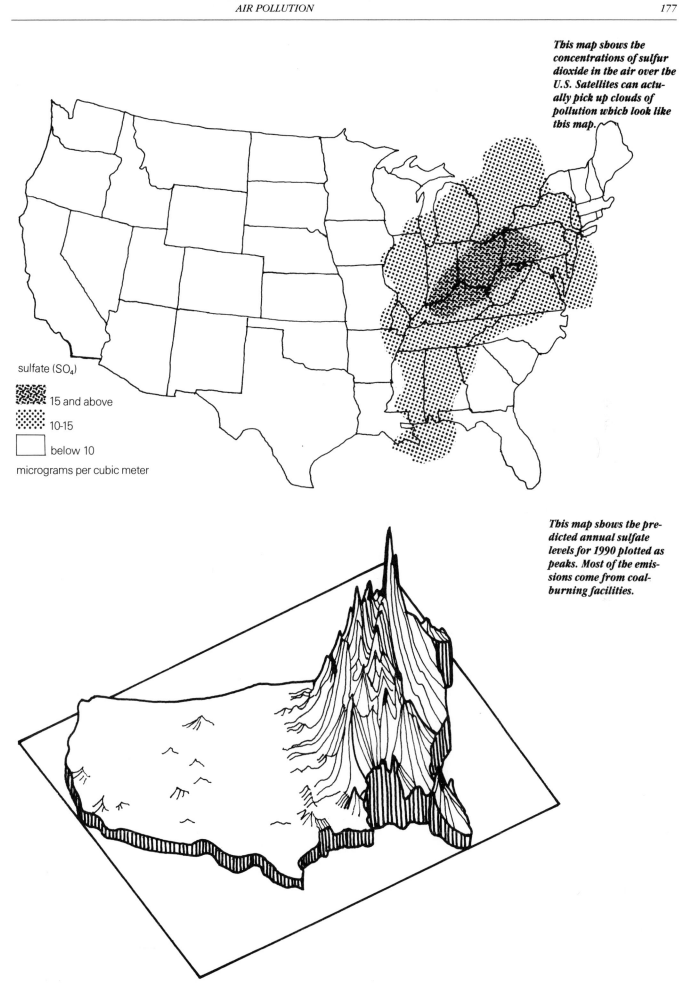

This map shows the concentrations of sulfur dioxide in the air over the U.S. Satellites can actually pick up clouds of pollution which look like this map.

sulfate (SO$_4$)

15 and above

10-15

below 10

micrograms per cubic meter

This map shows the predicted annual sulfate levels for 1990 plotted as peaks. Most of the emissions come from coal-burning facilities.

monoxide in the air caused heart pain to come on sooner and last longer during mild exercise (Anderson 1973).

In another study of air pollution and heart disease, angina sufferers were subjected to air from the Los Angeles freeway for ninety minutes. After they did mild exercise, angina pain came on sooner and lasted longer than in a control group who had breathed pure air for the same period of time before exercising (Aronow 1972).

In a study of the effects of carbon monoxide in the air, researchers found that levels of this chemical in the chambers of the heart rose significantly when subjects were given air to breathe comparable to the air on a polluted day in the city (Aronow 1972). The same study showed that carbon monoxide had significant

of air pollution.

In studies of cancer it has been found that, as air pollution increases, the incidence of lung cancer also increases. In England, for example, the incidence of lung cancer has increased 1,500 percent since the early 1920s.[4]

In the United States, deaths from lung cancer have increased from 9 per 100,000 in 1950 to 19.7 per 100,000 in 1967, a rise of nearly 220 percent in just over fifteen years (National Cancer Institute).

Lung cancer is most common among people in industrialized areas. According to a 1968 study by the National Cancer Institute, lung cancer in men costs 700,000 person years of life annually, which is 3.5 times higher than the rate for the next highest form of cancer, that is, cancer of the colon.

Particulate matter (dust) in urban air causes skin, cervix, and lung cancers. (*Homestead,* 1929, by John Kane. Oil on canvas, 24″ × 27″. Museum of Modern Art, New York. Gift of Abby Aldrich Rockefeller.)

adverse effects on the patterns of the heartbeat.

In a study of monkeys, researchers found that carbon monoxide in the air increased the incidence of ventricular fibrillation* (DeBias 1973). This is important, since ventricular fibrillation is a major cause of death after heart attacks.

In hospitals that take patients from inner city and industrial areas, the incidence of death from heart attacks increases with higher levels

Numerous studies have shown that the particulate matter (chemical dust) in urban air causes skin, cervical, and lung cancers in animal experiments (National Academy of Sciences 1972).

Benzo-a-pyrene, a common chemical released by burning fossil fuels and wood, has been shown to cause lung cancer in hamsters (Saffiotti 1970). The same chemical mixed with other common particulates and gases found in

*Disruption of the normal pumping cycles of the heart.

air pollution becomes a significantly more potent carcinogen.

Migrant studies seem to establish significant links between air pollution and lung cancer. For example, in studies of people moving from England (which has high levels of air pollution and correspondingly high incidences of lung cancer) to New Zealand (with low levels of air pollution and correspondingly low incidences of lung cancer), the migrants tend to adopt the disease patterns of the adopted country (Eastcott 1956).

Comparisons of matched control groups from rural and urban areas reveal much higher rates of lung cancer in the cities (Council of Europe 1972).

Death from lung cancer accounts for 13 percent of all deaths in people over 45 years of

points. Unhealthy ratings are anything between 100 and 500, as follows.

100–199: unhealthful. People begin to manifest mild symptoms, such as eye irritation or headache. People with chronic heart or lung diseases begin to manifest discomfort. The EPA recommends that at these levels people with existing heart or respiratory ailments should "reduce physical exertion and outdoor activity."

200–299: very unhealthful. Widespread symptoms are manifest in healthy people. Significant aggravation of heart and respiratory disease, with decreased tolerance for physical exercise. The EPA recommends that at these levels, elderly people and people with heart and respiratory disease should "stay indoors and reduce physical activity."

PSI Index 400-500. Hazardous. All persons should remain indoors, keeping all windows and doors closed. (*World Trade Center at Noon,* 1982, by Michael Samuels.)

age, according to the International Agency for Research on Cancer. The same group asserts that the present lung-cancer incidence is wholly environmental in its causes, and could be entirely prevented by: (1) the discontinuation of cigarette smoking; (2) the improvement of air-quality standards; and (3) the removal of air-pollution hazards in the workplace.

Extent of the Threat

Because of the importance of air pollution in human health, the government has established the Pollution Standard Index (PSI) for monitoring and evaluating sulfur dioxide, nitrogen dioxide, carbon monoxide, ozone, and total suspended particulates in the air.

The PSI is based on a scale of 0 to 500, with points given for each of the five pollutants. The most healthy air is rated from 0–49, with moderate pollution being between 50 and 99

300–399: hazardous. Onset of diseases such as asthma, bronchitis, heart attacks, angina, etc. Decreased exercise tolerance for everyone, including the most healthy people. The EPA recommends that at these levels everyone should avoid outdoor activity, and elderly people and people with chronic diseases should both stay indoors and reduce physical exertion.

400–500: hazardous. Death of ill and elderly, with healthy people manifesting severe symptoms. EPA recommends that at these levels "all persons should remain indoors, keeping windows and doors closed. All persons should minimize physical exertion and avoid traffic."

The EPA standards for the five air pollutants are as follows:

Sulfur dioxide: 80 micrograms per cubic meter of air.

Nitrogen dioxide: 10 micrograms per cubic meter of air (proposed).

Table 11.1: Unhealthy days in 40 U.S. cities[a]

Number of unhealthy days	City	Average number of days per year, 1976–1978	
		Unhealthful, very unhealthful, or hazardous days	Very unhealthful or hazardous days
More than 150 days	Los Angeles	242	118
	New York	224	51
	Pittsburgh[b]	168	31
	San Bernardino Riverside-Ontario	167	88
100–150 days	Cleveland	145	35
	St. Louis	136	29
	Chicago	124	21
	Louisville	119	12
50–99 days	Washington, D.C.	97	8
	Phoenix[c]	84	10
	Philadelphia	82	9
	Seattle	82	4
	Salt Lake City	81	18
	Birmingham[c]	75	19
	Portland	75	3
	Houston	69	16
	Detroit	65	4
	Jersey City[c]	65	4
	Baltimore	60	12
	San Diego	52	6
25–49 days	Cincinnati	45	2
	Dayton	45	2
	Gary-Hammond East Chicago	36	8
	Indianapolis	36	2
	Milwaukee	33	6
	Buffalo	31	5
	San Francisco	30	1
	Kansas City	29	6
	Memphis	28	2
	Sacramento	28	2
	Allentown[b]	27	1
0–24 days	Toledo	24	2
	Dallas	22	1
	Tampa	12	1
	Akron[c]	10	0
	Norfolk[c]	9	0
	Syracuse	9	1
	Rochester	6	0
	Grand Rapids	5	0

[a]From *Environmental Quality,* 1980, p. 154.   [b]Based on 1 year of data only.   [c]Based on 2 years of data only.

Carbon monoxide: 5 milligrams per cubic meter of air.
Ozone: 120 micrograms per cubic meter of air.
Total suspended particulates: 75 micrograms per cubic meter of air.

According to EPA records of the PSI for 23 major cities (not including N.Y.C.), there were 1,637 days with ratings of "unhealthful" or worse. Of these, 358 were "very unhealthful" or worse, while 15 days were "hazardous."

The actual relationship between increased mortality rates and air pollution is still not clear, partly because it is extremely difficult to establish accurate statistical curves showing how low levels of exposure will affect disease rates. However, a moderate statistical estimate (Lane and Seskin 1977) based on census data and air-quality data for standard metropolitan statistical areas arrived at a figure of 3.5 excess deaths per 100,000 people per microgram of sulfur dioxide in the air. For the total U.S. population, this means that 53,000 people die each year from air pollution. In terms of the average population of people who die from air-pollution-related causes, this would represent a total loss of nearly a million years of life annually. A study by Mendelsohn and Orcutt (1978) estimates more than three times as many deaths, but a study by Lipfert (1978) estimates half as many. A broad estimate, then, puts the excess deaths from air pollution in the United States at somewhere between 26,500 and 160,000.

Although it is difficult to find out exactly how many cancer deaths are related to air pollution, an average estimate, based on workers subjected to benzo-a-pyrene, is that it causes 1.7 excess cancer deaths per 100,000 people. For the 50 million people living in large cities

The progress that has been made in the past decade is significant. For example, between 1974 and 1978, the number of unhealthful days decreased 18 percent nationwide. The pollution of air with benzo-a-pyrene, the most potent carcinogen in normal air pollution, has decreased 88 percent from 1967 to 1977. This represents a reduction from 4 to .5 nanograms per cubic meter.

Severe air pollution problems continue. At present there are 27,000 major stationary sources of pollution. A major stationary source is any industry dumping in excess of 100 tons of pollutants into the air annually, operating with no pollution controls. These sources are shown in Table 11.3.

To get an idea of the amounts of sulfur dioxide, nitrogen dioxide, carbon monoxide,

Table 11.2: Unhealthy days in sample cities of the United States, 1978[a]

Name of city	Number of unhealthy days	Number of very unhealthy days	Type of pollutant
Chicago	150	25	Carbon monoxide
Denver	130	40	Carbon monoxide
Houston	75	25	Ozone
Los Angeles	100	100	Ozone
New York City	150	20	Carbon monoxide
Riverside, Cal.	75	75	Ozone
St. Louis	100	25	Ozone
San Francisco	25	3	Ozone
Washington, D.C.	75	5	Ozone

[a]From *Environmental Quality,* 1980, pp. 150–153.

Table 11.3: Major sources of air pollution: 1980[a]

Industry	Number of sources
Coal and oil power plants	700
Iron and steel plants	204
Primary smelters	28
Pulp and paper mills	475
Municipal incinerators	72
Petroleum refineries	214
Aluminum reduction	49
Portland cement	200
Sulfuric acid	262
Phosphate fertilizers	69
Coal cleaning	409
Gray iron	433
Asphalt concrete	2,862
Total	**5,977**

[a]**From** *Environmental Quality,* 1980, p. 175.

in the United States, this represents 1,000 cancer deaths annually (Wilson 1980). However, this estimate is based on the effects of a single carcinogen out of a long list of chemicals contained in air pollution, and does not include the effects of smoking; so the results must be considered extremely conservative.

Where It Is Found

Although progress has been made in recent years in reducing the amounts of the five criteria air pollutants and benzo-a-pyrene, air pollution continues to be a serious or even critical problem in Los Angeles and New York City. And unfortunately, in Houston, Chicago, and Kansas City, there has been a deterioration of air quality. Most of the progress we now see has resulted from government standards that restrict automobile exhaust and industrial emissions.

A broad estimate puts the excess deaths from air pollution in the U.S. somewhere between 26,000 and 160,000 per year. (Factories, 1918, by Joseph Stella. Oil on burlap, 56" × 46". Museum of Modern Art, New York. Acquired through the Lilly P. Bliss Bequest.)

Table 11.4: Air pollution emissions: 1977[a]

Source	Total suspended particulates	Sulfur oxides	Nitrogen oxides	Ozone	Carbon monoxide
Motor vehicles	1.1	.8	9.2	11.5	85.7
Burning of fossil fuels for elecricity, power and heat	4.8	22.4	13	1.5	1.2
Industry	5.4	4.2	.7	10.1	8.3
Solid waste	.4	0	.1	.7	2.6
Miscellaneous, including forest fires, agricultural, refuse and structural fires	.7	0	.1	4.5	4.9
Totals	12.4	27.4	23.1	28.3	102.7

[a]In million metric tons. Adapted from *Environmental Quality,* p. 000.

Some 27.8 million metric tons of volatile organic compounds are dumped into the air each year.
(*The End of the Day,* 1919, by George Grosz. Pen and brush and ink, 18″ × 14″. Museum of Modern Art, New York. A. Conger Goodyear Fund.)

and total suspended particulates dumped into the air each year, consider the following figures for 1978:

27 million metric tons of sulfur dioxide;

23.3 million metric tons of nitrogen dioxide;

102 million metric tons of carbon monoxide;

12.5 million metric tons of total suspended particulates.

In addition, 27.8 million metric tons of volatile organic compounds, including hydrocarbons, benzo-a-pyrene, and other ozone-producing substances, are dumped into the air each year.

Natural phenomena such as volcanic eruptions account for some of this air pollution. Mount St. Helens dumped somewhere between three and thirty tons of sulfur dioxide into the air per day, during the few days it was active. By comparison, the amount of sulfur dioxide dumped into the air by manmade sources is somewhere in the neighborhood of 74,000 tons per day, 365 days a year!

Indoor air pollution has also become a major concern in recent years, largely because of sealed buildings, central air conditioning, and increased time spent indoors. Indoor pollutants include carbon monoxide and nitrogen dioxide from stoves and heaters; formaldehyde from foam insulation, carpets, drapes, furniture, plywood, and particle board; and radon from cooking gases and from cement used in construction. In addition, there are suspended particles from cigarette smoking and wood fires. Air-conditioning systems in cities draw air from industrial sources and the street, each day pumping thousands of tons of specific pollutants through buildings where people are working and living.

In a model energy-efficient house constructed in Walnut Creek, California, researchers found that levels of nitrogen dioxide and carbon monoxide were higher in the kitchen than they were outdoors, and these indoor air-pollution levels exceeded proposed EPA standards for nitrogen dioxide. In numerous other studies it has been found that formaldehyde levels in the air of new homes actually exceed OSHA levels for the workplace.

Cigarette smoking in sealed, air-conditioned rooms is a serious form of air pollution. The amounts of total suspended particles in the air of a room where people are smoking can exceed federal pollution criteria standards for outdoor air by as much as 300 percent.

Finally, we should not forget that many of the specific organic chemicals dispersed in the air are not included as *criteria air pollutants* by the federal government. We have, however, covered most of these in Poisons List A. The most important toxic chemicals to consider are asbestos, benzene, arsenic, chromium, cadmium, vinyl chloride, beryllium, acrylonitrile, and trichloroethylene.

What You Can Do

For outdoor air pollution, political action, such as joining groups lobbying for stricter air-quality controls, is the best form of disease prevention we presently have. If a high incidence of respiratory infections, irritations, or allergic reactions is noticed in the workplace, suspect possible problems with air filtration, and contact OSHA for testing and recommendations for correcting such problems. If you live in an apartment house with central air conditioning and are suspicious of similar problems there, contact your county health department. (See the chapter on political action for names and addresses of groups working your area.)

Adequate ventilation of indoor work and

Vent all heaters and stoves both at home and in the workplace, to prevent buildups of the air pollutants associated with burning fossil fuels. The modern unvented kerosene heaters that have recently become popular release significantly high levels of air pollution contaminants. They are currently being investigated by the EPA.

Dying fires in fireplaces and wood stoves are not hot enough to carry carbon monoxide and other pollutants up the chimney, and so should be avoided. Gas burners emitting orange or sputtering flames are dangerous sources of carbon monoxide. Such problems can often be corrected by simple adjustments. Call your gas company for advice or assistance.

Many county health departments are equipped to test for formaldehyde in your

Table 11.5: Four hazardous pollutants found in air[a]

Name of pollutant	Source of pollutant
Asbestos	Asbestos mills, asbestos manufacturing plants, demolition of old buildings, insulation, fireproofing, road surface material, brake drums, water pipe
Beryllium	Extraction plants, ceramic factories, foundries, incinerators, rocket motor manufacturing, spark-plug factories, lantern mantles
Mercury	Ore processing, chlor-alkali manufacturing, sludge driers, incinerators, electrical-equipment manufacture, paint
Vinyl chloride	Ethylene dichloride manufacture, PVC manufacture, floor tile, vinyl fabrics, pipe, automobile manufacture, garbage-can/household-product manufacture

[a]From EPA data.

home spaces is important. Air-conditioning filters should be changed frequently to filter particles from the air. Areas where people smoke need 50 percent more ventilation than nonsmoking areas.

To reduce the adverse effects of smoking, smokers should use "smokeless ash trays;" these vary greatly in their effectiveness, but may be of some help in protecting nonsmokers. Guidelines for smokers can be established at work and home to protect nonsmokers: smoking and nonsmoking areas can be established; cigarettes should be thoroughly extinguished as quickly as possible; and adults should not smoke in the presence of children.

home. If you suspect this form of pollution may be present in your workplace, report the problem to your supervisor or OSHA. If formaldehyde is detected in a mobile home, contact the U.S. Department of Housing and Urban Development, 451 7th Street S.W. Washington, D.C. Plywood and particle board in new kitchen cabinets, bookshelves, and doors can be important sources of formaldehyde, and their effects can be reduced by painting or otherwise sealing these materials.

Household use of pesticides should be reduced or entirely discontinued. Nonpolluting pest control should include an effort to make structures less attractive to insects: careful cleaning of cabinets and food sources for pests; removing clutter, such as newspapers and rubbish, that provides shelter for pests; repair of screens on doors and windows; use of cleansers containing chlorine to discourage ants; and cleanup of damp or wet areas around the yard that may be breeding grounds for mosquitoes.

Indoor pollution caused by wood, gas, or kerosene stoves can be comparable to hazardous pollution days in cities such as Los Angeles and New York. (The Artist at Work, 1940, by George Ault. Oil on canvas, 20″ × 26.″ Collection of the Whitney Museum of American Art, New York.)

More information of this kind is available from Integrated Pest Management, California Department of Food and Agriculture, 1220 N Street, Sacramento, CA 95814.

To eliminate the problem of odors at work or in your home, don't use deodorizers, which may contain their own harmful air pollutants. Instead, seek out the sources of the odors and correct them. Deodorizers can cover up smells or anesthetize your sense of smell, but they don't remove hazardous substances.

Further Reading

Council on Environmental Quality. *Environmental Quality 1980.* U.S. Government Printing Office, 1980.

An up-to-date report of government figures, the information contained here, on both indoor and outdoor air pollution, is quite accessible to readers with non-technical backgrounds.

L. LANE AND E. SESKEN. *Air Pollution and Human Health.* Johns Hopkins University Press, 1977.

An excellent source of research on toxic and carcinogenic effects of air pollutants, written by leading researchers in the field.

A. J. FINKEL AND W. C. DULL, eds., for the American Medical Association. *Clinical Implications of Air Pollution Research.* Publishing Sciences Group, 1976.

Written for physicians and medical professionals, this book contains studies of the effects of air pollution on health. Specific clinical information on lung cancer, heart disease, respiratory disease, central nervous system disease, and childhood illness.

Air Pollution and Cancer in Man. International Agency for Research on Cancer, Lyon, France, 1977.

Reports of an international conference of researchers focused on lung cancer caused by air pollution. Written for researchers and medical professionals, the material contained here is quite accessible to readers with general technical backgrounds.

R. WILSON et al. *Health Effects of Fossil Fuel Burning.* Bollingen, 1980.

A highly technical compilation of research on air pollution and human health focusing on the five criteria pollutants and benzo-a-pyrenes. An excellent basic resource for researchers and medical professionals.

Poisons List B

Benzo-a-pyrene

What It Is: benzo-a-pyrene is produced wherever there is burning, whether it is from fossil fuels, wood, paper, rubbish, or the internal combusion engine. This is only one of the many hydrocarbons produced by burning, but it is the one most often monitored in exhaust gases from industrial stacks and motor vehicles.

Major Health Concerns (CA): benzo-a-pyrene has been tested in a variety of animal species and has been found to be carcinogenic in all of them.

In one study (Chu 1965), 50 percent of hamsters exposed to benzo-a-pyrene developed cancer.

Five out of 21 rodents exposed to this chemical combined with sulfur dioxide developed lung cancer (Laskin 1970).

Many researchers have demonstrated that benzo-a-pyrene painted on organs such as skin, cervix, or trachea produces cancer in these organs (National Academy of Sciences, 1972).

When administered by air, benzo-a-pyrene appears not to cause tumors if it is the only contaminant. However, when benzo-a-pyrene is joined with any one of a variety of other chemicals—sulfur dioxide, black powder, asbestos, iron, carbon, etc., all of which are now found in the air—it becomes a potent carcinogen.

One study (Menck 1974)* compared populations in areas

with high and low benzo-a-pyrene levels. Areas of low benzo-a-pyrene showed 43 cancers per 100,000 people; high areas produced 70 cancers per 100,000 people.

In an analysis of national benzo-a-pyrene emissions, one researcher found that lung cancer increased at the rate of 5 percent for each nanogram per cubic meter of air (Carnow and Meier 1972).*

Roofing workers, subjected to benzo-a-pyrene in the materials they use, had 60 percent more lung-cancer deaths than a control group not working with benzo-a-pyrene (Hammond 1976).

Exposure Levels/Standards: the health hazards of benzo-a-

*Both the Menck and the Carnow and Meier studies have been criticized for having insufficient data. Although no one has charged that cancer isn't caused by benzo-a-pyrene, the number of deaths occurring has been challenged.

When benzo-a-pyrene is joined with other chemicals in the air, it becomes a potent carcinogen. (*Wood Pulp Mill on Desert,* 1982, by Michael Samuels.)

Entering through the lungs, carbon monoxide is picked up by hemoglobin molecules in red blood cells and results in oxygen starvation. (Burning Coal to Produce Electricity, 1982, by Michael Samuels.)

pyrene have been recognized for nearly three decades. Government agencies and private enterprise have cooperated in lowering benzo-a-pyrene emissions significantly. In 1959 benzo-a-pyrene emissions were monitored at levels as high as 61 nanograms per cubic meter of air, with the national mean level being 6. In 1966 the mean level nationally was 3 nanograms per cubic meter, and in 1975 that figure was reduced to 1.

It is estimated that one nanogram per cubic meter of air causes between .1 and 1 cancer deaths per 100,000 people (Wilson *et al.,* 1980).

Where Found/What to Avoid: the major sources of benzo-a-pyrene in the U.S. at this time, are refuse burning, hand-stoked (coal) residential fires, coke ovens, forest fires, motor vehicles, and wood-burning stoves in private residences.

In a room where people are smoking, there are 2 to 4 nanograms of benzo-a-pyrene per cubic meter of air. A one-pack-a-day cigarette smoker gets the same amount of benzo-a-pyrene as a person living in an area with 3 nanograms of benzo-a-pyrene per cubic meter of air.

Asphalt workers, roofers, or people in their vicinity can receive up to 80,000 nanograms of benzo-a-pyrene per cubic meter of air.

In tunnels with motor vehicle traffic, levels can reach 70 nanograms per cubic meter.

Bioaccumulation Factor: not available.

Carbon Monoxide
Formula: CO

What It Is: a gas that results from burning fossil fuels, carbon monoxide is odorless and invisible. It is one of two pollutants most often found to be in the unhealthy range. Carbon monoxide is released wherever there is incomplete combustion; so *cleaner-burning* engines and furnaces have been recommended by both public and private agencies to reduce this contaminant in the air.

Major Health Concerns (TX): entering through the lungs, carbon monoxide is picked up by hemoglobin molecules in red blood cells. The hemoglobin, which is ordinarily a vehicle for carrying oxygen throughout the body, picks up carbon monoxide 200 times more easily than it picks up oxygen; so carbon monoxide in the air can starve the body of the oxygen it needs to carry out normal metabolic processes. The health effects of carbon monoxide are very similar to those of anemia. Since the heart and brain are the organs that have the highest priority for oxygen, it is in these organs that symptoms of oxygen deprivation show up most quickly. We have discussed these effects in Chapter Eleven, on air pollution (page 170). In summary they are: all persons have less tolerance for exercise; people with existing heart problems manifest symptoms more quickly in the presence of carbon monoxide; and there were increased mortality rates from heart attacks in regions with high carbon monoxide content in the air.

Exposure to low levels of carbon monoxide produces symptoms such as headache and fatigue. At *very* low levels of exposure, slight behavioral changes may be noted: loss of ability to distinguish between subtle differences in tone or visual pattern (Horvath 1970); loss of ability to estimate time (Beard 1967); loss of ability to distinguish between differences in the intensities of light (McFarland 1944); decreased intellectual abilities, such as in mathematics and grammar (Schulte 1963); altered alpha brain waves and decreased rapid eye movement (REM) sleep (Haider 1971). All these effects are important to note, since schools are often located near high traffic areas; behavioral problems and learning deficiencies may in part result from this contaminant. Similarly, adult sleep disturbances may be caused by high carbon-monoxide levels.

One researcher (Haider 1971) states that carbon monoxide causes functional changes on the same order as taking tranquilizers and coffee, except that with carbon monoxide the consumption is not elective. The same researcher states that carbon monoxide is associated with so-called "urbanization trauma," a disease so many physicians today find frustrating to treat: sleeplessness, irritability, restlessness, headaches, and anxiety.

Exposure Levels/Standards: EPA standards for carbon monoxide are 9 parts per million (approximately 10 milligrams per cubic meter of air).

The standard method for measuring the effects of carbon monoxide on humans is by monitoring the percentage of carboxyhemoglobin (COHB) in the blood. A healthy COHB, created by normal metabolic processes, is considered to be .36 percent. It should be noted here that at 9 parts per million (the EPA safety standard) COHB levels rise to 1.66 percent.

In a study of industrial workers in St. Louis, Missouri, one researcher (Kahn 1974) measured COHB at 1.38 percent in the blood of nonsmokers. Another group of nonsmokers working in the city in an area not close to factories producing high levels of carbon monoxide had COHB levels of .75 percent. Even in rural areas that were outside the study area, but still affected by air pollution, COHB levels were measured at .6 percent.

In a study done in Los Angeles (Aronow 1972), COHB levels around freeways reached 5 percent. Even in rural areas on nonpolluted days, COHB levels were 1 percent.

At 2.9 percent COHB, heart disease symptoms grow worse and are more frequent. At 5 percent, exercise limits are greatly reduced for normal people, and central nervous system symptoms appear in the 3 to 7 percent range.

In the person who smokes, depending on how much, COHB levels are usually high enough to cause the same symptoms as the worst urban air pollution from cars and factories. (In rooms where people are smoking, carbon monoxide can reach levels of 70 parts per million.)

From current data we can estimate that between 25 and 75 percent of the nonsmoking United States population has COHB levels above 1.5 percent (Stewart 1973).

Where Found/What to Avoid: the main sources of carbon monoxide are motor vehicles and fossil-fuel-burning furnaces in residences and industry. Automobile exhaust gases contain 7 to 30 percent carbon monoxide. Coal-burning exhaust

gases contain 10 to 30 percent carbon monoxide.

There are a number of cities where carbon monoxide was found in violation of EPA standards: Chicago; Denver; Louisville, Kentucky; New York City; Portland, Oregon; and Seattle, Washington.

Bioaccumulation Factor: not available.

Formaldehyde
Formula: HCHO

What It Is: formaldehyde is from a chemical family of aldehydes that are formed by incomplete combustion of fossil fuels; in this form it is an air pollutant. Formaldehyde is often used as a resin in adhesives for making plywood, particle board, and other wood compositions. It is also used in plastics production, especially foam-rubber padding, carpets, drapery textiles, and permanent-press fabrics. This chemical, when combined with hydrochloride in industry, forms bischloromethylethers (BCME), which we have already described in Poisons List A, page 000. BCME is extremely carcinogenic.

In recent years much interest has been focused on formaldehyde as an indoor pollutant. It produces a sharp, irritating odor.

Major Health Concerns (CA, BD, TX): a highly toxic chemical, its first common use was as a preservative for biological specimens.

This chemical has been shown to produce mutations in fruit flies (Auerbach 1966) and in *E. coli* bacteria (Demerec 1951). Mutations come about when formaldehyde causes DNA strands to bond with other protein materials in the cell.

Other research has shown that formaldehyde causes damage to DNA, which can result in cancer (Rosenkranz 1972).

This chemical, given to laboratory animals by inhalation, has resulted in nose and throat cancers (Swenberg 1980).

As an irritant this chemical can cause nausea, and it affects eyes, nose, and upper respiratory tract in humans. It injures cilia and the mucosal blanket that normally protects the lungs. When these defenses are injured or destroyed, other chemical materials in the air can easily enter the lungs, and either cause damage to the lungs or make their way into the lymph or blood systems of the body (United States Public Health Service 1964).

Exposure Levels/Standards: government standards for both indoor and outdoor exposure to this chemical are given as follows.

In the United States, the occupational standard as set by NIOSH is one part per million parts air; as set by OSHA, 3 parts per million. The American Industrial Hygiene Association recommends a level not to exceed .1 parts per million for outdoor air. (This compares to West Germany's outdoor standard of .025 parts per million.)

The United States has no standards established for indoor air. However, in Denmark, the Netherlands, Sweden, and West Germany, the indoor standards are from .1 to .12 parts per million. (It has been shown that one part per million produces significant irritation of mucosal tissue in eyes, nose, etc. and that levels of 10 parts per million cannot be endured.)

In the United States, tests of indoor air routinely show levels to be above .12 parts per million. In new buildings where plywood and particle board are used, the formaldehyde level often exceeds 3 parts per million.

Because carpets, draperies, and furniture contain this chemical, their installation often triples formaldehyde levels in the home. In addition, heating and cooking with natural gas indoors raises formaldehyde levels.

Indoor formaldehyde levels drop significantly with adequate ventilation of rooms.

Where Found/What to Avoid: formaldehyde is found in foam insulation, foam-rubber products, furniture, synthetic fabric and drapery materials, carpets, plywood, particle board, and household items such as cabinets and bookshelves constructed with these materials; it is a by-product of incomplete combustion, and is found in the air near industries using this chemical or producing adhesives and other bonding materials containing it.

Cigarette smoke contains formaldehyde at levels of 30 parts per million (Wynder 1976).

Bioaccumulation Factor: not available.

Nitrogen Dioxide
Formula: NO$_2$

What It Is: a reddish-brown gas with a sharp odor, created in burning any substance. As a substance burns, nitrogen and oxygen molecules join to form nitrogen dioxide.

Major Health Concerns (TX): research has shown that nitrogen dioxide damages large white blood cells in the alveoli of the lungs. This is a major health hazard, since these white blood cells are important defense mechanisms against disease (Voisin 1977, Samuelsen 1978).

It has been shown that nitrogen dioxide damages the mucosal tissue of the bronchi, as well as the cilia, in mice (Hattori 1973).

Studies have shown that, when challenged with strep bac-

Nitrogen dioxide from power plants damages white blood cells, and is thus a major health hazard, since these blood cells are important in the defense against disease. (*Pittsburgh,* 1922, by Louis Lozowick. Oil on canvas, 30″ × 17″. Collection of the Whitney Museum of American Art, New York.)

teria, laboratory animals whose respiratory systems had been subjected to nitrogen dioxide had high mortality rates (Gardner 1977). This indicates that nitrogen dioxide can lower resistance to infection.

In humans, numerous studies have shown that air passages are constricted by this contaminant, making asthma and other chronic respiratory diseases worse (Nakamura 1964, Shy 1970).

Exposure Levels/Standards: EPA safety standards are 100 micrograms of nitrogen dioxide per cubic meter of air. This is the same as .05 parts per million.

At levels of 150 to 280 micrograms per cubic meter, this chemical causes respiratory disease. It produces a characteristic pungent odor at levels of 200 micrograms.

There are routine violations of these standards in several areas of the U.S.: Chicago; Cleveland; the New York–New Jersey area (800 micrograms per cubic meter); Los Angeles (1,000 micrograms per cubic meter); southern Texas; Oklahoma; Mississippi; Ohio; Indiana; and Pennsylvania (400 micrograms per cubic meter).

Nitrogen dioxide levels of 200 micrograms per cubic meter provoke asthma attacks and lower the lungs' ability to resist infection. At 1,000 micrograms per cubic meter, mice die as a result of their inability to fight infection.

Where Found/What to Avoid: power plants and highway vehicles are about equal in contributing to nitrogen dioxide in the air. Space heating is the third highest contributor. These three sources account for approximately 23 million tons produced annually.

Bioaccumulation Factor: not available.

Ozone
Formula: O_3

What It Is: ozone is produced by a photochemical reaction. When a substance is burned, producing nitrogen dioxide, the nitrogen dioxide molecule is broken by ultraviolet rays from the Sun, and one of its two oxygen atoms breaks free to join with another oxygen molecule, forming ozone. In the cities this process begins the moment the Sun rises, immediately changing the nitrogen dioxide emitted by cars and factories into ozone. The ozone concentrations increase until about noon, when levels reach as high as 1,000 percent of the morning rate.

Major Health Concerns (TX): numerous studies have shown that ozone causes considerable damage to mucosal tissue and lung lining. It is the main eye irritant in smog.

At exposure levels of 200 micrograms per cubic meter, laboratory animals have less resistance to infection (Coffin 1968). Ozone causes this in several ways: by lowering the production of protective secretions in the lungs (Gardner 1971); by reducing macrophage activity (Hurst 1970); by changing cilia and dural cells (Stephens 1971); and by reducing lung elasticity and damaging alveoli cells (Bartlett 1974).

Ozone causes chest pain and breathing difficulty in children during exercise (Kagawa 1975).

Ozone at 500 micrograms per cubic meter of air provokes asthma attacks (Schoettlin 1961). At exposure levels above 588 micrograms, ozone increases the incidence of cough, chest pain, and headache (Hammer 1974). As ozone levels climb from 200 to 300 micrograms, eye irritation increases proportionately.

Ozone has significant effects on the central nervous system, even at low doses. It reduces *serotonin* production (a substance necessary for normal nerve transmission) in rats (Skillen 1961). A decrease in serotonin production leads to a decrease in perception and cognitive behavior. Indeed, at least one researcher (Lagerwerff 1963) has shown that ozone decreases visual acuity, peripheral vision, night vision, and visual field perception. Another researcher (Johnson 1976) has found that it depresses brainwave patterns much as reduced oxygen does. Ozone has also been found to produce temporary exhilaration followed by depression (Griswald 1957).

Exposure Levels/Standards: in 1979, the EPA relaxed standards for ozone levels from .08 parts per million (approximately 150 micrograms per cubic meter) to 1.2 parts per million (approximately 210 micrograms per cubic meter).

Ozone is one of the two air pollutants most frequently found in the unhealthy range in several cities: Los Angeles, Philadelphia, San Diego, St. Louis, Washington, D.C., and Houston. Ozone reaches levels of 600 to 1,200 micrograms per cubic meter of air in these cities. (At 1,000 micrograms the lung defenses of laboratory animals are greatly compromised. At 600 micrograms, normal people begin to suffer eye discomfort, chest pains, and cough, as well as difficulty in breathing.)

Many cities in the United States have ozone levels of 400 micrograms per cubic meter. At 400 micrograms exercising children experience difficulty in breathing and asthmatics have asthma attacks.

Where Found/What to Avoid: same as for nitrogen dioxide.

Bioaccumulation Factor: not available.

Sulfur Dioxide
Formula: SO_2

What It Is: a gas produced by the burning of fossil fuels. It is highly soluble in both air and water. Approximately 90 percent of the sulfur dioxide in the atmosphere is produced by humans. The remaining 10 percent is from forest fires, volcanoes, and other natural phenomena.

Major Health Concerns (TX): because sulfur dioxide is soluble, it is easily absorbed by human mucosal tissue. In normal breathing it is absorbed into your system through the mucosa of your nose and upper respiratory tract. With heavy breathing during exercise, it is also absorbed by the lungs.

When your body absorbs this chemical, the mucosal cells release fluids and histamines, causing swelling and a constriction of air passages, the result being difficulty in breathing (Weir 1973).

As little as one part per million of sulfur dioxide, for a period of six hours, has been shown to cause a constriction of air passages in humans (Andersen 1974).

When sulfur dioxide is combined with other pollutants, such as ozone, the adverse health effects are greater than the sum of the two pollutants measured individually (Bates 1973).

Increased mortality rates in New York City were related to high sulfur-dioxide levels (Buechley 1973 and 1975).

In Holland, as sulfur-dioxide pollution was decreased by pollution control, breathing functions of the general population improved (Van der Lende 1974).

In the United States, sulfur dioxide was related to upper (Douglas 1966) and lower (Hammer 1976) respiratory infections in children.

In London, during the eight-year period when air pollution standards were being improved, average phlegm production dropped in the general population (Fletcher 1976).

Many different studies have shown that asthma attacks and bronchitis are related to in-

creased amounts of sulfur dioxide in the air. The most dramatic of these studies has shown that an increase of 100 micrograms of sulfur dioxide per cubic meter of air increases mortality rates from asthma and bronchitis by 5 percent (Lane and Seskind 1977).

A study by Zarkower (1972) has shown that sulfur dioxide at levels of two parts per million inhibits antibody production in mice.

Exposure Levels/Standards: EPA studies of national air-pollution figures, of air monitored in both urban and rural areas, show that the year-round average levels of sulfur dioxide

are 40 micrograms per cubic meter of air. Since this is the *average* of both rural and urban air, the levels must be much higher than this in some regions of the country.

EPA studies have shown that there are many days when sulfur-dioxide levels exceed 200 micrograms per cubic meter of air, with some days exceeding 365 micrograms, in: Washington, D.C.; western Pennsylvania; eastern Ohio; southern Indiana; northern Kentucky; St. Louis, Missouri; and Indianapolis, Indiana. Days when sulfur-dioxide levels exceed 100 micrograms per cubic meter of air are also found in Arizona, Montana,

In normal breathing, sulfur dioxide is absorbed into the body through the mucosal tissue of the nose and upper respiratory tract. (*Pittsburgh,* 1927, by Elsie Driggs. Oil, 34″ × 40″. Collection of the Whitney Museum of American Art, New York.)

High sulfur dioxide levels have been found to be associated with increased mortality rates. This map shows predicted levels of sulfur dioxide for 1990 plotted as peaks.

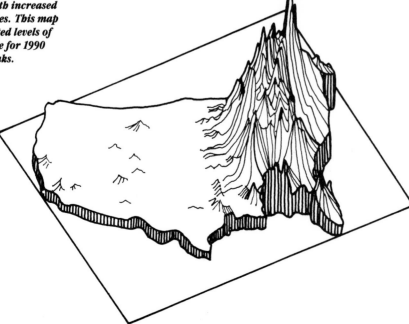

Nevada, Idaho, and New Mexico, as a result of coal-burning power plants.

Sulphur-dioxide levels as high as 2,607 micrograms per cubic meter of air have been measured directly downwind of short-stack power plants.

The EPA "safety" standard for sulfur dioxide is 80 micrograms per cubic meter of air, or .03 parts per million.

All the studies citing sulfur dioxide as a disease factor have measured it at levels of 80 to 150 micrograms per cubic meter of air. When combined with other pollutants, sulfur dioxide becomes a disease factor at less than the 80-microgram EPA standard.

Where Found/What to Avoid: the main source of sulfur dioxide is the burning of fossil fuels. By far the largest source is the coal-burning power plant. High concentrations of sulfur dioxide near plants burning fossil fuels have been reduced by the installation of tall stacks for exhausting these and other gases. Such stacks disperse the pollutants into the upper airstreams. With this dispersion, large areas are subjected to low levels of exposure instead of small populations being subjected to high levels, and the global situation will get worse as the number of coal-burning power plants increases.

In the upper levels of the airstreams, sulfur dioxide is converted to sulfuric acid (H_2SO_4), and comes back to earth as "acid rain."

Bioaccumulation Factor: not available.

Total Suspended Particulates

What It Is: the air is filled with suspended particulates that result from burning fossil fuels. These substances include sulfates, nitrates, and hydrocarbons, as well as soil and volcanic debris from natural sources. Sulfates make up more than half of the total suspended particulates. These are formed when sulfur dioxide, created in the burning of fossil fuels, rises into the higher air currents. In polluted air the sulfur dioxide, with the aid of nitrogen dioxide as a catalyst, rapidly picks up oxygen and turns into sulfates. Likewise, nitrogen dioxide turns into nitrates. Sulfates and nitrates bind with hydrogen from water drops, produce sulfuric acid and nitric acids, and eventually come down as acid rains. Large clouds of suspended particles are often observed by satellites over large cities and industrial areas. Particulates become vehicles that carry a large variety of substances, such as asbestos, beryllium, cadmium, chromium, or lead. (For the major health effects of these chemicals, see Poisons List A, pages 144 to 157.)

Major Health Concerns (TX, CA): experiments have shown that total suspended particulates from 1 to 3 microns in size cannot be filtered out by the nasal hairs and cilia in humans, and so make their way into the lungs and lodge in the alveoli. Then these particulates diffuse through the wall of the lungs, where they stay for months while the body's natural defenses attempt to break them down. The particulates, having come from the stacks of fossil-fuel-burning plants, are coated with contaminants, such as asbestos, mercury, and beryllium; so the particulates concentrate these toxic substances in the lungs. Some particulates actually penetrate the lung lining, and are carried by the lymph system throughout the body. This explains how cancers other than lung cancer can be created by breathing contaminated air.

Amdur (1973) has shown that sulfates in the air reduce the flow of air through the lungs in several ways: the natural defenses of the body, in an effort to protect against the contaminants, produce mucus, causing swelling in the air passages; smooth muscles in lung passages constrict, reducing air flow to the alveoli; with alveoli constricted, the passage of oxygen into the blood is compromised. According to the National Academy of Sciences (1979),

Particulate atmospheric pollutants may be involved in chronic lung disease pathogenesis, as causal factors in chronic bronchitis, as predisposing factors to acute bacterial and viral bronchitis, especially in children and cigarette smokers, and as aggravating factors for acute bronchial asthma and terminal stages of oxygen deficiency associated with chronic bronchitis and/or emphysema and its characteristic form of heart failure.

Exposure Levels/Standards: the EPA standard for total suspended particulates is 75 micrograms per cubic meter of air.

In 1977, of 4,000 stations monitoring particulates in the U.S, 17 percent reported violations of the EPA standard. From this and other data, it is estimated that the greater part of the U.S. population is breathing air with total suspended particulates exceeding 100 micrograms per cubic meter of air for at least 36 days of the year.

Where Found/What to Avoid: total suspended particulates are highest around industries burning fossil fuels, including coal-burning power plants. Because of the high stacks of these plants, even though the greatest concentration is in industrial areas, the problem is now global.

The highest populations exposed are in: Pennsylvania, Ohio, New Jersey, New York, Connecticut, and Massachusetts. Counties with highest concentrations are industrialized areas of the Ohio River Valley, the Great Lakes, the Tennessee Valley, and the refinery counties of Pennsylvania and New Jersey.

Bioaccumulation Factor: not available.

Suspended particulates from stacks of power plants are coated with asbestos, mercury, and beryllium. (Tall Stacks, 1982, by Michael Samuels.)

CHAPTER TWELVE

Human Health and the Living Earth: A Summary

In this part of the book we have focused on human health and on specific ways in which artificial substances adversely affect our well-being. Within this context it is easy to lose the broader perspective, that is, to fail to see the ways in which human health relates to the health of the living Earth. This is not to say that the welfare of the human species is a low priority; on the contrary, we are a part of the living Earth, active participants in a universal system far more complex and vital than anyone has yet been able to fully comprehend. We do know that, within the framework of today's environmental problems, human health can function as a barometer for the living Earth, a sensor for detecting too much, too little, or inappropriate inputs of matter, energy, or information.

People working together, first as individual sensors, and then joining to form the Earth's noosphere, are becoming increasingly aware of the global implications of environmental pollution. In this way both our illnesses and our intellectual awareness are becoming the motive force of at least one of the living Earth's homeostatic mechanisms. We have detected the error in our course and are beginning to take measures to correct it. If we fail to change both our own private habits and public policy, there will be poverty, human suffering, tremendous squandering of natural resources, and broad environmental destruction such as has never previously been experienced by the human race. The kind of inappropriate behavior that has led us up to this point cannot last for more than two or three more decades without radically changing the basic nature of the living Earth.

In recent years the subject of *acid rains* has received much attention in the media, since it is one of the ways in which artificial pollutants are directly threatening the normal functions of the living Earth. As we have said, acid rains are by-products of burning fossil fuels. With the construction of tall stacks on factories and power plants to vent exhaust gases into the higher air currents above the cities, sulfur dioxide and nitrogen dioxide mix with water vapors and form sulfuric and nitric acids. These acids, contained in the higher air currents, are dispersed globally. The pH factor of rains containing these substances is as low as 4.4, whereas normal rain has a pH of 7.6. These rains have highly unpredictable effects on everything living in the biosphere; they kill or stunt vegetation, kill fish, and destroy essential algae growths.

In addition to acid rains, our burning of fossil fuels produces vast quantities of carbon dioxide, adding to the "greenhouse" layer in the Earth's atmosphere. It is estimated that this layer has increased somewhere between 15 and 20 percent since the beginning of the Industrial Age (1800s), and that 7 percent of this increase has occurred since 1958. At a World Energy Conference in 1980, researchers estimated that concentrations of carbon dioxide could reach twice the preindustrial level by the middle of the 21st century unless our present policies about fossil-fuel burning change radically. Because the carbon-dioxide layer in the atmosphere traps infrared heat radiated by the Earth, increased atmospheric concentrations of this scope could raise global surface temperatures about $3°C$ ($5.4°F$), with average winter temperatures in the polar regions going up as much as $10°C$. Possible climatic effects include changes in wind direction and speed, and changes in ocean currents and rain patterns. If the warming persisted, polar ice caps could melt and sea levels would rise, reducing land surfaces and forcing mass human migrations from coastal regions. Although experts agree there would be broad agricultural and socioeconomic changes, the extent and nature of these changes are not completely predictable at this time.

For the living Earth the changes we describe here are somewhat equivalent to our drinking and eating highly acid foods and permanently changing our body temperature. Such changes would, of course, create radical shifts in our basic physiology and chemistry, assuming that our homeostatic capacities were not completely overloaded by the challenge.

In addition to acid rains and a buildup of the carbon-dioxide layer of our atmosphere, human innovation and industry are causing other global problems: atmospheric ozone depletion (as a result of chloroflurocarbon use); deforestation of tropical forests, resulting in soil loss; pollution from burning; loss of species (from clearing forests for building and agriculture); loss of biological diversity (as a result of agricultural and industrial chemicals, and the takeover of wilderness areas for new construction); soil loss (from cultivation of land); destruction of bacterial blooms living on the continental shelves of the ocean (as a result of dumping chemicals and silt into the waterways); and disturbance of the Earth's normal carbon cycles (by burning fossil fuels).

Most environmentalists agree that the living Earth can maintain a homeostatic balance

If present trends continue, the Earth may one day cease to be a living system; to survive we would have to become the maintenance engineers of a gigantic spaceship that no longer nurtures life of its own volition. (GT-4 EVA. Courtesy of NASA.)

This map shows the continental shelves under the oceans. They occupy an area as large as the African continent and may be essential for the homeostasis of our planet.

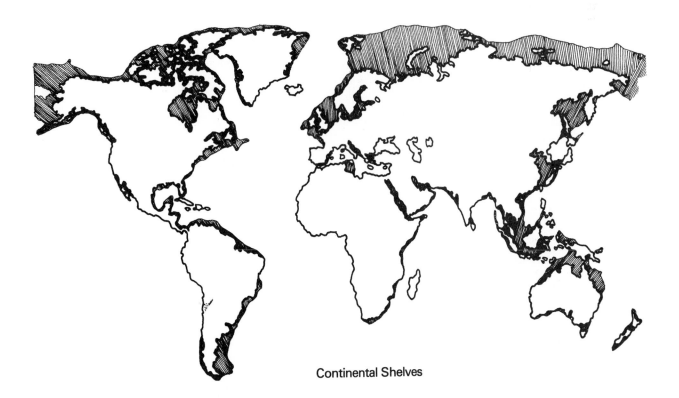

Continental Shelves

for itself, even though the adjustments it makes may radically alter human life as we presently know it. At some point, however, if present trends continue, the Earth will cease to be a living system. It will become a dead thing, and if we human beings are innovative enough to survive, we will find ourselves serving as maintenance engineers on a gigantic spaceship that itself no longer nurtures life. As Lovelock points out, "Each time we significantly alter part of some natural process of regulation or introduce some new source of energy or information, we are increasing the probability that one of these changes will weaken the stability of the entire system."[1]

In the midst of considering all our environmental problems, we may easily forget that our numbers are increasing at a tremendous

Earth's homeostatic mechanisms, those mysterious processes that regulate the Earth's health.

In considering the material in this chapter and the tremendous challenge to future generations that the questions here pose, it is all too easy to hear only the tolling of a death knell. If we respond to the challenge by merely defending our old ways of life, we are, indeed, doomed. But if in the challenge we find the inspiration to create a new and healthier way of life, we can look forward to a better future. The Hopis have a legend about passing from a confused, disrupted world to a brighter future. This is called the Hopi prophesy.

The emergence to the future fifth world has begun . . . You can read this in the Earth

*A Hopi legend describes how man emerged from a hole in the ground into our world. The Hopi built Kivas to symbolize the emergence. The emergence to the future (fifth) world has begun. (*Kiva,* 1983, by Michael Samuels.)*

rate. We are taking over larger and larger areas of the Earth, covering the surface with new highways, buildings, and factories, clearing billions of acres of what was once wilderness area and cultivating crops needed to feed our growing masses. As this growth continues, our global responsibility also grows, and to ensure the quality of life our planet has provided us, scrupulous care must be taken to maintain the

itself. Plant forms from previous worlds are beginning to spring up as seeds. This could start a new study of botany if people were wise enough to read them. The same kinds of seeds are being planted in the skies as stars. The same kinds of seeds are being planted in our hearts. All these are the same, depending how you look at them. That is what makes the Emergence to the next, Fifth World.[2]

A Prescription for Environmental Health

For the past four thousand years, human beings have been trying to gain mastery over nature. To some extent we have succeeded in that quest. By building weapons for killing animals larger than ourselves, by creating structures for protection from the elements, by cultivating grain crops and domesticating animals, by creating machines that can do our work, and by harnessing the atom and sending rockets into space, we have been putting our creative energies into learning how to control nature. Out of all this has been born, along with many valuable inventions, a view of nature as an adversary, on the one hand, and a resource to be endlessly exploited, on the other.

In the past two centuries, we have gone quite beyond the goal of controlling nature in order to survive. The momentum of our quest has carried us on to a point where our own inventions have become more life-threatening than anything presented by nature. Pollution could never have become so dangerously

We now enter a period of introspection, in an effort to gain mastery over the greatest threat the human race has ever faced. Our new quest is the search for balance between our own needs and nature's. (The False Mirror, 1928, by Rene Magritte. Oil on canvas, 21" × 31". Museum of Modern Art, New York.)

prevalent without our inventiveness.

The evidence that we have created threats to ourselves that are even greater than nature's threats comes in the form of disease, ranging from hypertensive complaints caused by overcrowding and highly competitive social structures, to a rising incidence of birth defects and cancer caused, in part, by artificial mutagenic substances. The diseases themselves signal the need for change, not only in the quest but in the attitudes fostered by that quest. The impulse to control must be redirected from manipulating the external world toward exploring and learning to master the inner world, that is, our own thoughts and feelings. We must now enter a period of introspection, in an effort to gain mastery over the greatest single threat the human race has ever faced. Our new quest is the search for a balance between our own needs and nature's.

Up to now the accumulation of wealth by the exploitation of our resources has been a central goal. And as René Dubos points out, this impulse has attained its

Caring must replace controlling; compassion must replace exploitation. We must replace adversarial roles with roles fostering competence. (*The Equatorial Jungle,* by Henri Rousseau. National Gallery of Art, Washington, D.C.)

apex in our present destructive power, represented by several thousand rockets armed with nuclear weapons. Valerius Geist states that,

> *because of the rapid changes and increasing artificiality of our environment, it is essential that an easily grasped theory of preventive medicine be generated and accepted as soon as possible. This cannot be left to medicine, [which views itself] as a science limited to dealing with organic dysfunctions.*[1]

The goal is to create an environment structured to ensure maximum health, both for ourselves as well as for the Earth; these together must be considered a whole. *Caring* must replace *controlling*. *Compassion* must replace *exploitation*. We must replace adversarial roles with roles that foster competence. To accomplish these ends, we must create an environment that in every way nurtures these values; otherwise these values simply will not exist, since the environment we create influences our lives and teaches us as much as we influence it.

What kind of environment do we have now? The myth is that we have never been healthier. It is true that our life expectancy has never been longer, and that we are relatively free of the fear of most infectious disease, but there is more to be considered.

In any one day in the United States, based on 1970 census figures, approximately 20 percent of our people are what Valerius Geist has called the "casualties of our lifestyle." Geist states that of our 203 million people, 2.1 million are institutionalized in mental hospitals, jails, homes for the handicapped, detention homes, homes for unwed mothers, and homes for abandoned children. Another 27 million are physically handicapped; 3.6 million are sick in bed; 90,000 are hospitalized with physical illness; and 4,500 die of environmentally linked diseases, such as heart attacks, cirrhosis, emphysema, bronchitis, suicide, and murder. There are 37 million people on public assistance, 3.2 million orphans, 6 million mentally retarded, 5 million congenitally deformed children, and 20 million people with sight, hearing, and speech dysfunctions. At least a million children are left unsupervised during the day while their parents work, 40,000 of them under the age of six. In addition, 3.5 million people are receiving some kind of treatment for psychological problems, and 50 percent of the total adult population are obese or hypertense, are cigarette smokers, or have high blood-cholesterol levels.[2]

This view of ourselves is not pleasant, but focusing on it for just a moment allows us to review where we have been and begin to form a plan of where we want to go. As we seek the new plan, we turn to evolutionary biologists and physiologists for suggestions about creating a caring environment. We know, for example, that animals in a balanced natural environment exhibit strong expressions of mutual care, deriving real pleasure from both expressing and receiving that care. This mutual caring serves an important function for the survival of the species. But as the environment becomes increasingly competitive—because of crowding, shortage of food, and the addition of stressors such as noise and air pollution—that level of caring gives way to defensiveness, aggression, and selfishness. The lack of caring, perhaps more than any other single symptom, indicates the degree of stress a society is feeling. Likewise, the opposite of caring, that is, a defensive or aggressive posture, is the outermost extreme of the loss of care, and is no more clearly seen than in our present nuclear policies, the ultimate assault on the environment. To turn this

Think globally but act locally. The best place to begin change is our own community with its fields, rivers, marshes, coastlines, roads, and streets. (*Flower Garden,* 1924. Watercolor and gouache, 14″ × 8″, by Paul Klee. Collection, The Museum of Modern Art, New York. Katherine S. Dreier Bequest.)

We must reduce the threats to well-being that we have created for ourselves. (*Old House by Creek,* 1982. Oil on canvas, 34" × 57", by Charles Burchfield. Collection of Whitney Museum of American Art, New York.)

trend around and create an environment where care is once more expressed, we must reduce the threats to well-being that we have created for ourselves.

When considering prescriptions for today's environmental ills, it is tempting to focus on global issues. But if we did so, we might obscure regional problems that have more immediate solutions. As René Dubos reflects,

Thinking at a global level is a useful and exciting intellectual activity, but no substitute for the work needed to solve practical problems at home. If we really want to contribute to the welfare of humankind and of our planet, the best place to start is in our own community, and its fields, rivers, marshes, coastlines, roads, and streets, as well as with its social problems.[3]

The preventive-medicine prescription we outline in the following pages is concerned with two general areas: (1) what you can change in your own life, at home and at work, and (2) what you can do in your community, to immediately start creating an environment of care, with health for the planet and for the human race being the final goal.

CHAPTER THIRTEEN

Lifestyle and Environmental Health

When we examine disease statistics, we see that not everyone becomes ill from every environmental pollutant. On the contrary, the evidence makes it clear that, just as with other diseases, there are multiple causes for environmentally induced illness. This does not mean, however, that our pollution problems should be underestimated. It is clear that chemicals, radiation, and psychosocial stress now constitute the major health problems of our planet, replacing microorganisms. The major challenge for medical science today is to prevent humanly-caused diseases that are side effects of life in the modern world. The quest for a cure must be launched with the same fervor that previously went into the search for medical controls over infectious diseases.

Every environmental factor, be it the pressure of daily commuting or the chemicals in the air we breathe, will have a significant effect on our physiology. Our bodies maintain themselves in a healthy state by means of the self-healing and self-regulatory mechanisms within us, but illness can and does occur when these homeostatic mechanisms are pushed beyond their limits, past the point where they can make adjustments that will maintain a healthy state. The power of our bodies to maintain and restore health is prodigious, but medical experts tell us that these capacities are strained by a variety of environmental problems; over some of these we could exercise immediate controls, but some are going to require much longer-range plans. If we are to fully enjoy the benefits of good health, we must learn more about how pollutants interact with our bodies —especially how these pollutants can reduce the effectiveness of our homeostatic capacities.

Human well-being is important, but we can address this issue only by addressing a still larger concern. Knowing what we know today about the interrelationships between the Earth and all living things, we cannot afford to adopt the simplistic view that only the human race is at risk with environmental pollution. Like the human body, the Earth itself has homeostatic limits, and once these limits are exceeded the Earth's health is threatened. It is therefore clear that human health and the Earth's health are intertwined and that only human beings, who created the problem, are in a position to effect a cure. Ironically, the correction lies in our discovery that we are an essential part of the Earth's homeostatic system. We are literally one of the Earth's self-healing mechanisms.

The Multiple Causes of Environmental Disease

The multiple causal factors of any environmental disease may be broken down into two categories. The first categories is *events*, which consist of inappropriate inputs of matter, energy, and/or information (see Chapter Four). Events can be chemical, psychosocial, or dietary, and include physical exercise and perceptions, shaped by past experiences, which determine how a person will react to an immediate stimulus. The second category is *genetic structure,* which includes such things as the body's ability to produce certain enzymes for digestion, the need for mothering in the early stage of life, the need for sleep, the need for particular foods, and the need for minimal levels of exercise.

Anything that affects any one of these factors, in large enough amounts, can have a detrimental effect on the organism. Similarly, a combination of disease factors, at relatively low levels, can also push the body's homeostatic mechanisms past their limits, ultimately manifesting as disease.

Our perceptions of any one or more of these disease factors are tremendously important. For example, if you perceive the daily commute to work as a threat to your well-being, fussing and fuming every time the traffic comes to a stop, your body will go through several important chemical changes. These chemical changes—largely involving the adrenal hormones—cause the body to go into what physiologists call the "fight-or-flight response," alerting the brain, cardiovascular system, and large muscles to get into readiness to encounter danger. If prolonged or repeated for enough years, these chemical changes can cause severe damage to a person's cardiovascular system.

Ideally the fight-or-flight response prompts a person to take action, to either escape from the perceived threat or to find a new pattern of behavior that reduces the extent of that threat. The simplest example of that is the animal who perceives the menace of a predator and takes flight to escape it. Unfortunately, environmental threats to health are seldom that obvious.

Our perceptions of health threats are shaped by both inner (or genetic) awarenesses of factors that might injure our body (fire and predators being good examples) and learning experiences after birth. For example, a person who has learned to regard commuting to work as a pleasant time to be alone and think will not react to that experience as a threat, and so there will be no fight-or-flight response. It is thus important to recognize that our perceptions of environmental threats may be far more flexible than we may think, providing us with a whole range of alternatives to getting frustrated with commute-hour traffic or other details in our daily lives.

Many of the environmental health threats we face today are new to our planet, created by us only in recent years; so the human body has not yet had a chance to develop an inner system for identifying them as a threat. For example, many chemicals that are toxic and carcinogenic have no perceivable scent, or may even be pleasantly scented. As a result, we don't sense them as threats in the way that we do when we smell fire. In fact, the only way we can identify many of our present environmental threats is intellectually, that is, by reading about scientific studies confirming the danger. But until we have that knowledge, we don't possess a way to identify the threat.

If no threat is perceived, no constructive action is likely to be taken, and our bodies begin to undergo changes. These changes can come in the form of genetic mutation, which causes birth defects and cancer; in the form of toxicity, which alters normal physiological functions; or in the form of allergic reactions, which usually disappear as soon as the threat is removed.

After we learn to identify environmental disease factors, we become able to take action to protect ourselves, and so prevent disease. Preventive action of this kind is what stress physiologists call a "coping response." Coping responses can be anything from reading food labels, in order to winnow out products containing harmful additives, to using public transportation, in order to avoid the stress of driving to work. Often these coping responses can be effective even after disease symptoms have begun to appear: if a man has high blood pressure, his physician may prescribe an exercise program; and if the man follows the program his blood pressure may return to normal. Making a decision about the disease factors that are most important in your own life is the first step toward creating environmental health.

```
PHOSPHORUS               10        20
MAGNESIUM                 8        10
ZINC                     25        30
COPPER                    8         8
*CONTAINS LESS THAN 2% OF THE U.S. RDA OF THIS
 NUTRIENT
```

INGREDIENTS LISTED IN ORDER OF PREDOMINANCE. INGREDIENTS: WHOLE WHEAT KERNELS, RAISINS, MALT FLAVORING, SALT, COCONUT OIL.

FORTIFIED WITH: VITAMIN E (VITAMIN E ACETATE), NIACIN (NIACINAMIDE), ZINC (ZINC OXIDE), VITAMIN A (VITAMIN A PALMITATE), VITAMIN B$_6$ (PYRIDOXINE HYDROCHLORIDE), VITAMIN B$_2$ (RIBOFLAVIN), VITAMIN B$_1$ (THIAMIN HYDROCHLORIDE), FOLIC ACID VITAMIN B$_{12}$ AND VITAMIN D$_2$.

KELLOGG COMPANY
BATTLE CREEK, MI 49016 U.S.A.
© 1982 BY KELLOGG COMPANY
® KELLOGG COMPANY
Pat. Pend.

CARBOHYDRATE INFORMATION

CEREAL	WITH MILK

Health begins with the "coping response," which can be anything from reading food labels to making the decision to use public transportation instead of driving to work. (Labels, 1983, by Michael Samuels.)

Stress

In Chapter Five, "The Manifold Nature of Disease," we described how stress causes disease. Here we'll discuss some of the most important kinds of psychosocial stress we face today, such as crowding, noise, and tough culture. Each has its own unique issues and slightly different approach in prevention.

Social Organization and Health

High population density need not, in itself, be unhealthy. Animal and human researchers have shown that only if groups are organized in a way that meets certain basic human needs for privacy and mutual respect can crowding be tolerated. Some excellent examples illustrate this point. One of the most famous is the Monkey Hill project.

In the 1920s, zoologists at the London Zoo

put together a program that, at least on paper, looked very good. Every effort was made to simulate a baboon's natural environment, complete with heated caves, climbing areas, and a balanced diet. In spite of the best intentions, the project was disastrous, because it failed to take social organization into account. In their natural habitat, baboons have a sophisticated social structure. Dominance and leadership roles are worked out from birth, with childhood play establishing clear relationships between the members of a community very early on. By the time a baboon has grown to adulthood, his or her position is specifically mapped out; each monkey knows its place in the social structure of the troop.

When the directors of the zoo brought the animals to Monkey Hill, they put together a

When the London Zoo put together a random collection of monkeys, without respect to sex or social position, more than a quarter of the animals died of stress-related diseases. (*Monkey Island,* 1982, by Michael Samuels.)

random collection of baboons without respect for their social origins. In other words, the monkeys that were to populate the hill as a community didn't know each other and had no defined perceptions about their social positions. Consequently, tensions were very high. Within six months, 27 of 100 males had died. Autopsies revealed a variety of stress-related diseases: atherosclerosis, pneumonia, ulcerative colitis, and kidney disease. Of 15 babies born in a five-year period at Monkey Hill, all but one died. The mothers appeared clumsy and inexperienced with their babies. Animals raised in this environment had minimal social assets, frequently becoming ill and dying as they found themselves in settings where their social skills proved inadequate, failing to help them make satisfying adjustments to the environment into which they had been thrust.[1]

Anthropologists have found similar patterns among human groups. For example, in 1972 the anthropologist C. M. Turnbill studied

a tribe of hunter-gatherers called the Ik, similar to the Kalahari Bush people we discussed earlier in this book. The Ik's nomadic way of life came to an end when political pressures forced them to live in villages. In a short period of time their social organization completely disintegrated. Family values such as caring, love, and sacrifice broke down. Marriages failed, and children were neglected. Along with these social stresses came diseases such as high blood pressure and atherosclerosis, as well as increased incidence of infection.[2]

We can hardly ignore the parallels between the diseases manifested at Monkey Hill, those among the disenfranchised Ik tribe, and those of our modern world. But what is the prescription for such ills? Based on studies of humans and animals, Valerius Geist has developed a model of social organization for health.

Geist's model begins with an extended family, that is, a family structure with daily contact and shared responsibilities across three generations. This would involve a couple raising from two to three siblings, spaced four to six years apart. Grandparents would be present to share in child-rearing and tutoring. There would be four to six such families, forming a social network of about thirty people. With an emphasis on cooperation, stress from competition with vastly larger groups would be reduced. Social support for everyone would reduce the need for highly aggressive impulses. Adults would get self-validation in part by teaching younger people.

Geist's model would emphasize: intellectual stimulation and education (language, music, art, and face-to-face teaching); emotional security (freedom from want of food and shelter); dependable social bonds among the adults raising the children; and freedom from fear of being attacked.

According to Geist, "The foregoing criteria are such that the individual gains competence and remains continuously master of his or her environment."[3] This mastery of the environment, the ability to have needs met by means of one's own efforts, is an essential part of every workable social organization. The opposite is true in most modern societies, according to Geist, and results in what he calls an "epidemic" of people who lack emotional security, and who continue to seek the primary needs for love and emotional security instead of developing skills for personal satisfaction and independence. Geist states that, "It cannot be stressed enough that individuals require emotional security, which in large part they gain by being competent masters at solving daily problems."[4]

By developing competence, the individual can visualize alternatives and solve problems. He or she can harmonize with a variety of people in many different circumstances, express and empathize with diverse moods, and detect selfish strategies in other people. This skilled person can maximize predictability in the social mileau, expressing and fostering a positive outlook toward life and confidence in meeting daily problems. Individuals in such groups would exercise their ability to make choices, to gain information, to explore and discover.

The importance of mastering the skills necessary for comfort and security has been dramatically demonstrated in animal experiments using "yoked" subjects. In these experiments, two monkeys are placed in identical environments, restrained in a special yoke for several hours each day. Both animals receive low levels of electric shock to their tails at the same time. The only difference between the two subjects' predicaments is that one has a button to push that *sometimes* stops the shock that both animals are receiving. In other words, one has some control over the negative stimulus; the other has none. Turning the electric current off also constitutes a skill the monkey must master.

Animals with no control of the shock manifest a high incidence of cancer, heart disease, and even infections. Animals with control are relatively healthy, even though they always get the same electric shocks as the other group. The yoked animal with no control over his environment goes through a predictable pattern: first comes despair, then deep depression, then disease, and finally death. The depression phase is particularly interesting to us here, since it presents a key for identifying social stress.

A family structure with daily contact and shared responsibilities fosters support and health. (A baby's transport on the Kalahari desert. Courtesy of the American Museum of Natural History.)

Physiological changes take place in our bodies when we feel helpless. (*Despair,* 1923, by Hugo Robus. Bronze, 12″ × 10″. Collection of the Whitney Museum of American Art, New York.)

A tough culture is one in which the goals valued by the society are accessible to only a few members: only the president is a success. (*Through the Mill,* 1940, by Phillip Evergood. Oil on canvas, 36″ × 52″. Collection of the Whitney Museum of American Art, New York.)

to action in the fight-or-flight response, the adrenal cortex sends out cortisone during the depressed response. Cortisone affects electrolyte balance in the body, reducing energy, excitement, and the ability to "feel" the world.

It has been speculated that depression was originally an adaptive mechanism, lowering aggression by helping animals adjust to rank or status in their community. In *The Lancet,* J. S. Price stated that, "Depression is calculated to lead to the idea of adjustment."[5] A depressed man withdraws and forgets memories that otherwise would help him build a sense of self-esteem. He loses his sex drive, and ceases to struggle for dominance over the problem he has been attempting to solve. He sees himself as unworthy and inferior, and in order to regain his sense of self, he may seek another situ-

Depression, Stress, and Tough Cultures

Depression is one of the most widespread emotional reactions in modern life. Indeed, Hans Selye, probably the foremost researcher on disease and stress, has noted that depression is one of two reactions to threatening situations, the other reaction being the fight-or-flight response.

According to Selye, when a person or animal is confronted with a problem that is perceived as insoluble, or is defeated or frustrated again and again by the same set of circumstances, physiological changes take place in the body. These changes involve the adrenal hormones: whereas the adrenal hormone known as epinephrine stimulates the muscles

ation in which he can feel better about himself.

When placed in the context of what anthropologists call a "tough culture," depression and the fight-or-flight response take on special meanings. A tough culture, according to J. Arsenian and J. M. Arsenian, is one in which the goals valued by the society are accessible to few members. Only the president of the company is a success; everyone below that is a failure. By contrast, in an "easy culture" social goals are accessible to everyone, with everyone's contribution to the community being seen as important, necessary, and valuable. In tough cultures, stress disease is extraordinarily high: symptoms of this stress include depression, violence, aggressive behavior, crime, neurosis, suicide, heart disease, and cancer.

If a society is organized with goals that are accessible to everyone, and if each member of that community receives preparation to be competent in the mastery of social skills, environmental diseases caused by stress will be greatly reduced. Disease symptoms arise either when the person fails to develop competence or when social changes are so radical that the individual's skills no longer serve him or her. In *Stress, Health, and the Social Environment,* Henry and Stephens state that,

A man living in a stable society, and well-equipped by his cultural background to deal with the familiar world around him, will not show a rise of blood pressure with age. This thesis holds whether he's a modern technocrat who became a fighter pilot early in life or a

the center of, or closely linked with, tough cultures; so tension and anxiety are everyday experiences, perhaps so familiar by now that we hardly notice them. Within this context, the ability to relax yourself at will can be one of the most important tools for health.

Mike and Nancy Samuels have written at length about relaxation. They observe that conscious relaxation is deceptively simple. Nevertheless, research has shown that relaxation produces significant physiological changes, resulting in a state quite different from everyday consciousness. Relaxation is characterized by turning inward and concentrating on one's own body and mind rather than on external events or concerns about the past or future. Inherent in the relaxed state is a feeling of detachment, a lack of concern for

During relaxation, heart rate, respiratory rate, oxygen consumption, and carbon dioxide production drop, enabling better self-healing. (*The Artist's Garden at Eragny,* 1898, by Camillo Pissarro. National Gallery of Art, Washington, D.C.)

Stoneage Bushman who is a skilled hunter-gatherer living in the Kalahari desert. However, when radical cultural changes disrupt his familiar environment with a new set of demands for which past acculturation has left him unprepared his social assets are then critical. Should they fail to protect him, he will be exposed to emotional upheavals and ensuing neuroendocrine disturbances that may eventuate in cardio-vascular disease."[6]

Conscious Relaxation

Most of us live in environments either at

how one is doing. Dr. Wolfgang Luthe describes it as "a casual, relaxed attitude involving minimal or no goal-directed voluntaristic efforts, in the sense of energetic striving, or apprehensive, tension-producing control of functions leading to the desired result."[7]

The inward-directed, nonstriving state has a predictable effect on the body's nervous system. This effect is called the relaxation response. What it means physiologically is that the body switches from a hypothalamic-sympathetic-adrenal arousal to a hypothalamic-parasympathetic-adrenal turn-off. In a sense, relaxation takes place when the body turns off the system that alerts it to external change or danger, and turns on a system that puts the body on a self-regulating, minimum-energy, self-healing mode. During relaxation, heart rate, respiratory rate, oxygen consumption, and carbon-dioxide production all drop.

Anyone can learn to relax by following a set of simple instructions. The maximum effects of relaxation can be achieved with only four to eight hours of instruction and twenty minutes of practice per day. There are many methods for learning to relax. No single method is significantly more effective than any other. The common aspects that are usually helpful are:

(1) a set of clear instructions and a belief in them;

(2) a comfortable position, so that muscles can relax;

(3) a passive attitude of *allowing* relaxation to take place;

(4) a quiet place; and

(5) deep, regular breathing.

As a preliminary, try an exercise designed to increase awareness of small amounts of muscular tension. Often our muscles are slightly tight, but we are not aware of it. The more nervous or tense we tend to be, the more likely we are to be unaware of constant, low-level tension that we have come to accept as *normal*.

To do this preliminary exercise, lie in a comfortable position with your hands resting lightly at your sides. Raise one hand slightly by bending it at the wrist; hold it up, and become aware of how this state of muscular tension feels. Now let your hand go limp. Be aware of how this relaxed state feels. Do this several times until you are fully familiar with the states of tension and relaxation.

Just as it is useful to know how muscular tension feels in order to relax, it is also important to learn the feeling of a passive attitude. A yogic exercise called "counting breaths" teaches concentration and can help everyone understand how the mind works. When you count breaths you quickly realize that thoughts constantly enter your mind one after another, and that you have only marginal control over the content of these thoughts. We have all had similar experiences during periods of tension, or while trying to solve a problem in our lives.

To count breaths, sit down in a comfortable position and concentrate on your breathing. Simply start counting your breaths: "one," as you inhale, "two," as you exhale, etc. Most people find their counting interrupted by thoughts about something they should be doing at that moment and they tend to stop their counting and get caught up in the thoughts that have intruded. If this happens to you, consciously remember that this moment of relaxation is as important as anything else you need to do. Bring your attention back to your breaths, and continue counting.

A yogic exercise called "counting breaths" teaches concentration and helps people relax their minds. (Kuan Yin, seventeenth century, Chinese. Metropolitan Museum of Art, Fletcher Fund.)

Which areas of your body are the most tense?

Everyone has certain muscles that get tense when he or she gets nervous or is under pressure. Although everyone has a different set of tension areas, the most common are:

eyes
neck and shoulders
jaw
lower back and pelvis

As you do any kind of relaxation exercises, be especially aware of these tension areas and give yourself as much time as necessary to relax them.

Deep Relaxation

Find a tranquil place where you will not be disturbed for ten or fifteen minutes. Lie down on your back, legs flat on the floor, arms resting lightly at your sides. Close your eyes. Inhale slowly and deeply. Pause. Exhale slowly and completely. Let your abdomen rise and fall as you breathe. Do this several times.

Notice how you are feeling calmer, more comfortable, and more relaxed. As you relax more deeply, your breathing will become slow and even. Mentally say to yourself, "My feet are relaxing. They are becoming more and more relaxed. My feet feel heavy." Rest for a moment, enjoying the sensations of your feet relaxing. Now repeat the same suggestions for your ankles, your lower legs, your thighs, pausing after each to enjoy the sensations of relaxing. Relax your pelvis. Rest and enjoy the sensations. Relax your back. Rest and enjoy how this feels. Relax your chest, your fingers, your hands. Relax and enjoy the sensations. Relax your upper arms and shoulders, your neck. Let your jaw and face be relaxed. Relax your tongue. Relax your eyes and forehead. Now just rest, enjoying the sensations of being deeply relaxed.

You are now in a deeply relaxed state. You can deepen this state by counting backward: breathe in, and as you exhale, say to yourself, "Ten. I am feeling very relaxed . . ." Inhale, and as you slowly exhale, say to yourself,

"Nine. I am feeling more relaxed." Breathe. "Eight. I am feeling even more relaxed." Breathe. "Seven. Deeper and more relaxed." "Six. More relaxed." "Five." Pause. "Four. More relaxed." Pause. "Three." Pause. "Two. Relaxed." Pause. "One. More and more relaxed."

You are now at a deeper and more relaxed level of awareness, a level at which your body feels healthy, your mind feels peaceful and open. You can stay in this relaxed state as long as you wish.

To return to your normal everyday state of being, say to yourself, "I am now going to move. When I count to three, I will raise my left hand and stretch my fingers. I will then feel relaxed, happy, and strong, ready to continue my everyday activities."

Every time you relax by this method, you

Evaluating the supportive dimensions of your social environment[a]

Do you confide in someone each day, once a week, less than once a week, never?

Do you feel secure in your environment each day, once a week, less than once a week, never?

Do you feel that you have some control over your environment each day, once a week, less than once a week, never?

Do you feel that people approve of you each day, once a week, less than once a week, never?

Do you have a close intimate time with someone each day, once a week, less than once a week, never?

Does your support come from family, friends, community?

Do you feel you have enough money? Usually? Sometimes? Never?

Do you have a strong set of personal beliefs? A strong religious affiliation?

A brief relaxation exercise

Whenever you feel tense, take a deep breath, let it out slowly, and recall the sensations of being deeply relaxed that you have experienced. Let your whole body remember these sensations, and as you do, you will find yourself relaxing almost as you would if you did a complete exercise.

---

will find it easier and easier to do, and you'll find yourself relaxing more deeply and more completely each time. The sensations of relaxation may include tingling, pulsing, warmth, heaviness, coolness, or an illusion of floating. After you have practiced conscious relaxation for some time, these sensations will be familiar to you, and you may even find yourself being able to experience them simply by taking a few deep breaths and allowing yourself to let go. Many people find it helpful to do this, pausing in their busy work schedule during the day to let themselves relax.

Noise Pollution

Environmental noise has become an important disease factor, not only because it means hearing loss for millions of people, but because our most recent medical research implicates noise in high blood pressure, ulcers, neurological disorders, alteration of body

---

Physical changes during deep relaxation

- Muscles are relaxed and blood flow within them slows.
- Breathing rate slows down.
- Oxygen consumption is reduced.
- Carbon dioxide elimination reduced.
- Heartbeat slows.
- Blood pressure is reduced.
- Cardiac output is slowed.
- Skin resistance increases.
- Brain waves change from theta to alpha.
- Blood lactate levels drop.
- Adrenal hormone levels drop.
- Blood flow to digestive system increases.

chemistry, and susceptibility to infectious disease. The mechanism by which it causes disease is fundamentally the same as with all other forms of stress: the body registers loud noises as warning signals. Even though most of the sounds we hear do not pose immediate danger —the roar of an airplane overhead, the din of city traffic outside the windows—our bodies still react to such sounds as real threats. In an EPA report on noise pollution, researchers note that "the body shifts gears. Blood pressure rises, heart rate and breathing speed up, muscles tense, hormones are released into the bloodstream, and perspiration appears."[8] When sounds are sudden, difficult to identify, or unexpected, they need not even be loud to trigger these physiological stress responses.

People living near airports, highways, or other high-noise areas are at greatest risk. These people have a significantly higher incidence of stress-related illness than people of matching socioeconomic background who live in quiet areas. One study on the effects of noise pollution showed that people living in residential areas near the Schiphol Airport in Holland had nearly twice as many visits to the doctor each week as comparable groups of people living in quiet areas.[9] Moreover, people living near airports had nearly three times as many psychological problems serious enough to seek medical help, and about twice as many complaints of lower back pain, spastic colon, stomach problems, allergic disease, tinnitus, dizziness, and headaches as people living in quiet environments. And finally, the people living near airports had twice as many visits to the doctor

Table 13.1: Sound levels of common noises in the environment

Sound level	Decibels[a]	Source
Very loud (harmful to hearing)	140	Jet engine (at 75 feet)
	130	Jet engine (at 300 feet)
	125	Loud "Walkman" type personal stereo
	120	Propeller airplane
Loud (potential hearing loss)	110	Live rock band
	100	Jackhammer or chipper
	100	Rapid-transit rail noise
	90	Large truck
	90	Noise in residence near freeway with average traffic flow
	80	Second-floor apartment in large city
Noisy	70	Private car passing residences in outskirts of city; average business office eight miles from airport
	60	Average conversational speech
Comfortable	50	Wooded residential area
	40	Field
	30	Whisper
	20	Inside a quiet rural dwelling
	10	Leaves rustling
	0	Hearing threshold

[a]Decibels are measured on a logarithmic scale; a 10 dB difference represents ten *times* as much noise.

Table 13.2: Allowable noise levels for unprotected ears[a]

Noise (in dB)	Length of time allowed per day
85	16 hours
90	8 hours
99	2 hrs 18 minutes
105	1 hour
111	26 minutes
115	15 minutes
121	6.6 minutes
124	4 minutes
130	1 minute

[a]30 percent of people exposed to these levels will still suffer some permanent hearing loss. OSHA data.

for high blood pressure and heart disease.

Many people living near airports claim that they adjust to the noise, and as proof of their adjustment they point out that they sleep well in spite of airplane or traffic noise at night. However, studies have shown that even though a person continues sleeping, and reports no sleep disturbance when awakened in the morning, loud sounds do produce stress responses that can affect health. An electrocardiograph revealed that sleeping people's heart rates jumped when recordings of street traffic were played at normal levels in the room. In another study of sleep, people subjected to noise at night showed mood shifts the following day, and these mood shifts correlated with noise stimuli during the previous night. Again, the groups studied neither complained of the noise nor were awakened by it during the study.[10]

The effects of noise on learning, especially in the formative years, can be important in a complex society like ours because education can make the difference between a comfortable and an uncomfortable lifestyle. In one study, schools located under takeoff and landing paths around the Los Angeles airport were compared with schools in quieter areas (Cohen 1982). Researchers found that school children in the airport corridors had greater difficulty solving puzzles and math problems than children from quiet schools. Moreover, there was no evidence whatsoever that children from these noisy areas ever adapted to the noise.

When considering the effects of loud noises on health, we need to recognize that human hearing evolved in a relatively quiet setting. Hearing was necessary for detecting subtle sounds. According to Valerius Geist, any "continuous exposure to noise above the level encountered, for instance, in a windy forest or

regenerate. There are sensory hairs for both high and low frequencies, and those in the higher registers are the first to be injured. Although no pain is involved in the destruction of the sensory hairs, the person gradually finds it harder to hear the human voice or musical instruments within that register. Once this destruction begins, it spreads to hairs in the lower registers.

It has been noted that one in every ten Americans—or 25 million people—are regularly exposed to noises loud enough to cause hearing loss. Approximately half of this is non-occupational exposure. This is why we have such a high incidence of deafness and partial deafness in this country. One interesting study compared Sudanese tribesmen to Americans, and discovered that the tribesmen, living in a

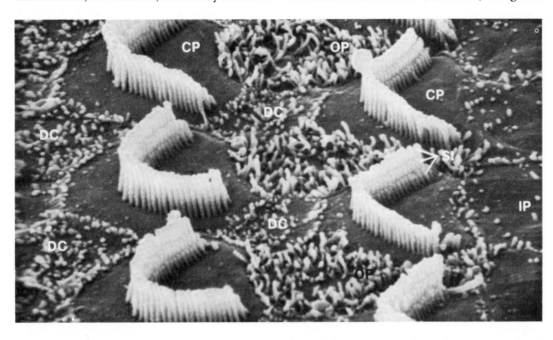

Loud sounds destroy sensory hair cells inside the organ of corti, located in the inner ear. (Hair cells in the organ of corti. Kessel and Kardon, *Tissues and Organs.*)

steppe, ought to lead to some sort of grief."[11]

Like ionizing radiation and microwaves, sound is an energy input, and when you exceed the levels of energy input the organism was designed to handle—in our case, the windy forest—the homeostatic mechanisms of the organism may be pushed beyond their capacities. We know that excessive inputs of sound cause a wide variety of diseases, from hearing loss to heart disease. Among the more dramatic findings was one that showed an increase in congenital deformities and a reduced capacity for learning language skills among infants subjected to continuous loud noise before their births (Arvay 1970).

Hearing loss itself has become a problem in our society. One study found that a third of all freshmen entering college had significant hearing losses, presumably as the result of listening to loud music.[12] Such hearing loss is not reversible. Loud sounds destroy sensory hair cells inside the inner ear, and these cells don't

natural environment where there were no loud noises, had little or no hearing loss as they grew older. Eighty-year-old men had hearing far better than thirty-year-old men who'd grown up in noisy cities.[13]

Among environmental disease factors, noise is probably the easiest for most people to control. For some, it will be a simple matter of turning down the volume of earphones (which can deliver up to 135 dB of sound, comparable to the noise behind a jet at takeoff). For others who live near airports or in the inner city, where sound levels can exceed the safe standards set by OSHA, soundproofing of rooms with drapes, rugs, and soft furniture may be helpful. Even better is a complete soundproofing, including double-thickness walls, sound insulation in the attic and walls, and the planting of trees in the yard to deaden noise.

If you are subjected to loud noises in the workplace, contact your labor union or OSHA for help. Current programs to protect workers include an annual hearing test, training in the use of ear protection, and the maintenance of close records on every employee's hearing.

Nutrition

Resistance to disease is important, whether we're talking about infection or any of the many illnesses caused by environmental pollution. In this respect, medical physiologists tell us that the "condition of the host" is at least as important in resisting illness as the presence of a microorganism, or other disease factor. First, many foods now bring the body in contact with a number of carcinogenic and toxic substances. Poor nutrition also reduces the abilities of the barriers between our bodies and the

Overall, 30-40 percent of all cancers in men, and 60 percent of all cancers in women, are related to diet. This means that a significant proportion of the deaths from cancer could be prevented by dietary means. (Bacon, 1975, by Michael Samuels.)

ishment." Overnourishment is the consumption of foods that push our bodies beyond their homeostatic limits, resulting in obesity, diabetes, atherosclerosis, angina, heart attacks, strokes, kidney disease, gall stones, arthritis, high cholesterol and high blood protein levels, chronic constipation, diverticulosis, and cancer. The foods implicated in such conditions include salt, refined sugar, fat, and processed foods.[14]

Diet, Nutrition, and Cancer

In 1980, the National Academy of Sciences asked the National Research Council to thoroughly review all research literature on the relationships between diet and cancer. This report was completed in 1982, and published in a

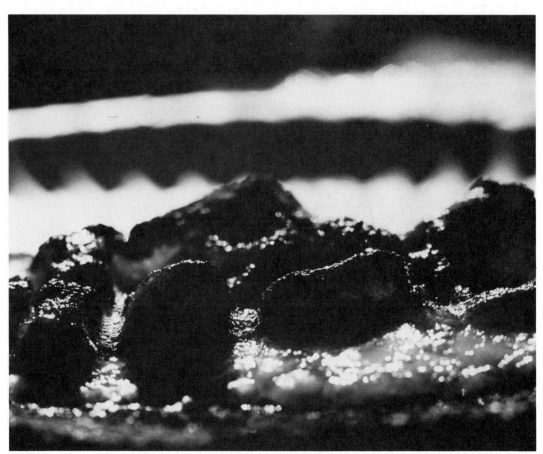

environment, diminishing the protective capacities of our skin and mucous membranes and of the cilia on epithelial surfaces. In addition, poor nutrition slows down the production of antibodies, the activity of phagocytes, and the production of complement, which is important in fighting bacteria that have entered our bodies.

Malnutrition has many facets. Although thousands are starving to death in third-world countries, the lives of thousands more, in the industrialized nations, are threatened by what the medical community now calls "overnour-

book entitled *Diet, Nutrition, and Cancer.* The following is a brief summary of the Council's findings.[15]

Fats. Epidemiological studies show associations between high fat intake and specific cancers, of the breast, prostate, and large bowel.

Protein. There is a "suggested association" between high protein diets and high incidence of cancer. In animals, doubling or tripling protein intake has resulted in those animals becoming more susceptible to chemical carcinogens in the environment.

Dietary Fiber. Colon cancer was reduced by high intake of dietary fiber.

Vitamin A. There is growing evidence that consumption of foods containing vitamin A decreases the incidence of cancer. In diets low in vitamin A, animals became more susceptible to chemical carcinogens.

Vitamin C. This vitamin protects against gastric and esophageal cancers and protects against formation of carcinogenic N-nitroso compounds, found in bacon and other foods containing nitrites.

Vitamin E. Like vitamin C, this vitamin inhibits the formation of N-nitroso compounds, which have been found to be carcinogenic.

Naturally occurring carcinogens. Nitrites and nitrates, used in the processing of meats, especially bacon and ham, are known carcinogens. These same carcinogens are also high in fruits and vegetables that have been grown in soils fertilized with nitrates.

Food additives. There are 3,000 chemicals added to foods in processing. Another 12,000 chemicals enter the food chain through packaging, spraying, etc. These include familiar chemical compounds such as saccharin, cyclamates, BHT, vinyl chloride, acrylonitrile, diethylstilbestrol, pesticides, and PCBs. Many of these are proven carcinogens, but because of their low content in foods, it is difficult to assess their importance in human cancer.

Table 13.3: Increased chance of death because of obesity in men 20% overweight[a]

Cause of death	Percent of increased risk of death
Heart disease	18–28%
Stroke	10–16%
Cancer	0–5%
Diabetes	100%
Digestive diseases	25–68%
All causes	20%

[a]Adapted from *Pediatric Clinics of North America,* **24** (1977).

The effects of malnutrition on resistance to disease and environmental factors

• Decreased production of lysozyme, a digestive enzyme found in saliva and tears. This enzyme breaks down bacteria, and when absent, it allows bacteria to proliferate in eyes, mouth, and vagina. (Scrimshaw 1968)

• Decreased complement activity. Complement is produced by the body and it forms a doughnut-shaped ring on bacteria that invade the body, exploding them much like exploding a balloon. (Chandron 1980)

• Decreased bactericidal activity of white blood cells. (Schopfer 1976)

• Diminished antibody response. (Ferguson 1974)

Minerals. High doses of selenium are protective against cancer, but the council does not recommend its use unless directed by a physician.

Iron. Deficiencies of this nutrient are "possibly associated with stomach cancer."

Heavy metals. Excesses of copper, zinc, molybdenum, lead, cadmium, and arsenic are linked to high incidences of cancer.

Alcohol. All forms of alcohol in excess are associated with increased risk of colon and rectal cancer, and act synergistically with cigarettes to increase the risk of cancer of the mouth, larynx, esophagus, and lungs.

Mutagens. High-temperature cooking, smoking, and charcoal broiling produce mutagenic and carcinogenic compounds, such as benzo-a-pyrenes, on the surface of the food.

Inhibitors. The Council has found "sufficient epidemiological evidence" that eating the following foods is associated with a reduction in cancers in humans: dark green and deep yellow vegetables (rich in vitamin A), cauliflower, broccoli, cabbage, and brussel sprouts.

Overall, 30 to 40 percent of all cancers in men, and 60 percent of all cancers in women, are related to diet. The Council reports that: "A significant proportion of the deaths from cancer could be prevented by dietary means and . . . dietary modifications would have the greatest effect on the incidence of cancer of the stomach and large bowel and, to a lesser extent, on cancers of the breast, endometrium, and the lung."[16]

To reduce the risk of cancer, the Council recommends the following: (1) reduce the intake of all fats, both saturated and unsaturated; (2) increase the intake of fruits, vegetables, and whole grains, especially citrus fruits and carotene-rich cabbage-type vegetables; (3) minimize the intake of salt-cured, salt-pickled, or smoked foods; (4) minimize the consumption of *all* foods contaminated with chemicals from *any* sources.*

Everything we can do to help our bodies resist chemicals from the environment is important, especially when we consider the long lists of chemicals now making their way into our food.

Chemicals in Food

Chemicals in food are intentionally added as additives, unintentionally added as packaging materials, and appear as remnants of environmental contamination from agricultural fertilizers and pesticides, industrial processing, and waste disposal. Some of these environmental contaminants, for example, the organochlorine pesticides, polychlorinated biphenyls, and polycyclic aromatic hydrocarbons, are known carcinogens. There isn't much current evidence that these chemicals, in food, are an important cause of cancer in humans, but they may very well act synergistically, compounding the effects of other carcinogens in ways still difficult to measure.

A small group of chemicals that are widely found in human food and are known carcinogens has been intensively studied. The following is a brief summary of these findings.

Saccharin. Although this artificial sweetener has been shown to be associated with an increased risk of bladder cancer, the evidence is not overwhelming. But it has *definitely* been

*The Task Force of the American Society for Clinical Nutrition has come to almost identical conclusions for dietary changes to prevent heart attacks.

Relative safety of common food additives[a]

Avoid:

All artificial colorings.
  Orange B (hot dogs)—causes cancer in animals
  Red #40 (soda, candy)—causes cancer in mice
  Red #3 (cherries, candy)—may cause cancer
BHT (in some cereals, potato chips)—may cause cancer
Saccharin (soda, diet foods, toothpaste)—causes cancer in animals
Sodium nitrite (bacon, ham, luncheon meats)—can be chemically transformed into cancer-causing nitrosamines, especially in fried bacon

---

Caution:

Artificial flavoring (soda, candy, gum, breakfast cereals)—may cause hyperactivity in children and some adults
BHA (cereals, potato chips)—needs testing
Gums (ice cream, beverages)—poorly tested, probably safe
Monosodium glutamate (soups, sauces, some Chinese food, Italian sauces)—damages brain cells in mice; causes headache and burning in head, neck, and arms in some people
Propyl gallate (soups)—poorly tested
Sodium bisulfite (wine, grape juice, dried fruits)—destroys vitamin B-1; otherwise, probably safe

---

Probably safe:

Alginate—seaweed gel
Alpha tocopherol (vitamin E)
Ascorbic acid (vitamin C)
Beta carotene (vitamin A)
Calcium propionate—preservative
Calcium stearoyl lactylate—dough conditioner
Citric acid—natural flavoring
EDTA—impurity trapper
Ferrous gluconate—iron
Gelatin—thickener made of animal by-products
Glycerin—natural fat
Lactic acid—natural acidifier
Lecithin—natural thickener
Polysorbate 60, 65, 80—synthetic emulsifiers
Sodium benzoate—preservative
Potassium sorbate—natural preservative made from berries
Vanillin—synthetic flavoring

[a]Adapted from Highland and Boyle, pp. 235–240.

shown to cause cancer in animals and to be mutagenic to bacteria (see Chapter 6).

Cyclamates. This artificial sweetener was banned in 1970 by the FDA, because tests showed it to be carcinogenic in mice and rats.

BHT (butylated hydroxytoluene). This widely used preservative has been shown not only to be carcinogenic in mice, but to promote existing tumors. In 1977, the FDA, after years of listing this chemical as safe, put it on an unsafe list and proposed guidelines to regulate its use.

Vinylchloride. This compound is widely used in plastic food packaging and containers. It has been found at staggering levels in some alcoholic drinks (.2 to 1 mg/liter), in vinegar (9.4 mg/liter), and in some products packaged or stored in PVC containers, such as edible oils (14.8 mg/liter). Acids, alcohols, and oils all leach chemicals out of plastic and store them in dissolved form. Vinylchloride is a potent carcinogen and mutagen (see page 157). The reason it is allowed in food preparation at all is that the FDA has declared it a contaminant, rather than an indirect additive.

Acrylonitrile. This plastic used in food packaging is widely found in foods. In margarine, olive oil, and bologna, concentrations were found up to 49 nanograms/kilogram. Although this concentration is not high, it is alarming because this chemical is such a potent carcinogen and mutagen (see page 145).

DES (diethylstilbestrol). This chemical is one of approximately 20 growth hormones used in animal feed. In 1979, the FDA terminated its use because it was found to be carcinogenic in both humans and animals. During the early 1970s, it was found in residues as high as 2 µg/kg in beef liver.

Pesticides. These agricultural products are widely found in foods, so much so that the FDA actually has set up acceptable daily intake levels. Like many other chemicals, pesticides are stored in body tissues, especially fat, and are excreted in mother's milk. Of the DDT ingested in the human diet, 40 percent comes from meat, fish, and chicken; less than 5 percent is found in grain products. Pesticide presence in fruit and vegetables varies greatly, depending on spraying times, rain, and cleaning.

Polyclorinated biphenyls (PCBs). This industrial chemical has gotten into the food chain indirectly through chemical spills and accidents. The major source of human exposure is diet. PCBs are found only in animal and dairy products. PCBs are also a potent carcinogen (see page 155).

Table 13.4: Concentrations of insecticides in mother's milk in Guatemala, 1971

Insecticide	Concentration in parts per million
DDT	.49 - 5.94
DDE	.60 - 6.13
DDD	.05 - .11
Total DDT	1.57 - 12.21
BHC	.01 - .06
Heptachlor	trace - .02
Dieldrin	trace - .01

Adapted from Olszyna-Marzys, 1973.

Benzo-a-pyrene (BaP). This is a highly carcinogenic by-product of the burning of fossil fuels. In 1971 it was reported that the average German ingested 1,200 micrograms per year, mostly from fruit and vegetables. Studies of foods grown near coal-burning power plants showed that the fruits and vegetables contained high levels of benzo-a-pyrene (Engst 1975). In more isolated rural areas, benzo-a-pyrene content was as low as .5 micrograms per kilogram, and approximately 20 percent of this could be washed off with water. Fruits grown in orchards near heavily traveled roads had up to 10 micrograms of benzo-a-pyrene; and fruit grown in orchards near heavy industrial areas had up to 30 micrograms per kilogram of fruit. Similarly, wheat grown in rural areas contained .73 micrograms of benzo-a-pyrene; lettuce grown in industrial areas had up to 150 micrograms per kilogram of weight. Consider also that more than 50 percent of all tumors are located in the gastrointestinal tract.

Poor nutrition can reduce the barriers between our bodies and the environment, diminishing the protective capacity of our skin, mucous membranes, and cilia. (Junk Foods, 1983, by Michael Samuels.)

The Body's Protective Factors

In recent years research has been focused on an enzyme called P450. Produced by our bodies on demand, this enzyme binds with fat-soluble chemicals, places them next to oxygen molecules, and thus breaks the foreign chemicals down. Thereafter they are expelled from the body without doing any damage. It is believed that this enzyme evolved to protect the human body from natural, nonnutritional substances in the environment, especially those which entered through the food chain.

P450 undoubtedly plays an important part in protecting us from today's environmental pollutants. But given the vast variety of complex, artificial chemicals this enzyme must deal with, we must assume that, like every other homeostatic mechanism we possess, this enzymatic process is being stressed to the limit.

Production of P450 can be encouraged by nutrition. We know, for example, that when protein in the diet is very low, the production of this enzyme is reduced. In selecting any diet, especially a vegetarian one, it is important to make certain you are receiving *complete* proteins. Meat, fish, and fowl supply complete proteins, as does a proper combination of grains and legumes. Research has shown that animals put on low-protein diets had less than half the ability to break down chemicals (such as DDT) as animals on average amounts of protein. Similarly, it was found that rats given high doses of vitamin A had more resistance to PCBs than rats on diets low in vitamin A.

Food grown in isolated communities contains far fewer pollutants than those grown near urban centers, where pollution is carried by the rain. (*Wivenhoe Park, Essex,* 1816, by John Constable. National Gallery of Art, Washington, D.C.)

At the supermarket, look for whole grains, fruits and vegetables, lean meats, and dairy products. (*Grapefruit,* 1972, by Michael Samuels.

Suggestions for reducing fat intake

1. Trim fat from raw meat; remove skin if possible; then roast, boil, or broil, instead of frying.

2. Switch to foods other than meat and eggs for breakfast and lunch: cereals, vegetarian sandwiches, and salads.

3. Eat low amounts of lean beef or pork; eat more ocean fish or fowl.

4. Cook with water rather than oils, lard, or shortening.

5. Reduce your intake of milk products, which are high in animal fats; use nonfat or lowfat dairy products, and skim-milk cheese.

6. Avoid butter, oil, and hard cheeses.

Table 13.5: Food values of some fast foods[a]

Food	Calories	Protein (grams)	Carbo-hydrates (grams)	Fat (grams)	Sodium (milli-grams)
Big Mac	540	26	39	31	962
Kentucky Fried Chicken (original)	830	52	56	46	2,285
Pizza Hut: half of 10″ pie	560	31	68	18	—
Taco Bell taco	186	15	14	8	79
Burger King french fries	214	3	28	10	5
MacDonald's chocolate shake	364	11	60	9	324
Recommended daily allowance	1,500–2,500	30–46	50–100	15–25	500

[a]Adapted from *The Well Child Book,* by M. Samuels and N. Samuels, 1982.

Flavones and indoles in fresh fruits and vegetables also increase P450 production.

Medical statistics reveal an increase in gastrointestinal disease as bulk is reduced in our diets. Bulk is the roughage in vegetables, fruits, and whole grains. This largely indigestible part of the food is often broken down, or refined out, in processed foods. Roughage in the diet allows the muscular channels of the intestines to move the stool at a particular rate. Low bulk slows this movement. Normal stool contains carcinogenic substances that are carried into our bodies by the food we eat. When the stool rests for long periods in our bodies, many of the chemicals carried in the food pose a real threat to health.

Maintaining a healthy calcium level in your body is particularly important because of environmental pollutants. A good storehouse of calcium prevents our bodies from taking up strontium 90, a by-product of all nuclear reactions, both natural ones and artificial. Once in our bones, strontium 90 can damage the genetic material of normal body cells, and cause them to become malignant.

Physical Exercise

The human body is simply not suited for the sedentary lifestyle that has developed in the twentieth century. The differences in attitude, in body chemistry, in immune-system responses, in bone and muscle consistency, and in cardiovascular efficiency between the

---

National health recommendations and diet goals[a]

Eat only enough calories to meet body needs (fewer if overweight).
Eat less fat and cholesterol.
Eat less salt.
Eat less sugar.
Eat more whole grains, cereals, fruits, and vegetables.
Eat more fish, poultry, beans, peas.
Eat less red meat.
Eat less additives and processed foods.

[a]From the Surgeon General's Report *Healthy People,* 1980.

Ways to reduce salt intake

Use fresh foods, emphasizing the natural flavors.
Use herbs and spices for seasoning.
Avoid bacon, bologna, salami, corned beef, sausage, hot dogs, sardines, anchovies, lox.
Avoid sauerkraut and olives; they are prepared in brine.
Avoid snack foods like crackers, pretzels, potato chips.
Avoid soups, bouillon cubes, some peanut butters, catsup, chili sauce.
Avoid "onion salt" and "garlic salt."
Avoid salting foods while cooking.
Avoid salting foods at the table.

person who regularly exercises and the person who doesn't are dramatic. A person in good physical condition not only has a greater resistance to disease, but also seems to recover more rapidly when he or she does get ill.

People who regularly exercise are better able to handle all kinds of stress—physical, emotional, and intellectual—than people who lead sedentary lives, because every cell in their brains and bodies is able to assimilate more nutrients, and because certain beneficial hormonal changes occur only with exercise.

Physical exercise can also strengthen your antibody system. This becomes obvious when you stop to consider that antibodies are produced and delivered to the sites of infection largely by the blood. Consider, too, that blood flow is increased with regular exercise. People

actually grow new networks of blood vessels, serving every part of their body.

Physical exercise, of course, requires heavy breathing, and with it comes a stimulation of the mucosal blanket that coats and protects your respiratory tract. Antibodies, present in this blanket, become increasingly effective as the blanket becomes more moist and active with exertion.

Vigorous exercise causes your body to secrete large quantities of norepinephrine. This hormone helps your antibody system indirectly, by releasing certain white blood cells that ordinarily cling to the walls of blood vessels. The hormone causes them to become very active, and to circulate freely, reducing infection.

While norepinephrine is being released, its

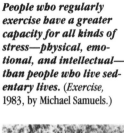

People who regularly exercise have a greater capacity for all kinds of stress—physical, emotional, and intellectual—than people who live sedentary lives. (Exercise, 1983, by Michael Samuels.)

companion hormone, *epinephrine*, flows through your body. This hormone speeds up your metabolic processes as much as 100 percent. Your heart rate and blood flow, carrying white blood cells and antibodies, become increasingly effective.

Norepinephrine also has profound effects on our emotions. Research shows that this hormone—secreted when the body is pressed into action—acts as a powerful mood elevator.

At Purdue University, Dr. A. H. Ismail tested the changes in body chemistry among a group of middle-aged college professors before and after a five-month jogging program. The research showed that even moderate exercise changed glucose and testosterone levels. There was also a marked reduction of *catecholamines* in the bloodstream, hormones

Physical Exercise Reduces the Effects of Stress

In a report to the American Heart Association, Ralph S. Paffenburger, M.D., of the Stanford University School of Medicine, stated that a person who burns up to 2,000 calories per week (from two to six hours of exercise) reduces the risk of heart attack by 64 percent. Paffenburger's research is based on a study of 4,000 San Francisco longshoremen. The longshoremen studied were employed in jobs that required vigorous physical exertion for long hours every day. Even though some of them smoked, were obese, or had prior coronary disease, hypertension, or abnormal glucose metabolism, this group had 49 percent fewer heart attacks than a similar, control group of

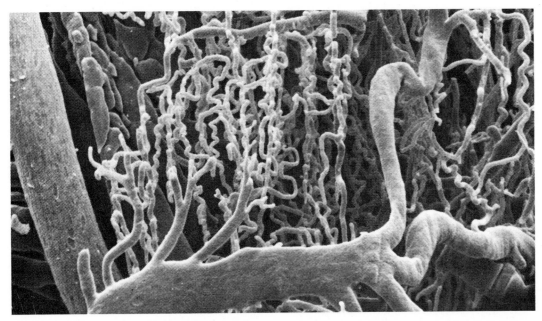

Aerobic exercise changes the body's physiology, reducing the chances of cardiovascular disease. Capillary beds in muscle increase, blood pressure drops and heart work with stress decreases. (Muscle capillary bed, × 155. R. G. Kessel and R. H. Kardon, *Tissues and Organs.*)

which are associated with states of aggression, anxiety, and depression. The research report stated that, after only ten weeks, the subjects who continued in the exercise program exhibited subtle but quite definite personality changes: "They became more open and extroverted. And their whole demeanor seemed more stable and self-confident."[17]

Exercise allows you to relax in ways that might otherwise be impossible. Chemicals released within your body during exercise continue to affect you for a number of hours. These hormones, plus substances produced in your muscle tissue while you exercise, induce a sense of well-being and relaxation, a physiological state not unlike meditation, wherein blood flow is increased to every area of the body, stimulating antibody production.

men whose lives did not include regular exercise. Moreover, the group that exercised had a dramatically lower rate of sudden death from heart attack than the nonexercising group.

Paffenburger has also studied groups of people from other socioeconomic backgrounds. In 1966, he studied 49,000 Harvard alumni. He discovered that physically active, nonsmoking men in this group had less than half as many heart attacks as the average Harvard graduates who did not exercise regularly.

As late as the 1940s, leading cardiologists prescribed six weeks to six months of total inactivity, often even prohibiting all "voluntary movements," as the standard treatment for heart attack victims (Price 1942). All cardiologists today prescribe early ambulation, and many cardiologists recommend intensive exercise programs beginning three months after the heart attack. One cardiologist (Kavanagh 1976) reports that seven of his patients, who followed his exercise program after heart at-

---

The effects of long-term physical training[a]

- Oxygen consumption, up 15%
- Cardiac output, up 8%
- Stroke volume, up 11%
- Heart rate (pulse), down 3%

[a]Adapted from Paffenberger.

---

tacks, finished the 26-mile Boston Marathon.

There are now more than 80 cardiac rehabilitation programs in the United States that include exercise regimens. One study (Wilhelmsen 1975) showed that 20 percent fewer heart attack deaths occurred among people who were on exercise programs as the result of heart attacks.

Exercise programs have also been shown to greatly benefit victims of angina pectoris, hypertension, diabetes mellitus, obesity, chronic obstructive lung disease, bronchial asthma, depression, and anxiety (Thomas 1979).

In his extensive work on stress and disease, Dr. Hans Selye even postulated that exercise may help cure or prevent cancer by providing a way to release tension. Although it is difficult to design a controlled scientific study to prove this point, there is some evidence to suggest that it may be true.

Dr. O. Carl Simonton, of the Simonton Center for Cancer Counseling and Research in Fort Worth, Texas, has done work on exercise and tumor reduction. Some of his success stories with terminal cancer patients are promising. He tells of one patient who completed the Honolulu Marathon even while receiving treatment for advanced lung cancer. After the race, the runner felt healthy, happy, and full of energy, with an extremely optimistic view of the future. Although nothing is proved by feats such as this, Simonton has been able to demonstrate that physical-exercise programs help cancer patients reestablish trust in their bodies and develop a feeling of being in control of their lives, two attitudes that have been shown to be characteristic of "survivors."

Most doctors recommend that if you have not been exercising regularly, are over 40, but are otherwise in good health, you should work with a physician or sports clinic to tailor an exercise program to match your present condition. Your cardiovascular system will build up rapidly, usually within two to three months, but if your life has been sedentary, your body and mind will need some encouragement to get started. Most communities have clinics where complete testing and guidance is available for little or no cost. In many communities, the YMCA offers such a service. There are no age limits for starting exercise programs. Increasing numbers of both men and women in their 60s, 70s, and even 80s are getting into shape, some even going on to compete in the growing number of "seniors" events.

Aerobic Exercise and Health

In the late 1960s, Dr. Kenneth Cooper published a book called *The New Aerobics;* in it he described the benefits of vigorous exercise in which the energy expended is supplied by oxygen breathed in at particular rates of intensity, duration, and frequency. According to Cooper, aerobic exercise provides the following benefits.

1. It strengthens the muscles of respiration and tends to reduce the resistance to air flow, ultimately facilitating the rapid flow of air in and out of the lungs.

2. It improves the strength and pumping efficiency of the heart, enabling more blood to be pumped with each stroke. This improves the ability to more rapidly transport life-sustaining oxygen from the lungs to the heart and ultimately to all parts of the body.

3. It tones up muscles throughout the body, thereby improving the general circulation, lowering blood pressure, and reducing the work of the heart.

4. It increases the total amount of blood circulating through the body, and increases the number of red blood cells and the amount of hemoglobin, making the blood a more efficient oxygen carrier. [18]

In his book, Dr. Cooper explains that a person must exercise at between 60 and 90 percent of maximum heart rate (a rate based on age) in order to enjoy the full benefits of aerobic exercise. To determine your maximum heart rate, subtract your age from the base number 220. Example: at age 40, the maximum heart rate would be 180 beats per minute (pulse taken at wrist or carotid artery in the neck.) That number would then be multiplied by 60 to 90 percent, giving you 108 to 162 beats per minute. Cooper calls this the *intensity* at which you should exercise.

Cooper's formula is to maintain 60 to 90 percent of your maximum heart rate for a *duration* of 15 to 60 minutes. Duration and intensity are inversely correlated. A 40-year-old person would receive the same aerobic benefits from exercising for 60 minutes at 60 percent of maximum heart rate as from exer-

Average exercise programs for aerobic benefits

Running:	6	miles per week
Bicycling:	30	miles per week
Swimming:	1.5	miles per week
Walking:	15	miles per week

cising for 15 minutes at 90 percent of maximum heart rate.

Cooper recommends that a person exercise a minimum of three days per week, preferably letting no more than a day elapse between sessions.

Sleep and Well-Being

Researchers are discovering more and more about sleep. Sleep puts the body and mind on a holding pattern, allowing our homeostatic mechanisms to catch up with the fatigue that has accumulated during our waking hours. As we sleep, the self-healing mechanisms work on repairing whatever has been damaged or worn out.

When deprived of sleep for long periods, we discover that even the simplest of tasks begin to seem stressful. We get jumpy, irritable, and short-tempered. Our appetites may diminish, or be expressed in strange food cravings. We find ourselves mentally distracted, making mistakes, unable to concentrate. Deprived of sleep for long enough, we even hallucinate, imagining situations that really aren't there. Our mental and emotional lives suffer, and our bodies suffer, because we become more susceptible to diseases of all kinds.

Most people look upon sleep as a totally passive state, a period during which nothing happens. We may stop interacting with the external world during this time, but events continue to take place inside us that are just as important as those that take place in the external world.

During sleep, the pituitary gland releases growth hormones. These are associated with a deep sleep state in which the brainwaves become slow and relaxed. In children these hormones stimulate bone growth; in adults, these hormones play an essential role in the renewal processes in bones, and in the production of blood cells within these bones.

Adrenal hormones (hydroxycorticosteroids) are also secreted during the deepest sleep stages. Experiments have shown that we have the highest levels of these hormones in our bloodstream in the first few hours after waking, and the lowest amounts just before we retire at night. These are important in the digestion of proteins and fats, and in the production of glucose in the blood, which supplies the cells with energy. Without these hormones, we would be unable to withstand physical or mental stress, and even minor infections or environmental irritations could become major sources of disease.

Scientists don't yet understand all the healing properties of sleep, but research has shown that our homeostatic mechanisms are at work during this time. During sleep new cells in the

Sleep puts your body and mind on a holding pattern, allowing your homeostatic mechanism to catch up with the fatigue that accumulated during working hours. (*Sleep,* 1972, by Michael Samuels.)

mucosal tissue of our mouths, needed to replace cells damaged by trauma, infection, and age, are produced much more rapidly than in our waking hours. As we sleep our arterial blood pressure drops, our pulse rates decrease, our skin vessels dilate, and muscles throughout our bodies become completely relaxed. Our overall metabolic rate goes down between 10 and 20 percent. Similarly, activity within our nervous system slows. Researchers in the future may be able to demonstrate that similar increased healing rates occur elsewhere in the human body as we sleep.

Sleep Patterns and Emotions

Normally we go from light sleep to deep sleep and back again to light sleep in approximately nintey-minute cycles. During parts of each cycle, we go into a state of consciousness that researchers call REM (Rapid Eye Movement) sleep, which is the period during which we dream.

Deprived of REM periods of sleep, people soon become moody and anxious, and find it difficult to concentrate. Muscular coordination goes awry, and cardiovascular rhythms are disrupted. In experiments in which animals are deprived of REM sleep, they eventu-

ally become mentally deranged, returning to normal only after they catch up on their sleep.

Dreams Ease The Tensions of Everyday Living

Dreams are a normal part of sleep, and although we don't always recall them upon waking, research shows that they are experienced universally. Like sleep, dreams affect our physical health through our minds, helping our bodies resist the problems of environmental pollution as well as infection by relieving stress.

The psychologist C. G. Jung believed that dreams were created from the material we store in our minds, and were an important health factor in our lives. According to Jung, dreams reflect the unconscious mind, wherein everyday experiences and wishes, dating back perhaps as far as when we were in the womb, are stored in a sort of poetic form in our minds. With a language rich in imagery and symbolism, it is as if their maker—the homeostatic mechanism?—has deliberately compressed them into well-hewn artifacts.

Working with his own dreams and the dreams of his patients, Jung discovered that two essential human needs are fulfilled through the poetry of the unconscious: the first is that dreams provide a way to store experiences the dreamer has collected throughout life; the second is that dreams provide the dreamer with a way to compensate for things that he or she couldn't do or had more sense than to do in real life. In their compensatory form, dreams can run the gamut, from the adolescent's dreams of sexual fulfillment to the adult's dream of domination over a tyrannical authority figure.

Civilized living requires constant compromise and negotiations that leave ragged edges of frustration even when we feel that our decisions to compromise or negotiate have been fair. Our ability to dream provides us with a theater for acting out feelings that, if acted out in real life, could prove dangerous, unfair to our loved ones, or just plain embarrassing.

Jung believed that dreams are important to health, that the ability to dream is one of the body's ways of maintaining harmony between all its various parts. In speaking of our mental and emotional life, he hypothesized that the unconscious mind, and the dream constituted

a self-regulating system that maintains itself in equilibrium as the body does. Every process that goes too far immediately and inevitably calls forth a compensatory activity. Without such adjustments a normal metabolism would not exist, nor would the normal psyche.[19]

Considering the power of sleep and dream-

Guidelines for improving sleep

Cut out all caffeine. Coffee, black tea, cola drinks, chocolate, many cold pills, and some headache remedies contain this drug.

Avoid recreational drugs. Alcohol and marijuana can inhibit your REM sleep or cause you to awaken during the night.

Drink warm milk before retiring. The effective ingredient of this folk remedy has recently been found to be L-tryptophan, a substance that induces drowsiness. Meat and green vegetables also contain this natural substance in significant amounts.

Meditate. Meditation empties your mind for sleep, relaxing your whole body.

Exercise lightly. If you are not getting aerobic exercise on a regular basis, try walking for a mile or so before retiring at night. Your muscles will relax, and you'll lie down with a feeling of well-being that will carry you toward sleep.

Seek help. Many people find that, night after night, they lie awake trying to solve problems. Working with a family counselor or some form of psychotherapy provides them with tools for solving these problems instead of allowing them to cause insomnia.

ing as healing instruments in our lives, we see better how dangerous noise and sleep-robbing drugs may be. These miraculous healing capacities must be protected, by avoiding chemicals that threaten them, and by creating quiet and comfortable sleeping environments for ourselves.

Prescriptions for Health

When we sit down to consider the multitude of environmental disease factors to which we're subjected in our lives, and the equal number of ways we have available for creating health, the sheer bulk of material we must deal with can become a source of confusion and stress. Where do we begin?

The first step is to get in touch with the issues that interest you the most. For example, as you look over this book, what subjects do you find most stimulating? Which issues seem to have the greatest impact in your life at this moment? What causes you the greatest discomfort? Your interest may result either because you have experienced actual symptoms from one or more of the disease factors we've outlined here or because you have an intellectual interest in one of the subjects. Whatever the source, trust that interest. Let it be the force the propels you toward change.

No matter what subject you choose, there will be something that you can do immediately in your own life. In diet it may be starting to purchase foods without unhealthy additives. In the use of household and hobby chemicals,

We can begin immediately to make changes for health, beginning with the area of most interest, be it sleep, diet, exercise, or relaxation. (Tobacco Medicine Bundle. Crow Indians, Montana. Courtesy of the Museum of the American Indian, Heye Foundation.)

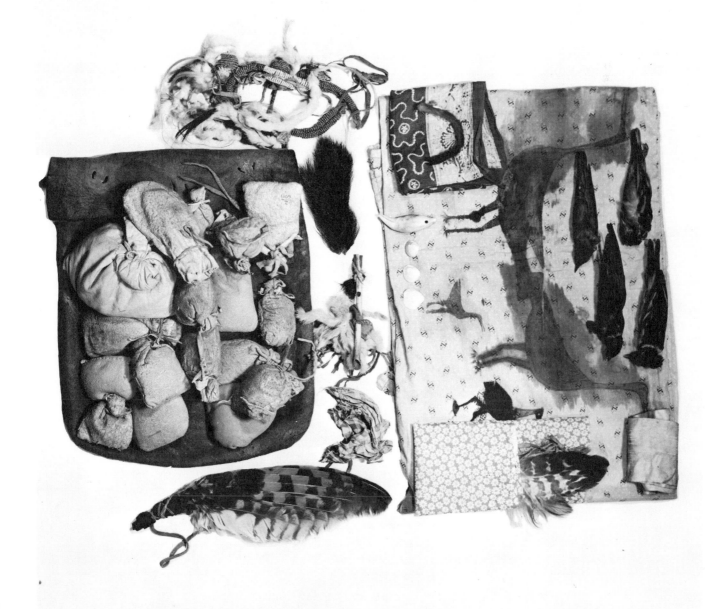

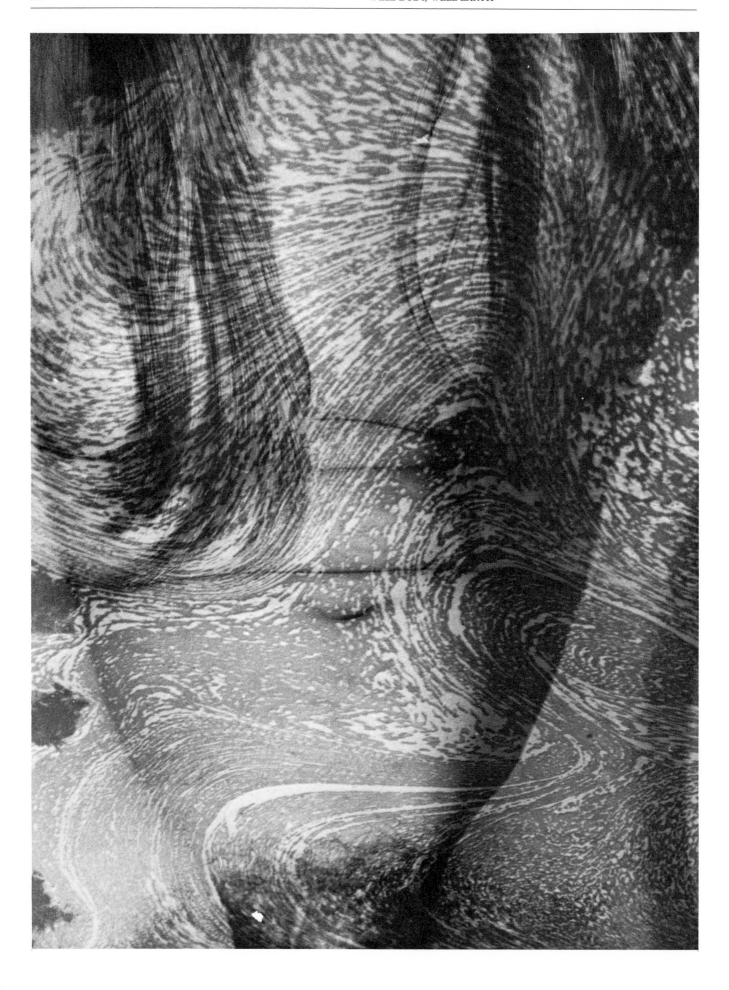

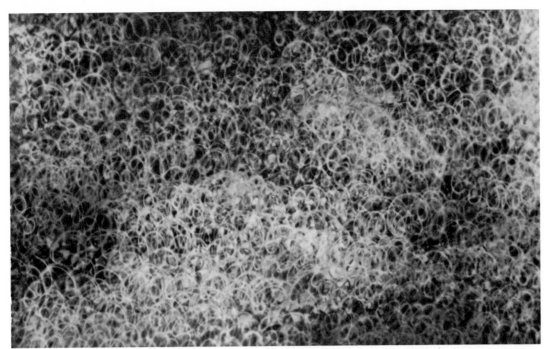

Picture yourself as part of the homeostatic mechanism of the Earth, and feel the energy of this system moving through you, being transformed and magnified by your own life force. (Untitled, 1969, by David Cummings. Synthetic polymer. 98″ × 156″. Collection of Whitney Museum of American Art, New York. Gift of the Larry Aldrich Foundation.) *Opposite: Water woman,* by Michael Samuels.

it may be a matter of studying our sections on chemicals and figuring out which toxic substances you can eliminate. If noise is a problem, you may want to buy ear protection for your job, or install acoustic material in your home.

Having started, you will soon begin to reap some benefits from your efforts, and you will automatically expand your exploration to find new, broader changes you might make. These further changes might involve long-term planning, such as seeking out an education for a new vocation in which you would not be subjected to pollutants. Or you might find yourself seeking out classes in your community where you could learn techniques for exercise and stress reduction.

Although we can immediately begin making changes to improve our own lives, many environmental issues will need to be addressed on a larger scale. This requires political action, which is the subject of Chapter Fourteen.

CHAPTER FOURTEEN

Political Action

Millions of people the world over are outraged by the pollution of our air and water, and of the soil in which we grow our foods. As little as ten years ago, we could do little more than look on in dismay as huge industries and power companies dumped billions of tons of pollutants into our environment each year. But that picture is changing.

Consumerism and Political Action

Today the antipollution movement is taking action against companies that spray our foods with toxic substances, against chemical companies that dump wastes into our streams and waterways, against politically powerful forces that seek to expand the nuclear industry. In addition, consumer groups are on the alert about the kinds of products being sold for home and hobby use, since such products may be toxic or threatening to our living Earth.

Organized consumerism officially began in the 1930s, after the publication of a book by Kallet and Schlink entitled *100,000,000 Guinea Pigs*. This book helped make the public aware of the differences in the quality of various products, and revealed how many manufacturers were misleading the public by selling them poorly made, useless, or harmful products. Following the publication of this book, consumer groups such as Consumers' Research, Inc., were formed (1936).

Today, private organizations, government agencies, and some conscientious manufacturers are participating in ongoing programs to maintain safety and quality in the products sold to the public. Most states now have a department of consumer affairs that acts as both an information center and a watchdog agency. Such consumer-oriented groups are invaluable for gathering and disseminating knowledge, and for bringing about public awareness.

Table 14.1 summarizes data from the California Department of Consumer Affairs, one of the better sources of such information available to the public. The table will help you choose nonpolluting products for use in your home.

Political Action as Preventive Medicine

As individuals, we can guard against exposure to toxic substances in our homes and hobbies, and even in the workplace. But we ultimately must realize that environmental pollution is a global problem requiring global solutions. Seeing ourselves as integral parts of the living Earth, we cannot help but see that all threats to the quality of our own lives—whether they are chronic irritations from smog in our cities, or elevated cancer rates as the result of chemical spills, or famine caused by the destruction of farmlands from overcultivation, or any of the multitude of problems we face today—are threats to the Earth as a whole.

History is filled with records of heroic peoples who have struggled for their freedom from repressive political powers, but never before in the history of the human race have we been confronted with a force as threatening as that of environmental pollution. We have seen people forced from their homes after discovering that those homes were built on toxic wastes, wastes known to cause birth defects and cancer. We have seen our waterways defiled by chemical dumping, and seen the fish of those waters, whose flesh once nourished us, turned into chemical repositories, no longer fit for human consumption. We have seen thousands of workers' lives destroyed or reduced to invalidism by asbestos, benzene, mercury, cadmium, and "nuclear accidents."

Arguments in favor of the technologies that are polluting the earth are all too convincing for most of us, accustomed as we are to living in a highly industrialized society. For decades we have been agreeing with the thesis that, with today's populations, we need chemi-

Table 14.1: Common household products: health effects and alternatives[a]

Product	Health effects	What you can do
Aerosol spray products, including many different kinds of health, beauty, and and cleaning products	Aerosol products release particles in air that can be inhaled into your lungs and then absorbed into your bloodstream. These particles can cause headaches, nausea, shortness of breath, eye and throat irritations, liver damage, heart problems, and possibly death. You should store these containers away from heat. Aerosol products will explode if they are exposed to heat, causing burns and very serious injury.	You can buy products in a non-aerosol form. Most products also come in creams, solids, liquids, and pump sprays. They will also save you money, because aerosol products are expensive. If you do use aerosol products, do not inhale them. Make certain aerosol containers are not exposed to heat.
Chlorine bleach	Chlorine bleaches can irritate and burn your skin and eyes. Even the fumes from chlorine bleach are irritating to your eyes and nose. *Never* mix chlorine bleach with ammonia, vinegar, toilet bowl cleaners, or other substances—these mixtures produce gases that can be deadly.	If you use chlorine bleach, handle it carefully. Instead of using chlorine bleach as a cleaning agent, make your own cleaning solution by mixing baking soda in water.
Paints	Chemical components in paints can irritate your eyes, skin, and lungs. Inhaling paint fumes can give you headaches and nausea. Other chemicals in paints can cause respiratory problems, muscle weakness, and liver and kidney damage. Some paints are flammable.	If you can, paint items outdoors. When you paint indoors, make certain you have adequate ventilation. Use of water-soluble paints can eliminate the need to use paint thinners, which contain additional toxic chemicals.
Shoe polish	Some shoe polishes may contain nitrobenzene and other extremely dangerous chemicals. Exposure to these chemicals can cause vomiting, and shallow and other severe breathing problems. If you drink alcohol and are exposed to these chemicals, which are absorbed through skin contact, death can result.	Read the product label. Do not buy shoe polish which doesn't list the contents, and don't use those products which contain trichloroethylene, methylene chloride, or nitrobenzene. After polishing shoes, make certain they are dry before they are worn.
Hobby materials: **Clay and stone**	If you inhale clay or rock dust, you can develop respiratory problems or lung cancer.	Kilns should be vented outdoors. You should wear a dust mask when grinding materials. Make certain you have good ventilation if you work indoors.
Hobby materials: **Papier-Mache**	Some supplies used in papier-mache materials contain asbestos. If inhaled, asbestos can cause cancer.	Avoid using products containing asbestos.
Hobby materials: **Metal work**	Hobby activities using metal materials often involve the use of dangerous chemicals. Many of these chemicals are eye, skin, and respiratory-tract irritants. Some can cause poisoning.	Wear goggles and gloves. Use an exhaust fan while welding metals. Work only in a well-ventilated area.

Table 14.1: Continued

Product	Health effects	What you can do
Hobby materials: **Glues and epoxy**	These substances are flammable. They are skin and lung irritants, and can make you more sensitive to a number of other substances. People have died after deliberately inhaling fumes from these products.	Read the product labels carefully. Wear gloves when you use them, and make certain you have good ventilation. Store these products away from children, in a cool place.
Hobby materials: **Photography supplies**	Many of the chemicals used to develop photographs are very dangerous. They are flammable and can cause skin, eye, and lung irritations. If swallowed, they cause poisoning. Many of these chemicals are acids, which can burn and blind you. Some of these chemicals cause cancer in laboratory animals.	Work with these materials only in a well-ventilated area. Wear goggles and gloves. Store these chemicals in unbreakable containers away from heat. Store acids in nonmetal containers away from heat. Never add water to acid to mix. Avoid products that contain benzene.
Rug and upholstery cleaners	These products contain some chemicals which, when inhaled, can cause nausea, anemia, liver damage, convulsions, and possibly coma.	Clean rugs and upholstery with a soap or nonaerosol shampoo. Wear gloves and make sure you have ventilation during cleaning.
Nonphosphate detergents	These products are highly alkaline, and can cause skin and eye irritations. They are very dangerous if they are swallowed.	Use soap. If you use phosphate detergents, remember: they build up and pollute our water systems; phosphates are not biodegradable.
Oven cleaners	Oven cleaners contain lye and other strong chemicals that can irritate and burn your skin and eyes.	Wipe your oven out after baking; this can reduce the need to use these strong cleaners. You can clean your oven with a homemade solution of ammonia, *or* baking soda dissolved in water. Apply this solution to the oven (be careful with ammonia!), wait, and wipe off.
Furniture and floor polish	These products contain chemicals, such as mineral spirits and petroleum distillates, that can irritate your skin, eyes, and nose. Some of these chemicals can cause photosensitization (sensitivity to light).	You can use soapy water to clean, and a soft cloth to shine some items. You can make your own polish by melting carnauba wax and mixing it with mineral oil.
Air fresheners	These products contain chemicals which can irritate and burn your skin. They also interfere with your natural sense of smell.	Open a window to ventilate unpleasant odors. A dish of hot vinegar can remove room odors, and a bouquet of flowers can give your room a pleasant smell. Put a box of baking soda in the refrigerator to remove strong odors.
Spray fabric finishes	These products are dangerous—if you get them in your eyes, the natural tearing process cannot wash them out. This can cause severe eye damage.	You can apply liquid fabric finishes with a brush. This is much safer, though not as convenient.

[a]Courtesy of the Department of Consumer Affairs, State of California

Never before in the history of the human race have we been confronted with a force as threatening as that of environmental pollution and nuclear technology. We have seen people forced from their homes after discovering that these homes were built on toxic wastes and we have seen whole cities destroyed by nuclear bombs. (*Love Canal Housing,* 1983, by Michael Samuels)

cal fertilizers and insecticides to increase farm production—even though we know the use of these chemicals is dangerous. And we can find ourselves agreeing with the logic that, with today's energy demands, we need nuclear power plants. To some extent, we can even agree that to maintain the standard of living enjoyed by the industrialized nations we must continue producing synthetic materials that subject thousands of workers and consumers to toxic substances. And what would we do for power without the huge smoke stacks spewing carbon dioxide and half a dozen other dangerous substances into the atmosphere, as we burn fossil fuels to run our factories and elec-

tric generators? But no matter how logical all these arguments may seem on the surface, there remains, just beneath that surface, the specter of a world in which air and water, the most basic of life's necessities, have become so contaminated that they are more threatening than beneficial to life.

During the past several decades the term "quality of life" has become synonomous with technological advancement, and in many ways the association has been justified. But as René Dubos points out in *Celebrations of Life,* there is a limit to the

betterment of human life through further

Practically all our advances in technology and in standard of living have brought in their train undesirable consequences. (*The Lone Tenement,* nineteenth century, by George Bellows. National Gallery of Art, Washington, D.C.)

technological and economic expansion: once a reasonable degree of affluence has been reached, further increase does not result in better health or more happiness; many persons seem to be more interested in leisure and simpler ways of life than in the acquisition of more wealth; practically all the advances in technology and in prosperity have brought in their train undesirable consequences.[1]

More and more people have become rightfully alarmed at the degradation of our environment, and the reduction in the quality of life, reflected as both major and minor disease, and the destruction of natural resources, such as fossil fuels, forests, and farmlands, as well as the fouling of our air, water, and food. In fact, many people now regard improving the quality of life in this sense as far more important that the acquisition of material wealth.

The fact that we are becoming concerned with these issues indicates that the noosphere is evolving, that the homeostatic consciousness of the living Earth has been alerted to the present threat and is responding. Reflecting this evolution, labor unions, public agencies, and private foundations have moved collectively to put pressure on the large companies producing and using substances that threaten the environment. These groups continue to expand their realms of influence, as more and more of us experience the diminution of the quality of our lives firsthand.

In Appendix A we provide the names and addresses of some of the more active groups you might consider supporting. Short descriptions of their special concerns give you an idea of what each group is doing, but you may want to send for literature describing their goals more fully before you commit yourself to donations of time or money.

If you belong to a labor union, explore its resources for addressing the problems of toxic substances in the workplace. If there is presently no resource of this kind in your union, and you are working in an industry that handles dangerous substances, you might consider forming a committee within your union to investigate work safety standards. An investigative committee of this kind might start by researching levels of exposure to toxic substances in and around the factory. If your committee is sanctioned by the union, a letter to your employer, on union letterhead stationery, will usually bring a response if you request information about toxins and toxic levels where you work. This book will be a resource for many of the more common chemicals and radiation problems likely to be confronted. If you need further assistance, either with monitoring or with seeking regulation of toxic substances, contact government agencies such as OSHA.

In the struggle for freedom from environmental pollution, the battle is ultimately won not by force but by healing, and within this framework we must all become healers. (Soaring, 1971, by Michael Samuels.)

In recent years we have witnessed a tremendous upsurge of grassroots movements that address regional pollution problems. Love Canal is a prime example of how a few people, armed with valid knowledge about the toxic waste that lay under their community, were able to move local politicians to act.

In any community action program, word of mouth is the most powerful tool. Let's say, for example, that you discover a local factory is dumping asbestos into a stream from which your township draws some of its water. You begin by gathering as much information as you can about the health hazards of asbestos. You contact both your county water-standards director and at least one private consultant to take water samples and write evaluative reports. You then put all your findings together

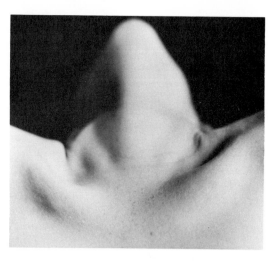

and literally carry them from door to door, spreading the word among neighbors and friends. Out of this you can develop a support group, people who will help, with time and money, to spread the message. Meanwhile you begin to attend water district and board of supervisors meetings; finally you contact these boards and ask for time on their agenda to present your findings. Schedule enough time to present your case fully, preferably using more than one speaker, and a slide show to give graphic illustrations of the problems you're addressing. Along with this presentation, you should have your support group, with at least half a dozen people.

It is important not to underestimate the power of the press. Two to three weeks before your scheduled presentation, invite local newspapers and television and radio stations to the meeting. Send the media a complete packet, with a description of the problem you're addressing, a copy of the speech you intend to deliver, copies of any supportive data you have, and photos, if relevant. What you are doing is highly "newsworthy," and you will get more media attention than you ever imagined if you take the time to put together press packets. Once you've gotten media exposure, your support group will tend to grow. Bear in mind that your power to effect change expands with the growth of your support group.

If you can make contact with environmental groups whose interests are similar to yours, by all means take advantage of whatever resources they can offer you. Check the advertising section of your telephone directory. You'd be surprised at the organizations listed and doubly surprised at how many people overlook this mundane resource. Environmental groups, both public and private, now have fairly extensive listings in most directories. Usually these are found under headings such as "Environmental, Conservation, and Ecological Organizations," and "Environmental and Ecological Services."

had once been a prosperous commercial and sportfishing resource.

The importance of attacking environmental problems at a regional level cannot be too highly emphasized. René Dubos, reflecting on the United Nations Conference on the Habitat in 1976, coined the slogan "Think Globally, but Act Locally." He pointed out that, "Our planet is so diverse, from all points of view, that its problems can be tackled effectively only by dealing with them at a regional level, in their unique physical, climatic, and cultural contexts."[2]

Though it may at times seem far removed from medicine, any effort we can make to protect or restore the natural environment—in our own backyards or over a vast geographical area—is an important healing process, benefit-

The Earth's ability to heal itself is prodigious. (Jamaica Bay, 1982, by Michael Samuels.)

No matter how desperate the picture of ecological disaster may seem, we should be reminded of the history of reclamation and restoration of areas once thought to be lost. We have, earlier in this book, spoken of Jamaica Bay, in New York, where the efforts of one man, Herbert Johnson, restored ecological health to one of the most polluted areas on the East coast, transforming it into one of the richest bird sanctuaries in that region. Similarly, a private organization called the Bronx River Planning and Action Group has taken over the restoration of the Bronx River, and their progress has been nothing short of miraculous. In the Great Lakes area wonderful progress has been made to restore fishing to a vast area of the Earth that in our own lifetimes was nearly turned into a network of dead seas, although it

ting ourselves as well as our planet. We are still learning about this new medicine, and will no doubt make errors along the way, but we should never lose sight of the fact that working with a labor union or neighbors to correct an environmental problem is as much a healing process for the living Earth as rest, exercise, and a healthy diet are for the person recuperating from a serious illness. In the struggle for freedom from environmental pollution, the battle is ultimately won not by force but by healing, and within this framework we must all become healers.

Notes

Introduction to Part I
1. Waters, p. 7.
2. Jung, p. 252.

Chapter One
1. Sagan, p. 133.
2. *Ibid.,* p. 257.
3. Marriott and Rachlin, p. 38.
4. Sagan, p. 258.
5. Eliade, p. 413.
6. Sagan, p. 258.
7. Aristophanes, *Birds,* lines 692-697, translated by Aidan Kelly.
8. Sagan, p. 258.
9. Weinberg, p. 2.
10. Waters, p. 3.

Chapter Two
1. Marriott and Rachlin, p. 38.
2. Waters, p. 5.
3. Sagan, p. 338.
4. Leakey, p. 125.
5. Marriott and Rachlin, p. 42.
6. Waters, p. 7.

Chapter Three
1. Montagu, p. 1.
2. Leakey, p. 249.
3. Marriott and Rachlin, p. 118.
4. Jones, in Lee and Devore, 1976, p. 322.
5. Sagan, p. 337.
6. Lee and Devore, 1968, p. 3.
7. Laughlin, in *ibid.,* p. 304.
8. Draper, in Lee and Devore, 1976, p. 201.
9. Katz, in *ibid.,* p. 286.
10. Yellem, in *ibid.,* p. 37.

11. *Ibid.,* p. 37.
12. Lee and Devore, 1968, p. 37.
13. *Ibid.,* p. 37.
14. Sahlins, in *ibid.,* p. 86.
15. Guenther, in Lee and Devore, 1976, p. 121.
16. *Ibid.,* p. 129.
17. Bronowski, p. 65.
18. Geist, p. 389.
19. Waters, p. 21.
20. *Ibid.,* p. 334.

Chapter Four
1. Waters, p. 7.
2. Money, p. 721.
3. Thomas, p. 145.
4. Lovelock, p. 9.
5. *Ibid.,* p. 146.
6. *Ibid.,* p. 74.
7. *Ibid.,* p. 147.
8. Thomas, p. 104.
9. Miller, p. 30.
10. Forresler, p. 110.
11. *Ibid.,* p. 205.
12. Thomas, p. 122.
13. Ehrlich and Ehrlich, p. 124.
14. Ferguson, p. 167.
15. Eccles, in *ibid.,* p. 323.
16. Einstein, in *ibid.,* p. 325. The following discussion of yoga is adapted from Mishra and from Eliade.
17. Chardin, 1961, p. 182.
18. *Ibid.,* p. 251.
19. *Ibid.,* p. 214.
20. *Ibid.,* p. 225.
21. *Ibid.,* p. 258.
22. *Ibid.,* p. 191.
23. James, p. 156.

Introduction to Part II
1. Chardin, 1961, p. 286.

Chapter Five
1. MacMahon, in Lee, Douglas, and Kotin, p. 2.
2. Dubos, pp. 107, 112.
3. Weiss, p. 109.
4. *Ibid.,* p. 2.
5. Jenkins, in Weiss, p. 42.
6. Weiss, p. 29.
7. *Ibid.,* p. 27.
8. *Ibid.,* pp. 27–28.
9. *Ibid.,* p. 167.
10. *Ibid.,* p. 167.
11. *Ibid.,* p. 1.
12. *Ibid.,* p. 167.
13. *Ibid.,* p. 173.

Chapter Six
1. Febrega, p. 81.
2. Thompson, p. 323.

Part III

Chapter Eight

1. Beebe *et al.,* p. 138.
2. Smith, Doll, and Radford, 1978.
3. BEIR, p. 342.
4. UNSCEAR, p. 414.
5. Gofman, p. 314.
6. *Ibid.,* p. 562; UNSCEAR, p. 52.
7. Gofman, p. 461.
8. Wang, p. 78.
9. Taylor, p. 6.
10. Gofman, p. 654.
11. *Ibid.,* p. 498.
12. *Ibid.,* p. 525.
13. *Ibid.,* p. 526.
14. NAS, 1979.
15. Wiltschko and Wiltschko, p. 62; Larkin and Southerland, p. 777; Bawin and Ross, p. 1999.
16. Konig, in Hanford Symposium, p. 74.
17. *Ibid.,* p. 218.
18. *Ibid.,* p. 218.
19. Wiltschoko and Wiltschoko, p. 75.

Chapter Nine

1. Hines and Randel, in Epstein, p. 52.

Poisons List A

1. Sittig, p. 98.
2. Epstein, p. 275.
3. *Ibid.,* p. 279.

Chapter Ten

1. Eliade, *Patterns,* p. 188.

Chapter Eleven

1. Eliade, *Patterns,* p. 43.
2. Lovelock, p. 113.
3. Wilson *et al.,* p. 219.
4. Mohr, p. 177.

Chapter Twelve

1. Lovelock, p. 131.
2. Waters, p. 334.

Introduction to Part Four

1. Geist, p. 411.
2. *Ibid.,* pp. 405–406.
3. Dubos, p. 200.

Chapter Thirteen

1. Zuckerman, 1932.
2. Turnbill, 1972.
3. Geist, p. 416.
4. *Ibid.,* p. 420.
5. Price, p. 62.
6. Henry and Stephens, p. 203.
7. Luthe, p. 75. See Samuels and Samuels, *The Well Child Book,* for further discussion of relaxation techniques.
8. Environmental Protection Agency, 1980.
9. *Raloff,* p. 379.
10. *Ibid.,* p. 379.
11. Geist, p. 431.
12. Raloff, p. 379.
13. *Ibid.,* p. 380.
14. Nutrition, p. 300.
15. NRC, pp. 1–16.
16. *Ibid.,* p. 14.
17. Andrews, p. 22.
18. Cooper, pp. 16–17.
19. Jung, p. 105.

Chapter Fourteen

1. Dubos, p. 106.
2. *Ibid.,* p. 108.

Political Action Groups

Action on Smoking and Health
2000 H Street, N.W.,
Washington, DC 20006.
Phone: 202-659-4310

A national group involved with problems of smoking and the rights of nonsmokers through legislative action.

Center for Science in the Public Interest
1757 S Street, N.W.,
Washington, DC 20009.
Phone: 202-322-4250

A group involved with nuclear energy, nutrition, energy conservation, toxic chemicals (especially in food), and the performance of voluntary health agencies. Publishes reports, books, and *Nutrition Action*.

Citizens Against Toxic Sprays
1385 Bailey Avenue
Eugene, OR 97402

Grassroots group against chemical spraying.

Coalition on Environmental and Occupational Health
106 K Street, Suite 200
Sacramento, CA 95814

Devoted to education about biohazards.

Commission for the Advancement of Public Interest Organizations
1875 Connecticut Avenue, N.W.,
Washington, DC 20009.
Phone: 202-462-0505

Supported by the Monsour Medical Foundation, the commission is concerned with establishing better working relationships between governmental, professional, and public-interest groups around issues such as control of environmental and occupational carcinogens.

Consumer Federation of America
1012 14th Street, N.W.,
Washington, DC 20005.

A national federation of labor groups, consumer groups, and co-ops, which lobbies for consumer protection. Publishes *Monthly News* and pamphlets.

Consumers Union
265 Washington Street
Mount Vernon, NY 10550
Phone: 914-664-6400

With a membership of approximately 200,000, this is the largest consumer group in the U.S. Devoted to testing effectiveness and safety of consumer products. Includes work concerning toxic and carcinogenic pollutants. Publishes *Consumer Reports* and *Consumers Union News Digest*.

Ducks Unlimited
Box 66300,
Chicago, Ill. 60666

Protects waterfowl breeding grounds.

Environmental Action
1346 Connecticut Avenue, N.W.,
Washington, DC 20036
Phone: 202-833-1845

A research and legislative group concerned with toxic and carcinogenic materials.

Environmental Defense Fund
1525 18th Street, N.W.,
Washington, DC 20036
Phone: 202-833-1484

A public-interest law firm specializing in toxic chemicals and carcinogens in water.

Environmental Improvement Associates
109 Chestnut Street
Salem, MA 08079
Phone: 606-935-4200

A group specializing in problems of smoking in the work place.

Federation of American Scientists
203 C Street, N.E.,
Washington, DC 20002
Phone: 202-546-3300

A group of scientists and engineers lobbying for safe use of science; concerned with carcinogens.

Federation of American Homemakers
P.O. Box 557
Arlington, VA 22205

A group specializing in consumer concerns, especially food and product safety.

Friends of the Earth
1045 Sansome Street
San Francisco, CA 94111

Environmental politics for our earth.

Health Policy Advisory Center
17 Murray Street
New York, NY 10007
Phone: 212-287-8890

A group that specializes in studying the health-care delivery system, and explaining it to consumer groups and workers, in its journal *Health-Pac Bulletin*.

Health Research Group of Public Citizens, Inc.
2000 P Street, N.W.,
Washington, DC 20036
Phone: 202-872-0320

A group that publishes legal reports; active in legislative work in health care.

International Union for the Conservation of Nature and Natural Resources
I.U.C.N. Avenue Du Mont Blanc, Ch 1196
Gland, Switzerland

A group of scientists and professionals devoted to the protection of endangered animals and other ecological issues.

League of Women Voters
1730 M Street, N.W.,
Washington, DC 20036

Political action group that has acted for air, water, land use, and energy causes; an admirable educational group also.

National Audobon Society
950 3rd Avenue
New York, NY 10022

An organization dedicated to protection of wildlife with an excellent educational service group.

National Clean Air Coalition
620 C Street, S.E.,
Washington, DC 20003
Phone: 202-543-0305

A group that lobbies for improving the Clean Air Act.

National Public Interest Research Group
1346 Connecticut Avenue, N.W.,
Washington, DC 20036
Phone: 202-833-3934

This is the national coordinator of local public-interest groups. Look in the phone book for your local PIRG.

National Resources Defense Council
15 W. 44th Street,
New York, NY 10036
Phone: 212-869-0150

Public interest law firm specializing in environmental health: radiation, chemicals, air, and water.

Northwest Coalition for Alternatives to Pesticides
Box 375
Eugene OR 97440

A group which fights the use of chemical sprays.

Rachel Carson Trust for the Living Environment
8940 Jones Mill Road
Washington, DC 20015
Phone: 301-652-1877

Resource group specializing in pesticides and toxic chemicals.

Sierra Club
530 Bush Street
San Francisco, CA 94108
Phone: 415-981-8634

A conservation group with legislative staff working for environmental protection.

Society for Occupational and Environmental Health
1341 G Street, N.W., Suite 308
Washington, DC 20005

A group of doctors and scientists who supply information on improving our environment.

Soil Conservation Society of America
7515 Northeast Ankeny Road
Ankeny IA 50021

A group dedicated to preserving our soil.

Urban Environment Conference
1302 18th Street, N.W.,
Washington, DC 20036
Phone: 202-466-6040

An educational group for legislative action.

Western Institute for Environmental/Occupational Sciences, Inc.
2520 Milvia Street
Berkeley, CA 94704

A group of concerned medical people who have done work on asbestos and microwave hazards.

Supplementary Tables and Charts

Table B.1: Radon levels found in houses and working places

	Number of buildings investigated	Type of building and material	Ventilation	Radon concentration mean and range (pCi l^{-1})
New York	1 (long-term measure)	Instrument room, cinder-block walls	Poor Recirculation	0.2 0.1-0.3
	1	Chemical laboratory	Good, filtration of ventilation air	~0.1
	1 (11 measurements)	Basement in laboratory	Low	6.0 3.6-7.8
	1	Fifth floor in laboratory	Normal	0.26
Boston area	7	One-family house, wooden frame, first floor	2-6 h^{-1}	(0.07) (0.005-0.23)
	7	One-family house, concrete basement	1-3 h^{-1}	(0.4) (0.1-0.94)
	3	Apartment, brick	5-9 h^{-1}	(0.9) (0.01-0.19)
	4	Office and laboratory, concrete and cinder block	6-14 h^{-1}	(0.05) (0.02-0.1)
Tennessee	15	Houses, most of them of concrete construction		(1.4) (0.13-4.8)
Florida	16	Houses, most of them of concrete construction		(1.3) (0.03-3.6)

Source: UNSCEAR, p. 78

Table B.2: Radioactive gases discharged into the air from reactors in various countries

Country and name of reactor	Start-up year	Net electrical power (MW(e))	Release (hCi)				Normalized release (Ci per MW(e) y)			
			1971	1972	1973	1974	1971	1972	1973	1974
PWR = pressurized-water reactor										
Belgium										
BR-3, Mol	1962	10		0.25				190		
France										
SENA, Chooz	1967	270	4.5	31.3	19.9		20	130	82	
Germany, Fed. Rep. of										
Obrigheim	1968	328	1.46	3.20	2.93	13.5	5.7	12		
Stade	1972	630		2.45	2.61	0.89		6.5		
Biblis	1974	1 147				0.06				
Italy										
Trino, Vercellese	1964	247	0.59	1.03			3.8	4.5		
Japan										
Mihama 1	1970	340	1.4	0.62	0.51	0.07	5.6	4.9	5.4	2.8
Mihama 2	1972	500		0.26	0.34	0.34		1.1	1.2	1.1
Takahama 1	1974	826				0.07				0.27
Netherlands										
Borssele	1973	447			0.31	5.83			4.0	18
United States										
Yankee Rowe	1961	175	0.013	0.018	0.035	0.040	0.08	0.25	0.29	0.38
Indian Pt. 1	1962	265	0.36	0.54	0.12	0.61	4.1	3.8	—	4.5
San Onofre	1968	430	7.67	19.1	11.0	1.78	21	59	42	5.0
Connecticut Yankee	1968	575	3.25	0.65	0.032	0.0074	6.8	1.3	0.12	0.015
R. E. Ginna	1970	420	31.8	11.8	0.58	0.76	100	43	1.5	3.2
Point Beach 1,2	1970/72	2 × 497	0.84	2.81	5.75	9.74	2.1	7.9	9.9	13
H. B. Robinson	1971	700	0.018	0.26	3.1	2.31	0.061	0.51	7.2	4.2
Palisades	1971	700		0.51	0.45	0.00003		2.3	1.7	0.0038
Maine Yankee	1972	790		0.002	0.16	6.36		0.04	0.41	16
Surry 1,2	1972/73	2 × 788		0.00001	0.87	55.0		0.0003	1.0	82
Turkey Pt. 3,4	1972/73	2 × 693			0.53	4.66			0.99	5.2
Indian Pt. 2	1973	873			0.015	5.58			0.38	15
Ft. Calhoun	1973	457			0.066	0.30			0.96	1.1
Prairie Island 1,2	1973/74	2 × 530			0.008	0.36			3.6	2.2
Oconee 1,2,3	1973/74	3 × 886			9.3	19.4			35	31
Zion 1,2	1973	2 × 1 050			0.004	2.99			0.052	5.6
Arkansas 1	1974	820				0.20				3.0
Kewaunee	1974	520				3.35				18
Three Mile Island	1974	810				0.92				3.8
Total			51.9	74.8	58.6	135.1				
BWR = boiling-water reactor										
Germany, Fed. Rep. of										
Kahl	1961	15	2.10	—	0.48	0.99	160		37	95
Gundremmingen	1966	237	6.50	11.0	23.7	4.15	29	53	120	19
Lingen	1968	174	8.70	5.1	2.6	9.5	75	84	18	180
Wurgassen	1972	640		0.59	0.56	0.05		9	2.4	0.9
Italy										
Garigliano	1964	152	640	290			4 800	6 000		
Japan										
Tsuruga	1969	331	42	4.9	5.2	5.6	170	19	18	33
Fukushima 1,2	1970/74	460/784	70	97	4.9	14	230	330	22	29
Netherlands										
Dodewaard	1968	52	2.76	8.32	6.70	4.16	60	220	160	130

Table B.2: Continued

Country and name of reactor	Start-up year	Net electrical power (MW(e))	Release (bCi)				Normalized release (Ci per MW(e) y)			
			1971	1972	1973	1974	1971	1972	1973	1974
BWR = Boiling-water reactor										
United States										
Dresden 1	1960	200	753	877	840	98.4	9 500	7 000	13 000	2 500
Big Rock Pt.	1962	70	284	338	230	188	7 200	5 900	4 800	4 900
Humboldt Bay	1963	69	514	430	350	572	14 000	10 000	7 300	13 000
Lacrosse	1969	53	0.53	30.6	91	49.0	21	1 100	4 000	1 300
Oyster Creek	1969	640	516	866	810	279	1 200	1 700	2 000	660
Nine Mile Pt.	1969	625	253	517	872	558	770	1 400	2 200	1 500
Dresden 2,3	1970/71	2 × 800	580	429	880	627	1 300	460	890	830
Millstone Pt. 1	1970	652	276	726	79	912	650	2 000	370	2 200
Monticello	1971	545	75.8	751	870	1 490	450	1 900	2 300	4 500
Quad Cities, 1,2	1972	2 × 800		132	900	950		300	780	1 000
Pilgrim 1	1972	655		18.1	230	546		200	490	2 400
Vermont Yankee	1972	514		55.2	180	63.9		1 100	880	220
Peach Bottom 2,3	1973/74	2 × 1 000			0.004	0.2				0.4
Browns Ferry	1973	1 050				64				150
Cooper Station	1974	760				1.6				7.6
		Total	4 024	5 587	6 376	6 438				

Source: UNSCEAR, p. 175

Table B.3: Radioactive tritium discharged into the water from reactors in various countries

Country and name of reactor	Start-up year	Net electrical power (MW(e))	Release (Ci)				Normalized release (Ci per MW(e) y)			
			1971	1972	1973	1974	1971	1972	1973	1974
PWR = pressurized-water reactor										
France										
SENA, Chooz	1967	270	706	1 762	1 849		3.2	7.2	5.7	
Germany, Fed. Rep. of										
Obrigheim	1968	328	311	243	326	149	1.2	0.89	1.2	0.51
Stade	1972	630		96.7	112	32.2		0.26	0.24	0.05
Biblis	1974	1 147				8.3				0.08
Italy										
Trino, Vercellese	1964	247	1 117	1 078			7.2	4.8		
Japan										
Mihama 1	1970	340	140	85	120	47	0.56	0.67	1.3	1.9
Mihama 2	1972	500		150	190	230	0	0.63	0.69	0.72
Takaham 1	1974	826				130				0.49
Netherlands										
Borssele	1973	447			1.8	171			0.02	0.53
Sweden										
Ringhals 2	1974	820				6.3				0.27
United States										
Yankee Rowe	1961	175	1 680	803	694	314	9.7	10.9	5.8	3.0
Indian Pt. 1	1962	265	725	574	138	684	4.7	4.0	—	5.0
San Onofre	1968	430	4 570	3 480	4 070	3 810	11.5	10.8	15.5	10.8
Connecticut Yankee	1968	575	5 830	5 890	3 900	2 240	11.6	12.0	14.1	4.5

Table B.3 : Continued

Country and name of reactor	Start-up year	Net electrical power (MW(e))	Release (bCi)				Normalized release (Ci per MW(e) y)			
			1971	1972	1973	1974	1971	1972	1973	1974
PWR = pressurized-water reactor										
R. E. Ginna	1970	420	154	119	286	195	0.47	0.43	0.74	0.81
Point Beach 1,2	1970/72	2 × 497	266	563	556	833	0.68	1.1	0.86	1.1
H. B. Robinson	1971	700	118	405	432	449	0.40	0.81	1.0	0.82
Palisades	1971	700		208	185	8.1		0.96	0.68	0.91
Maine Yankee	1972	790		9.2	154	219		0.17	0.40	0.53
Surry 1,2	1972/73	2 × 788		5.0	448	245		0.12	0.54	0.36
Turkey Pt. 3,4	1972/73	2 × 693			329	580			0.61	0.64
Indian Pt. 2	1973	873			27.5	47.9			0.69	0.13
Ft. Calhoun	1973	457			15.8	124			0.23	0.45
Prairie Island, 1,2	1973/74	2 × 530			10^{-4}	142			3.3 10^{-5}	0.89
Oconee 1,2,3	1973/74	3 × 886			70.7	350			0.26	0.55
Zion 1,2	1973	2 × 1 050				2.3				0.0043
Arkansas 1	1974	820				25.6				0.39
Kewaunee	1974	520				92.4				0.51
Three Mile Island	1974	810				130				0.54
		Total	15 617	15 471	13 905	11 265				
BWR = boiling-water reactor										
Germany, Fed. Rep. of										
Kahl	1961	15	1.4	1.2	1.7	7.9	0.11		0.30	0.76
Gundremmingen	1966	237	45.6	78.3	148	215	0.20	0.38	0.75	0.98
Lingen	1968	174		24.0	14.6	9.0		0.40	0.13	0.17
Würgassen	1972	640		3.2	5.9	3.6		0.05	0.03	0.06
Sweden										
Oskarshamm 1	1971	440				10.9				0.071
Ringhals 1	1974	760				2.0				0.23
United States										
Dresden 1	1960	200	8.7	43.3	18.5	18.8	0.12	0.34	0.29	0.47
Big Rock Pt.	1962	70	10.3	10.4	19.7	50.7	0.27	0.24	0.41	1.31
Humboldt Bay	1963	69	7.5	13.0	51.3	31.7	0.19	0.31	1.07	0.73
Lacrosse	1969	53	91.4	120.0	103.0	115.0	3.81	4.38	4.56	3.05
Oyster Creek	1969	640	21.5	61.6	35.9	14.1	0.047	0.12	0.087	0.033
Nine Mile Pt.	1969	625	12.4	27.8	46.5	18.7	0.036	0.075	0.12	0.50
Dresden 2,3	1970/71	2 × 800	38.5	25.9	25.8	22.6	0.084	0.028	0.026	0.030
Millstone Pt. 1	1970	652	12.7	20.9	3.7	24.1	0.030	0.058	0.017	0.059
Monticello	1971	545	0.6	0.0001	0	0	0.0036	2 10^{-7}	0	0
Quad Cities 1,2	1972	2 × 800		4.7	24.5	34.0		0.011	0.021	0.037
Pilgrim 1	1972	655		4.2	0.4	10.5		0.045	0.00092	0.046
Vermont Yankee	1972	514		0	0.2	0			0.00097	0
Peach Bottom 2,3	1973/74	2 × 1 000				10.0				0.017
Browns Ferry	1973	1 050				2.8				0.0064
Cooper Station	1974	760				1.7				0.0083
		Total	263	450	513	629				

Source: UNSCEAR, p. 182-3

Table B.4: Excess mortality from leukaemia and from all other cancers in Hiroshima and Nagasaki*

Period	Duration (years)	Man rad year (× 10^6)	Observed	Expected	Excess	Excess rate ($10^{-6} y^{-1} rad^{-1}$)	Ratio other cancers/leukaemia at end of period
			Leukaemia				

Compared with Japanese National Statistics

Period	Duration (years)	Man rad year (× 10^6)	Observed	Expected	Excess	Excess rate ($10^{-6} y^{-1} rad^{-1}$)	
1950-1954	4.25	8.24	24	4.5	19.5 (11.8-29.6)	2.37 (1.43-3.60)	
1955-1959	5	9.26	27	7.0	20.0 (11.6-30.7)	2.16 (1.25-3.31)	
1960-1964	5	8.77	16	2.2	13.8 (7.6-22.3)	1.57 (0.86-2.54)	
1965-1969	5	8.25	4	4.8	9.2 (3.3-17.5)	1.12 (0.40-2.13)	
1970-1972	3	4.68	3	2.7	0.3 (neg.-5.6)	0.06 (neg.-1.20)	

All Other Cancers

Period	Duration (years)	Man rad year (× 10^6)	Observed	Expected	Excess	Excess rate ($10^{-6} y^{-1} rad^{-1}$)	Ratio other cancers/leukaemia at end of period
1950-1954	4.25	8.24	146	128.4	17.6 (neg.-39.1)	2.14 (neg.-4.75)	0.79 (neg.-1.73)
1955-1959	5	9.26	193	184.0	9.0 (neg.-33.5)	0.97 (neg.-3.62)	0.57 (neg.-1.24)
1960-1964	5	8.77	258	215.2	42.8 (17.0-70.8)	4.88 (1.94-8.07)	1.17 (0.43-1.90)
1965-1969	5	8.25	301	238.4	62.6 (34.7-92.7)	7.59 (4.21-11.24)	1.90 (1.09-2.71)
1970-1972	3	4.68	177	153.0	24.0 (2.7-47.5)	5.13 (0.58-10.15)	2.22 (1.31-3.13)

*Males and females, all ages. Dose groups 10->200 rad T65
Note: The 90% confidence limits are indicated in parentheses.
Source: UNSCEAR, p. 403

Table B.5: Strontium-90 and Caesium-137 in total diet

Country or area	$^{90}Sr/Ca$ quotient ($pCi (gCa)^{-1}$)										^{137}Cs daily intake (pCi)									
	1966	1967	1968	1969	1970	1971	1972	1973	1974	1975	1966	1967	1968	1969	1970	1971	1972	1973	1974	1975
Northern hemisphere																				
Austria	25	15	15	14							135	53	60	51						
Denmark	14	10	8	8	7	8	8	6	7	6	79	44	39	38	32	38	31	15	18	18
Egypt	45		13																	
Faroe Islands	33	22	23	17	20	15	13	12	10	10	496	480	502	403	384	202	191	316	239	281
Finland	21										260									
France (1)	22	19	17	15	15	14	13	10	11	9										
France (2)			21	20	18	18	16	13	12	12			38	34	37	37	31	15	16	14
Germany, Fed. Rep. of	26	18	15	14	11	13	11	9	11	8	123	77	40	36	28	53	27	18	17	16
Greenland	15	9	7	8	6	8	9	6	5	6	89	297	346	61	137	51	55	71	54	29
India	12	28	10								6					3	20			
Japan (urban)	24	18	19	21	15	12		12	9	9	20	14	13	14	9	8		7	10	7
Netherlands	20	14	12	11	9	8	8				90	50	32	28	24	22	14			
Norway	38										420									
Sweden	22										132	88	71	65	58	50				
USSR (urban)	41	30	27	21	23	23	21	19			145	93	56	38	38	47	34	29		
United States																				
Country average	16	12									55	30	34	28	25	24	17	11		
Alaska	29	26																		
Hawaii	10	6									65	35								
New York City	17	16	14	12	12	13	11	10	9	8										
San Francisco	6	6	4	4	4	4	4	3	3	3										
Southern hemisphere																				
Argentina	7	7	5	6	5	5	5	4	3	3		24	19	18	17	17	15	13	11	4
Australia	7	6	5	5	6	7	6	5	4	4										

Source: UNSCEAR, p. 125

Table B.6: Chemicals in drinking water of U.S. cities

Chemical	New Orleans, La.	Miami, Fla.	Seattle, Wash.	Ottumwa, Ia.	Philadelphia, Pa.	Cincinnati, Ohio	Tuscon, Ariz.	New York, N.Y.	Lawrence, Me.	Grand Forks, N.D.	Terrebonne Parish, La.
Cancer in man											
Benzene	+	0.1		0.1	0.2	0.3					
Chloromethyl ether	+										
Vinyl chloride		5.6		0.3							
Cancer in animals											
Benzopyrene											
DDE, DDT	+					+					
Dieldrin	0.05	.002	.001	.002		.001					
Hexachlorocyclo-hexane						+					
Bis(2-chloroethyl) ether	+				0.5						
Carbon tetrachloride	+	+		+	+	+		0.13	0.1	0.1	+
Pentachloro-biphenyl						+					
Tetrachlorobiphenyl						+					
Trichlorobiphenyl						+					
Metabolized to carcinogen in animals											
Aldrin											
Carbon disulfide	+	+			+	+		+	+		
Recent studies, not published, re-vealing cancer in animals											
Chlordane											
Chloroform	133	301	21	1	65	38	0.08	44	32	40	130
Heptachlor and TCE	+	0.2		0.1	0.5	0.1					
Suspected carcin-ogens currently under test											
Acetaldehyde	+	+	0.1	+	0.1	+					
Bis (2-chloro-isopropyl) ether	0.18										
Hexachlorobenzene	+										
Tetrachloro-ethylene	+	0.1			0.2	0.4	0.3	+	0.5	0.07	0.2

Adapted from Hiatt et al., p. 312

Table B.7: 50-yr dose commitment from nuclear tests conducted before 1971, north temperate zone[a]

Source of Exposure	Dose Commitment, mrads:			Source of Exposure	Dose Commitment, mrads:		
	Gonads	Bone-Lining Cells	Bone Marrow		Gonads	Bone-Lining Cells	Bone Marrow
External exposure				*Internal exposure*			
Short-lived radionuclides	65	65	65	Hydrogen-3	4	4	4
Cesium-137	59	59	59	Carbon-14	12	15	12
Krypton-85	2×10^{-4}	2×10^{-4}	2×10^{-4}	Iron-55	1	1	0.6
				Strontium-90	—	85	62
				Cesium-137	26	26	26
				Plutonium-239[b]	—	0.2	—
				TOTALS[c]	170	260	230

[a]Data from U.S. Office of Radiation Programs.[22]

[b]Dose commitment to bone-lining cells has been taken to be equal to integrated dose over 50 yr to bone.

[c]Totals rounded to two significant figures.

Source: UNSCEAR, p. 53

Table B.8: Pesticides and other chemicals in drinking water

Compound	Maximum concentrations in water, µg/liter	Maximum dose producing no observed adverse effect, mg/kg/day	Uncertainty factor[1]	ADI[2] mg/kg/day	Suggested no-adverse-effect level from water, µ/liter assumption[3] 1	2
2,4-D	0.04	12.5	1,000	0.0125	87.5	4.4
2,4,5-T		10.0	100	0.1	700	35.0
TCDD		10^{-5}	100	10^{-7}	7×10^{-4}	3.5×10^{-5}
2,4,5-TP	detected	0.75	1,000	0.00075	5.25	0.26
MCPA		1.25	1,000	0.00125	8.75	0.44
Amiben		250	1,000	0.25	1,750.0	87.5
Dicamba		1.25	1,000	0.00125	8.75	0.44
Alachlor	2.9	100	1,000	0.1	700.0	35.0
Butachlor	0.06	10	1,000	0.01	70.0	3.5
Propachlor		100	1,000	0.1	700.0	35.0
Propanil		20	1,000	0.02	140.0	7.0
Aldicarb		0.1	100	0.001	7	0.35
Bromacil		12.5	1,000	0.0125	87.5	4.4
Paraquat		8.5	1,000	0.0085	59.5	2.98
Trifluralin	detected	10	100	0.1	700.0	35.0
Methoxychlor		10	100	0.1	700.0	35.0
Toxaphene		1.25	1,000	0.00125	8.75	0.44
Captan		50	1,000	0.05	350	17.5
Parathion (and Methyl parathion)		0.043	10	0.0043	30	1.5
Malathion		0.2	10	0.02	140	7.0
Maneb (and Zineb)		5.0	1,000	0.005	35	1.75
Thiram		5.0	1,000	0.005	35	1.75
Atrazine	5.1	21.5	1,000	0.0215	150	7.5
Propazine	detected	46.4	1,000	0.0464	325	16.0
Simazine	detected	215.0	1,000	0.215	1,505	75.25
Di-n-butyl phthalate	5.0	110	1,000	0.11	770	38.5
Di (2-ethyl hexyl)	30.0	60	100	0.6	4,200	210.0
Hexachlorophene	0.01	1	1,000	0.001	7	0.35
Methyl methacrylate	1.0	100	1,000	0.1	800	35.0
Pentachlorophenol	1.4	3	1,000	0.003	21	1.05
Styrene	1.0	133	1,000	0.133	931	46.5

1. Uncertainty factor—the factor of 10 was used where good chronic human exposure data were available and supported by chronic oral toxicity data in other species, the factor of 100 was used where good chronic oral toxicity data were available in some animal species, and the factor 1,000 was used with limited chronic toxicity data.
2. Acceptable Daily Intake (ADI)—Maximum dose producing no observed adverse effect divided by the uncertainty factor.
3. Assumptions: Average weight of human adult = 70 kg. Average daily intake of water for man = 2 liters.
Source: National Research Council, Safe Drinking Water Committee, 1977, p. 797

Table B.9: Vinyl chloride in water: findings of EPA survey

Water Utility	Year of Pipe Manufacture	Total Pipe Length, km	Total Wall Area, m²	Vinyl Chloride Concentration, µ/liter
Coolidge, Ariz.	Approximately 1964	2.7	540	< 0.03
Georgetown, Tex.	1975	20.0	7,920	1.3
Pioneer, Calif.	Approximately 1966	11.2	4,680	0.06
Roseburg, Calif.	1966-1967	5.58	1,260	0.03
Salados, Tex.	Approximately 1968	0.83	360	< 0.03

Source: National Research Council, Safe Drinking Water Committee, p. 68.

Table B.10: Known or suspected carcinogens found in drinking water

Compound	Highest observed concentrations in finished water, μg/liter	Upper 95% Confidence estimate of lifetime cancer risk per μg/liter[a]	Compound	Highest observed concentrations in finished water, μg/liter	Upper 95% Confidence estimate of lifetime cancer risk per μg/liter[a]
Human carcinogen			**Suspected animal carcinogens**		
Vinyl chloride	10	4.7×10^{-7}			
Suspected human carcinogens			*Bis* (2-chloro-ethyl) ether	0.42	1.2×10^{-6}
Benzene	10	I.D.	Endrin	0.08	I.D.
Benzo (*a*) pyrene	D.	I.D.	Heptachlor epoxide	D.	I.D.
Animal carcinogens					
Dieldrin	8	2.6×10^{-4}			
Kepone	N.D.	4.4×10^{-5}			
Heptachlor	D.	4.2×10^{-5}			
Chlordane	0.1	1.8×10^{-5}			
DDT	D.	1.2×10^{-5}			
Lindane (γ -BHC)	0.01	9.3×10^{-6}			
β -BHC	D.	4.2×10^{-6}			
PCB (Aroclor 1260)	3	3.1×10^{-6}			
ETU	N.D.	2.2×10^{-6}			
Chloroform	366	1.7×10^{-6}			
α -BHC	D.	1.5×10^{-6}			
PCNB	N.D.	1.4×10^{-7}			
Carbontetra-chloride	5	1.1×10^{-7}			
Trichloroethylene	0.5	1.1×10^{-7}			
Diphenyl-hydrazine	1	I.D.			
Aldrin	D.	I.D.			

I.D. = insufficient data
N.D. = not detected
D = detected but not quantified
Source: National Research Council, Safe Drinking Water Committee 1977, p. 794

Table B.11: Asbestos in water: findings of EPA survey

Location	pH	Alkalinity as Calcium Carbonate, mg/liter	Calcium Hardness, mg/liter	Aggressiveness Index	Average Chrysotile Fiber Count, fibers/liter
Pensacola, Fla.	5.2	1.0	1.4	5.34	5.52×10^{6}
King County Water District #58, Seattle, Wash.	7.2	14	14.5	9.51	0.66×10^{6}
Grant Hill Association, Bloomfield, Conn.	7.5	88	82	11.56	NSS[1]
Clark Counties Utilities, Northridge, Ohio	7.8	220	250	11.54	BDL[2]
Lockhart, Tex.	9.4	50	44	12.74	BDL
Cleburne, Tex.	9.7	36	39	12.85	BDL

1. NSS = Not Statistically Significant.
2. BDL = Below Detection Limit.
Source: National Research Council, Safe Drinking Water Committee, 1982, p. 52.

Table B.12: Air pollutants in the United States*, 1972

Name of pollutant	Natural sources (worldwide)	Energy	Manufacture	Mining	Processing	Transport	General use	Waste disposal	Total
Arsenic		0.73	0.84		4.6		3.01	0.30	9.48
Asbestos			0.49	5.81			0.41		6.71
Barium		3.76	0.06	0.10	3.7		0.18		7.80
Benzo(a)pyrene		0.27	0.02		0.11	0.03		2.72	3.15
Beryllium		316	0.06		21			0.54	337.6
Boron		4.52			2.4		0.02		6.94
Cadmium			0.01		1.7			0.01	1.71
Carbon monoxide	100,000	13,266	13,854		3,959	76,129	10.3	5,445	112,654
Chlorine		351	1.82		47.3	21	56.1		477
Chromium		1.9			8.3			3.06	13.2
Copper		0.17		0.15	9.7				10
Fluoride		20.1	17.1		80.9		3.30	1.04	122
Hydrocarbon		443	2,952		225	15,932	3,884	1,834	25,270
Iron		251	0.46		168			1.82	421
Lead (including gasoline)		17.4	3.19	0.06	10	224		5.01	260
Magnesium		50.6	38.7	8.48	11.4				110
Manganese		1.97	0.48		14.9			0.18	17.5
Mercury		0.11			0.05		0.3	0.01	0.5
Molybdenum		0.68		0.16	0.18				1.0
Nickel		3.73	0.06	0.14	0.63			0.04	4.6
Nitrogen oxides	500,000	12,715	516		117	8,508	21	194	22,071
Particulates		7,488	1,062		6,228	760	258	1,039	16,385
Phosphorus		22.5	21.7	0.31	13.4		0.02	0.08	58
Selenium		0.7	0.2		0.08				1.0
Silver		0.05	0.01		0.11		0.02	0.02	0.2
Sulfur oxides	11,000	23,836	2,172		39.55	622	33.2	75.6	30,694
Titanium		42.7	3.07	0.26	3.29				51.1
Vanadium		4.7		0.07	0.17				4.9
Zinc		4.9		0.05	92.8		2.50		100

*Kilotons per year.
Source: Adapted from Guthrie, Frank E., p. 3.

Table B.13: Amounts of airborne chemicals deposited in the Great Lakes*

Substance	Lake Superior	Michigan	Huron	Erie	Ontario
Total PCB	9.8	6.9	7.2	3.1	2.3
Total DDT	.58	.40	.43	.19	.14
α-BHC	3.3	2.3	11.6	1.1	.77
γ-BHC	15.9	11.2	11.6	5.0	3.7
Dieldrin	.54	.38	.55	.17	.13
HCB	1.7	1.2	1.2	.53	.39
p,p'-Methoxychlor	8.3	5.9	6.1	2.6	1.9
α-Endosulfan	7.9	5.6	5.8	2.5	1.8
β-Endosulfan	8.0	5.6	5.8	2.5	1.9
Total PAH	163.0	114.0	118.0	51.0	38.0
Anthracene	4.8	3.4	3.5	1.5	1.1
Phenanthrene	4.8	3.4	3.5	1.5	1.1
Pyrene	8.3	5.9	6.1	2.6	1.9
Benzo (a) Anthracene	4.1	2.9	3.0	1.5	1.1
Perylene	4.8	3.3	3.4	1.5	1.1
Benzo (a) Pyrene	7.9	5.6	5.8	2.5	1.8
Total Organic Carbon	2×10^5	1.4×10^5	1.5×10^5	$.66 \times 10^5$	$.46 \times 10^5$

*Metric tons per year.
Source: Council on Environmental Quality, 1981, p. 60.

Table B.14: Indoor pollutants: sources, possible concentrations, and indoor-to-outdoor concentration ratios

Pollutant	Sources of indoor pollution	Possible indoor concentration[a]	I/O concentration ratio	Location
Carbon monoxide	Combustion equipment, engines, faulty heating system	100 ppm	$\gg 1$	Skating rinks, offices, homes, cars, shops
Respirable particles	Stoves, fireplaces, cigarettes, condensation of volatiles, aerosol sprays, resuspension, cooking	100-500 $\mu g/m^3$	> 1	Homes, offices, cars, public facilities, bars, restaurants
Organic vapors	Combustion, solvents, resin products, pesticides, aerosol sprays	NA	> 1	Homes, restaurants, public facilities, offices, hospitals
Nitrogen dioxide	Combustion, gas stoves, water heaters, dryers, cigarettes, engines	200-1,000 $\mu g/m^3$	$\gg 1$	Homes, skating rinks
Sulfur dioxide	Heating system	20 $\mu g/m^3$	< 1	Removal inside
Total suspended particles without smoking	Combustion, resuspension, heating system	100 $\mu g/m^3$	1	Homes, offices, transportation, restaurants
Sulfate	Matches, gas stoves	5 $\mu g/m^3$	< 1	Removal inside
Formaldehyde	Insulation, product binders, particle board	0.05-1.0 ppm	> 1	Homes, offices
Radon and progeny	Building materials, groundwater, soil	0.1-30 nCi/m^3	$\gg 1$	Homes, buildings

Source: National Research Council, Committee on Indoor Pollutants, p. 23.

Table B.15: Reported health effects of Formaldehyde at various concentrations

Effects	Approximate formaldehyde concentration, ppm
None reported	0-0.05
Neurophysiologic effects	0.05-1.5
Odor threshold	0.05-1.0
Eye irritation	0.01-2.0[1]
Upper airway irritation	0.10-25
Lower airway and pulmonary effects	5-30
Pulmonary edema, inflammation, pneumonia	50-100
Death	100 +

1. The low concentration (0.01 ppm) was observed in the presence of other pollutants that may have been acting synergistically.
Source: National Research Council, Committee on Aldehydes, p. 324.

Table B.16: Summary of Aldehyde measurements
in nonoccupational indoor environments

Sampling Site	Concentration,[1] ppm: Range	Mean
Danish residences	1.8 (peak)	—
Netherlands residences built without formaldehyde releasing materials	0.08 (peak)	0.03
Residences in Denmark, Netherlands, and Federal Republic of Germany	2.3 (peak)	0.4
Two mobile homes in Pittsburgh, Pa.	0.1-0.8[1]	0.36
Sample residence in Pittsburgh, Pa.	0.5 (peak)[1]	0.15
Mobile homes registering complaints in state of Washington	0-1.77	0.1-0.44
Mobile homes registering complaints in Minnesota	0-3.0	0.4
Mobile homes registering complaints in Wisconsin	0.02-4.2	0.88
Public buildings and energy-efficient homes (occupied and unoccupied)	0-0.21 0-0.23[1]	— —

1. Formaldehyde, unless otherwise indicated.
Source: National Research Council, Committee on Aldehydes, p. 13.

Air pollutants, from Arsenic to Zinc, are the scourge of modern cities (see Table B.12). (*New York Skyline,* 1927, by Reginald Marsh. Courtesy of the Whitney Museum of American Art, a bequest of Felicia Meyer Marsh.)

Table B.17: Composition of mainstream and sidestream smoke

| Characteristic or Compound | Concentration, mg/cigarette: | | |
	Mainstream Smoke (1)	Sidestream Smoke (2)	Ratio, 2:1
General characteristics:			
Duration of smoke production, s	20	550	27.5
Tobacco burned	347	411	1.2
Particles, no. per cigarette	1.05×10^{12}	3.5×10^{12}	3.3
Particles:			
Tar (chloroform extract)	20.8	44.1	2.1
	10.2†	34.5†	3.4
Nicotine	0.92	1.69	1.8
	0.46†	1.27†	2.8
Benzo[a]pyrene	3.5×10^{-5}	1.35×10^{-4}	3.9
	4.4×10^{-5}	1.99×10^{-4}	4.5
Pyrene	1.3×10^{-4}	3.9×10^{-4}	3.0
	2.70×10^{-4}	1.011×10^{-3}	3.7
Fluoranthene	2.72×10^{-4}	1.255×10^{-3}	4.6
Benzo[a]fluorene	1.84×10^{-4}	7.51×10^{-4}	4.1
Benzo[b/c]fluorene	6.9×10^{-5}	2.51×10^{-4}	3.6
Chrysene, benz[a]anthracene	1.91×10^{-4}	1.224×10^{-3}	6.4
Benzo[b/k/j]fluoranthrene	4.9×10^{-5}	2.60×10^{-4}	5.3
Benzo[e]pyrene	2.5×10^{-5}	1.35×10^{-4}	5.4
Perylene	9.0×10^{-6}	3.9×10^{-5}	4.3
Dibenz[a,j]anthracene	1.1×10^{-5}	4.1×10^{-5}	3.7
Dibenz[a,h]anthracene, ideno-[2,3-ed]pyrene	3.1×10^{-5}	1.04×10^{-4}	3.4
Benzo[ghi]perylene	3.9×10^{-5}	9.8×10^{-5}	2.5
Anthanthrene	2.2×10^{-5}	3.9×10^{-5}	1.8
Phenols (total)	0.228	0.603	2.6
Cadmium	1.25×10^{-4}	4.5×10^{-4}	3.6
Gases and vapors:			
Water	7.5	298	39.7
Carbon monoxide	18.3	86.3	4.7
	—	72.6	—
Ammonia	0.16	7.4	46.3
Carbon dioxide	63.5	79.5	1.3
NO_x	0.014	0.051	3.6
Hydrogen cyanide	0.24	0.16	0.67
Acrolein	0.084	—	—
	—	0.825	—
Formaldehyde	—	1.44	—
Toluene	0.108	0.60	5.6
Acetone	0.578	1.45	2.5
Polonium-210, pCi	0.04-0.10	0.10-0.16	1-4

†Filtered cigarettes.

Source: National Research Council, Committee on Indoor Pollutants, p. 157.

Table B.18: Health effects observed from carbon monoxide exposure

Species	Exposure	Health effects observed
Human (normal)[3]	100 ppm, 1 h	Mean exercise time until exhaustion significantly decreased
Human (n = 18)[28]	200 ppm, 3 h	No significant effect on scotopic sensitivity, reaction time, eye movements, visually evoked cortical potentials
Human[29]	15-20 mg/m³, 13-18 ppm, 30 d	Increased albumin, β-globulins, total lipids, cholesterol, β-lipoproteins; decreased blood sugar
	10 mg/m³, 9 ppm, 90 d	None
Human (n = 19)[37]	50 ppm, 4 h	No significant changes in lung function
Human (n = 20)[43]	150 ppm, 3.5 h	No effect on critical flicker-fusion frequency; in monotonous situation, relative "activation" of subjective feelings
Human[44]	3.2-4.7% COHb	Increased errors in auditory discrimination in open office
	8% COHb	Less difficult task: no significant effects in isolation booth
	4.92% COHb	Less difficult task: no significant effects
Pigeon (normocholesterolemic and hypercholesterolemic)[2]	150 ppm, 52 and 84 wk	In hypercholesterolemic birds, atherosclerosis more severe
Rabbit (hypercholesterolemic)[10]	250 ppm, 10 wk	Coronary arterial atherosclerosis significantly higher
Dog (myocardial injury)[4]	100 ppm, 2 h	Decreased ventricular fibrillation threshold
Dog (anesthetized, normal, open-chested)[5]	100 ppm, 2 h	Decreased ventricular fibrillation threshold
Monkey[11]	100 ppm, 6 h, 9.3% (ave.) COHb	Ventricular fibrillation more easily induced
Rabbit[40]	180 ppm, 4 h	Focal intimal edema in aorta
Rat (n = 8-16)[6]	100 ppm, 200 ppm, 500 ppm; 4 h	Changes in blood glucose and lactic acid; no significant plasma corticosterone increase
Rat (n = 4)[7]	100-1,000 ppm, 1.5 h	Lever-pressing response rate decreased at increasing concentration
Rat (exposed prenatally)[14]	150 ppm, continuous, 15% COHb	Reduced birthweight, decreased weight gain, lower behavioral activity, altered central catecholamine activity, less total brain protein at birth

Source: National Research Council, Committee on Indoor Pollutants, p. 354.

Table B.19: PCB concentrations in continental air ($\times$ 10⁻⁹ g/m³)

Location and Date	No. Samples	Range	Comment
Kingston, R.I., 1973-75	6	1 - 15	Calculated as Aroclor 1254
Organ Pipe National Park, 1974	6	0.02 - 0.41	No reference to Aroclor
Hays, Kansas, 1974	3	0.03	No reference to Aroclor
Northwest Territories, Canada, 1974	3	0.002 - 0.07	No reference to Aroclor
La Jolla, Calif., 1974	6	0.5 - 14	No information on Aroclor
Vineyard Sound, Mass., 1973	2	4 - 5	Calculated as Aroclor 1254
Univ. R.I., 1973		2.1 - 5.8	Calculated as Aroclor 1254
Providence, R.I., 1973		9.4	Calculated as Aroclor 1254
Chicago, Ill., 1975-76	4	3.6 - 11.0	4% as 1242; 97% as "vapor"
Jacksonville, Fla., 1976		3 - 36	
Lake Michigan, 1976-78	6	0.57 - 1.6	74% as 1242; 88% as "vapor"
Milwaukee, Wis., 1978	2	2.7	59% as 1254; 27% as 1260; 84% as "vapor"

Source: National Research Council, Committee on Assessment of PCB's in the Environment, p. 32.

Table B.20: Proposed Superfund Priorities List December 1982, hazardous waste sites by state

Alabama: Mowbray Engineering, Greenville; Perdido Groundwater Contamination, Perdido; Triana-Tennessee River, Limestone and Morgan Counties.

Arizona: Indian Bend Wash Area, Scottsdale; Kingman Airport Industrial Area, Kingman; Litchfield Airport Area, Goodyear; Mt. View Mobile Home, Globe; Int'l Airport, Tuscon; 19th Ave. Landfill, Phoenix.

Arkansas: Cecil Lindsey, Newport; Crittenden Co. Landfill, Marion; Fritt Industries, Walnut Ridge; Gurley Pit, Edmondson; Industrial Waste Control, Ft. Smith; Mid-South, Mena; Vertac Inc., Jacksonville.

California: Aerojet, Rancho Cordova; Celtor Chemical, Hoppa; Coast Wood Preserving, Ukiah; Iron Mt. Mine, Redding; Jibboom Junkyard, Sacramento; Liquid Gold, Richmond; McColl, Fullerton; MGM Brakes, Cloverdale; Purity Oil Sales Inc., Fresno; Selma Pressure Treating, Fresno; Stringfellow, Glen Avon Heights.

Colorado: California Gulch, Leadville; Central City-Clear Creek, Idaho Springs; Denver Radium Site, Denver; Marshall Landfill, Boulder; Sand Creek, Commerce City; Woodbury Chem., Commerce City.

Connecticut: Beacon Heights, Beacon Falls; Laurel Park Inc., Naugatuck; Solvents Recovery System Inc., Southington, Yaworski, Canterbury.

Delaware: Army Creek, New Castle; DE City PVC Plant, Delaware City; Delaware Sand and Gravel, New Castle; Harvey Knott Drum Site, Kirkwood; New Castle Steel Site, New Castle; Tris Spill Site, New Castle; Tybouts Corner, New Castle County; Wildcat Landfill, Dover.

Florida: Alpha Chemical, Galloway; Amer. Creosote, Pensacola; Brown Wood, Live Oak; Coleman Evans, Whitehouse; Davie Landfill, Davie; Florida Steel, Indiantown; Gold Coast Oil, Miami; Hollingsworth, Ft. Lauderdale; Kassauf-Kimerling, Tampa; Miami Drum, Miami; Munisport, North Florida; NW 58th St., Hialeah; Parramore Surplus, Mt. Pleasant; Pickettville Landfill, Jacksonville; Pioneer Sand, Warrington; Reeves SE Galvanizing, Tampa; Sapp Battery, Cottondale; Schuylkill Metals, Plant City; Sherwood Medical, Deland; Taylor Rd. Landfill, Seffner; Tower Chemical, Clermont; Varsol Spill, Miami; Whitehouse Oil Pits, Whitehouse; Zellwood; 62nd St. Dump, Tampa.

Idaho: Arrcom, Rathdrum; Bunker Hill, Smelterville; Flynn Lumber Co., Caldwell.

Illinois: A&F Materials, Greenup; Acme Solvent/Morristown, Winnebago; Belvidere; Byron Salvage Yard, Ogle County; Cross Bros/Pembroke, Pembroke; Galesburg/Koopers, Galesburg; Johns-Mansville, Waukegan; Lasalle Elec. Util., La Salle; Outboard Marine Corp., Waukegan; Velsicol Ill., Marshall; Wauconda Sand and Gravel, Wauconda.

Iowa: Aidex Corp., Council Bluffs; Dico, Des Moines; Labounty Site, Charles City.

Kansas: Arkansas City Dump, Arkansas City; Doepke Disposal, Holiday; John's Sludge Pond, Wichita; Tar Creek, Cherokee County.

Kentucky: A.L. Taylor, Brooks; Airco, Calvert City; B.F. Goodrich, Calvert City; Distler Brickyard, West Point; Distler Farm, Jefferson County; Lee's Lane Landfill, Louisville; Newport Dump, Newport.

Louisiana: Bayou Bonfouca, Slidell; Bayou Sorrel; Cleve Reber, Sorento; Old Inger, Darrow.

Maine: McKin Co., Gray; O'Connor Site, Augusta; Pinette Salvage Yard, Washburn; Saco Tanning, Saco; Winthrop Landfill, Winthrop.

Maryland: Limestone Rd., Cumberland; Middletown Rd. Dump, Annapolis; Sand, Gravel & Stone, Elkton.

Massachusetts: Baird & McGuire, Holbrook; Cannon Engineering, Bridgewater; Charles-George, Tyngsboro; Groveland Wells, Groveland; Hocomoco Pond, Westborough; Industrial-Plex, Woburn; New Bedford; Nyanza Chemical, Ashland; Plymouth Harbor/Cordage, Plymouth; PSC Resources, Palmer; Re-Solve, Dartmouth; Silresim, Lowell; W. R. Grace, Acton; Wells G&H, East Woburn.

Michigan: Anderson Development, Adrian; Auto Ion, Kalamazoo; Berlin & Farro, Swartz Creek; Butterworth #2 Landfill, Grand Rapids; Cemetery Dump, Rose Township; Charlevoix Municipal Well, Charlevoix; Chem Central, Grand Rapids; Clare Water Supply, Clare; Cliff/Dow Dump, Marquette; Duell & Gardner Landfill, Muskegon; Electrovoice, Buchanan; Forest Waste Products, Otisville; G&H Landfill, Utica; Grand Traverse Overall Supply Co., Greilickville; Gratiot Co. Golf Course, St. Louis; Gratiot Co. Landfill, St. Louis; Hedblum Ind., Oscoda; Ionia City Landfill, Ionia; K&L Avenue Landfill, Kalamazoo; Kentwood Landfill, Kentwood; Liquid Disposal Inc., Utica; Littlefield Dump, Oden; Mason Co. Landfill, Ludington; McGraw Edison, Albien; Northernaire Plating, Cadillac; Novaco Ind., Temperance; Organic Chemicals, Grandville; Occineke, South Ossineke; Ott/Story/Cordova, Muskegon; Packaging Corp. of America, Filer City; Petoskey Mun. Wells, Petoskey; Rasmussen's Dump, Brighton; Rose Township Dump, Rose Township: SCA Landfill, Muskegon; Shiawassee River, Livingston Co; SW Ottawa Landfill, Park Township; Sparta Landfill, Sparta: Spartan Chem. Co., Wyoming; Spiegelburg Landfill, Brighton; Springfield Township Dump, Davisburg Tar Lake, Mancelona; U.S. Aviex, Niles; Velsicol Mich., St. Lewis; Verona Well Field, Pennafield Township; Wash King Laundry, Pleasant Plains TWP; Whitehall Wells, Whitehall.

Minnesota: Burlington Northern, Brainerd/Baxter; FMC, Fridley; Kopper's Coke, St. Paul; Lehillier; National Lead Taracorp, St. Louis Park; New Brighton; Oakdale; Reilly Tar, St. Louis Park; South Andover Site, Andover; Waste Disposal Engineering, Anoka Co.

Missouri: Arena 1, Moscow Mills; Arena 2; Fills 1&2, Imperial; Ellisville Site, Ellisville; Fulbright Landfill, Springfield; Syntex Facility, Verona; Times Beach.

Montana: Anaconda, Anaconda; Libby Ground Water, Libby; Milltown; Silver Bow Creek, Silver Bow/Deer Lodge.

New Hampshire: Auburn Rd. Landfill, Londonderry; Dover Landfill, Dover; Kes-Epping, Epping; Ottati & Goss, Kingston; Somersworth Landfill, Somersworth; Sylvester, Nashua, Nashua; Tinkham Site, Londonderry.

New Jersey: A.O. Polymer, Sparta; American Cynamid, Bound Brook; Asbestos Dump, Millington; Beachwood/Berkley Wells, Berkley; Bog Creek Farm, Howell Township; Brick Township Landfill, Brick Township; Bridgeport Rent. & Oil, Bridgeport; Burnt Fly Bog, Marlboro Township; Caldwell Trucking, Fairfield, Chemical Control, Elizabeth; Chemsol, Piscataway; Combe Fill North Landfill, Mt. Olive Township; Combe Fill South Landfill, Chester; CPS/Madison Industries, Old Bridge Township; D'Imperio Property, Hamilton Township; Denzer Schafer X-Ray, Bayville; Dover Municipal Well 4, Dover; Ellis Property, Evesham; Evor Phillips, Old Bridge; Fair Lawn Wellfield, Fair Lawn; Friedman Property, Freehold Township; Gems Landfill, Gloucester Township; Goose Farm, Plumstead Township; Helen Kramer Landfill, Mantua; Hercules, Gibbstown; Imperial Oil, Marlboro Township; Jackson Township Landfill, Jackson Township; JIS Landfill, South Brunswick TWP; Kin-Buc Landfill, Edison; King of Prussia, Winslow Township; Krysowaty Farm, Hillsborough; Lang

Table B.20: Continued

Property, Pemberton Township; Lipari Landfill, Pittman; Lone Pine Landfill, Freehold; M&T Delisa Landfill, Asbury Park; Mannheim Avenue Dump, Galloway Township; Maywood Chemical Sites, Maywood & Rochelle Pk; Metaltec/Aerosystems, Franklin Township; Monroe Township Landfill, Monroe Township; Montgomery Housing Dev., Montgomery Township; Myers Property, Franklin Township; N.L. Industries, Pedricktown; Pepe Field, Boonton; Pijak Farm, Plumstead; PJP Landfill, Jersey City; Price Landfill, Pleasantville; Reich Farms, Dover Township; Renora, Edison; Ringwood Mines/Landfill, Ringwood; Rockaway Boro Wellfield, Rockaway Boro; Rockaway Township Wells, Rockaway Township; Rocky Hill Municipal Well, Rocky Hill; Roebling Steel Co., Florence; Sayreville Landfill, Sayreville; Scientific Chemical Processing, Carlstadt; Shakey Landfill, Parsippany, Troy Hls; South Brunswick Landfill, South Brunswick; Spence Farm, Plumstead; Swope Oil and Chemical, Pennsauken; Syncon Resins, South Kearny; Toms River Chemical, Dover Township; Universal Oil Products, East Rutherford; US Radium, Orange; Vineland State School, Vineland; Williams Property, Swainton.

New Mexico: ATSF/CLOVIS, Clovis; Homestake, Milan; South Valley, Albuquerque; United Nuclear Corp., Churchrock.

New York: American Thermostat, South Cairo; Batavia Landfill, Batavia; Brewster Well Field, Brewster; Facet Enterprises, Elmira Heights; Fulton Terminals, Fulton; GE Moreau Site, South Glens Falls; Hooker-Hyde Park, Niagara Falls; Hooker-S Area, Niagara Falls; Hooker-102nd Street, Niagara Falls; Kentucky Ave. Wellfield, Horseheads; Love Canal, Niagara Falls; Ludlow Sand & Gravel, Clayville; Marathon Battery, Cold Springs; Mercury Refining, Albany; Niagara County Refuse, Wheatfield; Old Bethpage Landfill, Oyster Bay; Olean Wellfield, Olean; Pollution Abatement Services, Oswego; Port Washington Landfill, Port Washington; Ramapo Landfill, Ramapo; Sinclair Refinery, Wellsville; Solvent Savers, Lincklaen; Syosset Landfill, Oyster Bay; Vestal Water Supply, Vestal; Wide Beach Development, Brant; York Oil Company, Moira.

North Carolina: Chemtronics, Inc., Swannanoa; Martin Marietta, Sodyeco, Charlotte; PCB Spills, 210 Miles of Roads.

Ohio: Allied Chemical, Ironton; Arcanum Iron & Metal, Arcanum; Big D Campgrounds, Kingsville; Bowers Landfill, Circleville; Buckeye Reclamation, St. Clairsville; Chem Dyne, Hamilton; Coshocton City Landfill, Coshocton; E.H. Schilling Landfill, Ironton; Fields Brook, Ashtabula; Fultz Landfill, Byesville; Nease Chemical, Salem; New Lyme Landfill, Dodgeville; Poplar Oil, Jefferson; Pristine, Reading; Rock Creek/Jack Webb, Rock Creek; Skinner Landfill, West Chester; Summit National, Deerfield; Van Dale Junkyard, Marietta; Zanesville Well Field, Zanesville.

Oklahoma: Criner/Hardage, Criner; Tar Creek, Ottawa County.

Oregon: Gould, Inc., Portland; Teledyne Wah Chang, Albany.

Pennsylvania: Blosenski Landfill, West Chester TWP; Brodhead Creek, Stroudsburg; Bruin Lagoon, Bruin Boro; Centre County Kepone, State College; Craig Farm Drum Site, Parker; Douglasville Disposal, Douglasville; Drake Chemical Inc., Lock Haven; Enterprise Avenue, Philadelphia; Fischer & Porter, Warminster; Havertown PCP Site, Haverford; Heleva Landfill, West Ormrod; Hranica, Buffalo; Kimberton, Kimberton; Lackawanna Refuse, Old Forge; Lehigh Electric, Old Forge; Lindane Dump, Harrison Township; Lord Shope, Girard Township; Malvern TCE Site, Malvern; MCADOO, McAdoo; Metal Banks, Philadelphia; Moyers Landfill, Lower Providence TWP; Old City of York Landfill, Seven Valleys; Osborne, Grove City; Palmerton Zinc Pile, Palmerton; Presque Isle, Erie; Resin Disposal, Jefferson; Stanley Kessler, King of Prussia; Voortman, Upper Saucon TWP; Wade (ABM), Chester; Westline, Westline.

Puerto Rico: Barceloneta Landfill, Florida Afuera; Frontera Creek, Rio Abajo; GE Wiring Devices, Juana Diaz; Juncos Landfill, Juncos; RCA Del Caribe, Barceloneta.

Rhode Island: Davis Liquid, Smithfield; Forestdale, North Smithfield; L & RR-N Smithfield, North Smithfield; Peterson/Puritan, Cumberland; Picillo Coventry, Coventry; Western Sand & Gravel, Burrillville.

South Carolina: Carolawn, Inc., Fort Lawn; SCRDI Bluff Road, Columbia; SCRDI Dixiana, Cayce.

Tennessee: Amnicola Dump, Chattanooga; Galloway Ponds, Galloway; Lewisburg Dump, Lewisburg; Murray Ohio Dump, Lawrenceburg; North Hollywood Dump, Memphis; Velsicol Chemical Co., Toone.

Texas: Bio-Ecology, Grand Prairie; Crystal Chemical, Houston; French, Ltd., Crosby; Harris (Farley St), Houston; Highlands Acid Pit, Highlands; MOTCO, LaMarque; Sikes Disposal Pits, Crosby; Triangle Chemical, Orange County.

Vermont: Old Springfield Landfill, Springfield; Pine Street Canal, Burlington.

Virginia: Chisman, York County; Matthews, Roanoke County; Saltville Waste Disposal, Saltville; US Titanium, Piney River.

Washington: Colbert Landfill, Spokane; Com. Bay, Near Shore Tide Flat, Tacoma; Com. Bay, S. Tacoma Channel, Tacoma; FMC Yakima, Yakima; Frontier Hard Chrome, Vancouver; Harbor Island Lead, Seattle; Kaiser Mead, Mead, Lakewood; Pesticide Pit, Yakima; Western Processing, Kent.

West Virginia: Fike Chemical, Nitro; Follansbee Sludge Fill, Follansbee; Leetown Pesticide Pile, Leetown; West VA Ordnance, Point Pleasant.

Other State Sites: Plastifax, Gulfport, Mississippi; Arsenic Trioxide Site, Southeastern, North Dakota; Phillips Chemical, Beatrice, Nebraska; Whitewood Creek, Whitewood, South Dakota; Rose Park Sludge Pit, Salt Lake City, Utah; Baxter/Union Pacific, Laramie, Wyoming.

Source: Samuel Epstein M.D., Lester O. Brown and Carl Pope, 1982, revised 1983. *Hazardous Wastes in America*. Sierra Club Books.

Table B.21: Birth defects in Seveso, Italy after the 1976 Dioxin spill

Birth defect	1976	1977
Lung aplasia	—	1
Brain defects	—	1
Ear defects	—	1
Heart defects	—	8
Stomach defects	—	1
Hydrocephaly	—	1
Hypospadia	2	2
Anal defect	—	1
Abdominal defect	—	2
Cancer	—	2
Bone defect	—	1
Downs syndrome	2	2
Cleft palate	—	—
Limb defects	—	10
Spinal cord defects	—	1
Finger defects	—	3
Total	4	37

Adapted from Wagner, p. 186.

Table B.22: The effects of Dioxin on organs of laboratory animals

Organ	Mice	Guinea pig	Monkey
Adrenal	n	m	n
Bile duct	u	u	s
Bladder	n	m	n
Bone marrow	u	m	l
Kidney	n	m	l
Liver	s	n	n
Skin	n	n	s
Spleen	l	l	l
Testicle	m	s	
Thymus	s	s	s

S = strong   U = undetectable
M = medium   N = no effect
L = low   Adapted from Wagner, p. 171.

Table B.23: Pesticides in U.S. imported food

Food	Country	Number of pesticides found: Allowed in U.S.	Banned in U.S.
Bananas	Columbia Costa Rica Ecuador Guatemala Mexico	45	25
Coffee	Brazil Columbia Costa Rica Ecuador Guatemala Mexico	94	76
Sugar	Brazil Columbia Costa Rica Ecuador Guatemala India Thailand	61	34
Tomatoes	Mexico Spain	53	21
Tea	India Sri Lanka	24	20
Cacao	Costa Rica Ecuador	14	7
Olives	Italy Spain	20	14

Banned or heavily restricted pesticides include: DDT, Heptachlor, Lindane, 2,4,5-T, Kepone, Mirex, DBCP, Aldrin, Dieldrin, BHC, Silvex, Chlordane
Adapted from Weir, p. 82.

Table B.24: Longterm studies of Dioxin accidents

Location	Year	Number of people	Health effects observed
Nitro, W. Va. USA	1949	228	none noted
Ludwigshafen/ Rhein, Germany	1953	75	6 cancer deaths
Amsterdam, Holland	1963	106	8 deaths, 5-6 from heart disease
Bolsover, Derbyshire, UK	1968	90	1 death, heart attack
Seveso, Italy	1976	40,000	skin rash, swollen livers
Czechoslovakia	1965	80	5 deaths (2 cancer, 1 heart disease)

Adapted from Wagner, p. 177

Table B.25: Selected insecticides used by farmers on crops, 1964–1976

Insecticide	Pounds used (million)	Acres treated (million)	Pounds per acre
All insecticides, total			
1964	143	NA	NA
1966	138	43	3.3
1971	154	57	2.7
1976	162	75	2.2
Toxaphene			
1964	34	8	4.3
1966	31	5	5.8
1971	33	6	5.9
1976	31	5	6.3
Methyl parathion			
1964	10	7	1.5
1966	8	5	1.8
1971	28	12	2.3
1976	23	12	1.9
DDT[1]			
1964	35	12	2.9
1966	29	9	3.3
1971	14	3	4.5
1976	X	X	X
Carbofuran			
1964	NA	NA	NA
1966	NA	NA	NA
1971	3	4	0.8
1976	12	11	1.0
Ethyl parathion			
1964	6	5	1.3
1966	8	6	1.4
1971	9	10	0.9
1976	7	12	0.5
Aldrin/Dieldrin			
1964	12	14	0.8
1966	15	15	1.1
1971	8	8	1.1
1976	0.9[2]	0.5[2]	1.9[2]
All other			
1964	46	NA	NA
1966	46	NA	NA
1971	59	NA	NA
1976	90	NA	NA

Details may not add to totals due to independent rounding.
NA = Not available.
X = Not applicable due to restrictions on use.
DDT was banned for most uses in 1972, and aldrin/dieldrin in 1974.
[1]DDT includes its related compound TDE.
[2]Aldrin/dieldrin use in 1976 includes aldrin only. Because aldrin rapidly breaks down into its metabolite, dieldrin, most residues are dieldrin.
Source: Council on Environmental Quality, 1981, p. 241.

Table B.26: Various food additives and contaminants suspected or proven to be carcinogenic in laboratory animals[a]

Agent	Use/source in diet	Tumor site	Species	Reference
Intentional Food Additives				
Cyclamates	Nonnutritive sweetener	Bladder	Rats	International Agency for Research on Cancer, 1980
Saccharin	Nonnutritive sweetener	Bladder	Several species	International Agency for Research on Cancer, 1980
Dulcin (*p*-phenethylurea)	Nonnutritive sweetener	Bladder, liver	Rats	International Agency for Research on Cancer, 1976
Xylitol	Sweetener	Bladder	Female mice	Hunter *et al.*, 1978
Sucrose	Sweetener	Liver	Female mice	Hunter *et al.*, 1978
Amaranth (FD&C Red #2)	Food color	Nonspecific	Female rats	International Agency for Research on Cancer, 1975
FD&C Red #32	Food color	Lung, mammary tissue	Mice	International Agency for Research on Cancer, 1975
FD&C Orange #2	Food color	Intestinal, local	Mice	International Agency for Research on Cancer, 1975
Butter yellow (*N,N*-dimethyl-4-aminoazobenzene)	Food color	Liver	Rats and mice	International Agency for Research on Cancer, 1975
Safrole	Flavoring agent	Liver	Rats and mice	International Agency for Research on Cancer, 1976
Oil of calamus	Flavoring agent	Small intestine	Rats	Gross *et al.*, 1967
Cinnamyl anthranilate	Flavoring agent	Liver, kidney, and pancreas	Mice and rats	International Agency for Research on Cancer, 1978
Diethylpyrocarbonate	Preservative	Lung	Mice	Kraybill, 1977
8-Hydroxyquinoline	Preservative	Multiple sites	Rats and mice	International Agency for Research on Cancer, 1977
Thioacetamide	Seed grain mordant	Liver	Rats	International Agency for Research on Cancer, 1974
Butylated hydroxytoluene (BHT)	Antioxidant	Lung (promotor)	Mice	Witschi *et al.*, 1981
Trichloroethylene	Extractant	Liver	Mice	International Agency for Research on Cancer, 1979
Carrageenin	Emulsifier	Sarcomas	Rats	Cater, 1961
Myrj 45 (polyoxyethylene) monostearate)	Antistaling agent	Bladder	Rats	Kraybill, 1977
Tannic acid	Wine, fruits	Liver	Rats	International Agency for Research on Cancer, 1976
Tween-60 (sorbitan monostearate)	Antibloom agent in chocolates	Skin, also a promoting agent	Rats and hamsters	Kraybill, 1977
Carboxymethylcellulose	Ice cream stabilizer	Subcutaneous tissue	Rats	Kraybill, 1977
Unintentional Additives				
Polyvinyl chloride (vinyl chloride monomer)	Packaging material	Several sites	Several species	Feron *et al.*, 1951
Acrylonitrile	Packaging material	Forestomach, central nervous system, Zymbal's gland	Rats	Norris, 1977
DES (diethylstilbestrol)	Animal drug residue	Multiple sites	Several species	International Agency for Research on Cancer, 1979
Various organochlorine pesticides	Residues in diet	Liver	Mice	International Agency for Research on Cancer, 1974
Parathion	Residues in diet	Adrenals	Rats	National Cancer Institute, 1979
PAH's (polycyclic aromatic hydrocarbons), *e.g.*, benzo[*a*]pyrene	Air pollution; charcoal broiling	Several sites	Several species	International Agency for Research on Cancer, 1973
PCB's (polychlorinated biphenyls)	Freshwater fish, packaging materials	Liver	Rats	International Agency for Research on Cancer, 1978

Table B.26: Continued

Agent	Use/source in diet	Tumor site	Species	Reference
Cycads and cycasin	Cycad nuts	Liver, kidney, intestine	Rats	International Agency for Research on Cancer, 1976
Aflatoxin	Milk, mold in cereals, peanuts, corn	Liver, stomach, kidneys	Several species	International Agency for Research on Cancer, 1976
Nitrosamines	Nitrite and amines in foods	Several sites	Rats	National Academy of Sciences, 1981
Tannins	Tea, wine	Liver, sarcomas	Mice	International Agency for Research on Cancer, 1976
Bracken fern	Fern species	Bladder	Several species	Hirono et al., 1979
Thiourea	Laburnum shrubs	Several sites	Rats	International Agency for Research on Cancer, 1974
Pyrrolizidine alkaloids	Herbal medicine, teas, and food plants	Liver	Rats	International Agency for Research on Cancer, 1976
Patulin	Mold in apple juice	Local sarcomas	Rats	Dickens and Jones, 1961

[a]Adapted from *Diet, Nutrition, and Cancer,* National Research Council, pp. B-10, B-11

Table B.27: Carcinogenicity of various organochlorine pesticides

Pesticide	Acceptable daily intake (ug/kg bw)	Daily dietary intake (ug/kg bw), by year[b]	Mutagenicity and related tests	Carcinogenicity (oral administration only)[c]
Dieldrin	0.1 (total, including aldrin)	1975 - 0.0387 1977 - 0.0405 1979 - 0.0156	Negative in Ames test (McCann et al., 1975)	Significant increase in hepatocellular carcinoma in mice (National Cancer Institute, 1978b; Thorpe and Walker 1973), but not in rats (National Cancer Institute, 1978c)
DDT	5.0 (total, including dichlorodiphenyl-dichloroethylene [DDE] and trichlorodi-phenyldicholoro-ethylene [TDE])	1975 - 0.0152 1977 - 0.0057 1979 - 0.0041	Negative in Ames test (Bartsch et al., 1980; Marshall et al., 1976) and in host-mediated assay and dominant lethal tests in mice (Buselmaier et al., 1973)	Significant increase in hepatocellular carcinoma in several strains of mice (Innes et al., 1969; Terracini et al., 1973; Thorpe and Walker, 1973; World Health Organization, 1973); negative in mice and rats (National Cancer Institute, 1978d)
Captan	10.0	1975 - ND[d] 1977 - 0.0305 1979 - 0.0294	Positive in Ames test (McCann et al., 1975; Simmon et al., 1979), E. coli, S. cerevisiae, and B. subtilis (Simmon et al., 1979)	Significant increase in duodenal tumors in B6C3F$_1$ mice; inconclusive in rats (National Cancer Institute, 1977a)
Heptachlor and heptachlor epoxide	0.5 (total for both)	1975 - 0.0072 1977 - 0.0074 1979 - 0.0058	Negative in Salmonella with or without metabolic activation (Marshall et al., 1976) and in dominant lethal tests in mice (D. W. Arnold et al., 1977)	Significant increase in hepatocellular carcinoma in mice and in multiple tumors in female rats (Epstein, 1976; National Cancer Institute, 1977b)
Pentachloro-nitrobenzene (PCNB)	7.0	1975 - 0.0004 1977 - 0.0010 1979 - 0.0006	Negative in reversion tests in Salmonella, yeast, E. coli, and B. subtilis (Simmon et al., 1976)	Significant increase in hepatomas in one strain of male mice (Innes et al., 1969), but not in Osborne Mendel rats or B6C3F$_1$ mice (National Cancer Institute, 1978e)

Table B.27: Continued

Pesticide	Acceptable daily intake (ug/kg bw)	Daily dietary intake (ug/kg bw), by year[b]	Mutagenicity and related tests	Carcinogenicity (oral administration only)[c]
Hexachloro-benzene	NE[e]	1975 - 0.0046 1977 - 0.0019 1979 - 0.0032	Negative in yeast and in dominant lethal test in rats (Guerzoni et al., 1976; Khera, 1974)	Significant increase in liver cell tumors in mice (Cabral et al., 1979) and in hepatomas, liver hemangiotheliomas, and thyroid adenomas in hamsters (Cabral et al., 1977)
Methoxychlor	100[f]	1975 - 0.0037 1977 - 0.0078 1979 - 0.0032	Negative in Salmonella with or without metabolic activation, and in E. coli (Simmon et al., 1979)	No significant increase in tumors or decrease in age at which tumors occurred in mice (Deichmann et al., 1967) or rats (National Cancer Institute, 1978f)
Toxaphene	NE	1975 - 0.0072 1977 - 0.0802 1979 - 0.0035	Positive in Salmonella (Hooper et al., 1979); negative for dominant lethals in mice (Epstein et al., 1972)	Dose-related increase in hepatocellular carcinoma in mice and thyroid tumors in rats (National Cancer Institute, 1979g)
Lindane	10	1975 - 0.0031 1977 - 0.0038 1979 - 0.0038	Positive for chromosome aberrations, polyploidy and mitotic arrest in plant systems, and chromatid breaks in human lympho-cytes in vitro (International Agency for Research on Cancer, 1979)	Significant increase in liver tumors in two studies in mice (Nagasaki et al., 1971; Thorpe and Walker, 1973); inconclusive in rats (National Cancer Institute, 1977c)
Chlordane	1	*Oxychlordane* 1975 - 0.0017 1977 - 0.0025 1979 - 0.0041 *Trans-monachlor* 1975 - 0.0004 1977 - 0.0020 1979 - 0.0004	Not mutagenic in Ames test (Tardiff et al., 1976) and negative in dominant lethal tests in mice (D. W. Arnold et al., 1977); induced mutations in mammalian cells in culture (Ahmed et al., 1977)	Significant increase in hepatocellular carcinomas in CD-1 mice (Epstein, 1976) and in B6C3F$_1$ mice (National Cancer Institute, 1977d); inconclusive in Osborne Mendel rats (National Cancer Institute, 1977d).
Kepone (chlordecone)	NE	Not monitored in the Market Basket Surveys	Not mutagenic in dominant lethal assay in rats (Simon et al., 1978)	Significant dose-related increase in hepatocellular carcinomas in B6C3F$_1$ mice and Osborne Mendel rats (National Cancer Institute, 1976)

[a]ADI = Acceptable Daily Intake of pesticide residues in diet established periodically by the World Health Organization, based on standards established by the FAO/WHO Expert Committee on Food Additives (World Health Organization, 1958).
[b]Data from FDA Market Basket Surveys (U.S. Food and Drug Administration, 1980b).
[c]Doses used in these studies were many times higher (usually 100 times or more) than the amounts to which humans are exposed in the average U.S. diet.
[d]ND = Not detected.
[e]NE = ADI not established.
[f]Data from Food and Agriculture Organization, 1978.

Adapted from *Diet, Nutrition, and Cancer,* National Research Council, pp. 14-18, 14-19, (bibliographic sources).

Bibliography

Abbreviations used:

BEIR.   The Advisory Committee on the Biological Effects of Ionizing Radiation.
DHEW.   Department of Health, Education, and Welfare.
EPA.   Environmental Protection Agency.
NAS.   National Academy of Sciences.
NRC.   National Research Council.
UNSCEAR. United Nations Scientific Committee on the Effects of Atomic Radiation.

Abramson, F. D. 1973. "Spontaneous Fetal Death in Man." *Social Biology,* **20,** 375.

Alaranja, M., and I. Goldstein. 1977. "Report of Case Control Study of Cancer Deaths in Four Selected New York Counties in Relation to Drinking Water Chlorination." Report of EPA contract, **76, 224.**

Amdur, M. 1973. "Animal Studies." In NAS, 1973.

Andersen, I. 1974. "Human Response to Controlled Levels of Sulfur Dioxide." *Archives of Environmental Health,* **28,** 31.

Anderson, E. 1973. "Effect of Low-Level Carbon Monoxide Exposure on Onset and Duration of Angina Pectoris." *Annals of Internal Medicine,* **79,** 46.

Andrews, V. 1979. *The Psychic Power of Running.* Ballantine Books.

Aronow, W. 1972. "Effect of Freeway Travel on Angina Pectoris." *Annals of Internal Medicine,* **77,** 669.

Arsenian, J., and J. M. Arsenian. 1948. "Tough and Easy Cultures." *Psychiatry,* **11,** 377.

Auerback, H. A. 1966. *Methods and Principles of Psychotherapy,* Appleton Century Crofts.

Banbury Report. 1979. Assessing Chemical Mutagens. V. McElheny, ed. Cold Spring Harbor Laboratories.

Baranski, Stanislaw. 1976. *Biological Effects of Microwaves.* Dowden, Hutchinson, and Ross.

Bartlett, D. 1974. "Effects of Chronic Ozone Exposure on Lung Elasticity in Young Rats." *Journal of Applied Physiology,* **37,** 92.

Bates, D. 1973. "The Short-Term Effects of Ozone in the Human Lung." In NAS, 1973.

Bawin, S., and W. Adey. 1976. "Sensitivity of Calcium Binding In Cerebral Tissue to Weak Environmental Electrical Fields Oscillating at Low Frequency." *Proceedings of the NAS,* **73,** 1999.

Beard, R. 1967. "Behavioral Impairment Associated with Doses of Carbon Monoxide." *American Journal of Public Health,* **57,** 2011.

Beebe, G. W., H. Kato, and C. Land. 1978. "Studies of the Mortality of A-Bomb Survivors: 6, Mortality and Radiation Dose, 1956–1974." *Radiation Research,* **75,** 138–701.

BEIR. 1972. *The Effects on Populations of Exposure to Low Levels of Ionizing Radiation.* NAS, NRC.

Bennett, H. Z. 1979. *Cold Comfort; Colds and Flu: Everybody's Guide to Self-Treatment.* Clarkson Potter.

———. 1981. *The Doctor Within.* Signet.

Bennett, H. Z., and M. Samuels. 1973. *The Well Body Book.* Random House.

———. 1974. *Be Well.* Random House.

Bronowski, Jacob. 1973. *The Ascent of Man.* Little, Brown.

Buechley, R. 1973. "Sulfur Dioxide Levels and Perturbations in Mortality: A Study in the New York–New Jersey Metropolis." *Archives of Environmental Health,* **27,** 134.

———. 1975. "Sulfur Dioxide Levels and Perturbations in Mortality: A Further Study in the New York–New Jersey Metropolis." Report to the National Institute of Environmental Health Sciences.

Buncher, C. R. 1975. "Cincinnati Drinking Water—An Epidemiologic Study of Cancer Rates." Report to the Board of Health, Cincinnati, Ohio.

Calder, Nigel. 1978. *The Restless Earth.* Penguin.

Cantor, K. 1977. "Association of Halomethanes in Drinking Water With Cancer Mortality." National Cancer Institute.

Carlson, W. S., and J. Andoman. 1977. "Environmental Influences on Cancer Morbidity in the Pittsburg Region." Environmental Health Section, University of Pittsburg.

Carnow, B., and P. Meier. 1973. "Air Pollution and Pulmonary Cancer." *Archives of Environmental Health, 27,* 207.

Cattabeni, Flaminio et al. 1978. *Dioxin.* SP Medical and Scientific Books.

Chardin, Teilhard de. 1931. *The Spirit of the Earth.*

———. 1961. *The Phenomenon of Man.* Harper Torchbooks.

Chu, E. 1965. "An Inhibitory Effect of Vitamin A on Induction of Tumors to the Forestomach and Cervix in Syrian Hamsters by Carcinogenic Polycyclic Hydrocarbons." *Cancer Research, 25,* 884.

Cloud, Preston. 1978. *Cosmos, Earth, and Man.* Yale University Press.

Coffin, D. 1968. "Effect of Air Pollution on Alteration of Susceptibility to Pulmonary Infection." In *Proceedings of the Third Annual Conference on Atmospheric Contaminants in Confined Spaces,* p. 75.

Cooper, K. 1975. *The New Aerobics.* Bantam.

Council on Environmental Quality. 1980. *Environmental Quality.* U. S. Government Printing Office.

Council on Environmental Quality. 1981. U.S. Government Printing Office.

Council of Europe. 1972. *Working Party on Cancer Statistics.* Council of Europe.

DeBias, D. 1973. "Carbon Monoxide Inhalation Effects Following Miocardial Infarction in Monkeys." *Archives of Environmental Health, 27,* 161.

Douglas, J. 1966. "Air Pollution and Respiratory Infections in Children." *British Journal of Preventive Social Medicine,* **20,** 1.

Dubos, R. 1961. *Mirage of Health.* Doubleday.

———. 1981. *Celebrations of Life.* McGraw-Hill.

Eastcott, D. 1956. "Epidemiology of Lung Cancer in New Zealand." *Lancet, 1,* 37.

Eccles, John. 1953. *The Neurophysiological Basis of Mind.* Oxford University Press.

Ehrlich, Paul, and Anne Ehrlich. 1981. *Extinction.* Random House.

Eliade, Mircea. 1963. *Patterns in Comparative Religion.* Meridian.

———. 1969. *Yoga: Immortality and Freedom.* Pantheon, 2d, rev. ed.

Engst, W. 1975. *Nutrition in Health and Disease.* Allen Liss.

Environmental Defense Fund, 1977. See Harris.

EPA. 1976. *Quality Criteria for Water.* U.S. Government Printing Office.

———. 1978. *Noise: A Health Problem.* U.S. Government Printing Office.

Epstein, Samuel. 1979. *The Politics of Cancer.* Doubleday Anchor,

Ferguson, Marilyn. 1975. *The Brain Revolution.* Bantam.

Figueroa, W. G. 1973. "Lung Cancer in Chloromethyl Methyl Ether Workers." *New England Journal of Medicine,* **288,** 1096.

Finkel, A. 1976. *Clinical Implications of Air Pollution Research.* Publishing Sciences Group.

Fletcher, C. 1976. *The Natural History of Chronic Bronchitis and Emphysema.* Oxford University Press.

Fraumeni, Joseph. 1975. *Persons at High Risk of Cancer.* Academic Press.

Gardner, D. 1971. "Loss of Protective Factor for Alviolar Macrophages When Exposed to Ozone." *Archives of Inernal Medicine,* **127,** 1078.

———. 1977. "Relationship Between Nitrogen Dioxide Concentrations, Time, and Level of Effect Using an Animal Infectivity Model." *Proceedings of the International Conference on Photochemical and Oxidant Pollutants,* **1,** 513.

Geist, Valerius. 1981. *Life Strategies, Human Evolution, Environmental Designs.* Springer-Verlag.

Giese, Arthur. 1976. *Living With The Sun's Ultraviolet Rays.* Plenum Press.

Griswald, S. 1957. "Report of a Case of Exposure to High Ozone Concentrations for Two Hours." *Archives of Industrial Health,* **15,** 108.

Gofman, John. 1981. *Radiation and Human Health.* Sierra Club Books.

Guthrie, Frank E. and Perry, Jerome J. 1980. *Introduction to Environmental Toxicology,* Elsevier.

Haider, M. 1971. *Neuropsychologie.* Uber.

Hammer, D. 1974. "Los Angeles Student Nurse Study: Daily Symptoms Reporting and Photochemical Oxidants." *Archives of Environmental Health, 28,* 255.

———. 1976. "Air Pollution and Childhood Lower Respiratory Disease." In Finkel, 1976.

Hammond, E. C. 1976. "Inhalation of Benzopyrine and Cancer in Man." *Annals of the New York Academy of Science, 271,* 116.

Hanford Life Sciences Symposium. 1978. *Biological Effects of Extremely Low-Frequency Electromagnetic Fields.* Technical Information Center.

Hanna, M., ed. 1970. *Inhalation Carcinogenesis.* U.S. Atomic Energy Commission Symposium, 18.

Harris, Page T., and N. Reiches. 1977. "Carcinogenic Hazards of Organic Chemicals in Drinking Water." Environmental Defense Fund.

Hattori, S. 1973. "Alterations of Broncho-Alveolar System By Polluted Air." *Clinician, 219,* 408.

Henry, J. P., and P. N. Stephens. 1977. *Stress, Health, and the Social Environment.* Springer-Verlag.

Hiatt, H., ed. 1977. *Origins of Human Cancer.* Cold Spring Harbor Laboratory.

Higginson, John. 1976. "A Hazardous Society? Individual Versus Community Responsibility in Cancer Prevention." *American Journal of Public Health, 66,* 4.

Highland, Joseph, and R. H. Boyce. 1980. *Malignant Neglect.* Vintage.

Hinckle, —. "Illness, Life Experience, and Social Environment." *Annals of Internal Medicine.* 49: 1873, 1958.

Hogan, M. 1978. "Association Between Chloroform Levels in Finished Drinking Water Supplies and Various Site-Specific Cancer Mortality Rates." National Institute of Environmental Health Sciences.

Horvath, S. 1970. "Carbon Monoxide and Vigilance: Potential Danger From Existing Urban Concentrations." In *Project Clean Air, Vol. II.* Santa Barbara: University of California Research Project S-4.

Hudac, A. 1978. "Embryotoxic Effects of Benzene and Its Methyl Derivatives: Toluene and Xylene." *Toxicology, 11,* 55.

Hunt, V., and D. T. Janerich. 1973. "Epidemic Waves in the Prevalence of Anencephaly and Spina Bifida in New York State." *Teratology, 8,* 253.

Hurst, D. 1970. "Effects of Ozone Acid Hydrolases of the Pulmonary Alveolar Macrophage." *Journal of the Reticuloendotheleo Society, 8,* 288.

Infante, P. F. 1977. "Leukemia in Benzene Workers." *Lancet, 2,* 76–78.

Innes, J. R. 1969. "Bioassay of Pesticides and Industrial Chemicals for Tumorigenicity in Mice: A Preliminary Note." *Journal of the National Cancer Institute, 42,* 1101.

Jackson, G. C. 1960. "Susceptibility and Immunity to Common Upper Respiratory Viral Infection—The Common Cold." *Annals of Internal Medicine, 53,* 2.

James, William. 1929. *The Varieties of Religious Experience.* Modern Library.

Jastrow, Robert, and M. Thompson. 1979. *Astronomy: Fundamentals and Frontiers.* Wiley.

Jayne, W. A. 1925. *The Healing Gods of Ancient Civilizations.* Yale University Press.

Jensen, S., and A. Jernelov. 1969. "Biological Methylation of Mercury." *Nature, 223,* 753.

Johnson, B. 1976. "The Effect of Ozone on Brain Function." In Finkel, 1976.

Jung, Carl. 1959. "Dream Analysis in Its Practical Application." In *The Basic Writings of C. J. Jung.* Modern Library.

———. 1963. *Memories, Dreams, Reflections.* Vintage.

Kagawa, J., and T. Toyama. 1975. "Photochemical Air Pollution: Its Effects on Respiratory Function of Elementary School Children." *Archives of Environmental Health, 30,* 117.

Kahn, A. 1974. "Carboxyhemoglobin Sources in the Metropolitan St. Louis Population." *Archives of Environmental Health, 29,* 127.

Kavanaugh, T. 1976. *Heart Attack? Counterattack!* Van Nostrand.

Kimbrough, R. 1975. "Induction of Liver Tumors in Sherman Strain Female Rats by Polychlorynated Biphenyl Arochlor 1260." *Journal of the National Cancer Institute, 55,* 1453.

Knip, P. 1980. *Sound and Amsterdam Airport.* American Speech and Hearing Association.

Kociba, R. 1979. *Toxic and Applied Pharmacology.*

Kolonel, L. N. 1976. "Association of Cancer Rates With Renal Cancer." *Cancer, 37,* 1782.

Konig, H., A. Krueger, S. Lange, and W. Sonning. 1981. *Biologic Effects of Environmental Electromagnetism.* Springer-Verlag.

Kruse, C. 1977. *Chlorination of Public Water Supplies and Cancer.* Johns Hopkins University.

Kuschner, M. 1975. "Inhalation Carcinogenecity of Alpha Halo Ethers, III: Lifetime and Limited Period Inhalation Studies with BCME at .1 p.p.m." *Archives of Environmental Health, 30,* 73.

Kuzma, R. J., and C. M. Kuzma. 1977. "Ohio Drinking Water Sources and Cancer Rates." *American Journal of Public Health,* **67**, 725.

Lagerwerff, J. 1963. "Prolonged Ozone Inhalation and Its Effects on Visual Parameters." *Aerospace Medicine,* **34**, 479.

Lancranjan, I. 1975. "Reproductive Ability of Workmen Occupationally Exposed to Lead." *Archives of Environmental Health,* **30**, 396.

Larkin, R. P., and P. J. Southerland. 1977. "Migrating Birds Respond to Project Seafarer's Electromagnetic Field." *Science,* **195**, 777.

Laskin, S. 1970. "Studies in Pulmonary Carcinogenesis." In Hanna, 1970.

Lave, L., and E. Seskin. 1977. *Air Pollution and Human Health.* Johns Hopkins University Press.

Leakey, Richard. 1977. *Origins.* Dutton.

Lee, D., and P. Kotlin. 1972. *Multiple Factors in the Causation of Environmental-Induced Disease.* Academic Press.

Lee, Richard, and I. DeVore. 1968. *Man the Hunter.* Aldine.

———. 1976. *Kalahari Hunter-Gathers.* Harvard University Press.

Lemen, R. A. 1976. "Cancer Mortality Among Cadmium Production Workers." *Annals of the New York Academy of Sciences,* **271**, 273.

Lipfert, F. 1978. "The Association of Human Mortality With Air Pollution." Union Graduate School Thesis, Cincinnati, Ohio.

Lovelock, James. 1981. *Gaia.* Oxford University Press.

Luthe, W. 1970. *Autogenic Therapy,* Vol. IV. Grune & Stratton.

Lyapkalo, A. 1973. "Genetic Activity of Benzene and Toluene." *Gig. Tr. Prof. Zabol.* **17**, 24.

Maltoni, C. 1975. "Carcinogenicity Assays of Vinyl Chloride: Current Results." *Annals of the New York Academy of Sciences,* **246**, 195.

Mancuso, T. F., and W. Hueper. 1951. "Occupational Cancer and Other Health Hazards in a Chromate Plant: A Medical Appraisal: I, Lung Cancer in Chromate Workers." *Indiana Medical Surgery,* **20**, 358.

Manufacturing Chemists Association. 1977.

Marriott, A., and C. Rachlin. 1968. *American Indian Mythology.* New American Library.

Mason, T. J. 1975. *Atlas of Cancer Mortality for U.S. Counties: 1950–1969.* U.S. Government Printing Office.

McFarland, R. 1944. "The Effect of Carbon Monoxide and Altitude on Visual Thresholds." *Aviation Medicine,* **15**, 381.

McLain, R., and B. Baker. 1975. "Teratogenicity, Fetal Toxicity, and Placental Transfer of Lead Nitrate in Rats." *Toxicology and Applied Pharmacology,* **31**, 72.

Menck, H. 1974. "Industrial Air Pollution: Possible Effect on Lung Cancer." *Science,* **183**, 210.

Mendelsohn, R., and G. Orcutt. 1978. "An Empirical Analysis of Air Pollution Dose Response Curves." Institute for Social and Political Studies, Working Paper 800. New Haven, Connecticut.

Meyer, R. G., and R. J. Haggerty. 1962. "Streptococcal Infections in Families." *Pediatrics,* **29**, 539.

Miller, James. 1980. *Living Systems.* McGraw-Hill.

Mishra, R. S. 1973. *Yoga Sutras.* Doubleday.

Money, J. 1896. "The Ghost Dance Religion and the Sioux Outbreak of 1890." *Annual Report of the Bureau of American Ethnology,* Washington, D.C.

Montagu, Ashley. 1961. *Culture: Man's Adaptive Dimension.* Oxford University Press.

Mohr, U. 1977. *Air Pollution and Cancer in Man.* International Agency for Research on Cancer.

Nader, R., R. Brownstein, and J. Richard. 1981. *Who's Poisoning America: Corporate Polluters and Their Victims in the Chemical Age.* Sierra Club Books.

Price, F. 1942. "Noise Can Be Hazardous to Our Health." *Science News,* **121**, 379.

Price, J. S. 1967. "The Dominance Hierarchy and the Evolution of Mental Illness." *Lancet,* **2**, 243.

Raloff, S. 1982. "Noise Can Be Hazardous to Our Health." *Science News,* **121**, 379.

Regenstein, Lewis. 1982. *America the Poisoned.* Acropolis.

Safe Drinking Water Committee. 1980. *Drinking Water and Health.* NAS.

Saffiotti, U. 1970. "Experimental Respiratory Tract Carcinogenesis and Its Relation to Inhalation Exposures." In Hanna, 1970.

———. 1976. "Occupational Carcinogenesis." *Annals of the New York Academy of Sciences,* Vol. 271.

Sagan, Carl. 1980. *Cosmos.* Random House.

Salg, J. 1977. "Cancer Mortality Rates and Drinking Water in 346 Counties of the Ohio River Valley Basin." EPA PO-5-03-4528. University of North Carolina.

Samuels, M., and N. Samuels. 1975. *Seeing With the Mind's Eye.* Random House.

———. 1979. *The Well Baby Book.* Summit Books.

———. 1982. *The Well Child Book.* Summit Books.

———. 1983. *The Well Child Coloring Book.* Summit Books.

Schoettlin, C. 1961. "Air Pollution and Asthmatic Attacks in the Los Angeles Area." *Public Health Reports,* **76,** 545.

Schulte, J. 1963. "Effects of Mild Carbon Monoxide Intoxication." *Archives of Environmental Health,* **7,** 524.

Shy, C. 1970. "The Chattanooga School Children Study: Effects of Community Exposure to Nitrogen Dioxide." JAPCA **20,** 539.

Simmon, V. 1977. "Mutagenic Activity of Chemicals Identified in Drinking Water." Presented at Second International Conference on Environmental Mutagens, Edinborough, Scotland.

Sittig, Marshall, ed. 1980. *Priority Toxic Pollutants.* Noyes Data.

Skillen, R. 1961. "Brain 5-Hydroxytryptamine in Ozone-Exposed Rats." *Proceedings of the Society for Experimental Biological Medicine,* **108,** 121.

Smith, P., R. Doll, and E. P. Redford. 1978. "Age-and-Time-Dependent Changes in the Rates of Radiation-Induced Cancers." *Late Biological Effects of Ionizing Radiation,* **1,** 205.

Stephens, S. 1971. "Phenotypic and Genetic Effects of Neurospora Crassa Produced by Selected Gases and Gases Mixed With Oxygen." *Developmental Industrial Microbiology,* **12,** 346.

Stewart, R. 1973. "Carboxyhemoglobin Levels in American Blood Donors." *Journal of the American Medical Association,* **229,** 1187.

Swenberg, J. 1980. "Induction of Squamous Cell Carcinomas of the Rat Nasal Cavity by Inhalation Exposure to Formaldehyde Vapor." *Cancer Research,* **40,** 3398.

Taylor, F. 1966. "The Relationship of Mortality and Duration of Employment as Reflected by a Cohort of Chromate Workers." *American Journal of Public Health.* **56,** f218.

Taylor, K. W. 1979. "Variations in X-ray Exposures to Patients." *Journal of the Canadian Association of Radiologists,* **30,** 6.

Thomas, G., et al. 1979. *Exercise and Health; The Evidence and Policy Implications.* University of California Health Policy Program.

Thomas, J. A. 1975. *Advances in Sex Hormone Research.* University Park Press.

Thomas, Lewis. 1974. *The Lives of a Cell.* Viking.

Thompson, William. 1978. *Darkness and Scattered Light.* Doubleday, Anchor.

Thorpe, E., and A. Walker. 1973. "The Toxicology of Dieldrin in Mice With Dieldrin, DDT, Phenobarbitone, Beta-BCH, and Gamma-BCH." *Food and Cosmetics Toxicology,* **11,** 433.

Turnbill, C. M. 1972. *The Mountain People.* Simon and Schuster.

Turusov, V. 1973. "Tumors in CF-1 Mice Exposed for Six Consecutive Generations to DDT." *Journal of the National Cancer Institute,* **51,** 983.

UNSCEAR. 1977. *Sources and Effects of Ionizing Radiation.* United Nations.

Vasilenko, P. 1975. "Factors Relating to the Incidence of Cancer Mortality in New Jersey." Princeton University.

Viola, P. 1970. "Cancerogenic Effect of Vinyl Chloride." *Proceedings of the Tenth International Cancer Congress.*

Wagner, Sheldon. 1983. *Clinical Toxicology of Agricultural Chemicals,* Noyes Data Corporation.

Wang, Y. S. 1975. "Measurement of Ionizing Radiation from Color Television Receivers by Thermo-Luminescent Dosimeters." *Health Physics,* **28,** 78.

Waters, Frank. 1963. *Book of the Hopi.* Viking.

Wayne, W. 1967. "Oxidant Air Pollution and Athletic Performance." *Journal of the American Medical Association,* **199,** 901.

Weinberg, Steven. 1979. *The First Three Minutes.* Bantam.

Weir, David, and Schapiro, M. 1981. *Circle of Poison,* Institute for food and development policy.

Weir, F. 1973. *Effects of Sulfur Dioxide on Human Subjects Exhibiting Peripheral Airway Impairment.* American Petroleum Institute.

Weiss, S. 1981. *Perspectives on Behavioral Medicine.* Academic Press.

Wilhelmsen, L. 1975. "A Controlled Trial of Physical Training After Myocardial Infarction." *Preventive Medicine,* **4,** 491.

Wilson, R., S. D. Colome, J. D. Spengler, and D. G. Wilson. 1980. *Health Effects of Fossil Fuel Burning.* Bollinger.

Wiltschko, W., and R. Wiltschko. 1972. "Magnetic Compass of European Robins." *Science,* **176,** 62.

Wynder, E. L. 1976. "Tar and Nicotine Content of Cigarette Smoke in Relation to Death Rates." *Environmental Research,* **12,** 263.

Zarkower, A. 1972. "Alterations In Antibody Response Induced by Chronic Inhalation of SO and Carbon." *Archives of Environmental Health,* **25,** 45.

Zuckerman, S. 1932. *The Social Life of Monkeys and Apes.* Harcourt.

Index

Page numbers in italics refer to boxed lists or tables.